THE ONE YEAR BOOK OF

Praying through the Bible

CHERI FULLER

The ONE YEAR® BOOK OF PRAYING *through the* BIBLE

365 DEVOTIONS

Tyndale House
Publishers, Inc.
Wheaton, Illinois

Dedicated to the memory of

FLO PERKINS,

faithful intercessor, prayer mentor, loving friend

Visit Tyndale's exciting Web site at www.tyndale.com

The One Year Book of Praying through the Bible

Designed by Timothy R. Botts

Edited by Susan Taylor

Published in association with the literary agency of Alive Communications, Inc., 7680 Goddard Street, Suite 200, Colorado Springs, CO 80920.

Library of Congress Cataloging-in-Publication Data

Fuller, Cheri.
The one year book of praying through the Bible / Cheri Fuller.
p. cm.
Includes index.
ISBN 0-8423-6178-2 (sc)
1. Bible—Devotional use. 2. Devotional calendars. I. Title.
BS390 .F85 2003
242′.2—dc21 2003012633

Printed in the United States of America

09 08 07 06 05 04
7 6 5 4 3

CONTENTS

ACKNOWLEDGMENTS

How marvelous that although "everything comes from him; everything exists by his power and is intended for his glory" (Romans 11:36), yet the Lord gives us the opportunity to partner with him in his purposes! I am grateful for those who partnered with me on this project. Thank you, Peggy and Earl Stewart, Suzie Eller, Treasure Frosch, Lisa Cronk, Phama Woodyard, Kendra and John Smiley, and Vickey Banks, for your prayers, support, love for God's Word, and contributions to this book.

Special thanks to Jon Farrar, Susan Taylor, and the Tyndale House team for all their efforts on behalf of *The One Year Bible* and this devotional book, and for their commitment to helping God's Word come alive to people all around the world.

Thanks also to Janet Page and Jo Hayes for their ongoing prayers, and also to those who have prayed for and encouraged me along the journey.

Thanks and love to my husband, Holmes, who has stood by me, been my constant intercessor, and cheered me on in a variety of ways.

And most of all, thank you to the Living Word, Jesus, for giving his life for us that we might know him and for gifting us with the precious Word of God.

INTRODUCTION

Seventeenth-century French writer François Fénelon once said, "Listen less to your own thoughts and more to God's thoughts." When my heart reconnected with God in a renewing, enduring way when I was in my late twenties and I stopped listening to my own thoughts and focused on God's thoughts, I grew by leaps and bounds in my appreciation for the Bible, his love letter to us. Day by day as I studied and read his Word, I was amazed at the truth and grace it contained.

When I began reading through *The One Year Bible* each year, I found countless verses I could pray for my children, my husband, my own life, and those I regularly interceded for. The Bible began to shape my prayers, and I discovered that it was the best prayer manual of all, showing us how to pray and what to pray, and most of all through the Holy Spirit, providing constant inspiration for our prayers.

As I prayed God's Word, I was filled with confidence and faith in God's ability to answer and to act because I wasn't praying out of my own understanding or imagination but out of the Lord's heart and his intentions and desires for us, his people. As I prayed God's Word, fear, doubt, and discouragement left, and his peace renewed my heart and mind. I discovered the Bible contained promises concerning God's plans for our lives, for our children and loved ones and the body of Christ, the provision he has available and what he has in store for us both in this life and in the life to come. He wants us to pray these promises and verses, meditate on them, and trust in the Author's ability to move on our behalf.

What great gifts God has given us in the Bible and prayer! What a gracious invitation the Lord offers to bring our deepest concerns, our greatest needs to the One who cares for us affectionately and watchfully. And what an incredible supply of power is released when we pray. Prayer is meant to be our *first resource,* not a last resource, and it is our lifeline in uncertain times, in the best of times, and in the worst of times. Prayer is the greatest influence we can have on our children's lives and the best resource God has given us for making a difference and shining his light in our homes, our neighborhoods, our schools, our world. Watchman Nee, a classic prayer theologian said, "Our prayers lay the tracks on which God's power can come."

In *The One Year Book of Praying through the Bible* each devotional highlights a passage from that day's reading in *The One Year Bible* and contains a devotional thought, a prayer drawn from those verses to act as a springboard for your communication with God, and an insightful quote by a classic Christian.

Because *The One Year Book of Praying through the Bible* is meant to be used as a companion book to *The One Year Bible,* you may choose to read both at the same time of day. However, if doing so seems like more of a time commitment than you're prepared to make all at once, consider reading *The One Year Bible's* daily reading in the morning and *The One Year Book of Praying through the Bible* in the evening to help you go deeper into a portion of what you read in the morning. Another option is to read the devotional in the morning and then *The One Year Bible* in the evening to cement the idea and context of your morning reading in your mind.

In whatever way you approach your reading, as you read and pray through *The One Year Bible* and this devotional, I pray that you will be drawn closer to your Savior, that you will hear his voice and experience his presence and power in your life. As you pray along with the prayers of Paul, Isaiah, Hannah, Nehemiah, Jesus, and others from the pages of the Bible, may your heart be filled with hope and faith and your prayer life soar. As you pray prayers for help and prayers of praise, as David did in the Psalms, may God empower you to enjoy and worship God in new ways. May your life be increasingly yielded to the Lord so that he can live through you and love others through you. And as God's Word shapes your prayers, may you know him, follow him, trust him, and serve him with joy—not just for this year but for a lifetime!

Cheri Fuller

Fruitful Trees

This psalm, in which the wicked are contrasted with the godly, never fails to lead me to prayer—both for others and for myself. It is also the source of an ideal prayer for the new year—that we would delight in doing God's will, that his Word would be continually in our thoughts, and that we would bear fruit in the year ahead and in each season of our lives. None of this happens apart from God's Spirit and power working within us. But fruit bearing is the inevitable by-product of opening our hearts and lives to the power of his life within us. As we abide in Christ and his Word, our roots to go down deep in Christ, keeping us close to him, just as the roots of trees planted along the riverbank sink into the water source so that their leaves stay green and don't wither. And when we pray, the Spirit releases this wonder-working power that draws us to God, roots us deeper in him, and causes our faith to mature. Be assured of God's promise that as you draw near to him today and each day in the year ahead, he will draw near to you (James 4:8).

They delight in doing everything the Lord wants; day and night they think about his law. They are like trees planted along the riverbank, bearing fruit each season without fail. Their leaves never wither, and in all they do, they prosper.
Psalm 1:2-3

LORD, by your Spirit, draw me to the river of your love. Cause my roots to go deep into your streams of water, and make all that I do prosper. Give me the desire to read your Word and to meditate on it day and night. Most of all, empower me to do what it says. And for the fruit that is borne in the year ahead, I will give you all the glory!

A MAN WITHOUT PRAYER IS LIKE A TREE WITHOUT ROOTS. Pope Pius XII (1876–1958)

The One Year Bible readings for today are **Genesis 1:1–2:25; Matthew 1:1–2:12; Psalm 1:1-6;** and **Proverbs 1:1-6.**

JANUARY

2

reverving

Revering God

Fear of the Lord is the beginning of knowledge. Only fools despise wisdom and discipline.
Proverbs 1:7

As we look at the state of the world around us, at what has happened in the past and what we may face in the year ahead, there is much to fear: Will a sniper terrorize our community as has happened in other areas? Will the bottom fall out of the economy? Will my job be jeopardized? Will there be violence at my child's school? Fear about possibilities like these can consume us, producing increased stress and even illness. But today's verse tells us that there is only one thing to fear—God himself. This fear is not an unhealthy fear that leads to cringing and hiding as Adam and Eve did after they had disobeyed God. Rather, it is a humble and honest recognition of God's beauty, sovereignty, and preeminence so that worshiping and serving him take first place in our lives. It is a healthy reverence that leads to intimacy and an understanding that the power of God residing in us by his Spirit is greater than the power of our fears or of our enemy Satan. A deep sense of awe about who God is leads to the true knowledge and wisdom we desperately need for our lives today and in the year ahead.

LORD, develop in me a deep reverence of you that leads to life, wisdom, and greater intimacy with you. Open my heart to be teachable and to receive correction and discipline willingly. Grant that I would fear you, Father, and not my circumstances in the present or the what-ifs of the future. May I be so filled with your love that faith would replace my fear.

WHILE WE MUST NEVER ON THE ONE HAND LOSE THE FREEDOM TO ENTER BOLDLY AND JOYFULLY BY FAITH INTO GOD'S PRESENCE DURING OUR LIVES ON EARTH, WE MUST ALSO LEARN HOW TO REVERE GOD IN OUR RELATIONSHIP WITH HIM. . . . INTIMACY CANNOT OCCUR WITHOUT RESPECT.
John White

The One Year Bible readings for today are **Genesis 3:1–4:26; Matthew 2:13–3:6; Psalm 2:1-12;** and **Proverbs 1:7-9.**

shield

God Is My Shield

Have you ever felt as if someone was out to get you? as if you were surrounded by people who meant you harm in some way? When David wrote this psalm, he was crying out to God as he raced from the palace, pursued by enemies loyal to his son Absalom, who was trying to overthrow David's kingdom by force. As David prayed this God-centered prayer, he was exercising his confidence that in this situation the Lord would reveal himself as a shield and protector, as David's "glory and the one who lifts my head high." In the midst of hearing others telling David that there was no hope, that all was lost, he had hope. But the source of his hope wasn't in his mighty warriors or in the ability of another army to protect him. His hope was in God's character. Though David was surrounded by foes on every side, he knew that God heard him when he cried out to him. He was confident that God was his shield of protection, that he watched over David and would deliver him.

O Lord, I have so many enemies; so many are against me. So many are saying, "God will never rescue him!" But you, O Lord, are a shield around me, my glory, and the one who lifts my head high. I cried out to the Lord, and he answered me from his holy mountain.
Psalm 3:1-4

LORD, you are my shield and my eternal protector. When I am in danger or distress, help me trust in your character. Be my glory and the lifter of my head this day. Lift my gaze and my heart from everything on this earth to you, who reign over all. Thank you for answering me from heaven and acting on my behalf when I cry out to you. May you be glorified in my life.

THE ARMOUR IS FOR THE BATTLE OF PRAYER. THE ARMOUR IS NOT TO FIGHT IN, BUT TO SHIELD US WHILE WE PRAY. PRAYER IS THE BATTLE.
Oswald Chambers (1874–1917)

The One Year Bible readings for today are **Genesis 5:1–7:24; Matthew 3:7–4:11; Psalm 3:1-8;** and **Proverbs 1:10-19.**

JANUARY

4

safe

Safe in Him

You can be sure of this: The Lord has set apart the godly for himself. The Lord will answer when I call to him. . . . Many people say, "Who will show us better times?" Let the smile of your face shine on us, Lord. You have given me greater joy than those who have abundant harvests of grain and wine. I will lie down in peace and sleep, for you alone, O Lord, will keep me safe.
Psalm 4:3, 6-8

In this psalm David proclaimed his faith in God's ability to answer him when he called and to protect him even when he was pursued and slandered by his enemies. David's experiences with God had taught him that he did not have to wait to praise God until he was enjoying "better times." Though David was weary and may have been spending the night in a cave as he fled his enemies and didn't know the outcome of the danger he was in, his trust produced joy that was greater than the joy experienced by those celebrating a great harvest. And he could then lie down in peace and sleep because he knew God alone would keep him safe. What situation or problem could steal your sleep and your peace and joy? Call on the living God, who will answer when you call to him. And remember that you can close your eyes and rest because God's eyes never close. The One who never sleeps cares for you personally and watches over you.

LORD, thank you for setting apart each of us to know you and for answering when I call to you. Let the smile of your countenance shine on me this day. Grant me joy in Christ and peace in your presence, even before a turnaround or harvest comes. And when the night falls, grant me to "lie down in peace and sleep," for you alone keep me safe.

TALK TO HIM IN PRAYER OF ALL YOUR WANTS, YOUR TROUBLES, EVEN OF THE WEARINESS YOU FEEL IN SERVING HIM. YOU CANNOT SPEAK TOO FREELY, TOO TRUSTFULLY TO HIM.
François Fénelon (1651–1715)

The One Year Bible readings for today are **Genesis 8:1–10:32; Matthew 4:12-25; Psalm 4:1-8;** and **Proverbs 1:20-23.**

JANUARY

5

favor

The Favor of the Lord

This psalm is called the Inheritance Prayer and expresses a twofold blessing: First, we are recipients of great favor and a great inheritance. Second, the righteous—those in right standing with the Father by virtue of Christ's death and resurrection—are the Lord's own inheritance. Because we belong to him and are his heirs, God blesses our lives with deliverance, direction, and continual access into his presence. Because of his unfailing love for us, we can enter his throne room and receive his grace. When we ask him to tell us what to do, he will show us which way to turn and will always lead us on the right path. To top it all off, he encompasses, or encircles, us with the shield of his love, which means that he covers us with his favor and with the approval that he bestows on the righteous. This is a wonderful thing to petition the Lord for, on behalf of your loved ones and for your own life. Pray these verses today and in the days ahead, not only before job interviews and decisions, but for business relationships and daily encounters in ministry and life.

FATHER, thank you for the gift of being able to enter your house and worship at your temple every day. I ask you to lead me down right paths and to show me which way to turn. Thank you for protecting me from my enemies. You and you alone deliver me from them! Thank you for surrounding me with the shield of your love and favor.

Listen to my cry for help, my King and my God, for I will never pray to anyone but you. . . . Because of your unfailing love, I can enter your house; with deepest awe I will worship at your Temple. Lead me in the right path, O Lord, or my enemies will conquer me. Tell me clearly what to do, and show me which way to turn. . . . For you bless the godly, O Lord, surrounding them with your shield of love.

Psalm 5:2, 7-8, 12

MEASURE NOT GOD'S LOVE AND FAVOR BY YOUR OWN FEELING. THE SUN SHINES AS CLEARLY IN THE DARKEST DAY AS IT DOES IN THE BRIGHTEST. THE DIFFERENCE IS NOT IN THE SUN, BUT IN SOME CLOUDS. Richard Sibbs (1577–1635)

The One Year Bible readings for today are **Genesis 11:1–13:4; Matthew 5:1-26; Psalm 5:1-12;** and **Proverbs 1:24-28.**

JANUARY

6

Praying for Our Enemies

[Jesus said,] "You have heard that the law of Moses says, 'Love your neighbor' and hate your enemy. But I say, love your enemies! Pray for those who persecute you! In that way, you will be acting as true children of your Father in heaven."
Matthew 5:43-45

There are times when others will misunderstand, mistreat, or persecute us, and it's hard not to respond to such treatment by retaliating or rejecting those who act that way toward us. That would be the way the unredeemed world naturally reacts. But Jesus says in these verses that we are to offer a radically different response: we are to love and pray for our enemies; in other words, we are to respond with the energy of prayer instead of the energy of hate.

This approach upholds a basic foundation of our faith—that God is love, that his love is for all people, whether friend or foe toward us, and that he desires that not one would perish but that all would come to eternal life. When we pray for our enemies, we are not only partnering with Christ in his redemptive purposes but also becoming more like our Father in heaven. Ask God to give you a specific Scripture verse to pray for your "enemies" whenever they come to mind. Instead of dwelling on a negative thought about them, displace the negative thought. Praying God's heart for someone will soon produce a reflection of his love in your own.

LORD, please fill my heart with compassion for [insert name(s)]. Help me to pray for these people and to bless, not curse, them. I can do this only as I look to you as my example. Thank you for dying on the cross for me so that I could be reconciled to the Father. Let my heart respond to my enemies, even as your heart was poured out on their behalf.

NEVER CEASE LOVING A PERSON AND NEVER GIVE UP HOPE FOR HIM, FOR EVEN THE PRODIGAL SON WHO HAD FALLEN MOST LOW COULD STILL BE SAVED. THE BITTEREST ENEMY AND ALSO HE WHO WAS YOUR FRIEND COULD AGAIN BE YOUR FRIEND; LOVE THAT HAS GROWN COLD CAN KINDLE AGAIN. Søren Kierkegaard (1813–1855)

The One Year Bible readings for today are **Genesis 13:5–15:21; Matthew 5:27-48; Psalm 6:1-10;** and **Proverbs 1:29-33.**

prayer

The Value of Private Prayer

Jesus is our pattern and example for prayer, not only in giving us the Lord's Prayer but also in the way he practiced prayer himself during his life on earth. He often left the multitudes and his disciples and went apart to pray alone with his Father in heaven. He didn't just flash an eloquent prayer heavenward to impress his followers; he spent solitary, extended times talking and listening to God. In this passage he exhorts us to do the same. Jesus tells us not to pray like the Pharisees, whose goal was to impress others with their prayers, but to get alone with God and to "shut the door" behind us. That means setting aside our work and tasks, separating ourselves from family, from a spouse, and even from our prayer partners at times, in order to have intimate conversation with our Father in heaven. Then God, who sees and knows all secrets, promises to reward us.

LORD, my heart longs to hear your voice just as Jesus did. Help me to draw away from this frantic and busy world to be alone with you. Open my eyes to see what you want to show me, my ears to hear what you desire to tell me. Then and only then will I know what to pray in secret as I respond to your heart.

FROM THREE TO FOUR EACH MORNING—THAT IS MY HOUR. THEN I AM FREE FROM INTERRUPTION AND FROM THE FEAR OF INTERRUPTION. EACH MORNING I WAKE AT THREE AND LIVE AN HOUR WITH GOD. IT GIVES ME STRENGTH FOR EVERYTHING. WITHOUT IT I WOULD BE UTTERLY HELPLESS. Toyohiko Kagawa (1888–1951)

When you pray, don't be like the hypocrites who love to pray publicly on street corners and in the synagogues where everyone can see them. I assure you, that is all the reward they will ever get. But when you pray, go away by yourself, shut the door behind you, and pray to your Father secretly. Then your Father, who knows all secrets, will reward you.
Matthew 6:5-6

The One Year Bible readings for today are **Genesis 16:1–18:15; Matthew 6:1-24; Psalm 7:1-17;** and **Proverbs 2:1-5.**

JANUARY

8

Keep Asking

[Jesus said,] "Keep on asking, and you will be given what you ask for. Keep on looking, and you will find. Keep on knocking, and the door will be opened. For everyone who asks, receives. Everyone who seeks, finds."
Matthew 7:7-8

God is seeking people who will give themselves to earnest, persevering prayer. In these verses Jesus instructs us not to pray just once or twice for what we desire but to repeatedly come to him in the same way the persistent widow in Luke 18 did—to ask and keep on asking, to look and keep on looking, to knock and keep on knocking—and we will receive, find, and experience the opening of doors. If we could simply kneel down, ask for what we want, instantly get what we prayed for, and then run back to our own pursuits, our spiritual life and interaction with God would be superficial and minimal, and we would experience little growth. It is in the places where we have to persevere in prayer that we learn persistence in prayer, receive the most blessing, see our faith growing stronger, and most glorify God. It is when we persist in prayer that God prepares a person or works behind the scenes in the problem we are praying about.

Is there something about which you sense that God wants you to persevere in prayer until the answer comes? Write it down, and seek him today and every day until it's done!

LORD, thank you for your promise that those who ask receive and that when we seek, we will find. Grant me the grace to persevere, to keep on asking, seeking, and knocking until the answer comes. Thank you for the power and grace of your Spirit, who gives me the strength to persevere in prayer even when I am at my weakest moment and ready to give up.

IT IS NOT ENOUGH TO BEGIN TO PRAY, NOR TO PRAY ARIGHT; NOR IS IT ENOUGH TO CONTINUE FOR A TIME TO PRAY; BUT WE MUST PATIENTLY, BELIEVINGLY, CONTINUE IN PRAYER UNTIL WE OBTAIN AN ANSWER. George Müller (1805–1898)

The One Year Bible readings for today are **Genesis 18:16–19:38; Matthew 6:25–7:14; Psalm 8:1-9;** and **Proverbs 2:6-15.**

knowing

Knowing God

Those who know your name trust in you, for you, O Lord, have never abandoned anyone who searches for you.
Psalm 9:10

David was a man who knew the God he served. He hadn't just heard about the Lord. He had walked with him. That's why he loved God and could thank him with all his heart in good or bad times.

"To know, know, know him is to love, love, love him," says an old song about romantic love. We do not trust those we do not know. Throughout the Scriptures God gives us snapshots of his character as he reveals himself in his workings in history, in his people, and especially through his many names: Name above All Names, Jehovah Jireh (the Lord Our Provider), Jehovah Shalom (the Lord Our Peace), God Our Refuge and Strong Tower, Our Shepherd, and in this psalm, "a shelter for the oppressed, a refuge in times of trouble" (v. 9).

It is easy to focus our eyes on the things that shake our lives and the difficulties that try our souls and forget who God is. Although we can never plumb the depths of God's nature with our finite minds, we can pursue a lifelong quest to know him. Then his promise in today's verse—that God has never abandoned anyone who searches for him—will be true in our experience.

OH GOD, grant me the deepest desires of my heart—to know you and be known by you. Remind me of the marvelous things you have done for me so that I can tell others. Thank you for filling me with joy because your presence is near me and your Spirit dwells within me. Today I will sing forth your praises! I thank you with all my heart.

HOW SWEET THE NAME OF JESUS SOUNDS IN
A BELIEVER'S EAR!
IT SOOTHES HIS SORROW, HEALS HIS WOUNDS, AND
DRIVES AWAY HIS FEAR!

John Newton (1725–1807)

The One Year Bible readings for today are **Genesis 20:1–22:24; Matthew 7:15-29; Psalm 9:1-12;** and **Proverbs 2:16-22.**

JANUARY

10

Seek God's Understanding

Trust in the Lord with all your heart; do not depend on your own understanding. Seek his will in all you do, and he will direct your paths.
Proverbs 3:5-6

These verses from Proverbs can be a continual, lifelong, daily prayer for us to pray for all those we love, because our natural tendency is to lean on our own understanding and do things our way instead of depending on God's wisdom and ways. The longer I live, the more I realize that all of our responsibilities, all that God has called us to do, are beyond our own human ability. There is nothing I can do apart from God. In everything—whether it is parenting; relationships with my husband, children, grandchildren, and friends; ministry work; writing; speaking; or teaching—I need to depend on God, seek his higher understanding, his wisdom and his will, and then trust in his leading with all my heart. As I do these things, I become the recipient of God's wonderful promise in Proverbs 3:6—he will direct my path—a promise that is backed by all the honor of his name. Even when it seems that there is no way out, when we've hit our own limitations or a dead end, God will guide us and make a way for us.

LORD, help me to trust in you with all my heart today. Guard me from depending on my own limited understanding. Instead, help me to rely totally on you. I desire to seek your will in all I do today. Thank you for the promise that you will direct my paths so that I can walk hand in hand with you, depend on your higher understanding, and seek your will in all I do.

BECAUSE OUR UNDERSTANDING IS EARTHBOUND . . . HUMAN TO THE CORE . . . LIMITED . . . FINITE . . . WE OPERATE IN A DIMENSION TOTALLY UNLIKE OUR LORD . . . WHO KNOWS NO SUCH LIMITATIONS. WE SEE NOW. HE SEES FOREVER.
Charles R. Swindoll (b. 1934)

The One Year Bible readings for today are **Genesis 23:1–24:51; Matthew 8:1-17; Psalm 9:13-20;** and **Proverbs 3:1-6.**

faith

Increase Our Faith

Jesus got into the boat and started across the lake with his disciples. Suddenly, a terrible storm came up, with waves breaking into the boat. But Jesus was sleeping. The disciples went to him and woke him up, shouting, "Lord, save us! We're going to drown!" And Jesus answered, "Why are you afraid? You have so little faith!"
Matthew 8:23-26

The storm that came up that night struck terror in these veteran fishermen's hearts. Would they be shipwrecked? Would they perish? They panicked and doubted whether Jesus was aware of or even cared if they drowned. Like the disciples, we sometimes get into troubles that feel so overwhelming, storms that rage so furiously, that we're sure our boat is about to be swamped and we'll drown. It may seem to us—as it did to the disciples in today's verses—that Jesus is sleeping, that he is unconcerned and unaware of our plight, and we cry, "Lord, save us!" When we are panicked and overwhelmed, Jesus asks us as he did that day on the Sea of Galilee, "Why are you afraid? You have so little faith!"

Though the storms will come again and again, Jesus is always with us and is working within us through these experiences to develop a faith that can withstand any tumultuous trial, any waves of difficulty.

OH, LORD, we forget that you are in the boat with us, that you rule over the wind and waves and storms in our lives. Increase our faith so that even in the midst of great turbulence we will not panic but will trust you to care for us. Let our spirits be able to rest at all times because your presence is always greater than any stormy circumstance we will face.

IT IS FAITH THAT BRINGS POWER, NOT MERELY PRAYING AND WEEPING AND STRUGGLING, BUT BELIEVING, DARING TO BELIEVE THE WRITTEN WORD WITH OR WITHOUT FEELING.
Catherine Booth (1829–1890)

The One Year Bible readings for today are **Genesis 24:52–26:16; Matthew 8:18-34; Psalm 10:1-15;** and **Proverbs 3:7-8.**

JANUARY
12

medicine

Good Medicine

When he heard [the Pharisees' criticism], Jesus replied, "Healthy people don't need a doctor—sick people do." Then he added, "Now go and learn the meaning of this Scripture: 'I want you to be merciful; I don't want your sacrifices.' For I have come to call sinners, not those who think they are already good enough."
Matthew 9:12-13

When Jesus ate with the tax collectors, he caused a stir throughout the city. Many were men of ill repute who abused their power over their fellow citizens by overcharging them and then lining their own pockets with the difference. The Pharisees reasoned that if Jesus were truly the Messiah, he would not seek out these vile men but would eat with the righteous instead. When the Pharisees confronted Jesus about this, he silenced them with a challenge to discover the true meaning of mercy, defined by his own example. Rather than wait for the unbeliever to come to church, Christ brought a living gospel to the doorstep of their homes.

The challenge is no less compelling today. Right outside the walls of your local church are people who are seeking answers. There are those who need healing, who are lonely, and who may even be reviled by others in their community. You have good medicine to dispense—a gospel message that heals hearts and changes lives and reconciles sinners to a merciful Savior.

GOD, thank you for showing me that you desire that I be merciful rather than make sacrifices to you. You come to those of us who know that apart from you we are sick instead of to those who believe that they are well but are really sick at heart. Thank you for being my Great Physician and for never being too busy to attend to my needs or wounds. Guide me in joyfully dispensing to others the good medicine you pour out to me.

GOD IS NOT SAVING THE WORLD; IT IS DONE. OUR BUSINESS IS TO GET MEN AND WOMEN TO REALIZE IT. Oswald Chambers (1874–1917)

The One Year Bible readings for today are **Genesis 26:17–27:46; Matthew 9:1-17; Psalm 10:16-18;** and **Proverbs 3:9-10.**

workers

The Workers Are Few

Jesus saw the people not just as a whole massive group but as individuals suffering from pain, sickness, and grief. And while he felt deep compassion and healed them of every kind of disease and illness, he also enlisted his disciples to pray for more workers, for the harvest was ready, the kingdom was at hand, and the workers were few.

People are no different today. Many around us are lost and lonely. Their problems are great, and they don't know where to get real help and restoration for their broken lives. So the Lord of the harvest is imploring us to join him in the great commission by praying for laborers who will be his hands and feet on this earth, those who will bring lost sheep home to the shepherd.

LORD, I am so grateful that you heal every disease and illness that afflicts people. I pray that you will send laborers who will bring your healing and transforming power to the lives of people who don't know you. And while I am praying for workers, please make me willing by your Spirit to join you in the harvest fields. You and you alone are Lord of the harvest. Let your kingdom come on earth as it is in heaven!

THERE IS NO ROYAL ROAD TO BECOMING A WORKER FOR GOD. THE ONLY WAY IS TO LET GOD IN HIS MIGHTY PROVIDENCE IN ONE WAY OR ANOTHER GET THE LIFE OUT TO SEA IN RECKLESS ABANDON TO GOD. Oswald Chambers (1874–1917)

Wherever [Jesus] went, he healed people of every sort of disease and illness. He felt great pity for the crowds that came, because their problems were so great and they didn't know where to go for help. They were like sheep without a shepherd. He said to his disciples, "The harvest is so great, but the workers are so few. So pray to the Lord who is in charge of the harvest; ask him to send out more workers for his fields."

Matthew 9:35-38

The One Year Bible readings for today are **Genesis 28:1–29:35; Matthew 9:18-38; Psalm 11:1-7;** and **Proverbs 3:11-12.**

JANUARY

14

Words for Disciples

When you are arrested, don't worry about what to say in your defense, because you will be given the right words at the right time. For it won't be you doing the talking—it will be the Spirit of your Father speaking through you.
Matthew 10:19-20

Some of the traveling instructions that Jesus gave to his twelve disciples—such as don't take any money with you, and don't carry a bag or even an extra coat (Matthew 10:9-10)—may sound strange to our modern ears. But imbedded in Christ's words are important principles and, most important, a call for a deeper level of trust. In verse 19 Jesus carries that need to trust God even into the courtroom, advising his followers not to worry about relying on their own natural abilities to devise a clever defense, because God would give them the right words at the right time. Perhaps it is not a court trial you face but a job situation, a misunderstanding with a friend, or a problem with your teen. This chapter assures you of something wonderful: that God himself will give you the inspiration as you rely on him to do so. As you stay tuned-in to him and actively trust him and wait for his prompting, it won't be you doing the talking—it will be the Spirit of your Father. Rest today in the truth that the Lord will bring his words to your mind and that his words always accomplish the purposes for which they are sent.

LORD, I'm thankful that you desire to speak through me. Help me learn to depend completely on you and to trust you for the right words at the right time. Whenever I am in a tight spot, I know that you are especially with me then, giving me just the right words to say to bring your life, light, and hope to people surrounded by darkness. I will give you all the glory because you are the only One who can do this. Thank you for your wisdom and timing, which are always perfect.

IN PRAYER YOU ALIGN YOURSELF TO THE PURPOSES AND POWER OF GOD AND HE IS ABLE TO DO THINGS THROUGH YOU HE COULDN'T DO OTHERWISE. E. Stanley Jones (1884–1973)

The One Year Bible readings for today are **Genesis 30:1–31:16; Matthew 10:1-23; Psalm 12:1-8;** and **Proverbs 3:13-15.**

Of Infinite Value

Not even a sparrow, worth only half a penny, can fall to the ground without your Father knowing it. And the very hairs on your head are all numbered. So don't be afraid; you are more valuable to him than a whole flock of sparrows.
Matthew 10:29-31

God cares about even the smallest creatures that in the world's eyes are worth only a penny or less. The same God who created the expanse of the heavens, majestic mountains, glaciers, and everything else on earth and holds the whole world together by his powerful word knows the number of hairs on our heads—and watchfully and lovingly cares about each one of us individually. This one truth is worth rejoicing about all day—God cares about me! I am of infinite value to him. Nothing happens to me apart from his knowledge. He knows my name, my aches and struggles, and he loves me. We do not have to be afraid, for our heavenly Father is watching over us. Our part is to stay connected by trusting him.

LORD, thank you for your tender, watchful care. Help me to remember all through the day that you are with me. You know every detail about my life—who I am, what I like, where I go—nothing is hidden from you. I rejoice because I have no need to be afraid. Your love for me means more than anything else in this world. May I go about my days with quiet confidence and peace, knowing that I am safe in your hand.

WE HAVE BEEN PLANTED ACCORDING TO A DIVINE PATTERN, EVEN IF WE DO NOT ALWAYS UNDERSTAND THAT PATTERN. GOD IS INTERESTED IN EACH OF US "MICROSCOPICALLY" AS WELL AS "TELESCOPICALLY." THE HAIRS OF OUR HEADS HAVE BEEN COUNTED, BUT THE UNIVERSE IS ALSO IN HIS HAND. Corrie ten Boom (1892–1983)

The One Year Bible readings for today are **Genesis 31:17–32:12; Matthew 10:24–11:6; Psalm 13:1-6;** and **Proverbs 3:16-18.**

JANUARY

16

burden

His Burden Is Light

Then Jesus said, "Come to me, all of you who are weary and carry heavy burdens, and I will give you rest. Take my yoke upon you. Let me teach you, because I am humble and gentle, and you will find rest for your souls. For my yoke fits perfectly, and the burden I give you is light."

Matthew 11:28-30

What heavy burden is weighing you down and causing a heaviness and weariness in your spirit? Is it the need to take care of an elderly parent? a seemingly impossible deadline at work? juggling overwhelming responsibilities of a job plus parenting a houseful of kids? the burden of chronic illness? a difficult relationship with someone you love? financial struggles?

Whatever your "heavy burden" might be, Jesus invites you, just as he did the crowds he was teaching: *Come to me. Give me the heavy load you're carrying. And in exchange, I will give you rest.*

Whenever I read these verses from Matthew, I breathe a sigh of relief. Jesus knows the challenges and deadlines we face and the weariness of mind or body we feel. He understands the stress, tasks, and responsibilities that are weighing us down. As we lay all that concerns us before him, his purpose replaces our agenda, and his lightness and rest replace our burden.

LORD, thank you for your offer to carry my burdens for me. I give them all to you and I gladly receive your rest! I place myself under your yoke to learn from you. Teach me your wisdom that is humble and pure, and help me to walk in the ways you set before me. Thank you for your mercy and love that invite me to live my life resting and trusting in you!

WHEN HE SAYS TO YOUR DISTURBED, DISTRACTED, RESTLESS SOUL OR MIND, "COME UNTO ME," HE IS SAYING, COME OUT OF THE STRIFE AND DOUBT AND STRUGGLE OF WHAT IS AT THE MOMENT WHERE YOU STAND, INTO THAT WHICH WAS AND IS AND IS TO BE—THE ETERNAL, THE ESSENTIAL, THE ABSOLUTE. Phillips Brooks (1835–1893)

The One Year Bible readings for today are **Genesis 32:13–34:31; Matthew 11:7-30; Psalm 14:1-7;** and **Proverbs 3:19-20.**

enter

Who May Enter?

Who may worship in your sanctuary, Lord? Who may enter your presence on your holy hill? Those who lead blameless lives and do what is right, speaking the truth from sincere hearts.
Psalm 15:1-2

When we kneel at the altar, we present our hearts in reverent worship to God. It is our inward sacrifice of praise. In these verses the psalmist presents another side of worship—the worship that praises God with our lives. We offer this type of worship when we live in integrity and honesty in everyday situations. We offer it when we treat others with fairness in business deals and speak highly of others no matter who is listening. When we avoid the bitter tongue of gossip, tell the truth instead of resorting to a lie, or keep a promise we have made even at great cost, we are showing that our lives are a living sacrifice of worship to God.

I'm thankful that we don't have to be perfect to worship God. No one is without fault. However, when we endeavor to worship God through the way we live our lives, we offer him more than a show of worship. We present him with a heartbeat that sincerely desires to please him. Ask God today to help you live in such a way that your life is an offering of praise to his name.

GOD, I am far from perfect, but I desire to serve you in integrity and honesty. I realize that others watch my life and that my daily decisions influence others. I pray that they will see you in both my words and my actions. Lord, I sincerely desire to worship you not only with my heart but with my character. Help me to live a blameless life. Only you can do this. May I speak your truth from a sincere heart so that you will receive the glory and honor you deserve.

THE HEART THAT IS NOT ENTRUSTED TO GOD FOR HIS SEARCHING, WILL NOT BE UNDERTAKEN BY HIM FOR CLEANSING.
Frances Ridley Havergal (1836–1879)

The One Year Bible readings for today are **Genesis 35:1–36:43; Matthew 12:1-21; Psalm 15:1-5;** and **Proverbs 3:21-26.**

JANUARY

18

blessings

Unexpected Blessings

Do not withhold good from those who deserve it when it's in your power to help them.
Proverbs 3:27

Isn't it fun to watch television shows where people are surprised with unexpected blessings? The gift might be an elaborate wedding for a couple who couldn't afford it or a houseful of appliances for a struggling family. We delight in their joy, vicariously participating in their excitement. We may even imagine what it would be like if we had the same means of blessing others.

The fact is that we are surrounded with opportunities to share good things with others: a homemade apple pie to welcome a new neighbor, a note telling the youth pastor what a great job he is doing, a sincere compliment to a loved one. If we wait to do good to others until we can perform benevolent deeds on a grand scale, we miss the point and the opportunity. We have the power to act because Christ, who lives within us, came to serve. As we are yoked together with him, we will find ourselves ministering to others with his grace and love. What unexpected blessing can you share with someone today?

DEAR GOD, I realize that with you as my life, I have the power to encourage my brother or sister. I know that I also have the power to discourage people simply by withholding good things—whether great or small. Help me to look for opportunities today to delight someone with an unexpected blessing! Thank you for the chance to participate in showing your goodness to each person you place in my path.

GOD IS NOT GLORIFIED SO MUCH BY PREACHING, OR TEACHING, OR ANYTHING ELSE, AS BY HOLY LIVING. Catherine Booth (1829–1890)

The One Year Bible readings for today are **Genesis 37:1–38:30; Matthew 12:22-45; Psalm 16:1-11;** and **Proverbs 3:27-32.**

attention

God's Watchful Attention

In this prayer psalm David uses two vivid word pictures to invoke God's help for the danger that was pressing on him. "Guard me as the apple of your eye," he says. He is asking the Lord to keep his eye on him, to show his love by guarding David with his watchful attention. David's request "Hide me in the shadow of your wings" compares God's protection to the way a mother bird cares for and shields her own babies from danger by gathering them under her spread wings to hide them from predators.

David rested his petitions on the fact that God's very nature is to be loving, watchful, and protective. As you read these verses aloud, picture yourself as that little bird safe under God's wings. When we rest in his presence and protection, we can trust in God's care and infinite, unconditional love for us this day as well as in the days to come.

I am praying to you because I know you will answer, O God. Bend down and listen as I pray. Show me your unfailing love in wonderful ways. You save with your strength those who seek refuge from their enemies. Guard me as the apple of your eye. Hide me in the shadow of your wings.

Psalm 17:6-8

LORD, you are the God who cares for us watchfully and attunes your ears to our prayers, simply because we are your children. I ask that you show me your unfailing love today in whatever unexpected, wonderful ways you choose. I draw near to you and seek refuge from my enemies. Thank you for hiding me in the shadow of your wings. You guard me and give me life because I am the apple of your eye. Thank you for your tender, fatherly care.

ENTRUST YOURSELF TO GOD, AS A CHILD WOULD ENTRUST HIMSELF TO HIS FATHER. YOU WILL FIND THAT EVEN IN THE DARKEST HOUR HE WILL NOT LET YOU FALL. Mother Basilea Schlink (1904–2001)

The One Year Bible readings for today are **Genesis 39:1–41:16; Matthew 12:46–13:23; Psalm 17:1-15;** and **Proverbs 3:33-35.**

JANUARY
20

Worthy of Praise

I love you, Lord; you are my strength. The Lord is my rock, my fortress, and my savior; my God is my rock, in whom I find protection. He is my shield, the strength of my salvation, and my stronghold. I will call on the Lord, who is worthy of praise, for he saves me from my enemies.
Psalm 18:1-3

Hunted and chased like an animal, David had been in terrible distress and danger, but God had preserved his life and rescued him. Because of God's help, David hadn't just survived; he had emerged victorious. So he sings Psalm 18, a psalm of thanksgiving for all God has done and for who he is to David. It is a great song of worship and praise for the Lord's divine intervention in delivering David against all odds from his enemy Saul and for bringing David through his difficulties to a future and hope.

In singing God's praises, David uses vivid metaphors: "my rock" (stability and security), "my shield" (the one who guards and keeps me safe), "the strength of my salvation" (my source of strength when I'm weak), and "my stronghold" (the place I can go for protection). In David's darkest hour the Lord revealed himself in these ways, and he wants to reveal himself in our lives too—right where we are in our distress, in the problems that try us, and in our victories. Ask him to reveal himself in whatever you're facing today, and join David in praising the Lord who is "worthy of praise"!

LORD, when I am beset by difficulties, be my rock—my source of security in an uncertain world. In you alone I find protection. You are my stronghold; I need nothing else. Be my strength when I'm weak. Be my shield of protection from those who would harm me. Be the strength of my salvation when I call on you, and I will ever praise you because you are worthy.

GOD REVEALS HIMSELF UNFAILINGLY TO THE THOUGHTFUL SEEKER. Honoré de Balzac (1799–1850)

The One Year Bible Readings for today are Genesis 41:17–42:17; Matthew 13:24-46; Psalm 18:1-15; and **Proverbs 4:1-6.**

JANUARY

21

scars

Scars of the Past

Joseph made a hasty exit because he was overcome with emotion for his brother and wanted to cry. Going into his private room, he wept there.
Genesis 43:30

It has been said that the most painful cuts of all are those inflicted by others. Surely Joseph's life exemplified that truth. The sight of Benjamin, after Joseph's long separation from his family, was a raw reminder of his other brothers' cruel deception. Though God had granted Joseph favor during the dark days of his slavery and unjust imprisonment, the young boy standing in front of him represented undeniable proof of what Joseph had lost—not only a brother but a beloved father and a homeland. Surely Joseph was tempted to repay his brothers for their evil deeds. Instead, he invited them into his home to feed them. He devised a plan that would reconcile himself to his family. He could have punished his brothers a thousand times over for their actions. Instead, he chose to extend forgiveness.

When others affect the course of your life, you face a moment of decision. Though you cannot change the past, you can affect the future by your response to the wrong you suffered at their hands. You can feed the fire of bitterness, or you can hold your scars before God and ask for grace to forgive others for what they have done in the past.

LORD, I do not deny the pain that I have experienced, but by your grace I give you those painful wounds, no matter how deep they are. I realize that I am powerless to fix the past or to change others, but I also understand that your love can heal me. I give you my scars, O God, and I thank you for the peace and mercy and joy that will flourish within me in the absence of bitterness.

THE VOICE OF SIN IS LOUD, BUT THE VOICE OF FORGIVENESS IS LOUDER. D. L. Moody (1837–1899)

The One Year Bible readings for today are **Genesis 42:18–43:34; Matthew 13:47–14:12; Psalm 18:16-36;** and **Proverbs 4:7-10.**

JANUARY

22

lessons

Life Lessons

If you live a life guided by wisdom, you won't limp or stumble as you run.

Proverbs 4:12

We often find life's lessons in surprising places. When an elderly couple stares into each other's eyes with deep and genuine affection, they teach us that love can last forever. When a friend is struck with a terrible sickness and his faith remains intact, we learn that God will carry us through the hard times. When a baby falls while learning to walk and then doggedly pulls himself back up and tries again, he shares a lesson about tenacity. When storms come and bend a tree's massive branches to the ground, we learn that even those that are battered will stand straight again when the sun comes out the next day.

Many people define wisdom as knowing the rules and following them, yet it is so much more. You can find wisdom by heeding the examples of those who have gone before you, finding nuggets of truth in unexpected places or circumstances, opening your eyes to the magnitude of God through his magnificent creation. Wisdom is found by looking for God's lessons taught by those who surround us every day and then applying them to our lives.

LORD, thank you for lessons that come from the people you have placed in my path and from your creation of an intricate, amazing world. I pray that I will listen to those who have your wisdom and that I will learn from them. I'm thankful that your desire is not for me to limp or stumble along my path but to run the race accurately and quickly as I seek your wisdom to guide me to the finish line.

WISDOM IS OFTENTIMES NEARER WHEN WE STOOP THAN WHEN WE SOAR. William Wordsworth (1770–1850)

The One Year Bible Readings for today are **Genesis 44:1–45:28; Matthew 14:13-36; Psalm 18:37-50;** and **Proverbs 4:11-13.**

confession

Confession

Each of us has blind spots and lacks knowledge about all the sins and hidden faults in our lives, particularly those "lurking" in our hearts. But thank God that we have a Savior whose blood was spilled at Calvary for those very sins so that we can ask him to cleanse us from hidden faults and not allow deliberate sins to control our lives.

Both our hidden faults and our deliberate sins are the reasons we need to make time in our prayer and devotions for confession—for asking the Holy Spirit to search our hearts, to show us the behaviors and thoughts for which we need cleansing and that left unconfessed, can keep us from experiencing his grace.

Then what freedom, what joy Christ offers us—the breastplate of righteousness, the cleansing of our consciences, and right standing with God the Father, based not on our own works but on the grace of God alone. What hidden faults and sins are working in your heart? Spend some time in reflection today, writing down whatever the Spirit shows you and giving these to God.

How can I know all the sins lurking in my heart? Cleanse me from these hidden faults. Keep me from deliberate sins! Don't let them control me. Then I will be free of guilt and innocent of great sin. May the words of my mouth and the thoughts of my heart be pleasing to you, O Lord, my rock and my redeemer.

Psalm 19:12-14

LORD, I am blind to so much. There is no way I can know all the sins lurking in my heart. But you know them. I ask your Holy Spirit to shine your light on my blind spots, to cleanse me from hidden faults so that I can confess my sin and receive your forgiveness. Help me to grow in transparency and openness before you so that I might walk in your freedom and grace.

GOD IN HIS WISDOM ONLY GIVES THE GRACE OF SELF-KNOWLEDGE GRADUALLY. . . . BUT AS WE PERCEIVE AND CONQUER THE MORE GLARING FAULTS, HIS GRACIOUS LIGHT SHOWS US THE SUBTLER, MORE HIDDEN IMPERFECTIONS; AND THIS SPIRITUAL PROCESS LASTS ALL THROUGH LIFE. Jean Nicolas Grou (1731–1803)

The One Year Bible Readings for today are **Genesis 46:1–47:31; Matthew 15:1-28; Psalm 19:1-14;** and **Proverbs 4:14-19.**

legacy

A Father's Legacy

These are the twelve tribes of Israel, and these are the blessings with which Jacob blessed his twelve sons. Each received a blessing that was appropriate to him.
Genesis 49:28

The act of blessing in the Old Testament was much more significant than just an inheritance of gifts or money. A spoken blessing was a legacy that a father left to a son. When Jacob called his sons around him, the scene was much different from when he had stolen his brother Esau's blessing on their father Isaac's deathbed. At that time Jacob was known as "the deceiver." His sad example continued into the next generation, when his sons sold their brother Joseph into slavery. As Jacob lay on his deathbed, however, he could no longer be identified as a dishonest man. He had learned from his early mistakes and was now known as a man of honor. Though he bestowed spoken blessings on his sons, the example of his changed life was a living legacy that would have an impact on the generations that came after him.

We, too, will leave a legacy to those who will follow us. We have the opportunity to influence the outcome of our own destiny as we follow Christ, but we also have the chance to shape the lives of those who will follow in our footsteps. What kind of legacy are you leaving for the next generation?

FATHER, when I make wrong decisions, help me to be honest and transparent before you. Please help me to follow you faithfully so that I can be a blessing to those you've placed in my trust and to those around me who will be watching my example. As you have blessed me, your child, so I yearn to bless others.

THE POWER TO REPRODUCE GODLY OFFSPRING REMAINS PRIMARILY WITH THE PARENT WHO LOVES THE LORD, KNOWS AND OBEYS HIS WORD, AND IS COMMITTED TO THE DEPTH OF HIS HEART TO PRODUCE GODLY OFFSPRING. Bruce Wilkinson

The One Year Bible Readings for today are **Genesis 48:1–49:33; Matthew 15:29–16:12; Psalm 20:1-9;** and **Proverbs 4:20-27.**

JANUARY
25

know

I Know Him

Then [Jesus] asked them, "Who do you say I am?" Simon Peter answered, "You are the Messiah, the Son of the living God."
Matthew 16:15-16

How can people describe the ocean when they have not experienced it? How would they explain the waves that crash against the rocks or the shifting of the sand as the tide tugs at the shoreline? Are they able to put into words how the sand feels between their toes or describe the majesty of an endless blue horizon? Until they have taken a dip in the salty, white-frothed ocean, their descriptions would be limited.

Perhaps that is why Jesus asked the disciples to define their faith in him on a personal level rather than rely on what others had to say about him. Jesus challenged them to base their definition of who he was on the reality of what they had seen, heard, and experienced about him. Today, many stand in public platforms and attempt to define Jesus as a good man, a teacher, or a prophet while asserting that he could not possibly be the Messiah. Yet we who have experienced the depths of his grace and love can offer firsthand knowledge that he is real, that he has transformed our lives, and that his presence can bring light to a dark world.

Have you experienced the reality of who Christ is? Then you can confidently share the truth with others because you know him personally!

LORD, thank you for giving me a faith in you that is real and personal. There are so many who don't know you and need to hear the truth. Help me to share my faith in such a way that others will be drawn to you and will accept you as their Savior.

LIFE PASSES, RICHES FLY AWAY, POPULARITY IS FICKLE, THE SENSES DECAY, THE WORLD CHANGES. ONE ALONE IS TRUE TO US; ONE ALONE CAN BE ALL THINGS TO US; ONE ALONE CAN SUPPLY OUR NEED. Cardinal John Henry Newman (1801–1890)

The One Year Bible Readings for today are **Genesis 50:1 – Exodus 2:10; Matthew 16:13–17:9; Psalm 21:1-13;** and **Proverbs 5:1-6.**

mountains

Mustard Seeds and Mountains

The disciples asked Jesus privately, "Why couldn't we cast out that [boy's] demon?" "You didn't have enough faith," Jesus told them. "I assure you, even if you had faith as small as a mustard seed you could say to this mountain, 'Move from here to there,' and it would move. Nothing would be impossible."
Matthew 17:19-20

Did you know that an average-sized aspirin bottle holds more than 180,000 mustard seeds? One of those miniscule seeds, when planted in fertile soil, can produce a ten-foot bush within three months! How many times have we faced mountains and felt that our faith was small and insufficient? We might have asked ourselves how God could remove a mountain in light of the fact that our faith is so inadequate. Perhaps we've even considered surrendering to the circumstances that stand in our way.

When the disciples felt the sting of failure over their inability to heal the boy in today's reading, Jesus directed them to place their faith—no matter how small—in him rather than in their own abilities.

The mustard seed is a reminder to walk to the base of the mountain hand in hand with the all-powerful God. It is a tangible symbol that it is not your strength that will move the mountain; rather, it is the God in whom you place your faith that can move a mountain out of your way.

GOD, the mountain of my circumstances seems so large, yet when I look to you as the source of my strength, it becomes insignificant. My faith seems small, yet when I place it in the Creator's hands, it can produce a greater harvest than I could ever imagine. Lord, take my tiny seed of faith, and multiply it with your strength, wisdom, and guidance. Thank you for assuring my heart that nothing is impossible with you.

FAITH IS TO PRAYER WHAT THE FEATHER IS TO THE ARROW; WITHOUT FAITH IT WILL NOT HIT THE MARK. J. C. Ryle (1816–1900)

The One Year Bible Readings for today are **Exodus 2:11–3:22; Matthew 17:10-27; Psalm 22:1-18;** and **Proverbs 5:7-14.**

ordinary

I'm Ordinary!

Conflicting emotions arise when someone asks us to do something for which we feel unprepared or inadequate. We tend to look in the mirror and scrutinize our faults and shortcomings. But we can be thankful that God views us in a much different light. He sees the promises he placed inside us when we were conceived. God knows our talents, and he also knows our disabilities and weaknesses. In today's verses Moses focused on just one aspect of the task—speaking—but God saw a much broader picture. He understood the hardships that were ahead. He knew that Moses was not a skilled speaker but that it was not Moses' speaking ability that would lead God's people through the wilderness. Rather, it was the leadership skills, faith in God, and strength of character that God had developed in him that would guide a multitude out of Egypt. God can enable you to do what he asks of you when you obey him. Just as a silver urn can be used to hold fine wine, so can a common crock. It's what is on the inside that matters. When God uses ordinary people to perform the extraordinary, then his name is lifted up!

[God told Moses,] "Now go, and do as I have told you. I will help you speak well, and I will tell you what to say." But Moses again pleaded, "Lord, please! Send someone else."

Exodus 4:12-13

GOD, I am ordinary, but you are amazing! You created me, and you see things you have placed inside me that I may not recognize yet. When you ask something of me, you also understand what I need to complete the task. Please use me in extraordinary ways so that people will know that you are behind it all and will exalt your name!

DO YOU HAVE AN IMPOSSIBLE JOB TO DO? HAS THE LORD TOLD YOU TO DO IT? GO AHEAD! WHEN WE PRAY, WE ENTER GOD'S DOMAIN FROM THE DOMAIN OF OUR INABILITY.
Corrie ten Boom (1892–1983)

The One Year Bible Readings for today are **Exodus 4:1–5:21; Matthew 18:1-20; Psalm 22:19-31;** and **Proverbs 5:15-21.**

JANUARY

28

action

Love in Action

The king called in the man he had forgiven and said, "You evil servant! I forgave you that tremendous debt because you pleaded with me. Shouldn't you have mercy on your fellow servant, just as I had mercy on you?" Then the angry king sent the man to prison until he had paid every penny. That's what my heavenly Father will do to you if you refuse to forgive your brothers and sisters in your heart.

Matthew 18:32-35

We live in a world that paints word pictures of love. We love our families. We love our careers. We even say we love inanimate things such as a beautiful painting or a new pair of shoes. But that type of love can't change our world. *Agape* love is Christ's unconditional love toward us, but *agapao* love is what others see as our actions reflect our love for Christ. If Christians truly demonstrated *agapao* love, then our world couldn't help but be drawn to Christ.

The man who punished his servant in today's verses failed to demonstrate *agapao* love. His own master could have thrown him into jail until he repaid a massive debt he owed, but instead, he had forgiven that debt. But somehow the man forgot all about mercy when he encountered the man who owed him a small sum. He extended no leniency and realized his error only when he was forced to assume his former indebtedness.

As Christians, we have been forgiven a debt so massive that we could never repay it. If you want to show Christ to a world that is seeking love, remember what Christ has freely given you, and then extend that mercy to others.

LORD, you've forgiven me so many times that I've lost count. Each time I fail you, you scoop me up and put me back in right standing with you. When I owe a debt of forgiveness, remind me of the times you've forgiven me. Give me your heart for each person who wrongs or offends me. Help me to walk in forgiveness daily because daily you forgive me.

LOVE HAS HANDS TO HELP OTHERS. IT HAS FEET TO HASTEN TO THE POOR AND NEEDY. IT HAS EYES TO SEE MISERY AND WANT. IT HAS EARS TO HEAR THE SIGHS AND SORROWS OF ME. THIS IS WHAT LOVE LOOKS LIKE. Augustine of Hippo (354–430)

The One Year Bible Readings for today are **Exodus 5:22–7:25; Matthew 18:21–19:12; Psalm 23:1-6;** and **Proverbs 5:22-23.**

children

Blessing the Children

While the disciples were rebuking the children and those bringing them to Jesus, Jesus stretched out his arms to welcome and bless the children. God has always valued children and has invited them into vital, prayerful communication with him that they can maintain throughout their lives. He responds to children's prayer groups and answers the simple requests of an individual child. Are you welcoming the children you parent or teach to Jesus? Are you praying with them and teaching them to pray so that they will know God and not just know about him? Ask for his help. Model a vibrant prayer life with God yourself. Pray fervently for these children. Ask God to help them see Jesus in you. Teach them all you know about how to pray to their heavenly Father. Do all you can to bring them to the One who loves them even more than you do.

LORD, thank you for the children in my life. Whether they are mine or someone else's, draw them close. Help me teach them by example to go to you in times of need and times of praise to trust you with every part of their lives. Jesus, I will be your hands and feet in the lives of children. Show me how to bless them as you would.

HOLY FATHER, SAVE OUR CHILDREN
THROUGH LIFE'S TROUBLED WATERS STEER THEM,
THROUGH LIFE'S BITTER BATTLE CHEER THEM,
FATHER, FATHER, BE THOU NEAR THEM.

Amy Carmichael (1867–1951)

Some children were brought to Jesus so he could lay his hands on them and pray for them. The disciples told them not to bother him. But Jesus said, "Let the children come to me. Don't stop them! For the Kingdom of Heaven belongs to such as these." And he put his hands on their heads and blessed them before he left.

Matthew 19:13-15

The One Year Bible Readings for today are **Exodus 8:1–9:35; Matthew 19:13-30; Psalm 24:1-10;** and **Proverbs 6:1-5.**

JANUARY

30

Consider the Ant

Take a lesson from the ants, you lazybones. Learn from their ways and be wise! Even though they have no prince, governor, or ruler to make them work, they labor hard all summer, gathering food for the winter.
Proverbs 6:6-8

The life expectancy of an ant is only forty-five to sixty-five days. In that time, ants help organize a colony, find food, look after their young, and protect the queen from intruders. Ants are real team players. As they squeeze the juice from their food, they secrete a portion into a second stomach to share later with their fellow ants. No wonder Solomon pointed out their work ethic! The ant is a wonderful example of what hard work can accomplish.

God has provided tailor-made opportunities for each of us and has given us gifts that enable us to reach for those dreams. It is sad that we sometimes lose those opportunities by investing our time in things that matter little. God has given us the ability to dream big and to work hard. He has also given us the ability to discern between those things that are worthy of our time and those that rob us of the chance to realize our destiny. Today as you go about your work, pray for the wisdom to know the difference.

LORD, you've challenged me with hopes and dreams of having an impact on my world. I don't want insignificant things to rob me of that destiny. Give me wisdom to discern what really matters. Help me to set realistic priorities in my life and to use my gifts to achieve the dreams you have for me. Thank you for the gift of this day. Help me to focus on what is really important, not merely on what is "urgent."

EVERY MOMENT COMES TO YOU PREGNANT WITH A DIVINE PURPOSE; TIME BEING SO PRECIOUS THAT GOD DEALS IT OUT ONLY SECOND BY SECOND. ONCE IT LEAVES YOUR HANDS AND YOUR POWER TO DO WITH IT AS YOU PLEASE, IT PLUNGES INTO ETERNITY, TO REMAIN FOREVER WHAT YOU MADE IT. Archbishop Fulton J. Sheen (1895–1979)

The One Year Bible Readings for today are **Exodus 10:1–12:13; Matthew 20:1-28; Psalm 25:1-15;** and **Proverbs 6:6-11.**

solitude

Unwanted Solitude

Turn to me and have mercy on me, for I am alone and in deep distress.
Psalm 25:16

Some of us long for solitude, praying for a quiet retreat where we can gather our thoughts or rest our tired bodies. Yet sometimes we are faced with solitude we neither ask for nor desire. The psalmist found himself in that singular place. His thoughts were large in a wilderness that seemed vast and empty. It is interesting that David didn't ask God to take him out of the barren land but invited God to join him there. He knew from experience that God's presence could illuminate any dark night.

Our journeys through life will not always take us on straight paths. They are interspersed with thrilling mountaintop heights at times and with valleys and lulls in activity at others. Sometimes those valleys are lonely indeed. We might find ourselves there because of a move eight hundred miles away from family and friends or because we have a gnawing hole in our hearts when a child leaves the nest for the first time. These are places we do not willingly walk, but we do not have to face those lonely times alone. God is willing to join us and to walk with us step-by-step, holding our hands as we find our way through the valley together.

FATHER, I am hurting, and I need you. I am thankful that I do not have to face times of loneliness without you. When I am in the valley, show me every step I should take to find my way through the darkness. Help me to remember that even your precious Son was alone in Gethsemane before his crucifixion. Show me your face now, as you revealed yourself to him at his time of greatest need.

THE SOUL HARDLY EVER REALIZES IT, BUT WHETHER HE IS A BELIEVER OR NOT, HIS LONELINESS IS REALLY A HOMESICKNESS FOR GOD.
Hubert Van Zeller (1905–1984)

The One Year Bible Readings for today are **Exodus 12:14–13:16; Matthew 20:29–21:22; Psalm 25:16-22;** and **Proverbs 6:12-15.**

two sons

A Tale of Two Sons

[Jesus said,] "What do you think about this? A man with two sons told the older boy, 'Son, go out and work in the vineyard today.' The son answered, 'No, I won't go,' but later he changed his mind and went anyway. Then the father told the other son, 'You go,' and he said, 'Yes, sir, I will.' But he didn't go."
Matthew 21:28-30

In the parable of the two sons it seems that both sons were disobedient. One offered eloquent promises, but his actions revealed a heartbeat of rebellion. The other son was openly defiant but later realized his error ("changed his mind") and returned to work in the vineyard. Jesus was teaching his disciples that they should not base their opinion merely on outward appearances, for there is no protective facade when we stand before an omnipotent Father.

There is also a second lesson in this parable. Just as God discerns deceitful or rebellious hearts, he also recognizes those who return to him with broken and repentant spirits. Do you know people who have walked away from God's calling on their lives? If you look only at outward appearances, you may be tempted to give up on them. But don't write them off spiritually or distance yourself from them. Pray for them. Ask God to fill you with his love for them and to give you spiritual eyes that see them from his perspective. Believe that God is able to renew their hearts and save them. Ask the Holy Spirit to draw them back, and anticipate the day when they will turn away from disobedience and return to the arms of their Father.

LORD, help me to obey you wherever you lead me. I lift up those who have turned away from you. I believe, Lord, that you are able to draw them back to your heart, but help my unbelief. Help me to persevere in prayer and to stand in the gap until they turn to you as their Father.

THERE IS NOTHING THAT MAKES US LOVE A MAN SO MUCH AS PRAYING FOR HIM. William Law (1686–1761)

The One Year Bible Readings for today are **Exodus 13:17–15:18; Matthew 21:23-46; Psalm 26:1-12;** and **Proverbs 6:16-19.**

Godcan

God Can Do It Again!

It had been only days since the children of Israel watched the cloud and the pillar of fire hover between them and the camp of the Egyptians who were pursuing them. The cloud had protected the Israelites during the day and the pillar of fire had provided warmth and light at night while plunging their enemies into darkness. Then they had watched as the breath of God parted the Red Sea, so they could cross on dry land, and then brought the wall of water crashing down on their enemies. Yet when the children of Israel faced thirst, they complained and murmured, wondering out loud whether God had brought them to the desert to die. How could they so quickly forget God's miracles?

Perhaps their focus was on their thirst rather than on the God who had proved himself faithful many times over. When you are in a difficult place, find courage and comfort by recalling all the times God has provided for you in the past. Write down one specific moment when God delivered you or gave you a miracle in some way, and thank him. Then remind yourself that if God did it before, he can do it again!

When they came to Marah, they finally found water. But the people couldn't drink it because it was bitter. (That is why the place was called Marah, which means "bitter.") Then the people turned against Moses. "What are we going to drink?" they demanded.
Exodus 15:23-24

LORD, you have proved your faithfulness over and over. Many times when the smoke of the battle has cleared, I can see clearly that you were with me the entire time. Help me to remember your goodness and faithfulness to me no matter what circumstances I may face today. Thank you for never forgetting about me!

IF WE HAVE NOTED THE LORD'S ANSWERS TO OUR PRAYERS AND THANKED HIM FOR WHAT WE HAVE RECEIVED OF HIM, THEN IT BECOMES EASIER FOR US, AND WE GET MORE COURAGE, TO PRAY FOR MORE. Ole Hallesby (1879–1961)

The One Year Bible Readings for today are **Exodus 15:19–17:7; Matthew 22:1-33; Psalm 27:1-6;** and **Proverbs 6:20-26.**

FEBRUARY

3

burnout

On the Brink of Burnout

"This is not good!" his father-in-law exclaimed. "You're going to wear yourself out—and the people, too. This job is too heavy a burden for you to handle all by yourself."
Exodus 18:17-18

Moses not only led thousands of people in a hostile environment but also served as judge in every argument, small or large. When Moses' father-in-law saw that Moses stood all day listening to the minor complaints of the people, he counseled him to slow down before he burned out. Moses wisely heeded the advice and delegated tasks to other capable leaders. This allowed him not only to rest in body but also to refresh himself spiritually so that he could accomplish the calling God had laid on his heart.

Sometimes we get caught in the same trap as Moses. It is easy to convince ourselves that no one can do the job quite like we can. Yet delegation is the most effective form of leadership. It fosters maturity in potential leaders and provides a wider foundation of talents for meeting diverse needs. Have you allowed others to share the joys and burdens of ministry, or are you wearing yourself out with a burden too heavy for you to handle all by yourself? Working as part of a team helps you to retain the pleasure of ministering to others without finding yourself exhausted and on the brink of burnout.

DEAR GOD, when I try to do things by myself, I am easily overwhelmed. Sometimes I'm tempted to give up because I am so tired. Give me the wisdom to listen to the wise counsel of others as Moses did. Thank you for always hearing me and for having all the answers even before I know what questions to ask! Help me to share my burden with others and to stop trying to do it all alone.

A BURDEN SHARED IS A LIGHTER LOAD. Anonymous

The One Year Bible Readings for today are **Exodus 17:8–19:15; Matthew 22:34–23:12; Psalm 27:7-14;** and **Proverbs 6:27-35.**

camel

There's a Camel in My Soup

Blind guides! You strain your water so you won't accidentally swallow a gnat; then you swallow a camel!
Matthew 23:24

Picture this: We reach over to pick a gnat out of our brother's soup only to discover a large, hairy camel sitting in our own bowl. When we lean in to get a better look, he spits in our eye. It's a camel, all right! Jesus paints a humorous picture of a serious subject—legalism. It's so easy to find fault with a brother or sister. After all, it's right there where we can see it plainly. Yet as we point out the gnats—those tiny, pesky faults in others that hover and annoy us—we have shortcomings the size of camels in our own lives!

When it comes to judging, what we need to do is offer our own hearts and minds daily to God so that his grace can redeem our failures. Then we can rejoice in our victories because we know that they are gifts from him. Even when we feel as if we have "arrived" and no longer have any imperfections, we still cannot judge our brother, for now we have a new camel in our soup—pride. Take a moment today and ask God to help you take your eyes off of others' faults and to help you examine your own heart.

PRECIOUS JESUS, the world judges others by what they look like, what they own, and what they believe. I know that you are a holy God and that sin grieves you, but let my judgment be reserved for my own heart. Help me to show mercy to my brother rather than condemnation. Thank you for extending mercy to me as I extend mercy to others.

WHEN ONE KNOWS ONESELF WELL, ONE IS NOT DESIROUS OF LOOKING INTO THE FAULTS OF OTHERS. John Moschus (ca. 550–619)

The One Year Bible Readings for today are **Exodus 19:16–21:21; Matthew 23:13-39; Psalm 28:1-9;** and **Proverbs 7:1-5.**

FEBRUARY

5

worship

Worship the Lord

Give honor to the Lord, you angels; give honor to the Lord for his glory and strength. Give honor to the Lord for the glory of his name. Worship the Lord in the splendor of his holiness.

Psalm 29:1-2

David had seen a powerful thunderstorm sweep across the land and attributed it to the power of the Lord. In this psalm, he calls on the angels and all God's people to join him in ascribing honor and glory to the Lord for his strength, his glory, and his holiness. "Give God the credit for the great things he does! Worship the Lord in the splendor of his holiness!" he urges us. David knew that the greatest thing in all our lives is to worship God. That's what we were created to do. When we give honor to God, he blesses us and lights our path. When we look at his glory and holiness, he gives us his perspective, and everything else pales in comparison. But when our busyness pushes worship aside and our focus gets off of God and onto the things of this world or ourselves, we lose our way. Darkness and emptiness begin to envelope us. Do you want the joy of knowing God and experiencing his love? Take a few minutes to read Psalm 29 aloud and worship the Lord in the splendor of his holiness!

LORD, forgive me for getting wrapped up in myself and my tasks and forgetting to give you credit for all you have done in my life and in the world around me. Create in me a heart of worship. This day I give honor to you and worship you for the glory of your name, for your amazing strength and might, for the splendor of your holiness!

WE ARE SAVED TO WORSHIP GOD. ALL THAT CHRIST HAS DONE FOR US IN THE PAST AND ALL THAT HE IS DOING NOW LEADS TO THIS ONE END.
A. W. Tozer (1897–1963)

The One Year Bible Readings for today are **Exodus 21:22–23:13; Matthew 24:1-28; Psalm 29:1-11;** and **Proverbs 7:6-23.**

A Change of Season

When leaves begin to curl and crimson starts to creep into the trees' color scheme, it is a subtle sign that fall has arrived. When leaves float from majestic trees to the ground below and the air becomes crisp, it is an announcement that winter is approaching. We recognize these signs and adapt. We add heavier clothing to ensure that we will be warm and comfortable. We do not wish to be unprepared for what we know is certain to come. Jesus has promised that he will come back for his church. He described activities symbolic of an ordinary day—two women grinding grain and two men in the field, indicating that he will burst into our everyday existence. But we do not have to be unprepared for that wonderful day. Though we do not know the hour that the Lord will come, the Bible speaks of signs, both subtle and drastic, that announce his approach. These signs not only allow us to anticipate meeting our Savior, they also encourage us to prepare others for that day by sharing the gospel.

LORD, let it be forever settled in my heart that you are returning. Help me to be sensitive to the changing seasons, both in my life and in the lives of those around me. Help me to share your life with others who yearn to know more about you. Open my eyes to the signs that are all around me so that I might prepare for and anticipate your return.

He will send forth his angels with the sound of a mighty trumpet blast, and they will gather together his chosen ones from the farthest ends of the earth and heaven. Now learn a lesson from the fig tree. When its buds become tender and its leaves begin to sprout, you know without being told that summer is near. Just so, when you see the events I've described beginning to happen, you can know his return is very near, right at the door.
Matthew 24:31-33

THE ONLY WAY TO WAIT FOR THE SECOND COMING IS TO WATCH THAT YOU DO WHAT YOU SHOULD DO, SO THAT *WHEN* HE COMES IS A MATTER OF INDIFFERENCE. IT IS THE ATTITUDE OF A CHILD, CERTAIN THAT GOD KNOWS WHAT HE IS ABOUT. [ITALICS ADDED.] Oswald Chambers (1874–1917)

The One Year Bible Readings for today are **Exodus 23:14–25:40; Matthew 24:29-51; Psalm 30:1-12;** and **Proverbs 7:24-27.**

FEBRUARY

7

management

You're in Management

The master replied, "You wicked and lazy servant! You think I'm a hard man, do you, harvesting crops I didn't plant and gathering crops I didn't cultivate? Well, you should at least have put my money into the bank so I could have some interest."

Matthew 25:26-27

We are all managers to some degree. Students manage their time so they can study to make good grades. Parents manage their homes and children. Business owners manage employees and company operations. Some of us even attempt to manage our checkbooks! We also have a responsibility to manage our talents. God has gifted some of us with creative talent; others he has given a talent for teaching or for playing musical instruments. Others are leaders who have the ability to motivate and encourage people to action. Still others are gifted artists or athletes. You may think your own talent seems small in comparison with those of other people, but does that really matter? All God asks of us is that we invest what we do have. Have you hidden your talent, waiting to use it "someday"? We all have seasons where we are able to plant in greater abundance, but where can you plant your gifts today? When we sow our talents into a hurting world, God reaps the harvest.

DEAR GOD, it's easy to look at others and think that I have nothing to offer. But you are not a hard master; you have blessed me with talents and gifts that the world needs. Help me to plant my talents, to look for opportunities to sow a seed. Thank you for helping those seeds to flourish and grow, and thank you for reaping a wonderful harvest.

IF YOU HAVE A TALENT, USE IT IN EVERY WHICH WAY POSSIBLE. DON'T HOARD IT. DON'T DOLE IT OUT LIKE A MISER. SPEND IT LAVISHLY LIKE A MILLIONAIRE INTENT ON GOING BROKE.

Brendan Francis

The One Year Bible Readings for today are **Exodus 26:1–27:21; Matthew 25:1-30; Psalm 31:1-8;** and **Proverbs 8:1-11.**

listening

Are You Listening?

This passage of Scripture always reminds me of what is important to Jesus and how he wants us to join him in his work on earth. It is so easy to be busy doing many things: taking care of our households, a business or ministry, or projects we're interested in. But then it also becomes easy to miss the thing that's most important: extending mercy to the "least of these," caring for those who are hungry, poor, sick, or imprisoned. Our response to these needs doesn't affect only our future, eternal destiny. It also affects our present prayer life.

Prayer theologians of the past emphasized that the Lord will not hear us if we aren't listening to him and responding to what he asks of us. We can't feed all the hungry people, help all the homeless, or visit every sick or incarcerated person. But we can listen to the voice of the One who loves all of them and doesn't want them to perish without knowing his mercy and compassion through the hands of his followers. Ask what he would have you to do to reach out to them. And remember, he promises that when you come under his yoke, it will be easy, and his burden will be light because it is full of grace.

Come, you who are blessed by my Father, inherit the Kingdom prepared for you from the foundation of the world. For I was hungry, and you fed me. I was thirsty, and you gave me a drink. I was a stranger, and you invited me into your home. I was naked, and you gave me clothing. I was sick, and you cared for me. I was in prison, and you visited me.

Matthew 25:34-36

LORD, I want to join you in what you are doing to rescue those who are perishing, to feed those who are hungry and thirsty with your Bread of Life and Living Water. Forgive me when I don't listen and instead pursue my own agenda. Help me to hear and obey when you call on me. Empower me to be your hands and your feet in the place where I live.

IF WE WILL NOT LISTEN TO THE POOR WHEN THEY CRY UNTO US IN THEIR NEED, GOD WILL NOT LISTEN UNTO US WHEN WE CRY UNTO HIM IN OUR NEED. R. A. Torrey (1856–1928)

The One Year Bible Readings for today are **Exodus 28:1-43; Matthew 25:31–26:13; Psalm 31:9-18;** and **Proverbs 8:12-13.**

FEBRUARY

9

incense

Sweet-Smelling Incense

Each evening when [the priest] tends to the lamps, he must again burn incense in the Lord's presence. This must be done from generation to generation. Do not offer any unholy incense on this altar, or any burnt offerings, grain offerings, or drink offerings.

Exodus 30:8-9

The priests in the Old Testament nurtured the tender flame—symbolic of the prayers of the children of Israel—to make sure the fire didn't smolder and die. They burned only special incense on the altar so that the continual sweet fragrance wafted before God. Today we no longer have to burn candles or incense when we come into God's presence because we can freely fellowship with him anywhere. Yet sometimes we place other things on the altar and allow the busyness of our days to cause our prayer life to smolder. We lose precious one-on-one time with God. When we pray, we connect with the Lord and climb into the shelter of his love. It is in our quiet time with God that we seek answers and find guidance. Is daily prayer a part of your life? When you make prayer a priority, you will walk in closeness with the Lord, and his peace will encompass your life. Prayer not only strengthens you, it is also a sweet fragrance before a God who longs to talk with his children.

FATHER, I love the fact that you want to spend time with me. Thank you for our sweet fellowship together. Help me to teach others by my example the importance of daily prayer and fellowship with you. Sometimes I let so many things get in the way of our time together. Today, Lord, I will reserve a portion of my day just for you and me!

PRAYER IS A KIND OF CALLING HOME EVERY DAY. AND THERE CAN COME TO YOU A SERENITY, A FEELING OF AT-HOMENESS IN GOD'S UNIVERSE, A PEACE THAT THE WORLD CAN NEITHER GIVE NOR DISTURB, A FRESH COURAGE, A NEW INSIGHT, A HOLY BOLDNESS, THROUGH CALLING HOME THAT YOU'LL NEVER, NEVER GET ANY OTHER WAY. Earl G. Hunt Jr.

The One Year Bible Readings for today are **Exodus 29:1–30:10; Matthew 26:14-46; Psalm 31:19-24;** and **Proverbs 8:14-26.**

forgive

Forgive Me

There are many reasons that we hide our sin from God. It might be that we don't want to face our shortcomings or that we are ashamed. Unconfessed sin weighs heavily on us because we do not have the means to forgive our own sins. Rest assured that God seeks us when our sin separates us from him. The Holy Spirit follows us into the hidden places to draw us back to a place of safety.

The wonderful thing is that we don't have to run from God when we have fallen short of his standards. He paid a costly price—the sacrifice of his own Son—to redeem us from our sins. Wouldn't it be better to run to him and lay our sins at his feet than to continue to carry such a heavy burden? Take a few moments and allow God free rein in your heart. Ask him to reveal any areas where you have tried to hide your sin. Openly confess whatever wrong motives, actions, or words the Holy Spirit shows you, and allow his gentle mercy to remove the heavy weight you've carried for far too long.

When I refused to confess my sin, I was weak and miserable, and I groaned all day long. Day and night your hand of discipline was heavy on me.
Psalm 32:3-4

GOD, I thought I could fix it myself. I hid my sin because I was ashamed and felt as if I had failed you. When you called my name, I ran from you, yet I longed to be in your presence. Please forgive the sins—large or small—that hide in my heart. When you discipline me, it is for good, because you long for us to have fellowship together, with our hearts joined as one.

IN CONFESSION . . . WE OPEN OUR LIVES TO HEALING, RECONCILING, RESTORING, UPLIFTING GRACE OF HIM WHO LOVES US IN SPITE OF WHAT WE ARE. Louis Cassels (1922–1974)

The One Year Bible Readings for today are **Exodus 30:11–31:18; Matthew 26:47-68; Psalm 32:1-11;** and **Proverbs 8:27-32.**

FEBRUARY

meeting

A Special Meeting Place

Whenever Moses went out to the Tent of Meeting, all the people would get up and stand in their tent entrances. They would all watch Moses until he disappeared inside. As he went into the tent, the pillar of cloud would come down and hover at the entrance while the Lord spoke with Moses.
Exodus 33:8-9

The people lingered outside their tents, watching, waiting for the moment when the tent closed around Moses. It was evident that wondrous events were taking place within the confines of the tabernacle. The Israelites worshiped from a distance as their leader sat in the presence and glory of God and spoke to him as a man speaks with a friend.

There are times when we may feel as if a vast distance separates us from God. There are moments, even days, when it seems as if we are standing outside our own tent, watching as others embrace spiritual intimacy with God. Yet the good news is that we don't need to find a special place to share our hearts or use special words to communicate our thoughts, needs, even our fears to God. Our sacred tent of meeting is as close as a whisper because Christ lives in us. He invites you to come freely to him and to sit in his presence, talk with him as you would with a friend, and continue that dialogue as you work, live, and walk through your day.

OH, LORD, it is when I am in your presence that you reveal your love for me. In those quiet moments I can express my thoughts, fears, and longings to walk with you through joyous times and even the times when I feel I am in the wilderness. I am so thankful that you are as close as my heartbeat. Thank you for the privilege of daily being able to meet with you!

PRAYER IS NOT ARTFUL MONOLOGUE
OF VOICE UPLIFTED FROM THE SOD;
IT IS LOVE'S TENDER DIALOGUE
BETWEEN THE SOUL AND GOD.

John Richard Moreland (1880–1947)

The One Year Bible Readings for today are **Exodus 32:1–33:23; Matthew 26:69–27:14; Psalm 33:1-11;** and **Proverbs 8:33-36.**

power

Amazing Power

Sometimes it seems as if the forces of evil are winning and godless rulers and superpowers are dominating our world. But these verses remind us of who is really in charge and calling the shots: the Lord Almighty. The same God who created the world with a word can shatter the plans of the nations and thwart all their schemes. No matter how out of control things may appear, God's plan remains in place. He is running the show and knows the end from the beginning. No one is higher or mightier than the Lord! He governs our world, his kingdom will come, and his sovereign will shall be done on earth as it is in heaven! God's intentions can never be shaken, and his plans stand firm forever. His amazing power is at work in the world, and he will carry out his eternal purpose to the last detail.

THANK YOU, LORD, for the assurance your Word gives me that you reign over heaven and earth and that no one can thwart your plans for my life—and for the whole world. I put my trust in you today. Only you understand everything—even those things that are mysteries to me. Because you have all authority on earth and in heaven, I can rest in you.

The Lord looks down from heaven and sees the whole human race. From his throne he observes all who live on the earth. He made their hearts, so he understands everything they do. The best-equipped army cannot save a king, nor is great strength enough to save a warrior. Don't count on your warhorse to give you victory—for all its strength, it cannot save you.
Psalm 33:13-17

GOD IS NEVER IN A PANIC, NOTHING CAN BE DONE THAT HE IS NOT ABSOLUTE MASTER OF, AND NO ONE IN EARTH OR HEAVEN CAN SHUT A DOOR HE HAS OPENED, NOR OPEN A DOOR HE HAS SHUT. GOD ALTERS THE INEVITABLE WHEN WE GET IN TOUCH WITH HIM. Oswald Chambers (1874–1917)

The One Year Bible Readings for today are **Exodus 34:1–35:9; Matthew 27:15-31; Psalm 33:12-22;** and **Proverbs 9:1-6.**

FEBRUARY

13

Freedom from Fear

I prayed to the Lord, and he answered me, freeing me from all my fears. Those who look to him for help will be radiant with joy; no shadow of shame will darken their faces.
Psalm 34:4-5

These verses tell us that although fear is a normal, human reaction to danger or crisis, God has an antidote for our fear. We may fear death, failure, or people. We may be frightened about taking a new step, fearful of suffering, or anxious about what may happen tomorrow. Whatever the circumstances, we don't have to be ashamed of being afraid or stuff our fears down inside and try to look brave. The very fear that plagues us can cause us to press into God's presence. He invites us to pray to him and lay down our fears instead of being paralyzed by them, to fear and revere him (David mentions this fifteen times in Psalm 34) instead of anything or anyone else. An amazing thing happens when we give God our fears: in return for our fears he infuses us with faith, hope, and love. As F. B. Meyer said, "God incarnate is the end of fear; and the heart that realizes that he is in the midst . . . will be quiet in the midst of alarm."

LORD, I give you all my fears today and look to you for help. Do a deep work in my heart concerning those things that strike fear in me. I know that your perfect love will cast out all my fears. Thank you for your promise to answer me when I call to you, to free me from fear and shame, and to make me radiant with joy.

FEAR IMPRISONS, FAITH LIBERATES; FEAR PARALYZES, FAITH ENCOURAGES; FEAR SICKENS, FAITH HEALS; FEAR MAKES USELESS, FAITH MAKES SERVICEABLE—AND, MOST OF ALL, FEAR PUTS HOPELESSNESS AT THE HEART OF LIFE, WHILE FAITH REJOICES IN ITS GOD.
Harry Emerson Fosdick (1878–1969)

The One Year Bible Readings for today are **Exodus 35:10–36:38; Matthew 27:32-66; Psalm 34:1-10;** and **Proverbs 9:7-8.**

help

Promised Help

Someone once said that when we sail through life without a trial or a sorrow, we may slide by without knowing Jesus, but in our suffering we discover true fellowship with him. God never promised us a problem-free Christian life, but this psalm gives us several assurances about how God responds to us when troubles come. He promises his watch care, his attentiveness to our cries for help, his closeness, and his deliverance. Even the fact that we are counted among "those who do right," or "the righteous," and are thus eligible to receive this promised assurance is a result of the finished work of Christ on the cross. No matter what we are going through today, these are powerful reasons for praise. So speak to God, for he hears you. And remember, when your heart is breaking, he is most close to you, and he rescues those whose spirits are crushed.

The eyes of the Lord watch over those who do right; his ears are open to their cries for help. . . . The Lord hears his people when they call to him for help. He rescues them from all their troubles. The Lord is close to the brokenhearted; he rescues those who are crushed in spirit.
Psalm 34:15, 17-18

LORD, it is such a comfort to know that your eyes watch over me and that your ears hear my cries for help. Thank you for hearing my cries, for rescuing me when I am crushed in spirit. You are always close to the brokenhearted, to those who are in dire straits. I praise you for the hope and courage your promises give me when I am face-to-face with the most difficult of circumstances!

GOD PUTS HIS EAR SO CLOSELY DOWN TO YOUR LIPS THAT HE CAN HEAR YOUR FAINTEST WHISPER. IT IS NOT GOD AWAY OFF UP YONDER; IT IS GOD AWAY DOWN HERE, CLOSE UP—SO CLOSE UP THAT WHEN YOU PRAY TO HIM, IT IS MORE A WHISPER THAN A KISS. Thomas De Witt Talmage (1832–1902)

The One Year Bible Readings for today are **Exodus 37:1–38:31; Matthew 28:1-20; Psalm 34:11-22;** and **Proverbs 9:9-10.**

FEBRUARY

15

purpose

His Purpose, Not Mine

This messenger was John the Baptist. He lived in the wilderness and was preaching that people should be baptized to show that they had turned from their sins and turned to God to be forgiven.
Mark 1:4

John the Baptist's camel-hair cloak should not be confused with the luxurious, woven garments found in upscale stores today. His was most likely a tanned, hairy hide held together with a leather belt. He did not preach in the comfort of a temple but baptized in the stark setting of the wilderness. He was well known for his not-so-gentle speeches. His diet was meager, consisting of locusts and wild honey. Though these facts alone set John apart from other religious men, it was his single-minded dedication to his calling that etched his name in history. John never forgot his purpose. When John's disciples left to follow Jesus, his loyal friends complained bitterly, yet John assured them that this was exactly what he hoped would happen. He wanted to decrease so that Christ could increase. His whole mission in life was to point the way to Jesus. When God gives us a particular ministry, it is easy to assume ownership. We birth it. We pray over it. Yet our calling was never ours in the first place. Just like John the Baptist's, our purpose is to point others to Christ, not to ourselves.

LORD, thank you for the ministry you have entrusted to me. If others praise me, help me to remember that my one purpose should be that your gospel is proclaimed and you are exalted. In everything I do, may I be a stepping-stone instead of a stumbling block so that others may come to know you as Savior and Lord.

OUR METHOD OF PROCLAIMING SALVATION IS THIS: TO POINT OUT TO EVERY HEART THE LOVING LAMB, WHO DIED FOR US, AND ALTHOUGH HE WAS THE SON OF GOD, OFFERED HIMSELF FOR OUR SINS. Count Nikolaus von Zinzendorf (1700–1760)

The One Year Bible Readings for today are **Exodus 39:1–40:38; Mark 1:1-28; Psalm 35:1-16;** and **Proverbs 9:11-12.**

sin

Taking Sin Seriously

If you bring a sheep as your gift, present it to the Lord.

Leviticus 3:7

Sin was serious business for the ancient Israelites. The sacrifices they placed on the altar were spotless, prized animals, to remind the people of the high cost of their sins. To sacrifice an animal, the priests killed it and drained its blood. This reminded the people that the animals were dying in their place.

Since Christ died on the cross, we no longer need to offer animal sacrifices because Jesus, the spotless Lamb of God, was the ultimate sacrifice for our sins! Oftentimes we offer God a mumbled prayer asking for forgiveness. We forget that God offered his perfect Son, whom he loved and prized. When we sin casually, we ignore the fact that Christ carried the weight of our sins on his shoulders as he bled and died. When we fail to ask for forgiveness, we miss the opportunity to receive mercy as we sit in the presence of a holy God. Have you thanked him for the sacrifice he gave for you? We take sin seriously when we remember Christ's sacrifice and offer him a thankful and repentant heart.

JESUS, thank you for giving yourself as an offering so that I could be free! I confess that I sometimes take my sin lightly and forget what you suffered on the cross. Help me to remember your sacrifice and not to grieve you with a callused and forgetful heart. As I receive the Father's forgiveness through your offering of yourself, I will praise you and thank you for the freedom that forgiveness gives!

SIN IS LIKE ICE IN OUR PIPES—OUR SPIRITUAL LIVES HAVE BEEN "FROZEN." THERE IS ONLY ONE SOLUTION, AND THAT IS REPENTANCE TO CLEAR THE BLOCKAGE AND RESTORE THE FLOW OF THE HOLY SPIRIT. Billy Graham (b. 1918)

The One Year Bible Readings for today are **Leviticus 1:1–3:17; Mark 1:29–2:12; Psalm 35:17-28;** and **Proverbs 9:13-18.**

FEBRUARY

17

God's Unfailing Love

Your unfailing love, O Lord, is as vast as the heavens; your faithfulness reaches beyond the clouds. Your righteousness is like the mighty mountains, your justice like the ocean depths. You care for people and animals alike, O Lord. How precious is your unfailing love, O God! All humanity finds shelter in the shadow of your wings.

Psalm 36:5-7

It has been said that a picture is worth a thousand words. In today's verses the psalmist uses just a few words to paint some dramatic pictures. With a series of metaphors this psalm describes some of the many blessings for believers because of God's character: His ever faithful, ever loyal love is truly "out of this world" because it is so great that it reaches beyond the clouds and heavens. The Lord's righteousness is as steady as the highest mountains, and his judgments are as deep as the ocean. But the metaphor that gives us the greatest insight into the heart of God is in verse 7: we can find shelter in our Lord just as baby chickens take refuge under the shelter of the mother hen's wings. Because God loves us, his arms are open to us today; all we have to do is run to him, and he will provide shelter and protection.

YOUR UNFAILING LOVE, LORD, is as vast as the heavens. Your faithfulness reaches beyond the clouds. Your righteousness is as glorious as the mighty mountain, and your justice is as deep as the deepest ocean. Thank you for caring for people and animals alike with your unfailing love. Thank you for the shelter that I find in the shadow of your wings. I rejoice because your unfailing love is the most precious thing to me!

GOD'S LOVE IS MEASURELESS. IT IS MORE: IT IS BOUNDLESS. IT HAS NO BOUNDS BECAUSE IT IS NOT A THING BUT A FACET OF THE ESSENTIAL NATURE OF GOD. HIS LOVE IS SOMETHING HE IS, AND BECAUSE HE IS INFINITE, THAT LOVE CAN ENFOLD THE WHOLE CREATED WORLD IN ITSELF AND HAVE ROOM FOR TEN THOUSAND TIMES TEN THOUSAND WORLDS BESIDE. A. W. Tozer (1897–1963)

The One Year Bible Readings for today are **Leviticus 4:1–5:19; Mark 2:13–3:6; Psalm 36:1-12;** and **Proverbs 10:1-2.**

contest

No Contest

When evil people prosper, it may cause believers to ask why. It doesn't seem fair that the wicked succeed when the righteous struggle, but we can't judge prosperity by the world's standards. Much of what society considers success is temporary and shallow. God offers lasting rewards. He gives joy that overflows in spite of circumstances. He grants abundant peace in the midst of chaos. He offers comfort when we grieve and guides us when we are lost. We serve a God who knows everything about us and still loves us. That same God understands the desires of our hearts. How then can we compare material goods or fame with a loving God such as this? There is no contest! When it looks as if life is falling apart at the seams, trust God to take you safely through the hard times. Delight in him, and rejoice because he will give you eternal gifts that cause temporal rewards to pale in comparison.

Don't worry about the wicked. Don't envy those who do wrong. For like grass, they soon fade away. Like springtime flowers, they soon wither. Trust in the Lord and do good. Then you will live safely in the land and prosper. Take delight in the Lord, and he will give you your heart's desires.
Psalm 37:1-4

COMPASSIONATE AND LOVING FATHER, many people have material goods and success, but they still search for something that is real and lasting. Thank you for joy that runs deep. Thank you for peace that only you can give. Help me not to take what I have been given for granted but to be filled with gratefulness.

GOD IS MY BEING . . . MY STRENGTH, MY BEAUTITUDE, MY GOOD, MY DELIGHT.
Catherine of Genoa (1447–1510)

The One Year Bible Readings for today are **Leviticus 6:1–7:27; Mark 3:7-30; Psalm 37:1-11;** and **Proverbs 10:3-4.**

FEBRUARY

19

Seed Sowers

The farmer I talked about is the one who brings God's message to others.
Mark 4:14

In West Africa people customarily sing as they work in the fields. They lift their voices as they plant in anticipation of the harvest. Perhaps this is how the farmer in the parable appeared as he walked through the field. As he tossed seed, it fell in various types of soil—some hard, some weedy, some shallow, and some good and fertile. Not once did Jesus describe the farmer as anxious; rather, he portrayed the sower as faithfully carrying out his job.

Sometimes we treat evangelism as a heavy burden. Instead of cheerfully scattering seed everywhere, we become soil testers, trying to determine whether or not the seed will flourish even *before* we plant. We hover over the tender shoots, trying to thwart weeds. When a seed doesn't produce the desired fruit, we may declare ourselves failures as farmers. But God has called us to plant the message of the gospel in whatever field he places us. It is the Lord of the harvest who nourishes the tiny seeds and causes them to grow. You may never see the bushels of souls that result from seeds you planted, but you can sing as you sow and anticipate a harvest of thirty, sixty, and even a hundredfold.

GOD, I can scatter seeds in my job, my neighborhood, my family, and plant seeds of hope in people I encounter every day. Help me to sing as I plant and be confident that many of those seeds will take root in soil that will someday produce a harvest.

PLANT A WORD OF LOVE HEART-DEEP IN A PERSON'S LIFE. NURTURE IT WITH A SMILE AND A PRAYER, AND WATCH WHAT HAPPENS.
Max Lucado (b. 1955)

The One Year Bible Readings for today are **Leviticus 7:28–9:6; Mark 3:31–4:25; Psalm 37:12-29;** and **Proverbs 10:5.**

share

Share Your Story

When Jesus got back into the boat, the man who had been demon possessed begged to go, too. But Jesus said, "No, go home to your friends, and tell them what wonderful things the Lord has done for you and how merciful he has been."

Mark 5:18-19

The demon-possessed man roamed the land of the dead, living in a cemetery because the living feared him. Loose chains hung from his body where he had broken free from his shackles, but his spirit was still in captivity. Jesus commanded the demons to leave the man, and his tormentors fled in response. It is no wonder that the man begged to follow Jesus. His home held only painful reminders of the misery he had endured. Yet Jesus encouraged him to stay behind and to tell others what had happened. He knew that the testimony of this healed man would have a great impact on those who were once witnesses to his agony.

It isn't easy to live in a place where painful memories abide, but those same memories are an opportunity to share what God has done for you. Your testimony may open the door for hope to flourish in another's heart. The God moments that happen not only affect us but also have the power to rescue others from despair. Today, ask the Lord to give you the courage and power to share your story and proclaim the Good News to those you live and work with.

LORD, I have benchmarks in my life where I can see that you rescued me. Sometimes I avoid those places because they hold painful memories. Let me see my past hurts as opportunities to share how you have healed me so that my life's story can give hope to someone else. Thank you that neither bad memories nor difficult circumstances can silence how you intervened in my life, showed me your mercy, and rescued me.

IF YOU HAVE BECOME A PART OF THE STORY OF GOD, THEN YOU HAVE A STORY TO SHARE WITH THE PEOPLE AROUND YOU. THEY ARE EAGER TO HEAR IT. THEY ARE *DYING* TO HEAR IT. Leighton Ford

The One Year Bible Readings for today are **Leviticus 9:7–10:20; Mark 4:26–5:20; Psalm 37:30-40;** and **Proverbs 10:6-7.**

FEBRUARY

21

trust

Just Trust Me

She had heard about Jesus, so she came up behind him through the crowd and touched the fringe of his robe. For she thought to herself, "If I can just touch his clothing, I will be healed." Immediately the bleeding stopped, and she could feel that she had been healed! . . . While he was still speaking to her, messengers arrived from Jairus's home with the message, "Your daughter is dead. There's no use troubling the Teacher now." But Jesus ignored their comments and said to Jairus, "Don't be afraid. Just trust me."

Mark 5:27-29, 35-36

In this amazing chapter of Mark's Gospel we read of two miracles Jesus performed: the healing of the woman with a hemorrhage and the raising of Jairus's daughter from the dead. The doctors had given up on the woman, taken all her money, and instead of healing her had left her worse than before. Yet with just the touch of her finger on Jesus' robe, all the blood dried up and all the disease was gone from her body. Likewise, no one had hope for Jairus's daughter; she had died, and the neighbors were already bringing food and mourning with the family. But one touch from Jesus raised her to new life.

But that happened way back in Bible days, we may think. *It's not relevant to my life today.* On the contrary, the same power that went out through the hem of Jesus' garment and through his words "Get up little girl!" is available to us today. God desires that through the Holy Spirit, we know and understand the unlimited, surpassing greatness of his power for us when we trust him. Voice your needs and cares to God, and then receive these words he speaks to you, his child, this day: "Don't be afraid. Just trust me."

FATHER, I praise you that the same power that raised Jairus's daughter from the dead, healed the woman with a hemorrhage, and raised Jesus from the dead is available to us through your Spirit! Open the eyes of my heart to see, know, understand, and believe in the working of your power in and for us who believe.

GOD HAS IN HIMSELF ALL POWER TO DEFEND YOU, ALL WISDOM TO DIRECT YOU, ALL MERCY TO PARDON YOU, ALL GRACE TO ENRICH YOU.
Thomas Benton Brooks (1608–1680)

The One Year Bible Readings for today are **Leviticus 11:1–12:8; Mark 5:21-43; Psalm 38:1-22;** and **Proverbs 10:8-9.**

days

Our Days Are Numbered

The average life span of a mayfly is a brief twenty-four hours. A rare number of them reach ancient status, living up to fourteen days, but some live only two hours. This tiny winged insect is born, reaches maturity, mates, and dies in just *one* of our days! It would seem foolish to us for the mayfly to waste even one moment in light of such a short life span. To an eternal God our life is but a brief flash, yet we often flit along like the mayfly, acting as if we have unlimited days in front of us. Our time on earth is brief, and each moment has potential. It is only when we view time through God's eyes that we can truly understand how precious a gift is every hour that we exist. Do you make the most of your numbered days, or is time an empty commodity? Ask God today how you can make the most of the time that you have been given. Seize each moment, for life will quickly pass away.

Lord, remind me how brief my time on earth will be. Remind me that my days are numbered, and that my life is fleeing away. My life is no longer than the width of my hand. An entire lifetime is just a moment to you; human existence is but a breath.
Psalm 39:4-5

ETERNAL GOD, help me to see time as a valuable asset that you have entrusted to me. When you gave me life, you intended that I live life abundantly and that I experience joy, fulfillment, and purpose. Help me not to squander time on meaningless endeavors but to understand that my days are numbered and that each one counts. And although an entire lifetime is just a moment to you, let my days be filled to overflowing with the glory of your presence.

DO NOT WALK THROUGH TIME WITHOUT LEAVING WORTHY EVIDENCE OF YOUR PASSAGE.
Pope John XXIII (1881–1963)

The One Year Bible Readings for today are **Leviticus 13:1-59; Mark 6:1-29; Psalm 39:1-13;** and **Proverbs 10:10.**

FEBRUARY

23

deeds

God's Wonderful Deeds

O Lord my God, you have done many miracles for us. Your plans for us are too numerous to list. If I tried to recite all your wonderful deeds, I would never come to the end of them.

Psalm 40:5

Remembering all the wonderful things God has done in our lives can produce so much gratefulness that we won't be able to keep quiet about God's goodness to us. We'll spontaneously talk about his faithfulness and saving power to those around us (Psalm 40:10). But just as the Israelites quickly forgot the miracles God did for them when he delivered them from bondage in Egypt, we, too, can easily forget what God has done for us and begin to grumble and complain. We tend to forget answered prayers or other "little things." But throughout the Scriptures, we see reminders to remember what God did. When we recall and recite God's goodness to us and praise him for it, we gain renewed hope for the future because we realize that his plans—and blessings—are too numerous for us to list! Recount the ways God has worked in your life. You might want to write them down. Then on rough days, you can read them and see how God has worked. Praise him for all he has brought you through and for the wonderful deeds you have seen him accomplish.

OH, LORD, you have done many miracles for us. Thank you that your plans are bigger than all of us put together! How I praise you for your wonderful deeds! Help me to remember your goodness to me. Give me courage to talk to others about your faithfulness and saving power and to live my life in a way that would draw them to you.

IF YOU DISCERN [GOD'S] LOVE IN EVERY MOMENT OF HAPPINESS, YOU WILL MULTIPLY A THOUSANDFOLD YOUR CAPACITY TO FULLY ENJOY YOUR BLESSINGS. Frances J. Roberts

The One Year Bible Readings for today are **Leviticus 14:1-57; Mark 6:30-56; Psalm 40:1-10;** and **Proverbs 10:11-12.**

mercies

Tender Mercies

Lord, don't hold back your tender mercies from me. My only hope is in your unfailing love and faithfulness. For troubles surround me—too many to count! They pile up so high I can't see my way out. They are more numerous than the hairs on my head. I have lost all my courage. Please, Lord, rescue me! Come quickly, Lord, and help me.
Psalm 40:11-13

Like the psalmist, each of us encounters seasons when we face not just one problem but waves of troubles that crash into our lives like breakers incessantly battering the shore. If we are not experiencing that now, we surely will somewhere down the road: Perhaps a child becomes chronically ill, or a teenager rebels and breaks our hearts. Our mother may be diagnosed with Alzheimer's and move in with us so that we're providing care 24/7, juggling a stressful job, and finding ourselves assailed by financial difficulties. Our troubles pile up so high that we can't see our way out, and we understand what the psalmist was feeling when he said that they are more numerous than the hairs on our heads. Life seems to unravel, we are weary, and courage drains away as we wonder, *Can I handle all of this? What if something else happens?* This is the time to lift up our heads to heaven, to cry out, as the psalmist did, for God's tender mercies, to say, "Come quickly, Lord, and help me" (v. 13), and to put our hope in his unfailing love and faithfulness.

LORD, today as troubles surround me, I turn my focus to you. Come quickly, Lord, and help and rescue me. Don't hold back your tender mercies in my life—release them, I pray! May showers of mercy and blessing come down from you. My only hope is in your unfailing love and faithfulness. You are my helper and my savior.

GOD HATH TWO WINGS, WHICH HE DOTH EVER
MOVE,
THE ONE IS MERCY, AND THE NEXT IS LOVE;
UNDER THE FIRST THE SINNERS EVER TRUST,
AND WITH THE LAST HE STILL DIRECTS
THE JUST.

Robert Herrick (1591–1674)

The One Year Bible Readings for today are **Leviticus 15:1–16:28; Mark 7:1-23; Psalm 40:11-17;** and **Proverbs 10:13-14.**

FEBRUARY

25

bread

Christ Our Bread

About this time another great crowd had gathered, and the people ran out of food again. Jesus called his disciples and told them, "I feel sorry for these people. They have been here with me for three days, and they have nothing left to eat. And if I send them home without feeding them, they will faint along the road. For some of them have come a long distance." "How are we supposed to find enough food for them here in the wilderness?" his disciples asked. "How many loaves of bread do you have?" he asked. "Seven," they replied.

Mark 8:1-5

Jesus enlisted his disciples to help him feed the multitude of people gathered to hear the Good News. They had no idea how the hungry hoard could be satisfied; they had so little to offer them. But when they gave Jesus the resources they had, a miracle occurred, and there was plenty of food for everyone.

Jesus asks us the same question today that he asked his disciples then: "How many loaves of bread do you have?" We may feel that we have no resources to give, but there are hungry people to feed. When we give Jesus our "bread," whether it is our time, money, or special talent or skills, he is able to take it—however little it is—and make it life and refreshment for many. Christ is our sufficiency when our personal resources are insufficient. He is our adequacy when we are inadequate. And when we yield all that we are and have to him, he can do more with it than we could ask or think. Express your desire for the Lord to use you today. Then be obedient to what he directs you to do with the "bread" you have.

THANK YOU, LORD, for the miracle you performed to feed the multitude and thank you for the ways you are still doing miracles today as we give what we have to you. There are so many in the wilderness, people who are physically and spiritually hungry. Strengthen me, use me, and prepare me to partner with you in what you are doing on earth.

CHRIST IS THE BREAD FOR MEN'S SOULS. IN HIM THE CHURCH HAS ENOUGH TO FEED THE WHOLE WORLD. Ian Maclaren (1850–1907)

The One Year Bible Readings for today are **Leviticus 16:29–18:30; Mark 7:24–8:10; Psalm 41:1-13;** and **Proverbs 10:15-16.**

presence

Recognizing God's Presence

Jesus had just miraculously fed the multitude, yet the Pharisees demanded more signs, more miracles. Like them, we sometimes fix our hopes on miraculous, stupendous events: our ship coming in so that all our financial woes disappear in a moment, or our wheelchair-bound friend getting up to walk again. Jesus is just as able to do those things as he was to feed the five thousand, but what about the fact that the sun rises each morning or that God has given us new birth into a living hope through what Jesus did on the cross? Aren't those things manifestations of his miraculous power?

We see signs of God's presence everywhere: in a bank of daffodils, in the encouraging words of a friend, in the gentle rain, in the ways he provides all we need. We don't need a miraculous sign—we just need Jesus! Ask him to help you to recognize anew the ways in which he is with you, for you are never outside of his loving arms or without his Spirit, who lives in you. Ask him to give you glimpses of his nature and character wherever you go and to turn your heart toward him in gratitude.

DEAR LORD, forgive me when I demand evidence of your working and power instead of thanking you for all you do. Please open my eyes to be aware of your presence, to sense your nearness, and to see the works of your hand everywhere I look. With all my heart I welcome your presence today, however you choose to reveal yourself to me. And don't let me forget to thank you.

When the Pharisees heard that Jesus had arrived, they came to argue with him. Testing him to see if he was from God, they demanded, "Give us a miraculous sign from heaven to prove yourself." When he heard this, he sighed deeply and said, "Why do you people keep demanding a miraculous sign? I assure you, I will not give this generation any such sign." So he got back into the boat and left them, and he crossed to the other side of the lake.

Mark 8:11-13

WE NEED NEVER SHOUT ACROSS THE SPACES TO AN ABSENT GOD. HE IS NEARER THAN OUR OWN SOUL, CLOSER THAN OUR MOST SECRET THOUGHTS.
A. W. Tozer (1897–1963)

The One Year Bible Readings for today are **Leviticus 19:1–20:21; Mark 8:11-38; Psalm 42:1-11;** and **Proverbs 10:17.**

FEBRUARY
27

doubts

Dealing with Our Doubts

[The boy's father said,] "The evil spirit often makes him fall into the fire or into water, trying to kill him. Have mercy on us and help us. Do something if you can." "What do you mean, 'If I can'?" Jesus asked. "Anything is possible if a person believes." The father instantly replied, "I do believe, but help me not to doubt!"
Mark 9:22-24

The desperate father had already asked Jesus' disciples to cast the evil, destructive spirit out of his son, but they had failed. It seems the father wasn't the only one in the story struggling with doubt! The disciples, the Pharisees, and the crowd were filled with doubt and unbelief. Since the disciples lacked the faith to heal the boy, the father turned to Jesus, who responded in compassion and inquired not only into the boy's condition but also into the condition of the father's heart. We need not be afraid to follow this humble man's model and be honest with God about our doubts. But at the same time we can pray as he did, asking Jesus to strengthen our faith and help us when we struggle to believe. Then we will see, as the boy's father in Mark's account saw, that with the dynamic combination of belief and prayer, anything is possible.

LORD, you know my deepest thoughts, all the places within my heart. When my faith is weak or I struggle with doubts about your care for me, enable me to turn to you and be honest about it. I believe in your power to accomplish anything, but grant me greater trust and faith in you.

EVERY STEP TOWARD CHRIST KILLS A DOUBT. EVERY THOUGHT, WORD, AND DEED FOR HIM CARRIES YOU AWAY FROM DISCOURAGEMENT.
Theodore Ledyard Cuyler (1822–1909)

The One Year Bible Readings for today are **Leviticus 20:22–22:16; Mark 9:1-29; Psalm 43:1-5;** and **Proverbs 10:18.**

first

The First Shall Be Last

In this passage the disciples fussed and argued about who would be the greatest in the kingdom of God. The startling aspect of this argument is that it occurred shortly after Jesus informed the disciples that he would soon die. Not only did they miss an opportunity to comfort their leader, but they also missed the point entirely. Christ had lived a selfless life as their example. He had taught them that he would die an agonizing death so that they, and generations after them, might live eternally. But they didn't understand because their focus was on themselves. So Jesus attempted to teach them one more lesson: that anyone who wants to be first (that is, in importance) must be last. It is only when we take the spotlight off of our own ambitions and desires that our eyes can be open to the needs of those around us. Then we can become humble servants and welcome the innocent, hungry, hurting, and broken. Jesus said that in doing this, we also welcome him, and we embrace the heart of God.

[Jesus said,] "Anyone who wants to be the first must take last place and be the servant of everyone else." Then he put a little child among them. Taking the child in his arms, he said to them, "Anyone who welcomes a little child like this on my behalf welcomes me, and anyone who welcomes me welcomes my Father who sent me."
Mark 9:35-37

JESUS, society teaches me to grab for all that I can. Yet you desire more for me than a selfish existence. Help me not to be "inward" focused but rather to see a world much bigger than my own needs and ambitions. You are my example. You came to serve when, of all people, you deserved to be waited upon. I look to you for guidance on how I, too, can serve those who are in need today.

IN GOD'S FAMILY, THERE IS TO BE ONE GREAT BODY OF PEOPLE: SERVANTS. IN FACT, THAT'S THE WAY TO THE TOP IN HIS KINGDOM.
Charles R. Swindoll (b. 1934)

The One Year Bible Readings for today are **Leviticus 22:17–23:44; Mark 9:30–10:12; Psalm 44:1-8;** and **Proverbs 10:19.**

MARCH
1

confidence

Calling with Confidence

Wake up, O Lord! Why do you sleep? Get up! Do not reject us forever. Why do you look the other way? Why do you ignore our suffering and oppression? . . . Rise up! Come and help us! Save us because of your unfailing love.
Psalm 44:23-24, 26

The writer of today's psalm mourns a massive military defeat and calls on God not to reject his people forever. Without God's help in battle, his people are plundered, and their enemies taunt them. So they cry to God to rouse himself and act on their behalf as a God of saving, delivering love. Just as the psalmist experienced, when we live day after day under difficult circumstances without a word from the Lord, it can cause deep frustration, worry, and fear. We, too, may begin to question whether God is paying attention to our lives at all: "Why do you sleep? Why do you look the other way? Why do you ignore our suffering and oppression?"

Even when God seems silent, we need never fear if the Lord is in the boat with us through the storm. Uncomfortable circumstances may continue, but God will prove himself our sure refuge because he has promised he will never forsake us. His name Emmanuel means "God with us." Because of this truth we can continue to call on the Lord with confidence that he will hear and respond because of his unfailing love.

LORD, thank you for your promised presence with me today. Although my circumstances may seem overwhelming, I call to you with confidence because you are all powerful and you love me. Come and help me! Save me because of your unfailing love and help me experience you as my sure refuge. I wait expectantly to see you move in a mighty way in my life today.

IF THE VESSEL OF OUR SOUL IS STILL TOSSED WITH WINDS AND STORMS, LET US AWAKE THE LORD, WHO REPOSES IN IT, AND HE WILL QUICKLY CALM THE SEA. Brother Lawrence of the Resurrection (1605–1691)

The One Year Bible Readings for today are **Leviticus 24:1–25:46; Mark 10:13-31; Psalm 44:9-26;** and **Proverbs 10:20-21.**

praying

Praying Specifically

When the blind beggar Bartimaeus heard that Jesus was nearby, he cried out for mercy and compassion. But as soon as Bartimaeus came to Jesus, Christ led him to be even more specific in his request by asking, "What do you want me to do for *you* [italics added]?" The blind man, in only a few words, prayed the most heartfelt prayer: "Teacher, I want to see!" In complete faith he asked for God's healing because the Lord had led him to ask. Jesus prompted the man's request by asking him to speak his heart's desire.

Christ asks you the same question: *What do you, [your name], want me to do for you?* When we approach God in prayer, he wants us to come with as much wholehearted desire and longing as Bartimaeus had and to trust him for the answer. As his Spirit leads us in praying more specifically and honestly, we will begin to see and be awed by his grace, goodness, and glory. The faith that it takes to voice sincere, deeply felt, and earnest prayers places us in a position to experience great and mighty things from a great and mighty God.

"What do you want me to do for you?" Jesus asked. "Teacher," the blind man said, "I want to see!" And Jesus said to him, "Go your way. Your faith has healed you." And instantly the blind man could see!
Mark 10:51-52

LORD, help me to follow as your precious Spirit leads me to pray about the deep longings of my heart . . . for your glory. Thank you for caring about every detail of my heart and my life. I long to please you, Lord, in every request I make before your throne of grace.

GOD SEES TO IT THAT WHEN THE WHOLE MAN PRAYS, IN TURN THE WHOLE MAN SHALL BE BLESSED. E. M. Bounds (1835–1913)

The One Year Bible Readings for today are **Leviticus 25:47–27:13; Mark 10:32-52; Psalm 45:1-17;** and **Proverbs 10:22.**

MARCH

3

grudges

From Grudges to Grace

[Jesus said,] "Listen to me! You can pray for anything, and if you believe, you will have it. But when you are praying, first forgive anyone you are holding a grudge against, so that your Father in heaven will forgive your sins, too."
Mark 11:24-25

God's Word reveals what is necessary for effective prayer, and these verses point to the key of forgiveness. Although it is contrary to the world's pattern, it is at the heart of the life Jesus calls us to. Christ explained that holding grudges proves detrimental to our oneness with the Father, hinders our prayers, and causes God to withhold forgiveness from us.

Our fellowship with God is restored through our own repentance and confession. Jesus provided for this through his finished work on the cross. He died so that we would be pardoned and restored to the Father. When we come to Jesus, he forgives our sins of the past and all the sins we will ever commit. But we who are forgiven much must love and forgive others much! Do you need to forgive someone today? What relationship needs restoration? Ask the Holy Spirit to show you any areas where you need to practice forgiveness.

God is ready to provide the grace to enable us to forgive and to experience being fully forgiven ourselves. Then we will know the joy God gives as we move from grudges to grace and are ready for prayer.

OH, FATHER, help me to have a forgiving heart. I need to learn how to receive your forgiveness and how to forgive those who have wronged me. I don't want to cause your presence in my life to be quenched because of unforgiveness. Create in me a free and forgiving spirit that sees others as you do, responds to them with your heart, and prays for them with your love.

MAY THE FATHER OF MERCY GRANT TO ALL OF HIS CHILDREN THAT DEEP CONTRITION, SO THAT THEY MAY BE LED INTO THE BLESSEDNESS OF HIS PRESENCE AND ENJOY THE FULLNESS OF HIS POWER AND LOVE. Andrew Murray (1828–1917)

The One Year Bible Readings for today are **Leviticus 27:14—Numbers 1:54; Mark 11:1-26; Psalm 46:1-11;** and **Proverbs 10:23.**

sing

Sing Praise

Sing praise to God, sing praises; sing praise to our King, sing praises! For God is the King over all the earth. Praise him with a psalm!
Psalm 47:6-7

God absolutely loves to hear his children sing. He cherishes and delights in lavish worship and praise that come from the heart in song. Spending time singing to the Lord is vital to our life with God. Our songs shouldn't be merely a means to an end or preparation in a church service or the "first step" in a prayer model like the "Four Steps of Prayer." They should reflect our joy at being in God's presence. Just as parents delight in their young children's songs even when they're off-key, our heavenly Father hears past our broken chords of harmony, the strained efforts at melody, and the obscure rhythms and rhymes. There is no sound more pleasing to God than the voice of his child singing of his wonderful character and marvelous glory. The only thing resounding throughout his throne room is the gratitude of our hearts, which to him is irresistible. In prayer, lift your voice in extravagant worship of the Lord, singing praises to his name. Worship him because he is the perfect, holy, almighty Creator and king of the universe and yet calls you into intimate relationship with him.

LORD, grant me the grace to enter into true praise and to experience your delight in me. I want to be lost in wonder, love, and praise. I want to sing songs that lift your name and character high. Give me fresh revelation today, Lord, of who you are. Inspire me so that I will sing of your greatness and glory forever! You are the king over all the earth. I love you, Lord.

WHEN ALL THY MERCIES, O MY GOD!
MY RISING SOUL SURVEYS,
TRANSPORTED WITH THE VIEW, I'M LOST.
IN WONDER, LOVE, AND PRAISE.

Joseph Addison (1672–1719)

The One Year Bible Readings for today are **Numbers 2:1–3:51; Mark 11:27–12:17; Psalm 47:1-9;** and **Proverbs 10:24-25.**

MARCH

5

love

The Greatest Commandment

[A teacher of religious law asked Jesus,] "Of all the commandments, which is the most important?" Jesus replied," . . . 'You must love the Lord your God with all your heart, all your soul, all your mind, and all your strength.' The second is equally important: 'Love your neighbor as yourself.' No other commandment is greater than these."
Mark 12:28-31

As Jesus entered Jerusalem, the religious leaders were watching and waiting to confront him with their manipulative questioning and to attempt to trap him by hypocritically challenging his authority. Nonetheless, one religious leader, noticing that Jesus was giving them good answers, asked him which was the most important commandment. Jesus did not answer with a complicated code of laws, rituals, and customs. Instead, he reduced their binding law to two simple ideas—loving God and loving others—and focused on the one thing central to the Christian life: the principle of love. Oh, how often we miss living in the grace of God when we confine our walk of faith to the observance of rituals and laws. God sent his Son to save us from anything that could hinder our living the liberated life in Christ. This is salvation—the power of his life within us enabling us to love the Father and to love others with all of our heart, soul, mind, and strength. Spend a few moments basking in Christ's love for you, expressing your love for him, and asking him to fill you to overflowing with his love for people.

FATHER, I am often too busy and distracted to remember the most important thing of all: your love. Help me to lay aside all else and order my day around my love for you. Teach me how to love you and how to love people as Christ loves them. As you fill me with your love, Father, lead me to those who need to know your love today.

LOVE IS NOT THE WORK OF THE HOLY SPIRIT, IT IS THE HOLY SPIRIT—WORKING IN US. GOD IS LOVE, HE DOESN'T MERELY HAVE IT OR GIVE IT; HE GIVES HIMSELF—TO ALL MEN, TO ALL SORTS AND CONDITIONS. Joseph Fletcher

The One Year Bible Readings for today are **Numbers 4:1–5:31; Mark 12:18-37; Psalm 48:1-14;** and **Proverbs 10:26.**

giving

Giving All to Him

When Christ said that she "has given everything she has," he was specifying more than a monetary sacrifice. He was drawing our attention to the woman's *life* sacrifice, her practice of living in complete surrender and loyal devotion to God. The story of the poor widow teaches more than just how to sacrifice through our monetary offerings. Her sacrificial giving is a demonstration of a life fully offered into the loving care of the Master's hands.

Why is it so difficult for us to yield all that we have and are to God? Is there fear that we'll be left without? It is only as we yield ourselves to him in complete faith and trust that we can experience true oneness with the Father, true freedom in Christ, and true, abundant, joy-filled living. As you prayerfully offer all that you have and are to the Father, his Holy Spirit will lovingly teach you and lead you to the joy that comes from wholehearted sacrifice.

[Jesus] called his disciples to him and said, "I assure you, this poor widow has given more than all the others have given. For they gave a tiny part of their surplus, but she, poor as she is, has given everything she has."

Mark 12:43-44

LORD, I fully yield myself to you—all that I have, all that I am, and all that I hope to be. I give you everything about me . . . my strengths as well as my weaknesses. They are yours to do with as you please. I submit my heart, mind, and will to you, Lord Jesus. You alone are Lord of my life. I am thankful that I can trust you with anything that involves me in any way, whether big or small.

ONLY THE HOLY SPIRIT HIMSELF CAN TEACH YOU WHAT AN ENTIRE YIELDING OF THE WHOLE LIFE TO GOD CAN MEAN. Andrew Murray (1828–1917)

The One Year Bible Readings for today are **Numbers 6:1–7:89; Mark 12:38–13:13; Psalm 49:1-20;** and **Proverbs 10:27-28.**

MARCH

7

coming

He's Coming Back

[Jesus said,] "Since you don't know when [these things] will happen, stay alert and keep watch. The coming of the Son of Man can be compared with that of a man who left home to go on a trip. He gave each of his employees instructions about the work they were to do, and he told the gatekeeper to watch for his return. So keep a sharp lookout! For you do not know when the home-owner will return—at evening, mid-night, early dawn, or late daybreak. Don't let him find you sleeping when he arrives without warning."

Mark 13:33-36

Christ compared his return with that of a businessman who went on a trip. The businessman left specific instructions on how to take care of matters while he was away. It was clear that this was a task for which he would hold the employees accountable. He instructed them to watch for his return, though they were not sure what hour or moment he would arrive.

Christ's return is a certainty, but do we act as if it is? One day the sky will split open, the trumpet will sound, and our Savior will return for his church. It is intended to be a glorious reunion, but what will Christ find? Will it be a neglected kingdom or a church actively reaching out to lost souls and making disciples? Will he find a sleeping bride or discover believers waiting with expectant hearts? Jesus promised that he would prepare a place for us in heaven. That's good news! But while we wait for that day, we have instructions to build his kingdom. Jesus is coming. What will you be doing when he returns? Are you watching and waiting for that hour?

LORD Jesus, you promised to come back for your church. Help me to be diligent while I anticipate that day. I want to share the Good News with my loved ones who don't know you. Please prepare their hearts to receive that message. Help me not to lose sight of what you have called me to do while I am here on earth and to wait for your return with expectation and hope.

LOOK UP! THE KING IS COMING AND THOSE WHO ARE COMING WITH HIM ARE THE CALLED AND CHOSEN AND FAITHFUL. THAT'S YOU! THAT'S US, MY FRIEND! PERSEVERE, FOR HE IS COMING AND HIS REWARD IS WITH HIM. Kay Arthur

The One Year Bible Readings for today are **Numbers 8:1–9:23; Mark 13:14-37; Psalm 50:1-23;** and **Proverbs 10:29-30.**

broken jar

Living as a Broken Jar

Jesus was in Bethany at the home of Simon, a man who had leprosy. During supper, a woman came in with a beautiful jar of expensive perfume. She broke the seal and poured the perfume over his head.
Mark 14:3

As we read this description of exorbitant devotion, so often we hone in on the fact that this was a costly, dear, and precious thing, a fragrant, expensive perfume worth more than a year's wages, that Mary lavishly sacrificed in reverencing her King. Yet her extravagance moves us to ask ourselves, What thing that we consider costly and dear might the Lord want us to offer up to him: a relationship? a habit? a cherished possession? Perhaps it is one of the gifts God has given us that lies hidden or saved for use for a time that never comes. These very treasures could bring light to restore someone's faith, to touch someone's heart, to change a life. One of these important things could be the very "jar" that he wants us to break before him. Notice, Mary broke open the jar, representing that her life was no longer centered in herself but in Christ Jesus, that she counted him as the treasure above all others.

Is your life a broken jar, the contents poured out in joyful abandonment to the Lord? Of those who live as broken jars, Jesus says, they have "done a beautiful thing to me" (Mark 14:6, NIV).

DEAR LORD, please show me the things that I consider dear and precious that need to be broken so that I, too, may do a beautiful thing to you. The most costly gifts I can give you are my life and my love in ways that are pleasing to you. I give you also the gifts and treasures you have given me, and I offer them up for your use. Today, let the fragrance of my brokenness bring joy to you.

PRAYER THRIVES IN THE ATMOSPHERE OF TRUE DEVOTION, FOR GOD DWELLS WHERE THE SPIRIT OF DEVOTION RESIDES. E. M. Bounds (1835–1913)

The One Year Bible Readings for today are **Numbers 10:1–11:23; Mark 14:1-21; Psalm 51:1-19;** and **Proverbs 10:31-32.**

MARCH

9

tree

Like an Olive Tree

I am like an olive tree, thriving in the house of God. I trust in God's unfailing love forever and ever.
Psalm 52:8

In Bible times the olive tree was considered the most valuable of trees. Throughout Scripture it symbolizes value, prominence, peace, and a promise of better times to come. The olive tree was also known as a tree that persevered, for it stood with great endurance under any adverse condition. The man who is secure in God's presence is a symbol of God's power. When David compared himself with an olive tree, he was declaring his faith and trust in God as the One who enabled him to be strong, not only to survive but also to thrive and bear fruit no matter how his enemies pursued him. He voiced, through the symbolism of the olive tree, his determination to grow in God's presence and live a life of faith, seeking only to fulfill the will of God and become his alone. In whatever circumstances you may find yourself, the Holy Spirit dwelling within you can empower you to stand as a mighty, flourishing olive tree, full of the vitality that comes from living anchored in God's unfailing love.

LORD, just like your servant David, I want not just to survive today but to thrive. Help me to display your splendor. Just as olive trees produce fruit, let my life produce the fruit of the Holy Spirit. Let others see the oil of joy, of healing, and of your very presence in my life, not only for my sake, but for the sake of those who so desperately need to see that you really do exist and dwell among us.

LET HIM DO WHAT HE PLEASES WITH ME: I DESIRE ONLY HIM, AND TO BE WHOLLY DEVOTED TO HIM.
Brother Lawrence of the Resurrection (1605–1691)

The One Year Bible Readings for today are **Numbers 11:24–13:33; Mark 14:22-52; Psalm 52:1-9;** and **Proverbs 11:1-3.**

MARCH
10

faith

Through the Eyes of Faith

One weekend I arrived at a beach, looking forward to walking in the lovely white sand. What awaited me was the most awful-smelling seaweed I've ever seen—not one pile but miles and miles of it brought in by a storm. The first two days all I could see (or smell) was that stinky seaweed. I barely noticed the beautiful things about those two days. The next morning when I went out, the seaweed was still there, but this time the Lord turned my gaze to the dazzling blue Texas sky, the blonde toddler splashing in the waves, a dad and his son making an intricate sand castle. Oh, the seaweed was still there, but this time it didn't spoil my enjoyment because my focus was somewhere else.

Joshua and Caleb were the kinds of leaders who saw that the land they explored was "exceedingly good" (v. 7, NIV). But the other men saw only giants and obstacles and were filled with fear. Joshua and Caleb saw the possibilities, but the others spread a bad report. Ask the Lord to help you to look up and keep your focus on him—and to not miss the beautiful things along the way.

LORD, open my spiritual eyes to see those "exceedingly good" things in my path. Forgive me for focusing on the problems and the "stinky seaweed" in the world around me. As I keep my eyes on you and the goals you've put before me, may I go forth in faith, not in fear, so that I don't miss the beauty and blessings of each day.

HAVING THUS CHOSEN OUR COURSE, LET US RENEW OUR TRUST IN GOD AND GO FORWARD WITHOUT FEAR AND WITH MANLY HEARTS.
Abraham Lincoln (1809–1865)

Two of the men who had explored the land, Joshua son of Nun and Caleb son of Jephunneh, tore their clothing. They said to the community of Israel, "The land we explored is a wonderful land! And if the Lord is pleased with us, he will bring us safely into that land and give it to us. It is a rich land flowing with milk and honey, and he will give it to us! Do not rebel against the Lord, and don't be afraid of the people of the land. They are only helpless prey to us! They have no protection, but the Lord is with us! Don't be afraid of them!"
Numbers 14:6-9

The One Year Bible Readings for today are **Numbers 14:1–15:16; Mark 14:53-72; Psalm 53:1-6;** and **Proverbs 11:4.**

MARCH

11

pleasing

Pleasing the Crowd

They shouted back, "Crucify him!" "Why?" Pilate demanded. "What crime has he committed?" But the crowd only roared the louder, "Crucify him!" So Pilate, anxious to please the crowd, released Barabbas to them. He ordered Jesus flogged with a lead-tipped whip, then turned him over to the Roman soldiers to crucify him.

Mark 15:13-15

Pilate knew that an innocent man stood before him. He knew that the true instigators were the chief priests and that their motivation was envy. He also understood that Barabbas was a convicted, dangerous criminal. Yet he went against his own instincts, his responsibilities as an official, and the facts before him. Pilate sold out, and he knew it. When he handed Jesus over to the guard, Pilate set into motion events that would likely haunt him for the rest of his life. He not only killed an innocent man and endangered the safety of his community, he also betrayed himself. He appeased an angry mob, but he did so at great expense.

Sometimes we hear voices from every corner telling us what we should or should not do. As believers our first priority is to do what is right and to be true to God's Word. It's not always easy to take the high road, but it is the road God asks us to travel. Take a moment and ask God to help you to do the right thing. Determine to please him in your job, your decisions, and your relationships no matter what the crowd thinks.

LORD, I want to please you rather than people. That's not always easy, but you didn't travel an easy road either. You embraced the Father's will rather than your own. You shut out the noise of the crowd by finding a place of solitude to seek God. Today I will shut myself in with you, for my heart's desire is to please you. Help me to do the right thing no matter what the crowd might say.

WHATEVER ELSE LOVE MAY ASK OF US, IT DOES NOT ASK US TO BE DOORMATS OR COMPULSIVE PLEASERS OR PEACE-AT-ANY-PRICE PERSONS. THE PRIMARY GIFT OF LOVE IS THE OFFERING OF ONE'S MOST HONEST SELF THROUGH ONE'S MOST HONEST SELF-DISCLOSURE. John Powell

The One Year Bible Readings for today are **Numbers 15:17–16:40; Mark 15:1-47; Psalm 54:1-7;** and **Proverbs 11:5-6.**

care

He Will Take Care of You

Give your burdens to the Lord, and he will take care of you. He will not permit the godly to slip and fall.
Psalm 55:22

There are times when, like the psalmist, we feel pursued by enemies or surrounded by difficulties. Our enemy may be financial trouble, ill health, or a person who misjudges or opposes us so that our "heart is in anguish" (v. 4). At that point we may be tempted to run away, retreat, or give up. But the Lord offers us something better. In this psalm, trials and problems cause us to cry out to him. Someone once said, "If you are swept off your feet, it's time to get on your knees." God encourages us to turn to him and call on him in our distress so that he can rescue us and keep us safe in the midst of the trouble. He may not immediately take us out of the situation, but he will guide us through the circumstances. He gives us a wonderful promise: If we give our burdens to him, he will take care of us and not allow us to slip and fall.

LORD, I give you every burden and concern I face today. And I thank you for your promise of care, provision, and safety. You will not allow me to slip or fall. I will trust in you because you are faithful forever to those who love you. I consider it a joy and privilege to be counted among the many who love you. Thank you for the freedom to ask for and receive your help.

WHATSOEVER IT IS THAT PRESSES YOU, TELL YOUR FATHER; PUT OVER THE MATTER INTO HIS HAND, AND SO YOU WILL BE FREE FROM THAT DIVIDING, PERPLEXING CARE THAT THE WORLD IS FULL OF.
Archbishop Robert Leighton (1611–1684)

The One Year Bible Readings for today are **Numbers 16:41–18:32; Mark 16:1-20; Psalm 55:1-23;** and **Proverbs 11:7.**

MARCH

13

Laying Hold of His Words

When I am afraid, I put my trust in you. O God, I praise your word. I trust in God, so why should I be afraid?
Psalm 56:3-4

The scene in this psalm is very familiar: the psalmist has been attacked, slandered, and maligned by his enemies. He even feared death and had every human reason to be afraid. But as he reminded himself of the Lord's care and concern, as he meditated on God's power and majesty, and as he trusted and praised God's Word, his fear began to flee.

When circumstances cause us to be afraid, the only way we can avoid being overwhelmed by fear and genuinely trust in almighty God is by experiencing and declaring who he says he is in his Word. It is there that we learn of him and come to know him. As he speaks, his very words and presence bring peace, calmness, rest, and stillness in our inmost being. Therefore, as the psalmist said, we trust in God, so why should we be afraid? As children of God, we learn to live by his precious, powerful Word so that we can walk before him in the light of life. We can trust him and not give way to fear.

LORD, when I am afraid, I trust in you, and I praise you for the sustaining power of your Word. Help me to lay hold of your words to me, for they alone bring me life, health, and peace. Let my trust in you continue to grow deep and wide so that I can fulfill the plans you have for me in order for your kingdom to increase. Thank you for the gift of your Word, which comforts, inspires, and guides my path each day.

THE BIBLE IS ALIVE, IT SPEAKS TO ME; IT HAS FEET, IT RUNS AFTER ME; IT HAS HANDS, IT LAYS HOLD OF ME. Martin Luther (1483–1546)

The One Year Bible Readings for today are **Numbers 19:1–20:29; Luke 1:1-25; Psalm 56:1-13;** and **Proverbs 11:8.**

MARCH
14

cry

A Heartfelt Cry

I cry out to God Most High, to God who will fulfill his purpose for me.
Psalm 57:2

The idea of crying out to God usually implies distress, great need, testing, or simply a strong desire to experience or hear from God in a specific way. That was exactly where David found himself, surrounded by enemies who set a trap for him, fierce as lions whose tongues cut like swords. However, he directed his heartfelt cry not to just any god, but to the God who had proven himself faithful again and again and who would fulfill his purpose for David. In this psalm David proclaimed his confidence that God would "send help from heaven" to save him (v. 3). Just as David did, we are meant to build on every experience of God's help and faithfulness in the past so that our hearts will be confident in him and sing his praise (v. 7). What are you facing today? Give it—along with the burden and worry you feel—to the Lord, and trust in his promise that he will fulfill his purpose for you.

LORD, in my distress I still choose to trust and have hope in the fulfillment of your purposes for my life. Help me not to hide my troubled heart from you but to cry out to you, for you alone know the depth of my need. Thank you for your promise that you will fulfill your purpose for me. I lay at your feet any pressure I feel to take matters into my own hands. You are able to turn any troubles I face into a fulfillment of my destiny to be more like you!

GOD IS READY TO ASSUME FULL RESPONSIBILITY FOR THE LIFE WHOLLY YIELDED TO HIM.
Andrew Murray (1828–1917)

The One Year Bible Readings for today are **Numbers 21:1–22:20; Luke 1:26-56; Psalm 57:1-11;** and **Proverbs 11:9-11.**

MARCH

15

obeying

God's Will God's Way

[The angel said to Balaam,] "I have come to block your way because you are stubbornly resisting me. Three times the donkey saw me and shied away. . . . " Then Balaam confessed to the angel of the Lord, "I have sinned. I did not realize you were standing in the road to block my way. I will go back home if you are against my going." But the angel of the Lord told him, "Go with these men, but you may say only what I tell you to say."
Numbers 22:32-35

In today's reading Balaam was going forth to do as God had instructed him, but he was going with the wrong motives. His wholehearted obedience turned half-hearted because of his greed for wealth and prestige. His covetousness blinded him to the angel of the Lord who was blocking the path on which he traveled, because his eyes were focused on hoped-for riches and not on the hope-filled mission. Balaam ceased to reside in prayer—in a conscious awareness of God's presence. However, three times God was there narrowing the road in attempts to stop Balaam and get his attention. What path is God "narrowing" in your life so that you feel his resistance? God loves us enough that if we persist in doing things our way and ignore his presence or resist his will, he will derail us, just as he did Balaam's talking donkey, in order to get our attention and restore our fellowship with him.

LORD, thank you for your love that opens my eyes to see you on every path of life and leads me in obeying your will your way! Help me to follow you, whether it is to move forward into new territory or to return to a previously visited place. Only you know the direction I need to go. I will trust in your leadership and rely on your character. Thank you for leading me exactly where I need to go!

GOD CAN'T GIVE US HAPPINESS AND PEACE APART FROM HIMSELF BECAUSE THERE IS NO SUCH THING. C. S. Lewis (1898–1963)

The One Year Bible Readings for today are **Numbers 22:21–23:30; Luke 1:57-80; Psalm 58:1-11;** and **Proverbs 11:12-13.**

Savior

I Have Seen the Savior!

Many people saw Jesus that day and passed him by, taking no notice, but Simeon, who had eagerly expected the Messiah, was overjoyed and broke out in praise to God. Simeon had prayed for, hoped for, and waited for this moment. Getting to see the Christ was the highlight of Simeon's life, and he shared that joy by proclaiming Christ's glory and light to those around him.

Getting a glimpse of Jesus can light up our lives as well. We can be like those who must have passed him by in the temple on the day of his dedication—too busy to seek him and spend time with him. We can take him for granted and miss the blessing of his presence or be distracted by other things in the world. But if we eagerly look for Christ in our everyday goings and comings, draw close to him through prayer in our families, our work, our difficulties and trials, we, too, will get a new glimpse of God. Our hearts will be renewed, and others will come to know him through us.

FATHER, thank you for letting me see the Savior! I rejoice as Simeon did long ago. Jesus is alive, he has come and is coming again! Lord Jesus, thank you for being a light to reveal God to the nations so that more people can know and worship our Father. Thank you for bringing us out of darkness and into your marvelous light. I want to shine your light everywhere I go so that everyone around me will be drawn to you.

I HAVE ONE PASSION ONLY: IT IS HE! IT IS HE!
Count Nikolaus von Zinzendorf (1700–1760)

There was a man named Simeon who lived in Jerusalem. He was a righteous man and very devout. He was filled with the Holy Spirit, and he eagerly expected the Messiah to come and rescue Israel. . . . When Mary and Joseph came to present the baby Jesus to the Lord as the law required, Simeon was there. He took the child in his arms and praised God, saying, "Lord, now I can die in peace! As you promised me, I have seen the Savior you have given to all people. He is a light to reveal God to the nations, and he is the glory of your people Israel!"
Luke 2:25, 27-32

The One Year Bible Readings for today are **Numbers 24:1–25:18; Luke 2:1-35; Psalm 59:1-17;** and **Proverbs 11:14.**

MARCH
17

devotion

Wholehearted Devotion

Anna, a prophet, . . . was now eighty-four years old. She never left the Temple but stayed there day and night, worshiping God with fasting and prayer. She came along just as Simeon was talking with Mary and Joseph, and she began praising God. She talked about Jesus to everyone who had been waiting for the promised King to come and deliver Jerusalem.
Luke 2:36-38

Anna was wholehearted in her devotion, her worship, and her witness. For decades she had waited with hope. She worshiped the Lord with fasting and prayer. Though she was in one of the outer courtyards where women were allowed, *not* in the inner circle of priests, she was in the temple at the very hour and moment when the Christ child was dedicated. When she saw Jesus in the temple, she burst out with joy and praise, telling all who were waiting for the King about his coming.

We may think our lives are much more distracted and divided than Anna's, and we are not widows who live in the temple. Yet God calls us to Anna's place of devotion as well. When our hearts are divided, we can yield them to him again and ask him to help us and to draw us back to wholehearted devotion to him. When we do, the Lord gives us his grace and enables us to center our lives in him.

LORD, I want to let go of my divided desires and be wholeheartedly devoted to you. Capture and renew my heart today. May I be like Anna, who waited joyfully for you her whole life. I may not yet see you with my physical eyes, but let the eyes of my heart be awakened to see you and to rejoice in you today. You are worthy of all of my praise and adoration!

GOD OFFERS HIMSELF, GIVES HIMSELF AWAY, TO THE WHOLEHEARTED WHO GIVE THEMSELVES WHOLLY TO HIM. Andrew Murray (1828–1917)

The One Year Bible Readings for today are **Numbers 26:1-51; Luke 2:36-52; Psalm 60:1-12;** and **Proverbs 11:15.**

shelter

The Shelter of Your Wings

O God, listen to my cry! Hear my prayer! From the ends of the earth, I will cry to you for help, for my heart is overwhelmed. Lead me to the towering rock of safety, for you are my safe refuge, a fortress where my enemies cannot reach me. Let me live forever in your sanctuary, safe beneath the shelter of your wings!
Psalm 61:1-4

In contrast to yesterday's verses from Luke 2:36-38, this psalm was not penned by someone in the safety and comfort of the temple's walls but by one who was surrounded by his enemies or perhaps even imprisoned in the midst of a war. As he longs to escape to the rocky wilderness, he feels overwhelmed and weak. But instead of focusing on his inadequacy and spiraling into despair, he focuses on God, cries out to him, and finds strength in who the Lord is—his refuge, his fortress, his towering rock of safety. But the psalmist didn't seek God's protection and presence only for that particular time. He yearned for the day he would live safely under the shadow of God's wings forever. Are you overwhelmed today? Do you feel inadequate or weary? Look to God, your towering rock of safety, for help. He has promised never to fail you or forsake you. Read Psalm 61 aloud as your expression of love and worship today.

LORD, I cry to you for help, for you are my refuge. Even though my heart feels overwhelmed, you alone can lead me to your towering rock of safety. You are my fortress, Lord, and my enemies scatter in your presence. I long to dwell with you forever and to rest beneath the shelter of your wings. Thank you for providing such a safe place for me to live—in your presence.

SAFE IN JEHOVAH'S KEEPING,
SAFE IN TEMPTATION'S HOUR.
SAFE IN THE MIDST OF PERILS,
KEPT BY ALMIGHTY POWER.
SAFE WHEN THE TEMPEST RAGES,
SAFE THOUGH THE NIGHT BE LONG;
E'EN WHEN MY SKY IS DARKEST
GOD IS MY STRENGTH AND MY SONG.

Sir Robert Anderson (1841–1918)

The One Year Bible Readings for today are **Numbers 26:52–28:15; Luke 3:1-22; Psalm 61:1-8; Proverbs 11:16-17.**

MARCH

19

waiting

Quietly Waiting

I wait quietly before God, for my hope is in him. He alone is my rock and my salvation, my fortress where I will not be shaken. My salvation and my honor come from God alone. He is my refuge, a rock where no enemy can reach me.
Psalm 62:5-7

In this psalm David pours out his heart to God, describing his difficulties, the enemies that are trying to kill him, and the lies and curses others have spoken against him. But on the battlefield of life, in the midst of every trouble, David has a Godward focus. He is honest about his complaints and problems, but he has purposed to direct his gaze to the God of all faithfulness, putting his trust in the One who alone is his rock, salvation, fortress, and refuge. He then can wait quietly before God because he has put his hope, and his very life, in the Lord's hands. He doesn't trust in human nature because it is no more secure than a breath. He doesn't put his hope in riches because he knows that wealth will not save him. His hope, confidence, and trust are in the Lord Almighty.

If, like David, we are waiting for God to act when we are in the midst of trouble, we can wait frantically or impatiently. But to wait quietly in hope takes a deep confidence in knowing the One we are waiting for. He will never disappoint us.

LORD, I lift my eyes up to you, my rock, my salvation, my fortress, and my refuge. Quiet my heart to wait on you, for my hope is in you. Help me to wait for you in the storms, in the light, and in the darkness. Let my confidence not be shaken by what my heart may feel, circumstances may say, or my mind may think. I thank you that my confidence rests on the One who is my rock and that ***you*** *will never be shaken.*

WE MUST WAIT FOR GOD, LONG, MEEKLY, IN THE WIND AND WET, IN THE THUNDER AND LIGHTNING, IN THE COLD AND THE DARK. WAIT, AND HE WILL COME. Frederick William Faber (1814–1863)

The One Year Bible Readings for today are **Numbers 28:16–29:40; Luke 3:23-38; Psalm 62:1-12;** and **Proverbs 11:18-19.**

life

Better Than Life Itself

O God, you are my God; I earnestly search for you. My soul thirsts for you; my whole body longs for you in this parched and weary land where there is no water. I have seen you in your sanctuary and gazed upon your power and glory. Your unfailing love is better to me than life itself; how I praise you! I will honor you as long as I live, lifting up my hands to you in prayer.

Psalm 63:1-4

This psalm contains the words of a man who knows what it means to earnestly seek and lay hold of the Lord. David has experienced God, seen him in his sanctuary, and gazed on his power and glory. That is why in the wilderness, in the desolate, dry places of life, his soul thirsts for the Lord, his whole body longs for communion with him.

Although the experience of soul-thirsting after the Lord eludes us from time to time, the same experience that David had is available for each one of us. Jesus has opened the way for us to experience communion and harmony with our Creator. This is what we were made for! Our eyes can wander to other places; we can get distracted from seeking the Lord, but then we will wind up in a dry and weary land where there is no water. God calls us throughout Scripture to rise above the problems in the parched places in our lives and proclaim as David did that God's unfailing loving-kindness is better than anything in life—better than life itself.

OH, LORD, I earnestly search for you this day in this parched and weary place in my life. Let me see you and gaze on your power and glory. Draw me into intimacy with you by your Spirit to truly experience your loving-kindness. May I proclaim with the psalmist that your unfailing love is better to me than life itself. How I praise you! I will honor you as long as I live, lifting up my hands to you in prayer. Thank you for your promise that those who seek you will find you.

SEEKING WITH FAITH, HOPE AND LOVE PLEASES OUR LORD AND FINDING HIM PLEASES THE SOUL, FILLING IT FULL OF JOY. AND SO I LEARNT THAT AS LONG AS GOD ALLOWS US TO STRUGGLE ON THIS EARTH, SEEKING IS AS GOOD AS SEEING.
Julian of Norwich (1342–ca. 1413)

The One Year Bible Readings for today are **Numbers 30:1–31:54; Luke 4:1-30; Psalm 63:1-11;** and **Proverbs 11:20-21.**

MARCH
21

amazed

Amazed at Jesus

Jesus went to Capernaum, a town in Galilee, and taught there in the synagogue every Sabbath day. There, too, the people were amazed at the things he said, because he spoke with authority. . . . Amazed, the people exclaimed, "What authority and power this man's words possess! Even evil spirits obey him and flee at his command!"
Luke 4:31-32, 36

[Simon] was awestruck by the size of their catch, as were the others with him.
Luke 5:9

Throughout today's passage in Luke, Jesus taught in the temple, delivered people from demons, and healed Simon's mother-in-law and scores of others. Everywhere he went, those who were paying attention and heard him were filled with amazement and wonder at his authority and power. Later, when Jesus told Simon to take a different approach and cast the fishing net into deeper water, the attempt produced a catch so huge that it almost caused the boat to sink, and Simon was awestruck.

Although it is the same God who still does miracles and brings in a "catch" bigger than we can ask or think, who rules and reigns in our world today, many of us have lost our sense of awe and wonder and thus have ceased to truly worship him. If the weight of the burdens you're carrying has snuffed out your sense of awe, picture yourself in the boat with Simon or at the bedside of his mother-in-law or as one of those healed by Jesus' word. Ask the Holy Spirit today to open your eyes to see God's marvelous works in your life and to fill you with wonder at what a great God he is.

LORD, restore my sense of wonder and awe as I look for you at every turn in my everyday, walkaround life. I want to be like those who heard you teach and were amazed at the things you said. Speak to my heart, and give me ears to hear. Open my spiritual eyes to see that you are working in the world around me. May I be filled with wonder and gratefulness at your great deeds.

IF FOR ONE WHOLE DAY, QUIETLY AND DETERMINEDLY, WE WERE TO GIVE OURSELVES UP TO THE OWNERSHIP OF JESUS AND TO OBEYING HIS ORDERS, WE SHOULD BE AMAZED AT ITS CLOSE TO REALIZE ALL HE HAD PACKED INTO THAT ONE DAY. Oswald Chambers (1874–1917)

The One Year Bible Readings for today are **Numbers 32:1–33:39; Luke 4:31–5:11; Psalm 64:1-10;** and **Proverbs 11:22.**

prayer

Confidence in Prayer

When we pray, we are talking to the all-powerful God who created the earth by the power of his word, whose wonders fill the earth—and who faithfully answers our prayers with awesome deeds! Prayer is how he has designed his mighty power to be released on the earth, in our lives, and in the lives of those who desperately need God's help. It's like the huge generator one of the children in my prayer group drew to show what he had learned about prayer.

"That's God," Grant said. "He's got all this power for us." Then he drew a long diagonal line from the big generator to some stick figures representing a family. "That's who needs help. And the power flows along the cord as we pray!" Realizing God's awesome power changes the way we pray and the way we live. His power is available for every situation and need so that we "can do everything with the help of Christ who gives [us] the strength [we] need" (Philippians 4:13). This is a God we can trust and lean on. This is the all-powerful God in whom we can have confidence when we pray.

You faithfully answer our prayers with awesome deeds, O God our savior. You are the hope of everyone on earth, even those who sail on distant seas. You formed the mountains by your power and armed yourself with mighty strength.
Psalm 65:5-6

LORD, we praise you for your power. We believe, but help our unbelief, and fill us with fresh faith through the power of your Word. Enlarge our circle of prayer, not just for our needs and our own family but for those who are hurting, oppressed, and lost around us. You are our hope and the hope of everyone on the earth!

OUR PRAYERS LAY THE TRACK DOWN ON WHICH GOD'S POWER CAN COME. LIKE A MIGHTY LOCOMOTIVE, HIS POWER IS IRRESISTIBLE, BUT IT CANNOT REACH US WITHOUT RAILS.
Watchman Nee (1903–1972)

The One Year Bible Readings for today are **Numbers 33:40–35:34; Luke 5:12-28; Psalm 65:1-13;** and **Proverbs 11:23.**

MARCH

23

Unclogging the Pipes

Come and listen, all you who fear God, and I will tell you what he did for me. For I cried out to him for help, praising him as I spoke. If I had not confessed the sin in my heart, my Lord would not have listened. But God did listen! He paid attention to my prayer. Praise God, who did not ignore my prayer and did not withdraw his unfailing love from me.

Psalm 66:16-20

What sobering verses! When we come to God with a burden or request, oh, how we want him to hear us and answer. In today's verses David gives clear instruction: when we're crying out to God for help, we should first come to him in confession and ask him to cleanse our hearts. Then he will pay attention and will not ignore our prayer.

I illustrated this lesson for some children one Sunday with a piece of transitional pipe that I stuffed with brown Play-Doh and held to my ear. Sin clogs communication between God and us—the way the Play-Doh clogged the pipe, keeps us from hearing God, and keeps him from hearing us. But when we ask his Spirit to search our hearts and show us anything that displeases him, he will reveal what we need to confess. When we bring that sin to the cross, Jesus is faithful to cleanse us from all unrighteousness, as he promises in 1 John 1:9. Out goes the Play-Doh representing our sin—and the paths of communication are open again! Now we can proclaim with David: Praise God, who paid attention to my prayer, who answered me from his holy hill!

LORD, I ask you, search my heart. Shine your light on my sin. Forgive me. I am crying out to you for help. Thank you for hearing me, answering the cry of my heart, and continuing to show your unfailing love in my life.

EITHER SIN IS WITH YOU, LYING ON YOUR SHOULDERS, OR IT IS LYING ON CHRIST, THE LAMB OF GOD. NOW IF IT IS LYING ON YOUR BACK, YOU ARE LOST; BUT IF IT IS RESTING ON CHRIST, YOU ARE FREE, AND YOU WILL BE SAVED. NOW CHOOSE WHAT YOU WANT. Martin Luther (1483–1546)

The One Year Bible Readings for today are **Numbers 36:1–Deuteronomy 1:46; Luke 5:29–6:11; Psalm 66:1-20;** and **Proverbs 11:24-26.**

MARCH
24

sinners

Jesus, Friend of Sinners

Jesus answered them, "Healthy people don't need a doctor—sick people do. I have come to call sinners to turn from their sins, not to spend my time with those who think they are already good enough."
Luke 5:31-32

Isn't it great that our lives don't have to be fixed up, patched up, and cleaned up to have a relationship with Jesus? He came to call people who were broken and needy and whose lives were a mess to turn from their sins. He didn't have time for the self-righteous Pharisees, who thought they were already good enough and had no need of what he offered: a brand-new life and salvation from their sins. He was reaching out to those who were humble enough to honestly admit their need.

When Christ calls us out of darkness into his marvelous light, he wants us to tell others that there is hope for them. If a great doctor's skills had healed us of a life-threatening illness, we wouldn't fail to share the source of our health and the name of the doctor with those who are still suffering. We have a great physician, a savior who has transformed and healed our lives. Ask God to give you his heart to see people set free from their sins and sorrows and to renew your desire to tell others of his life-changing power. Then be his willing vessel to a waiting world, the largest intensive-care unit in the universe.

LORD, thank you for shedding your light on my life to show me that I needed you, the Great Physician, to heal my woundedness. Thank you for calling me to repent and to come to you and for your tender mercies in my life. Jesus, give me your heart for those who are hurting, sick, and lost in sin, just as your heart reached out to me in my time of greatest need.

GOD EXPECTS OF US ONLY WHAT HE HAS HIMSELF FIRST SUPPLIED. HE IS QUICK TO MARK EVERY SIMPLE EFFORT TO PLEASE HIM, AND JUST AS QUICK TO OVERLOOK IMPERFECTIONS WHEN HE KNOWS WE MEANT TO DO HIS WILL.
A. W. Tozer (1897–1963)

The One Year Bible Readings for today are **Deuteronomy 2:1–3:29; Luke 6:12-38; Psalm 67:1-7;** and **Proverbs 11:27.**

MARCH

25

glad

Be Glad in God's Presence

Let the godly rejoice. Let them be glad in God's presence. Let them be filled with joy. Sing praises to God and to his name! Sing loud praises to him who rides the clouds. His name is the Lord—rejoice in his presence! Father to the fatherless, defender of widows—this is God, whose dwelling is holy.
Psalm 68:3-5

The Lord is infinitely worthy in so many ways that we will never plumb the depths of his nature. Whether our situation puts us in the brightness of sunshine or in darkness of shadow, we are to be glad in God's presence, for he has created us and given us new life in Christ Jesus. He has provided for our needs and made us part of his eternal family. In the midst of the psalmist's praise of God, he proclaims one of God's most precious attributes: The Lord is a father to those without fathers and a strong defender of widows. The same God who reigns over the universe, rides the clouds, and defeats and scatters the enemy takes tender, fatherly care of those who are alone. In the amazing wideness of his mercy, he places the lonely in families where they can be loved and nurtured. Start a new habit of being glad in God's presence. Proclaim his unfailing love and mercy. Get up in the morning singing praises, and go to bed thanking God for his faithfulness. And look around you to those who may be lonely or leading solitary lives. Ask the Lord to help you to reach out and bring them into the circle of your family's love.

LORD, I praise you for your greatness and goodness, for the way you reign over all and yet care for the "least of these." Your mercy is over all your works! I sing praises to your name, Father of the fatherless, defender of widows, almighty and victorious King. Grant me grace to be glad in your presence and filled with joy as I walk with you today and to be open to those you want me to love with your love.

WE ALL SIN BY NEEDLESSLY DISOBEYING THE APOSTOLIC INJUNCTION *TO REJOICE* AS MUCH AS ANYTHING ELSE. C. S. Lewis (1898–1963)

The One Year Bible Readings for today are **Deuteronomy 4:1-49; Luke 6:39–7:10; Psalm 68:1-18;** and **Proverbs 11:28.**

wind

Inherit the Wind

Those who bring trouble on their families inherit only the wind. The fool will be a servant to the wise.
Proverbs 11:29

It's not difficult to imagine receiving your grandmother's treasured brooch, but what would it be like to inherit the wind? It sounds grand until you consider the magnitude of the gift. The wind is forceful, unruly, and can strike without warning. It may only whisk your hat off your head, but it also has the power to send ships careening off course. It goes where it wishes, whipping the small, the fragile, and the unrestrained where it will. We risk danger when we open the door and allow trouble to march in to our homes. Unwelcome guests with names such as unrestrained anger or petty arguments can whip through our homes and drive family members apart. Selfishness nudges joy out the window as love and kindness and gentleness fall to the ground like brittle, dead leaves. Our families were intended to be a sanctuary—a safe place for each of us. We all face trouble from time to time, but it should never be because we willingly allow it into our homes. Instead, let your home be characterized by a legacy of kindness, godly character, and faith. Choose today to bring good things to your family and to leave trouble outside the door.

FATHER, my loved ones are precious to me. I want them to inherit more than the wind. Forgive me for the times when I have allowed uninvited guests into my home. Help me to keep rage and petty arguments and selfishness far away. If I have willingly brought trouble to my family, help me to make amends. I don't want the destructive wind of trouble to invade my home and family. I invite the gentle breeze of your Spirit to abide in us.

LET YOUR HOME BE YOUR PARISH, YOUR LITTLE BROOD YOUR CONGREGATION, YOUR LIVING ROOM A SANCTUARY, AND YOUR KNEE A SACRED ALTAR.
Billy Graham (b. 1918)

The One Year Bible Readings for today are **Deuteronomy 5:1–6:25; Luke 7:11-35; Psalm 68:19-35;** and **Proverbs 11:29-31.**

MARCH
27

enemy

Destroy the Enemy

[Moses said,] "When the Lord your God brings you [the Israelites] into the land you are about to enter and occupy, he will clear away many nations ahead of you: the Hittites, Girgashites, Amorites, Canaanites, Perizzites, Hivites, and Jebusites. These seven nations are all more powerful than you. When the Lord your God hands these nations over to you and you conquer them, you must completely destroy them. Make no treaties with them and show them no mercy.

Deuteronomy 7:1-2

God gave clear instructions to the Israelites to conquer their enemies completely. They were not to show mercy or compromise in any way, or they could lose what they had gained. The seven enemies were all more powerful than the Israelites and clearly had the potential to keep them from occupying the Promised Land. But God had already handed the Israelites' enemies over to them, assuring them that they would reach their destination.

When God delivers us from a life of sin, we must not recross the bridge that God has brought us over. There should be no place in our lives where we would entertain the things that once had the power to destroy us. God is leading each of us to a place where we can discover his greatest intentions for our lives. Compromises large or small allow the enemy to slip in and distract, delay, or keep us from reaching that destination. Determine today to show no mercy to the old enemies that once had a hold on your life. Thank God that he saved you, and praise him that because of the finished work of Christ, he has conquered the enemy once and for all.

PRECIOUS SAVIOR, once the enemy stood in my way, yet you saved me. Help me to give my enemies no part in my life. I will not make treaties with them or compromise in any way. I will show no mercy to the things that once threatened to destroy my life. I will embrace you, God, for you moved those things out of my way so that I could respond to your higher calling.

IT IS NEVER WISE TO UNDERESTIMATE AN ENEMY. WE LOOK UPON THE ENEMY OF OUR SOULS AS A CONQUERED FOE, SO HE IS, BUT ONLY TO GOD, NOT TO US. Oswald Chambers (1874–1917)

The One Year Bible Readings for today are **Deuteronomy 7:1–8:20; Luke 7:36–8:3; Psalm 69:1-18;** and **Proverbs 12:1.**

soil

Good Soil

Farmers scattering seed by hand were a familiar sight in Jesus' time. The soil was rich for the most part, but there were thornbushes and fields full of stones. Travelers walked through the fields, beating down the ground and disturbing the seeds. Some seeds fell on thin soil that hid the stones underneath. Other seeds were blown into thornbushes. Neither were good environments for the new plants.

Jesus knew this. He wanted them—and us—to ask some probing questions: Are our hearts hard, like the paths worn down by travelers, so that it's easy for Satan to steal away God's truth after we hear it? Is the soil of our hearts thin and rocky so that the roots of God's Word can't go very deep? Or are we thorny-ground folks who are so worried and anxious about our lives that the seed never produces good fruit or grows into maturity? God's Spirit is always ready and willing to make our hearts good soil so his Word can grow strong in us. Ask him to do that today.

LORD, I want to receive the seed of your message, apply it to my life, and be obedient to you. If my heart is hard, soften it with your love. If my roots aren't deep, enrich the soil. Deliver me from being consumed with the cares, riches, and pleasures of this world. Bring forth, by your Spirit, a great harvest in my life!

"I HAVEN'T TIME!" OF COURSE YOU HAVE TIME! TAKE TIME, STRANGLE SOME OTHER INTERESTS, AND MAKE TIME TO REALIZE THAT THE CENTER OF POWER IN YOUR LIFE IS THE LORD JESUS CHRIST.
Oswald Chambers (1874–1917)

"The seed is God's message. The seed that fell on the hard path represents those who hear the message, but then the Devil comes and steals it away. . . . The rocky soil represents those who hear the message with joy. But . . . their roots don't go very deep. . . . They wilt when the hot winds of testing blow. The thorny ground represents those who hear and accept the message, but all too quickly the message is crowded out by the cares and riches and pleasures of this life. . . . But the good soil represents . . . people who hear God's message, cling to it, and steadily produce a huge harvest."
Luke 8:11-15

The One Year Bible Readings for today are **Deuteronomy 9:1–10:22; Luke 8:4-21; Psalm 69:19-36;** and **Proverbs 12:2-3.**

MARCH

29

faith

A Living Faith in the Living God

[Moses said,] "Commit yourselves completely to these words of mine. Tie them to your hands as a reminder, and wear them on your forehead. Teach them to your children. Talk about them when you are at home and when you are away on a journey, when you are lying down and when you are getting up again. Write them on the doorposts of your house and on your gates, so that as long as the sky remains above the earth, you and your children may flourish in the land the Lord swore to give your ancestors.
Deuteronomy 11:18-21

Parents often spend energy and time helping children develop in sports, academics, and the arts. These are valuable activities, but from God's perspective, helping children develop a living faith in the living God is far more important than anything else. In Deuteronomy 11:21 the Lord tells the Israelites that only when they love and worship him wholeheartedly will he bless them and cause them to flourish. Failing to teach this to our children would be the greatest disservice.

How do parents, teachers, and others go about this? By being examples of those who are wholly devoted to loving, serving, and obeying Christ. By talking about God's truth wherever we are. Pointing children to God and the life-giving power of his Word is one of the greatest things we can do because it has eternal consequences. If you are a parent, make a new commitment to pass on God's truth to your children. If you are not a parent, look for opportunities to share God's truth with children with whom you spend time.

LORD, I want to love you with all my heart and soul and lead children to love and honor you as well. Help me to live in such a way that they will be drawn to you. Show me practically how to talk with children—mine or others'—about your truth, teach them your principles, and help them apply your Word to their lives.

THERE'S NO DOUBT THAT IT IS THE JOB OF US AS PARENTS—NOT THE PRIESTS, KINGS, OR PROPHETS—TO TEACH GOD'S TRUTH TO OUR CHILDREN. WHY? BECAUSE WHEN OUR CHILDREN LEARN FROM US, THEY WILL MORE READILY MOVE BEYOND JUST KNOWING TO OBEYING.
Bruce Wilkinson

The One Year Bible Readings for today are **Deuteronomy 11:1–12:32; Luke 8:22-39; Psalm 70:1-5;** and **Proverbs 12:4.**

passing

Passing It On

The psalmist, now old, is looking back on his life and the history of his people. Although he has been assailed by the wicked and seen troubles, many and bitter, his first resource has always been God. He is confident that the same God he trusted as a youth will lead him through his present trials to restoration and blessing. Woven throughout Psalm 71 is a theme of gratefulness for God's faithfulness and protection in the past, even when the psalmist was suffering loneliness, betrayal, and great hardship. However, the psalmist isn't content just to reminisce about the good things the Lord has done in the past or merely praise God in front of others. His greatest desire is to proclaim the Lord's power and mighty miracles to the next generation. He calls on God, knowing that he needs divine help to pass on a heritage of faith in the one true God to all who will come after him. We, too, have a great responsibility and privilege to declare God's power to the next generation. Ask God for the grace and strength to be a role model in your faith, witness, and prayer life to those who follow you.

I will tell everyone about your righteousness. All day long I will proclaim your saving power, for I am overwhelmed by how much you have done for me. I will praise your mighty deeds, O Sovereign Lord. I will tell everyone that you alone are just and good. O God, you have taught me from my earliest childhood, and I have constantly told others about the wonderful things you do.

Psalm 71:15-17

LORD, let me proclaim your power to this new generation and tell my children, grandchildren, and youth in my church and nation the wonderful things you have done for us. Thank you for your faithfulness in my life through troubles and joy. I pray that a new generation will rise up and be devoted to you.

EACH GENERATION OF CHRISTIANS, AND EACH PEOPLE TO WHICH THE CHRISTIAN GOSPEL IS PREACHED, MAKES ITS OWN CONTRIBUTION TO THE UNDERSTANDING OF THE RICHES OF JESUS CHRIST. C. B. Moss

The One Year Bible Readings for today are **Deuteronomy 13:1–15:23; Luke 8:40–9:6; Psalm 71:1-24;** and **Proverbs 12:5-7.**

MARCH
31

possible

Mission Possible

Late in the afternoon the twelve disciples came to him and said, "Send the crowds away to the nearby villages and farms, so they can find food and lodging for the night. There is nothing to eat here in this deserted place." But Jesus said, "You feed them." "Impossible!" they protested. "We have only five loaves of bread and two fish. Or are you expecting us to go and buy enough food for this whole crowd?"

Luke 9:12-13

After a time of ministry, the disciples wanted to have Jesus all to themselves and enjoy some rest and relaxation away from the crowds. But the multitudes found out where the Messiah was and flocked to him. If that weren't enough frustration, now Jesus was asking the disciples to do something that looked impossible—feed more than five thousand men plus hundreds of women and children with what were ridiculously meager resources. The disciples, having been given the instruction "You feed them," could have been the vehicle for the miracle had they obeyed in faith. Instead they watched as Jesus took the food, asked God to bless it, and then broke and distributed it to the multitudes. What seemingly impossible task is God asking you to do? What do you not have enough resources for? Does parenting an unruly toddler—or teen—look like "mission impossible"? Do job demands seem more than you can handle? Are financial needs insurmountable? Give all you have to Jesus. Ask him to multiply your resources, time, and skills, and listen for his instruction. Then be ready to experience his amazing power in your life.

DEAR LORD, this task (or situation) looks impossible. Yet you said that with you, nothing is impossible if we believe. Strengthen my trust in your ability and your resources. I want to be your vessel and be used by you. I give you myself—my heart, my time, my gifts—and ask you to multiply them for your purposes. May you be glorified in my life.

GOD CALLS US TO LIVE A LIFE WE CANNOT LIVE, SO THAT WE MUST DEPEND ON HIM FOR SUPERNATURAL ABILITY. WE ARE CALLED TO DO THE IMPOSSIBLE, TO LIVE BEYOND OUR NATURAL ABILITY. Erwin W. Lutzer (b. 1941)

The One Year Bible Readings for today are **Deuteronomy 16:1–17:20; Luke 9:7-27; Psalm 72:1-20;** and **Proverbs 12:8-9.**

strength

Strength of My Heart

The psalmist had tested and experienced the beauty, glory, and excellency of the Lord; that is why he could proclaim that there was nothing or no one in all the earth that he wanted or treasured more than God. He had seen God as he truly was—as his shepherd, his counselor, his victory, his refuge, and his sustainer. Therefore, he knew that all his needs and desires were fulfilled in God and that he would always be the strength of his heart and life, even when his health failed or the aging process brought weakness.

If we see and experience Jesus as he is, we, too, will value him above every earthly pleasure, possession, or relationship. Though our vision of God is often dim and "we see things imperfectly as in a poor mirror" (1 Corinthians 13:12), we can ask for the spiritual eyes to see the Lord and for our hearts to so experience his presence that we will treasure him and be more thrilled by him than by anything on earth. Dedicate some time today for praising and thanking God that he is and always will be the strength of your heart and yours forever.

Whom have I in heaven but you? I desire you more than anything on earth. My health may fail, and my spirit may grow weak, but God remains the strength of my heart; he is mine forever.
Psalm 73:25-26

LORD, I want to know, see, and experience you in fresh ways so I can truly say that I desire you more than anything on earth! You and you alone are the strength of my heart. You are all that I need, and I am so thankful that you are mine forever. Nothing can separate me from your love. Open my eyes, and grant me fresh vision to constantly see your beauty and your love for me.

JESUS INTENDS FOR YOU TO EXPERIENCE THE PLEASURE AND REASSURING PEACE OF HIS PRESENCE AT THE CORE OF YOUR LIFE.
Joseph Stowell

The One Year Bible Readings for today are **Deuteronomy 18:1–20:20; Luke 9:28-50; Psalm 73:1-28;** and **Proverbs 12:10.**

The ONE YEAR BIBLE

APRIL

2

harvest

The Harvest Is Here

These were [Jesus'] instructions to them: "The harvest is so great, but the workers are so few. Pray to the Lord who is in charge of the harvest, and ask him to send out more workers for his fields. Go now."
Luke 10:2-3

Jesus selected seventy of his disciples and sent them out in pairs in order to strengthen their witness and give them fellowship as they traveled. He gave them specific instructions—travel light, take no extra baggage, and be cautious because they were embarking on dangerous work—like lambs evangelizing among wolves; their preaching mission was urgent, so they were to make haste and focus on spreading the good news of the kingdom, healing the sick, and delivering the oppressed. Jesus also urged them to pray for more workers, for the harvest was great.

Those instructions still apply to us today. God doesn't want anyone to perish; he wants all to hear the gospel and have eternal life. All over the world, fields are white for harvest. There are still many unreached people groups who need to hear the Good News. There are villages where children and parents and the elderly have never known a savior. So in the midst of whatever ministry or work we are doing, we are to pray that the Lord of the harvest will send out more laborers for his fields.

LORD, raise up and send out laborers to every tribe and nation, every people group, and every unreached child. Raise up missionaries, doctors, teachers, businessmen and women, Bible translators, and musicians to share the goodness of Jesus Christ and to bring in a harvest of souls. Help me to see that the harvest is right before my eyes. Come, Lord Jesus, your harvest awaits!

THINE IS THE SEED TIME. GOD ALONE
BEHOLDS THE END OF WHAT IS SOWN;
BEYOND OUR VISION WEAK AND DIM
THE HARVEST TIME IS HID WITH HIM.

John Greenleaf Whittier (1807–1892)

The One Year Bible Readings for today are **Deuteronomy 21:1–22:30; Luke 9:51–10:12; Psalm 74:1-23;** and **Proverbs 12:11.**

APRIL
3

praise

A Heart of Praise

As for me, I will always proclaim what God has done; I will sing praises to the God of Israel.
Psalm 75:9

Often when we thank God, we are responding to what he does, how he is answering our prayers and working out his plan in our lives. When we worship, on the other hand, we are adoring, honoring, and embracing God simply for who he is. Worship is the overflow of hearts that are thankful and full of wonder. We worship God when we lift our hearts and voices in grateful acknowledgment of how he has revealed himself in our lives: our faithful and trustworthy provider, protector, redeemer, refuge, comforter, healer, sustainer, source of strength, helper, father, and friend. On and on the list goes. With praise-filled hearts we can proclaim all that God is and has done in our lives. Nothing delights the heart of our Father more than songs of praise from the lips of his children. It's what we were created for, and it deepens our dependence on him. What an awesome God we serve! Express to the Lord your desire to worship him with all your heart, soul, and mind. Spend time in his presence meditating on all God has done and who he is to you.

OH, LORD, how I praise the wonders of your works! May I be found faithful in proclaiming through a heart of praise all that you are and have done in my life. You are so many things to me—you are my everything! Thank you for the privilege of receiving a heart that is able to praise you every single day of my life.

THE HEART MUST HAVE IN IT THE GRACE OF PRAYER TO SING THE PRAISES OF GOD.
E. M. Bounds (1835–1913)

The One Year Bible Readings for today are **Deuteronomy 23:1–25:19; Luke 10:13-37; Psalm 75:1-10;** and **Proverbs 12:12-14.**

APRIL

4

work

One True Work

[Jesus said,] "There is really only one thing worth being concerned about. Mary has discovered it—and I won't take it away from her."
Luke 10:42

In the story of Mary and Martha we see not only how busy Martha is with preparations for dinner but also her frustration because Mary is sitting with Jesus instead of helping her. However, as much as Martha yearned for her sister's help, her words to the Lord indicate an even greater problem: she could not control Mary. She went to the Lord saying, "Tell her to come and help me," in hopes that he would get Mary to do as Martha wanted.

So often, the Martha in us tries to control another person's choices, especially if we would benefit in some way, but we find ourselves in the same flustered state Martha was in. Mary wisely chose listening to the Lord over any service she may have done for him at that particular time. She was also living beyond her sister's control and was discovering the one true work worth being concerned about—sitting at the feet of Jesus. What concerns you? The time we spend in prayer means more to him than any other work we could ever do. Jesus desires that we "sit at his feet" daily in prayer and learn from his infinite supply of love and knowledge.

LORD, I want to be like Mary, to rest in your presence and converse with you. Help me to discover today what it is like to lay aside everything else and focus on you. Without these times alone with you, my spirit would surely be dry and weary. I love you and need your guidance on how to spend time alone with you every single day.

PRAYER IS NOT THE OPPOSITE OF WORK; IT DOES NOT PARALYZE ACTIVITY. RATHER, PRAYER ITSELF IS THE GREATEST WORK; IT WORKS MIGHTILY.
E. M. Bounds (1835–1913)

The One Year Bible Readings for today are **Deuteronomy 26:1–27:26; Luke 10:38–11:13; Psalm 76:1-12;** and **Proverbs 12:15-17.**

head

The Head and Not the Tail

When reading Deuteronomy 28, it is pleasant to focus on the blessings in Moses' message, yet we cannot avoid the fact that there were two sides to this oracle. Blessings would rain on the children of Israel as a result of their obedience, but harsh consequences awaited those who served other gods. It is hard to imagine a compassionate God raining down such curses on his children, for we know that God longed to bless his people. When the children of Israel turned from God, they would return to him only when they realized that they had placed themselves under the yoke of a far less benevolent master. Therein lies the curse—willingly abandoning a loving God to follow one whose intent is not to bless but to destroy. God still longs to bless us, but there is another who prowls about seeking to destroy those who are precious to God. Choose today to serve the God who longs to make you the head and not the tail.

If you listen to these commands of the Lord your God and carefully obey them, the Lord will make you the head and not the tail, and you will always have the upper hand. You must not turn away from any of the commands I am giving you today to follow after other gods and worship them.
Deuteronomy 28:13-14

MERCIFUL GOD, when I was created you forged a path for me to follow. But there is an enemy who desires that I lose my way. He seeks to destroy the destiny you have had for me from the beginning. I choose blessings because today and every day, I choose you! Thank you for the many blessings that have come from serving a compassionate, living, and mighty God. Thank you for making me the head and not the tail.

IN DARKNESS THERE IS NO CHOICE. IT IS LIGHT THAT ENABLES US TO SEE THE DIFFERENCES BETWEEN THINGS; AND IT IS CHRIST WHO GIVES US LIGHT. Augustus Hare (1792–1834)

The One Year Bible Readings for today are **Deuteronomy 28:1-68; Luke 11:14-36; Psalm 77:1-20;** and **Proverbs 12:18.**

APRIL

6

senses

Bring Me to My Senses

To this day the Lord has not given you minds that understand, nor eyes that see, nor ears that hear!
Deuteronomy 29:4

The Israelites had watched as God split open the Red Sea to allow them to walk across on dry ground. They saw God's daily provision of food fall from heaven. They were shielded night and day from their enemies. Yet they complained, longing for what they did not have and failing to recognize what God had given them. It is easy to forget the blessings that surround us every day and instead clamor for greener pastures. How many of us thank God for our health, the breath that we breathe, the shelter over our heads, work to do, children that fill the house with sound and energy, a spouse who kisses us good-bye in the morning, good friends? Unfortunately, many of us experience the awakening of dulled senses only when we lose what we took for granted when it was right under our noses. What blessings surround you right now? Take some time to try listing them. Even the smallest things become great when we realize how much they enrich our lives. As you name the ways God has blessed you, ask him for eyes to see, ears to hear, and a heart to perceive the wonders that surround you every day.

FATHER, thank you for the sweet smell of honeysuckle. Thank you for the food in my cupboard. Thank you for the child who gave me sticky kisses on my cheek. Thank you for the comfortable chair where I rest after a hard day of work. Thank you for those who love me. Thank you for giving me eyes to see what I have and ears to hear. Thank you for a heart to respond in thankfulness for all that you have given me. Help me never to take any of it for granted.

CULTIVATE THE THANKFUL SPIRIT! IT WILL BE TO YOU A PERPETUAL FEAST. John MacDuff (1818–1895)

The One Year Bible Readings for today are **Deuteronomy 29:1–30:20; Luke 11:37–12:7; Psalm 78:1-31;** and **Proverbs 12:19-20.**

shoes

Size-Twelve Shoes

Have you ever been asked to follow in the footsteps of someone that you respect as a leader? If you have, then you may know something about how Joshua felt as he stood before Moses. Joshua understood the enormity of the task before him. He had watched Moses enter the tent of meeting, burdened and heavy laden, to seek guidance and strength from God. He had heard the murmuring among the people. He had participated in the battles. Would he be able to lead the Israelites into the Promised Land without the guidance of Moses? Whether Joshua felt capable and ready or not, it was time.

When God calls you to assume leadership, you may feel inadequate, as if you are placing size-nine feet in size-twelve shoes. Take heart. Just as the Lord assured Moses and Joshua, his promises are for your encouragement today. He will be with you; he will neither fail you nor forsake you. Remember, you are not filling a person's shoes; rather, you are placing your feet in the footsteps of the One who called you. With God's help, you can do it!

Moses called for Joshua, and as all Israel watched he said to him, "Be strong and courageous! For you will lead these people into the land that the Lord swore to give their ancestors. You are the one who will deliver it to them as their inheritance. Do not be afraid or discouraged, for the Lord is the one who goes before you. He will be with you; he will neither fail you nor forsake you."
Deuteronomy 31:7-8

LORD, thank you for trusting me to lead others. Help me to trust you each step of the way. When I encounter difficulties, may I carry my burden to you so that you may dispense wisdom and counsel. When the task seems too great, help me to trust you to show me the way. Thank you for going before me. I will follow your footsteps as you lead me one step at a time. I will not be afraid or discouraged, because I know that you are right beside me.

A TRUE AND SAFE LEADER IS LIKELY TO BE ONE WHO HAS NO DESIRE TO LEAD BUT IS FORCED INTO A POSITION OF LEADERSHIP BY THE INWARD PRESSURE OF THE HOLY SPIRIT AND THE PRESS OF THE EXTERNAL SITUATION. A. W. Tozer (1897–1963)

The One Year Bible Readings for today are **Deuteronomy 31:1–32:27; Luke 12:8-34; Psalm 78:32-55;** and **Proverbs 12:21-23.**

APRIL

8

ready

Are You Ready?

[Jesus said,] "Be dressed for service and well prepared, as though you were waiting for your master to return from the wedding feast. Then you will be ready to open the door and let him in the moment he arrives and knocks. There will be special favor for those who are ready and waiting for his return. I tell you, he himself will seat them, put on an apron, and serve them as they sit and eat! He may come in the middle of the night or just before dawn. But whenever he comes, there will be special favor for his servants who are ready!"

Luke 12:35-38

Just the thought of living so that we are ready when Christ returns should fuel all God's children to be about his kingdom work with consecrated energy and zeal. Whether we have the strength, time, and vigor to do his will depends on our readiness and openness to hearing his voice in prayer. Prayer is absolutely necessary if we wish to carry on God's work successfully. God has designed it so that he will sufficiently and energetically work through us in proportion to how much we give ourselves to prayer and so live ready for Christ's return. As we see the time of his return drawing near, we evaluate how we are spending our days by asking, "What am I to be doing?" The Lord has planned and purposed so much for our lives, given us so much work to do for his glory. However, so that we can be truly ready, God beckons us to his glorious throne room to pour out our hearts and concerns and to listen for his marching orders. Then as we work with him in fulfilling his Word and purposes, we will do so in his power, love, and grace. Are you ready? Living ready begins on our knees . . . and continues as we stay there.

DEAR FATHER, I desire to live ready! Help me to first fall on my knees in prayer before beginning a work with you. Thank you, too, for your promise of "special favor" for those who are prepared when Jesus returns! I desire to be found ready in your eyes and to please you in everything I do.

THE SUCCESS OF OUR LIVING READY IS DEPENDENT ON OUR GIVING OURSELVES IN PRAYER. E. M. Bounds (1835–1913)

The One Year Bible Readings for today are **Deuteronomy 32:28-52; Luke 12:35-59; Psalm 78:56-64;** and **Proverbs 12:24.**

God's Everlasting Arms

Our world seemed to be falling apart. My husband was severely depressed, and his business was crumbling. As I tried to support and nurture our children, help my husband, and take up the slack financially, I became drained physically, spiritually, and mentally. I cried out to God in exhaustion, and I felt his everlasting arms underneath me. Quieting my racing heart, the Lord reminded me that although my own resources might be exhausted, his resources were limitless.

During that difficult season I experienced God as my refuge when there was nowhere else to turn, and I felt his security in the middle of a very uncertain, insecure time.

In today's passage Moses praises the Lord and assures the Israelites that God will be with them no matter what adversity or trial they encounter—that he is their refuge and underneath them are his everlasting arms. Do you need to feel God's everlasting arms carrying you today because your strength is exhausted? Do you know someone who is in desperate straits and needs God's help? Pray these verses for yourself or for someone else, and proclaim God's faithfulness.

LORD, there is no one like you! You ride across the heavens in majestic splendor to help us when we cry out to you. May we experience you today as our refuge and sense your everlasting arms of protection and love holding us. I praise you for your faithfulness and unparalleled power!

WHEN YOU ARE AT THE END OF YOUR ROPE, GOD IS THERE TO CATCH YOU—BUT NOT BEFORE.
Erwin W. Lutzer (b. 1941)

There is no one like the God of Israel. He rides across the heavens to help you, across the skies in majestic splendor. The eternal God is your refuge, and his everlasting arms are under you.
Deuteronomy 33:26-27

The One Year Bible Readings for today are **Deuteronomy 33:1-29; Luke 13:1-21; Psalm 78:65-72;** and **Proverbs 12:25.**

APRIL
10

obedience

Blind Obedience

Jesus asked the Pharisees and experts in religious law, "Well, is it permitted in the law to heal people on the Sabbath day, or not?" When they refused to answer, Jesus touched the sick man and healed him and sent him away. Then he turned to them and asked, "Which of you doesn't work on the Sabbath? If your son or your cow falls into a pit, don't you proceed at once to get him out?"
Luke 14:3-5

The Pharisees, along with the priests, were administrators of the law. They studied, interpreted, and observed the law in their homes and in the temple. Therefore, it made sense that Jesus would pose his question to them. Yet over generations the Pharisees' ancestors had heaped new definitions and traditions on top of the individual laws. Their intent was to avoid sin, but the original meaning of the law became diluted because of all the complicated stipulations. The observance of the law became burdensome. It also made it difficult for the Pharisees to provide a clear answer to Jesus' question. Jesus was not breaking the law of the Sabbath when he healed the man. He showed compassion for one who was helpless to heal himself. We practice only blind obedience when we follow dogma or tradition or adhere to rules and regulations and yet fail to understand and practice the heart of Christianity. "Love God with all your heart, soul, and mind, and love your neighbor as yourself." There is no higher law.

JESUS, forgive me when I get caught up in tradition or legalism and follow those things instead of seeking and following you. It's easy to get tangled in religious activities and forget that there is a world outside the four walls of my church. I love you, Lord. Bring me into harmony with you. Help me to live in such a way that others will see you at work in my heart.

IF YOU HAVE RECEIVED THE SPIRIT AND ARE OBEYING HIM, YOU FIND HE BRINGS YOUR SPIRIT INTO COMPLETE HARMONY WITH GOD, AND THE SOUND OF YOUR GOINGS AND THE SOUND OF GOD'S GOINGS ARE ONE AND THE SAME.
Oswald Chambers (1874–1917)

The One Year Bible Readings for today are **Deuteronomy 34:1 – Joshua 2:24; Luke 13:22–14:6; Psalm 79:1-13;** and **Proverbs 12:26.**

mentality

A Rival Mentality

Come back, we beg you, O God Almighty. Look down from heaven and see our plight. Watch over and care for this vine that you yourself have planted, this son you have raised for yourself.
Psalm 80:14-15

The people of Judah had to contend with rebellious family members who had caused tremendous conflict. When the Assyrians overcame them and took them into captivity, it would have seemed natural for the people of Judah to rejoice. However, instead of seeing the captives as their enemy, Judah immediately perceived their pain as their own and cried out for God to restore the fallen nation.

Unfortunately, we sometimes see our brothers and sisters in Christ as rivals. Do others recognize our efforts? Is our church congregation the largest in the city? Is our Easter pageant the most spectacular? A rival mentality, whether within our own church body or among the churches in our community, causes division and weakness and makes us less effective in reaching a lost world. When a wounded brother falls, we can embrace a rival mentality and rejoice in his failure, or we can stand in the gap and pray for his restoration. Rather than concentrate on beating others to the finish line, ask for the grace to pray for and support our fellow churches and our own church family so that we can run the race together as brothers and sisters in Christ.

LORD, thank you for the churches in my community. Please bless their pastors and leaders with strength and unity, and help their congregations to grow! Help us to work together to reach our community for you. Help me to be an encouragement to my brothers and sisters in Christ and not to forget that we are all running the race together!

THERE CAN BE NO UNITY, NO DELIGHT OF LOVE, NO HARMONY, NO GOOD IN BEING, WHERE THERE IS BUT ONE. TWO AT LEAST ARE NEEDED FOR ONENESS. George Macdonald (1824–1905)

The One Year Bible Readings for today are **Joshua 3:1–4:24; Luke 14:7-35; Psalm 80:1-19;** and **Proverbs 12:27-28.**

APRIL

12

don't tell

Don't Tell Me What to Do!

A wise child accepts a parent's discipline; a young mocker refuses to listen.
Proverbs 13:1

No one likes to be told what to do. We are self-sufficient creatures who would rather stumble along until we get it right. A natural shield zips into place when we feel the zing of correction coming our way. But how much time, effort, and frustration could we avoid if we listened to the counsel of those older and wiser? Many times their life experiences have sharpened their insights. Think of the misfortune we might have missed if we had heeded their instruction. Of course, not every piece of advice is valuable, but we can weigh it in light of God's Word. When someone rebukes you, pause and examine what you hear. Is there truth in the instruction? Is the Lord trying to show you something through it? What practical steps will you take to apply the instruction to your life?

Although it's not easy to welcome discipline or instruction from others, it has the potential to shape your character and make your journey through life a little less bumpy. Ask God today to develop in you a teachable heart that accepts discipline and correction and listens to those he puts in your path to teach you and prepare you for what is ahead.

FATHER, thank you for people who will be honest with me and even correct me when I need it! Help me to be receptive rather than defensive and to grow in maturity and character. One day I will be older and wiser, but until then, thank you for those who share their insights with me. Help me to discern what is helpful, to examine instruction in the light of your Word, and to grow!

DISCIPLINE IS A PROOF OF OUR SONSHIP.
Erwin W. Lutzer (b. 1941)

The One Year Bible Readings for today are **Joshua 5:1–7:15; Luke 15:1-32; Psalm 81:1-16;** and **Proverbs 13:1.**

steward

Are You a Good Steward?

[Jesus said,] "Unless you are faithful in small matters, you won't be faithful in large ones. If you cheat even a little, you won't be honest with greater responsibilities."
Luke 16:10

Each day we make decisions about matters that seem small. If a cashier gives us too much change, it may be only a few cents, but the larger issue is honesty. Our use of time in the workplace may not seem all that important, but the larger issues are integrity and loyalty. It's how we handle the "small" details of life that define our character. God wants us to be faithful stewards, not just with resources such as our time, money, or talent, but in our work ethic, our business dealings, and in everyday details that affect others. The steward in the parable Jesus told in Luke 16 was not diligent with his employer's money until he realized that he might lose his job and be forced to beg. His irresponsibility became relevant only when it affected him. In today's society, honesty and diligence are respected but not expected. Many people consider cheating a little, especially if it advances your cause, a small matter. But God calls us to a higher standard. Take a moment and examine your life. What type of steward are you when no one is watching? Are you diligent in the small matters as well as in the large? Expose your heart to the searchlight of God's Spirit and truth, and ask him to make you faithful in the little so that he will be able to trust you with bigger responsibilities and larger territory in his kingdom.

DEAR GOD, sometimes I think that the little things don't matter much until I remember that even if no one else notices, they matter to you. Help me to define honesty and loyalty by your Word rather than the way society sees them. A temporary reward gained from laziness or dishonesty is not worth the loss of integrity, and that's enough reason for me to be a faithful steward.

FAITHFULNESS IN LITTLE THINGS IS A BIG THING.
Saint John Chrysostom (ca. 347–407)

The One Year Bible Readings for today are **Joshua 7:16–9:2; Luke 16:1-18; Psalm 82:1-8;** and **Proverbs 13:2-3.**

APRIL

14

counsel

Godly Counsel

"This bread was hot from the ovens when we left. But now, as you can see, it is dry and moldy. These wineskins were new when we filled them, but now they are old and cracked. And our clothing and sandals are worn out from our long, hard trip." So the Israelite leaders examined their bread, but they did not consult the Lord. Then Joshua went ahead and signed a peace treaty with them, and the leaders of Israel ratified their agreement with a binding oath. Three days later, the facts came out—these people of Gibeon lived nearby!

Joshua 9:12-16

On the surface the evidence seemed to match the travelers' story. Their wineskins were tattered, and their clothing and sandals were worn. Their bread was moldy. They certainly looked as if they had traveled a great distance. Their story seemed so authentic that the Israelite leaders entered into an unbreakable covenant with them. But the leaders had forgotten to seek the counsel of God before they signed on the dotted line. They realized too late that the men were deceitful, but they had no choice but to honor the covenant.

It's not always easy to keep a promise, but it's especially difficult to honor a promise gained through the deceitful actions of another. When you make an important decision, you may have a tendency to weigh the facts as you see them. It's important to assess the reputation of an individual or organization. It's advisable to pore over figures on a balance sheet or to check references. All of these things are wise, but don't forget to seek the counsel of God, to ask for wisdom and discernment. Praying before you make important decisions can save you a great deal of trouble down the road.

WISE FATHER, you know what is best for me. You see what I cannot. Thank you for that check in my spirit that tells me to wait or not to do something at all. Help me to heed it. Thank you for the peace that floods my soul when I am taking a step in the right direction. I will turn to you first when making important decisions. Thank you for caring about the decisions in my life.

THOSE WHO ARE IN HEAVENLY PLACES SEE GOD'S COUNSELS IN WHAT TO THE WISDOM OF THE WORLD IS ARROGANT STUPIDITY.
Oswald Chambers (1874–1917)

The One Year Bible Readings for today are **Joshua 9:3–10:43; Luke 16:19–17:10; Psalm 83:1-18;** and **Proverbs 13:4.**

Pilgrimage

Because we can worship God anyplace and anytime, we might fail to understand the psalmist's longing. In Old Testament times a person made a pilgrimage to worship God. It was a yearly event and often involved a lengthy journey. That is why the psalmist sang of a dwelling place where he could be in the presence of the Lord. It's why he expressed a desire to be even a lowly gatekeeper in God's house (v. 10) so that he could worship God every single day! We have available to us what the psalmist could only hope for. When Christ hung on the cross, the heavy veil separating the Holy of Holies from the rest of the temple ripped from top to bottom. This symbolic act shouted to the world that believers were no longer required to stand at a distance. We can walk into God's presence and commune with him by name. Today many religions continue to require a pilgrimage to worship their gods. Christ made a way for you by making a pilgrimage of his own—the long, lonely walk to the cross—so that you could praise him wherever you are.

How lovely is your dwelling place, O Lord Almighty. I long, yes, I faint with longing to enter the courts of the Lord. With my whole being, body and soul, I will shout joyfully to the living God.

Psalm 84:1-2

JESUS, I am thankful that I can worship you right where I am. I will enter your courts with thanksgiving. I will kneel at the mercy seat and find forgiveness. I will call out your name in praise. Lord, I pray for those who do not have intimacy with the living God. You have already made the pilgrimage for them. Open their eyes to see that they can find you right here, right now.

TRUE PEACE IS FOUND BY MAN IN THE DEPTHS OF HIS OWN HEART, THE DWELLING PLACE OF GOD.
Johann Tauler (ca. 1300–1361)

The One Year Bible Readings for today are **Joshua 11:1–12:24; Luke 17:11-37; Psalm 84:1-12;** and **Proverbs 13:5-6.**

APRIL

16

child

Through the Eyes of a Child

Jesus called for the children and said to the disciples, "Let the children come to me. Don't stop them! For the Kingdom of God belongs to such as these. I assure you, anyone who doesn't have their kind of faith will never get into the Kingdom of God."

Luke 18:16-17

When children discover a new treasure, they are not content to simply look at it. They touch, smell, and explore it. With wide-eyed delight they share the treasure with others. Even if the "treasure" is a creepy crawling insect or a wide-eyed toad, it's beautiful to the one who found it! As adults we sometimes miss the joy of experiencing the treasures that surround us. One of those treasures is our faith. As time passes, we might forget our first love for God or even take our faith for granted. Our lives become busy and complicated, and it becomes easy to get caught up in what we think are more "important" matters. Sometimes we intellectualize the Bible or our relationship with God and completely miss the simplicity and beauty of it.

The excitement and joy of new believers is like that of a child who has discovered a treasure. They marvel at it, delight in it, and can't help but share it with others. Revisit the moment you accepted Christ as your Savior and ask God to restore the excitement of your first love for him.

PRECIOUS SAVIOR, I sometimes take my faith for granted. Forgive me for the times I make my faith complicated or cumbersome. I want to embrace the freshness I felt when I first knew you and rejoice in the simplicity of my Father's love, but there are also new depths that you wish to show me. I ask you to take my faith to the next level, and then help me to share it with others.

GENTLE JESUS, MEEK AND MILD,
LOOK UPON A LITTLE CHILD,
PITY MY SIMPLICITY,
SUFFER ME TO COME TO THEE.

Charles Wesley (1707–1788)

The One Year Bible Readings for today are **Joshua 13:1–14:15; Luke 18:1-17; Psalm 85:1-13;** and **Proverbs 13:7-8.**

God

You Alone Are God

All the nations—and you made each one—will come and bow before you, Lord; they will praise your great and holy name. For you are great and perform great miracles. You alone are God.
Psalm 86:9-10

In our pluralistic world we can pluck our choice of deities from a hat or fashion our own faith to suit our ideologies. But this doesn't negate the fact that there remains a living God—the one true God. What sets our God apart from the other gods of this world? There is none like him! He is a God whom we can experience and know. He is a God who sacrificed himself for us and then rose three days later triumphant. He heals the brokenhearted. He is our shelter in tumultuous times. He is our comfort when we grieve. He gives joy that no tongue can describe. He pours out peace that passes all understanding. He sets free those who are bound by sin! Our God is not confined to a temple or found in rituals. One day all the nations will bow down before him, acknowledging that the creator of the universe reigns. Have you acknowledged him today? Take a moment and praise him for the attributes that set him apart from every other god of this world.

JEHOVAH, you alone are God. Even creation worships you! The oceans sing your praises. The angels call you Lord. Forgive us for failing to recognize your sovereignty. I acknowledge that you are God. I praise you today and pray that I will bring pleasure to you. I pray for my nation. May its leaders look to you in turbulent times, and may its people acknowledge you as the one true God.

THERE IS BUT ONE GOD, THE MAKER, PRESERVER AND RULER OF ALL THINGS, HAVING IN AND OF HIMSELF, ALL PERFECTIONS, AND BEING INFINITE IN THEM ALL; AND TO HIM ALL CREATURES OWE THE HIGHEST LOVE, REVERENCE AND OBEDIENCE.
James Montgomery

The One Year Bible Readings for today are **Joshua 15:1-63; Luke 18:18-43; Psalm 86:1-17;** and **Proverbs 13:9-10.**

APRIL
18

lost

Seek and Save the Lost

Jesus responded, "Salvation has come to this home today, for this man has shown himself to be a son of Abraham. And I, the Son of Man, have come to seek and save those like him who are lost."
Luke 19:9-10

Zacchaeus was a Jewish tax collector with both wealth and influence. What prompted a prominent man like him to perch in a tree to catch a glimpse of Jesus? Was it only his short stature? Whatever the reasons, we do know that his life was forever changed the moment he met Christ. When the crowd looked into the branches of the tree, they saw a despised tax collector, but Jesus saw a son of Abraham. The people saw a sinner, but Jesus saw a potential friend. Even as Jesus was approaching the day of his death, he continued to seek and save those who were lost. He sought out Zacchaeus by pushing through the crowd to speak to him. He reached out and befriended him by inviting himself to dinner. He gave Zacchaeus a reason to turn away from sin. What a beautiful pattern of how to reach our world! Who are the Zacchaeuses in your life? Let them know that God has marked them with destiny. Though others may see only what's on the surface, God sees deeper. There is potential within them. Let them know that God has marked them with destiny. You might even make a new friend and because of your relationship, which points him to Christ, you will see him in heaven.

JESUS, you reached out to Zacchaeus even when others despised him. Thank you for seeking and saving those who are lost. Lord, there are people like Zacchaeus all around me. Open my eyes that I might see them and reach out. Help me to look beneath the surface and discover the person within, who was created in your image. Help me to have a burden for the lost and to be a friend to those who are seeking you.

WE DO NOT SEEK GOD—GOD SEEKS US.
Frederick William Robertson (1816–1853)

The One Year Bible Readings for today are **Joshua 16:1–18:28; Luke 19:1-27; Psalm 87:1-7;** and **Proverbs 13:11.**

rocks

Rocks Won't Take My Place!

Some of the Pharisees among the crowd said, "Teacher, rebuke your followers for saying things like that!" He replied, "If they kept quiet, the stones along the road would burst into cheers!"
Luke 19:39-40

When Jesus, on the back of a colt, rode past the crowd, the disciples broke into enthusiastic shouts of praise. They believed their Messiah deserved a crown, but the crown of thorns that lay ahead was not what they envisioned. Perhaps the disciples did not fully understand the majesty of Jesus, but their unabashed love for him was a balm as he prepared for the events ahead. The Pharisees were embarrassed by this loud display of affection and attempted to quiet the disciples. But Christ rebuked the Pharisees and pointed to the stones on the ground. He announced that even they would burst into cheers if his followers failed to praise him. Can you imagine a rock breaking out in a hymn or song? What if the towering mountains and deep caverns shouted his praises? What if the gravel on the road danced before him? Rocks are versatile, but there is one thing that rocks should never do: they should not take our place in worship, for it is we who were created to praise! Will a rock take your place? Determine today to do your part to worship almighty God!

JESUS, no rock will ever take my place in worship! I thank you for your love for me. I praise you for faith that is real and deep. I praise you for your Holy Spirit and for the Word that teaches me. I will not be quiet and keep my love for you hidden. Just as the disciples called out your name, I will praise you, for I serve an amazing and wonderful Savior.

PREPARE THE WAY! A GOD, A GOD APPEARS
A GOD, A GOD! THE VOCAL HILLS REPLY,
THE ROCKS PROCLAIM TH' APPROACHING DEITY
LO, EARTH RECEIVES HIM FROM THE BENDING
SKIES!

Alexander Pope (1688–1744)

The One Year Bible Readings for today are **Joshua 19:1–20:9; Luke 19:28-48; Psalm 88:1-18;** and **Proverbs 13:12-14.**

honor

Honor the Son

" 'What will I do?' the owner asked himself. 'I know! I'll send my cherished son. Surely they will respect him.' But when the farmers saw his son, they said to each other, 'Here comes the heir to this estate. Let's kill him and get the estate for ourselves!' So they dragged him out of the vineyard and murdered him. What do you suppose the owner of the vineyard will do to those farmers?" Jesus asked.

Luke 20:13-15

When the master of the vineyard sent his servants to collect a portion of the harvest, the farmers killed them. So he sent his son, believing that the farmers would surely honor his flesh and blood, but they killed the son as well. When Jesus shared this parable, the Pharisees became furious. They knew that he was referring to them. Just like the farmers in the parable, the Pharisees had taken ownership of the vineyard—the religion of their fathers. Just as the farmers didn't accept the master's son, the Pharisees could not accept that Jesus was sent from God; thus they plotted to kill him. It is ironic that as they walked away that day, planning Jesus' arrest, they resembled the farmers even more than they realized. God so loved the world that he sent his only Son, and yet that Son was met with death and dishonor. His resurrection proved once and for all that he was indeed the Son of God. Surely there is no better way to celebrate the season of spring than to honor the Father by remembering the Son.

DEAR GOD, today I rejoice over the resurrection of your precious Son! I won't forget what he has done for me. You sent him to earth and he was dishonored, but I pray that I will honor him by remembering the cross. I will acknowledge his sacrifice and celebrate his resurrection. Thank you that he burst from the tomb to live inside us.

OUR GREAT HONOR LIES IN BEING JUST WHAT JESUS WAS AND IS. TO BE ACCEPTED BY THOSE WHO ACCEPT HIM, REJECTED BY ALL WHO REJECT HIM, LOVED BY THOSE WHO LOVE HIM AND HATED BY EVERYONE WHO HATES HIM. WHAT GREATER GLORY COULD COME TO ANY MAN?
A. W. Tozer (1897–1963)

The One Year Bible Readings for today are **Joshua 21:1–22:20; Luke 20:1-26; Psalm 89:1-13;** and **Proverbs 13:15-16.**

APRIL

21

letters

Letters from God

An unreliable messenger stumbles into trouble, but a reliable messenger brings healing.
Proverbs 13:17

A U.S. ambassador resides in a foreign country and yet lives on U.S.–owned property. Though the laws of that land may differ from ours, the ambassador is still responsible to uphold the laws and rules of his own government. His words and actions can never be wholly his for he does not act in his own capacity. When he speaks, he is a messenger for his government. When he acts, his deeds reflect on the country he represents. We are Christ's ambassadors and therefore his messengers. Too often we think that the message we preach reflects our faith. However, on a much deeper level it is the message of our everyday words and actions that are influential. We are the letter from God that people read. We become unreliable messengers when we speak crudely, gossip about a neighbor, or act dishonestly.

Our words and actions reflect God, who lives inside us, to people who may never open a Bible or enter a church. Never forget that you are an ambassador for Christ and a messenger of hope. Ask his Spirit to empower you to deliver the Good News with your life and words.

LORD, thank you for allowing me to be your ambassador. Let my message be honest and true. Help me to encourage others and to go out of my way to speak a kind word. Forgive me for times when I have spoken without thinking. Let me live in such a way that my words and actions represent you so that my message may be one of love and hope.

A CREDIBLE MESSAGE NEEDS A CREDIBLE MESSENGER BECAUSE CHARISMA WITHOUT CHARACTER IS CATASTROPHE. Peter Kuzmic

The One Year Bible Readings for today are **Joshua 22:21–23:16; Luke 20:27-47; Psalm 89:14-37;** and **Proverbs 13:17-19.**

APRIL
22

point

Point the Way

[Joshua said,] "So honor the Lord and serve him wholeheartedly. Put away forever the idols your ancestors worshiped when they lived beyond the Euphrates River and in Egypt. Serve the Lord alone. But if you are unwilling to serve the Lord, then choose today whom you will serve. . . . But as for me and my family, we will serve the Lord." The people replied, "We would never forsake the Lord and worship other gods."
Joshua 24:14-16

Joshua was nearing the end of his life the day he stood before the generation of young men. For most of them, the flight from Egypt was something their grandfathers spoke about. They knew about God. They had seen the walls of Jericho fall as Joshua led them around the fortified city, but they had also watched their fathers stray away to worship idols. Joshua knew that it was time for these men to choose their God. If they chose other gods, the foundation of the nation would crumble.

Though it can be flattering, our ministries, accomplishments, and endeavors mean little if they exalt a man or woman or a program rather than God. Just as Joshua pointed the way to God, each of us has the same opportunity. Ask God to help you examine your ministry or work. Whether you're a teacher, a salesperson, a mom, a pastor, or a computer technician, are you pointing the way to God? Will those who follow your leadership remember your deeds—or the God who accomplished them through you?

DEAR GOD, I remember the times that you rescued me, healed me, guided me, and pushed obstacles out of my way. Thank you for allowing me to lead others, whether in the home or the workplace. I pray that those who look to me for leadership will be drawn to you through me. Help them to choose to serve you and no other.

THE TRUE LEADER WILL HAVE NO DESIRE TO LORD IT OVER GOD'S HERITAGE, BUT WILL BE HUMBLE, GENTLE, SELF-SACRIFICING AND ALTOGETHER AS READY TO FOLLOW AS TO LEAD, WHEN THE SPIRIT MAKES IT CLEAR THAT A WISER AND MORE GIFTED MAN THAN HIMSELF HAS APPEARED.
A. W. Tozer (1897–1963)

The One Year Bible Readings for today are **Joshua 24:1-33; Luke 21:1-28; Psalm 89:38-52;** and **Proverbs 13:20-23.**

home

Our Home

Lord, through all the generations you have been our home! Before the mountains were created, before you made the earth and the world, you are God, without beginning or end.
Psalm 90:1-2

One day I was wrestling with God about our impending move. This was the first house where I'd felt at home and the first one we owned in our ten years of marriage. It was small, but it was all ours. We had painted it lovely colors, wallpapered the kitchen, prepared a nursery for our baby, and built a wooden fort in the backyard for our sons. I didn't want to pack the boxes. I didn't want to move *again*, and I wrestled with God over this matter as I strolled my little ones around our beloved neighborhood. *Lord, you know how hard we worked to fix up this house and how I love living here.* As I continued telling him all the reasons I wanted to stay, his gentle whisper interrupted me. *I am your dwelling place. Through all generations I have been and will be your home.* Seeing God as my dwelling place that day changed the way I looked at moving—and at houses. No matter where I live, and we have lived in a number of houses since that first one, the Lord is my heart's true home and will be for all eternity.

LORD, through all my life, you have been my true home. Through all generations, even before you made the earth, you have been our dwelling place. You are God, without beginning or end. I am thankful that wherever I go, I don't have to feel insecure or anxious because you are there! Thank you for your faithfulness and loving-kindness that follows me all the days of my life.

TO ME REMAINS NOT PLACE OR TIME;
MY COUNTRY IS IN EVERY CLIME;
I CAN BE CALM AND FREE FROM CARE
ON ANY SHORE, SINCE GOD IS THERE.

Madame Guyon (1648–1717)

The One Year Bible Readings for today are **Judges 1:1–2:9; Luke 21:29–22:13; Psalm 90:1–91:16;** and **Proverbs 13:24-25.**

APRIL
24

needs

He Needs You, Too

Then at the proper time Jesus and the twelve apostles sat down together at the table. Jesus said, "I have looked forward to this hour with deep longing, anxious to eat this Passover meal with you before my suffering begins."
Luke 22:14-15

At the Last Supper, Jesus expressed his desire to be surrounded by his friends. It wasn't a casual comment but rather an expression of "deep longing." Jesus was approaching the time of his crucifixion and his beloved disciples would be a comfort to him. Perhaps before that moment, the disciples had not realized that Jesus needed them because he was the One who had always given. He had taught them, led them, and poured himself like an offering over their lives. What did they have to offer? As they sat around the table, they realized that there was something they could give back to their Savior—themselves. Have you ever stopped to consider God's longing for you? It may seem impossible for us to think in these terms, especially in light of what God has done for us. But God created each of us to commune with him. Jesus longs to be one with his own. We may feel as if we have little to offer God. It is easy to forget that God longs for our presence just as we long for his. Take time to open your heart and commune with God as a friend today. He's waiting for you.

LORD, you have done so much for me. I often think I have nothing to offer you. The thought that you long for my friendship is almost overwhelming because you've given so much and I've given so little. I love to be in your presence. I rejoice that you want to be with me. Help me to devote a portion of each day to communion with you.

AS OUR LOVE IS THE BEST THING WE HAVE, AND NONE DESERVES IT MORE THAN GOD, SO LET HIM HAVE OUR LOVE, YEA, THE STRENGTH OF OUR LOVE, THAT WE MAY LOVE HIM WITH ALL OUR SOULS, AND WITH ALL OUR MIND, AND WITH ALL OUR STRENGTH. Richard Sibbs (1577–1635)

The One Year Bible Readings for today are **Judges 2:10–3:31; Luke 22:14-34; Psalm 92:1–93:5;** and **Proverbs 14:1-2.**

obeyng

Obeying Anyway

[Jesus prayed,] "Father, if you are willing, please take this cup of suffering away from me. Yet I want your will, not mine." Then an angel from heaven appeared and strengthened him. He prayed more fervently, and he was in such agony of spirit that his sweat fell to the ground like great drops of blood.
Luke 22:42-44

As Jesus prayed in Gethsemane, his sweat fell like drops of blood. Only Luke's Gospel recounts this. But Luke was a physician, so he understood the physical agony this represented and recorded it in the Gospel. Modern-day doctors describe this sweating-of-blood phenomenon as a physical reaction to extreme psychological stress. Jesus faced an agonizing choice that night. The suffering that he was to endure was not a result of his own wrongdoing, for he was without sin. He could have called ten thousand angels to whisk him away, yet he gave his life rather than give in to his own anguish.

Sometimes believers suffer even when they obey, for we share in Jesus' suffering as well as in his joy. Sometimes the work before us is difficult or painful, but there is a greater purpose behind our difficulties, and we have the opportunity to share in God's plan when we do his will in spite of how we feel.

JESUS, I sometimes must be reminded that we share in your suffering just as we share in your joy. The road you choose for me will not always be easy. Help me to remember that to love you is to obey you. Thank you for following your Father's wishes that night in Gethsemane. Help me to choose the Father's will in my life as well.

OBEDIENCE TO JESUS CHRIST IS ESSENTIAL, BUT NOT COMPULSORY; HE NEVER INSISTS ON BEING MASTER. WE FEEL THAT IF ONLY HE WOULD INSIST, WE SHOULD OBEY HIM. BUT OUR LORD NEVER ENFORCES HIS "THOU SHALTS" AND "THOU SHALT NOTS"; HE NEVER TAKES MEANS TO FORCE US TO DO WHAT HE SAYS. Oswald Chambers (1874–1917)

The One Year Bible Readings for today are **Judges 4:1–5:31; Luke 22:35-53; Psalm 94:1-23;** and **Proverbs 14:3-4.**

APRIL
26

Sing a New Song

Sing a new song to the Lord! Let the whole earth sing to the Lord! Sing to the Lord; bless his name. Each day proclaim the good news that he saves. Publish his glorious deeds among the nations. Tell everyone about the amazing things he does.

Psalm 96:1-3

Every day we cross paths with someone who needs to hear the good news that the Lord saves. We can never fully plumb the depths of God's character and attributes, but with every day and every experience we can discover new facets about God, new songs to sing to him. To "publish" means to share and that refers not only to writing books and delivering sermons about God but also to sharing what the Lord has done in our own lives so that others might be drawn to him. Each of us can purpose to do that. The most powerful evangelism doesn't take place within the four walls of a church building. It occurs as we share with others in our neighborhood and workplace the good news of what God has done for us individually and for the whole world in the life, death, and resurrection of Jesus Christ. Ask God to bring people across your path today who need to hear the good news that God saves and that he loves them. And then ask him for the compassion and courage to share the reason for your hope and to pray for those people.

LORD, I want to sing a new song to you and bless your name. I want to tell everyone about the amazing things you do. Help me to start today, right where I am, to proclaim the good news of salvation and to publish your glorious deeds everywhere I go. Give me the words to share from your heart with those I will meet.

O FOR A THOUSAND TONGUES TO SING
MY GREAT REDEEMER'S PRAISE!

Charles Wesley (1707–1788)

The One Year Bible Readings for today are **Judges 6:1-40; Luke 22:54–23:12; Psalm 95:1–96:13;** and **Proverbs 14:5-6.**

impossible

Impossible Odds

The odds were against Gideon's winning the war. He had only thirty-two thousand men. The Midianites—the enemy—were as numerous as locusts. Imagine Gideon's surprise when God asked him to whittle down his army by twenty-two thousand. Surely winning was impossible! But God tested Gideon's faith even further by asking him to use only the men who lapped up water like dogs. Now only three hundred men remained. Later that night the small group of warriors encircled the enemy's camp. In one accord they broke their clay jars holding torches, and light flooded the night. They blew their ram's horns and shouted and watched in amazement as the enemy defeated itself without a single casualty in Gideon's army! Without a doubt Gideon and his men understood that God was with them even when it seemed there was no way out. When you face overwhelming circumstances, you are in a perfect position for God to intervene on your behalf. It is in those times that, like Gideon, you learn to trust God and discover that he is always with you, even when you face impossible odds.

The Lord said to Gideon, "You have too many warriors with you. If I let all of you fight the Midianites, the Israelites will boast to me that they saved themselves by their own strength. Therefore, tell the people, 'Whoever is timid or afraid may leave and go home.' " Twenty-two thousand of them went home, leaving only ten thousand who were willing to fight. But the Lord told Gideon, "There are still too many! Bring them down to the spring, and I will sort out who will go with you and who will not."
Judges 7:2-4

HEAVENLY FATHER, when I am in a battle, you shine in the midst of that battle. When I am unsure about which direction to turn, you give me wisdom. When I need advice, I can listen for your voice. Many times I have felt there was no way out, only to discover that you were making a way for me. You give me victory when it seems impossible. Thank you for being my warrior!

THERE'S NOTHING WRITTEN IN THE BIBLE . . . THAT SAYS IF YOU BELIEVE IN ME, YOU AIN'T GOING TO HAVE NO TROUBLES. Ray Charles (b. 1930)

The One Year Bible Readings for today are **Judges 7:1–8:17; Luke 23:13-43; Psalm 97:1–98:9;** and **Proverbs 14:7-8.**

APRIL

28

prayer

Answered Prayer

The Lord is king! Let the nations tremble! He sits on his throne between the cherubim. Let the whole earth quake! The Lord sits in majesty in Jerusalem, supreme above all the nations. Let them praise your great and awesome name. Your name is holy! . . . Moses and Aaron were among his priests; Samuel also called on his name. They cried to the Lord for help, and he answered them.
Psalm 99:1-3, 6

God is worthy of our praise, and in Psalm 99 the psalmist encourages us to praise God for two reasons: for his essential character—his greatness, majesty, and radiant holiness—and because he has designed and initiated prayer as a means of blessing, restoring, and helping his people. While the holy God sits in majesty, he calls us into an intimate relationship with him and chooses to work in this world through our prayers. He invites us to call to him, and he answers our call and shows us great and mighty things that we do not know (Jeremiah 33:3). From his throne he dispenses grace, healing, and strength, so as we come to him in prayer as Moses, Aaron, and Samuel did, we experience his presence, and he answers us in his way, in his time, and for his glory and our good. Take a few minutes to reflect on the many times you have prayed for God's help and the different ways he has answered, and thank him today.

LORD, awesome and holy is your name! You sit on your throne in majesty; you are King and yet you hear my cries and answer me. You are worthy of our praise simply because of who you are—supreme above all nations and yearning for every person to come to know you. Worthy are you, Lord! I will sing about your holy name throughout the day!

I THINK WE SOMETIMES DISCOURAGE OURSELVES BY A MISCONCEPTION OF THE EXACT MEANING OF THE EXPRESSION "ANSWER," TAKING IT TO MEAN ONLY GRANT. NOW, AN ANSWER IS NOT NECESSARILY ACQUIESCENCE. IT MAY BE A REFUSAL, AN EXPLANATION, A PROMISE, A CONDITIONAL GRANT. IT IS, IN FACT, SIMPLY ATTENTION TO OUR REQUEST EXPRESSED. IN THIS SENSE, BEFORE WE CALL HE WILL ANSWER, AND WHILE WE ARE YET SPEAKING, HE WILL HEAR.
Mary B. M. Duncan

The One Year Bible Readings for today are **Judges 8:18–9:21; Luke 23:44–24:12; Psalm 99:1-9;** and **Proverbs 14:9-10.**

APRIL
29

promises

Golden Promises

Before Jesus sent out the disciples to take the message of the gospel to all the nations, he assured them of his promise to send the Holy Spirit. That promise motivated them to continue with one accord in prayer (Acts 1:14). God's promises are provided to stir us and inspire us to pray. Those precious promises—there are hundreds throughout the Bible—show us things God has purposed and wants us to ask for, just as he wanted the disciples to ask for the Holy Spirit so they would have power for ministry. These golden promises teach us about how to pray, and they build our faith. "If I am to have faith when I pray," said American evangelist R. A. Torrey, "I must find some promise in the Word of God on which to rest my faith. . . . If there is no promise in the Word of God, and no clear leading of the Spirit, there can be no real faith." Today, ask the Lord which of his promises he wants you to pray about. The Holy Spirit will fill you with power from on high to accomplish what needs to be done.

[Jesus told them,] "Now I will send the Holy Spirit, just as my Father promised. But stay here in the city until the Holy Spirit comes and fills you with power from heaven."
Luke 24:49

THANK YOU, FATHER, for the promises in your word. May they be incentives for me to continue in prayer so that your will may be accomplished and your kingdom will come in my life, family, nation, and world. Holy Spirit, thank you for dwelling within me and for filling me with your power. Let my prayers be pleasing to you, Father, as your Spirit leads me in praying in light of your promises.

THOUGH THE BIBLE BE CROWDED WITH GOLDEN PROMISES FROM BOARD TO BOARD, YET THEY WILL BE INOPERATIVE UNTIL WE TURN THEM INTO PRAYER. F. B. Meyer (1847–1929)

The One Year Bible Readings for today are **Judges 9:22–10:18; Luke 24:13-53; Psalm 100:1-5;** and **Proverbs 14:11-12.**

APRIL

30

revealed

God Revealed

No one has ever seen God. But his only Son, who is himself God, is near to the Father's heart; he has told us about him.
John 1:18

When Jesus came on the stage of history, the majority of Jews did not perceive or receive him as the revelation of God the Father. The Gnostics refused to believe that deity would manifest itself in a human body because they believed that matter is evil. It is just as easy for us to have faulty ideas about God. If we base our view of God on the media's opinions or on what liberal professors say about him, we will have an incorrect picture. If our opinions about God are the result of pain left over from childhood or from our experience with an unloving or absent earthly father, we may see him through a dark filter and not accept his love for us. But God revealed himself in his Son. And his Word is his love letter to us, calling us to come home to his heart. Jesus declared who God is and showed God's heart to humankind so that we would be drawn to him and could know him. His life, miracles, teaching, death, and resurrection have given a glorious revelation of the Father. Through his Word we can see the Father accurately in his splendor, love, grace, and light.

DEAR LORD, I praise you for revealing yourself in your Son Jesus. Wipe off the lens of my heart that I might see you accurately and love you more each day. Thank you for your Word, which reveals your love and your purpose for my life. Thank you for Jesus, who has made it possible for me to have clear vision with which to see you, Father.

INSTEAD OF COMPLAINING THAT GOD HAS HIDDEN HIMSELF, YOU SHOULD GIVE HIM THANKS FOR HAVING REVEALED SO MUCH OF HIMSELF.
Blaise Pascal (1623–1662)

The One Year Bible Readings for today are **Judges 11:1–12:15; John 1:1-28; Psalm 101:1-8;** and **Proverbs 14:13-14.**

character

His Consistent Character

Our world has seen more change from 1900 to the present than in all history recorded before 1900, and things continue to accelerate rapidly. As time speeds by, measured not just in minutes or seconds but in nanoseconds (billionths of a second), everything changes. Technology changes so fast in our twenty-first-century world that we can barely keep up with the upgrades on our computers. Our bodies undergo the inevitable aging process, and we witness constant upheaval in the nations of the world. Material things change and deteriorate. Even the flowers of the field and the stars in the heavens will fade away. But you, Lord, are always the same, says the psalmist in these verses. The changes in the world do not change God one bit or thwart his plans. He's the same yesterday, today, and forever, and his love extends to the next generation and the next. This psalm reminds us that our security can't be found in any of the things in this ever-changing world. Instead, our security is in God and his promises, including the wonderful ones in these verses: that the children and grandchildren of God's people will live in security and will thrive in the Lord's presence.

In ages past you laid the foundation of the earth, and the heavens are the work of your hands. Even they will perish, but you remain forever; they will wear out like old clothing. You will change them like a garment, and they will fade away. But you are always the same; your years never end. The children of your people will live in security. Their children's children will thrive in your presence.

Psalm 102:25-28

UNCHANGING LORD, I praise you and worship you for your love and faithfulness that extend from one generation to the next. Thank you for this reminder that although our circumstances may change and the things around us pass away, you remain the same forever. Help me to find my security in your eternal sameness.

GOD IS NOT AFFECTED BY OUR MUTABILITY; OUR CHANGES DO NOT ALTER HIM. . . . HE IS STILL THE UNALTERABLE I AM. THE SAME YESTERDAY, TODAY, AND FOREVER. Frederick William Robertson (1816–1853)

The One Year Bible Readings for today are **Judges 13:1–14:20; John 1:29-51; Psalm 102:1-28;** and **Proverbs 14:15-16.**

MAY

2

attributes

Pleading God's Attributes

He forgives all my sins and heals all my diseases. He ransoms me from death and surrounds me with love and tender mercies. He fills my life with good things. My youth is renewed like the eagle's! The Lord gives righteousness and justice to all who are treated unfairly. He revealed his character to Moses and his deeds to the people of Israel. The Lord is merciful and gracious; he is slow to get angry and full of unfailing love.

Psalm 103:3-8

Christians of times past felt that prayer found its greatest inspiration in the Lord himself, and they had a term called "pleading God's attributes," in which they would recount particular attributes of God's character to him and then ask him to answer their prayer on the basis of those attributes: "Lord, you are merciful and gracious, so have mercy on me." "Lord, you are full of unfailing love. Show us your love in this situation." "Lord, you delivered your servant Daniel; I pray for your deliverance in my life." "You revealed your character and deeds to Moses and your people. Likewise, please reveal yourself to me!" Since God's attributes are numerous throughout Scripture, they provide a never-ending source of inspiration for our prayer life. Praying God's attributes renews our faith and confidence and reminds us of his greatness and his ability to save. Choose one of the attributes of God from this psalm to "plead" as you pray today.

LORD, you are _______ [merciful, gracious, full of unfailing love]. I ask you to reveal this in my life today. Thank you for revealing your wondrous attributes to us in your Word. As I read it, continually open my eyes to who you really are so that my prayers will rest on the solid foundation of your character. May my prayers have power because they are based on the truth about you.

RIGHTLY VIEWED, ALL THE PERFECTIONS OF DEITY BECOME PLEAS FOR FAITH.
Charles Haddon Spurgeon (1834–1892)

The One Year Bible Readings for today are **Judges 15:1–16:31; John 2:1-25; Psalm 103:1-22;** and **Proverbs 14:17-19.**

Boundless Love

God so loved the world that he gave his only Son, so that everyone who believes in him will not perish but have eternal life. God did not send his Son into the world to condemn it, but to save it.
John 3:16-17

It is a marvelous and profound truth that although God loves the whole world generally, he also loves us personally and individually so much that Christ died for each of us as if there were only one of us. Because of his love for us, he poured out his life on the cross while we were still sinners. He didn't wait for us to get our lives all cleaned up and fixed up first—we couldn't have anyway. Instead, he demonstrated his grace in saving us even though we didn't deserve it. That would be amazing enough, yet this gift of love isn't for just a few. It's not just for me or a select group of people, for those in particular families, denominations, or nationalities—but for those from every tribe and tongue, people, group, and nation. We can hardly conceive of such a limitless, boundless love! But we can rejoice in the truth of John 3:16—everyone who believes in Jesus Christ will not perish but will have eternal life.

FATHER, thank you for loving me even beyond what I could ever imagine. It amazes me that you would love me—even when I didn't love you—and would send your Son to pay the ultimate price so that I could know you and experience eternal life. Let your love flow through me so that even more people may experience your boundless love.

GOD'S LOVE IS MEASURELESS. IT IS MORE: IT IS BOUNDLESS. IT HAS NO BOUNDS BECAUSE IT IS NOT A THING BUT A FACET OF THE ESSENTIAL NATURE OF GOD. HIS LOVE IS SOMETHING HE IS, AND BECAUSE HE IS INFINITE, THAT LOVE CAN ENFOLD THE WHOLE CREATED WORLD IN ITSELF AND HAVE ROOM FOR TEN THOUSAND TIMES TEN THOUSAND WORLDS BESIDE. A. W. Tozer (1897–1963)

The One Year Bible Readings for today are **Judges 17:1–18:31; John 3:1-21; Psalm 104:1-23;** and **Proverbs 14:20-21.**

MAY

4

beauty

God's Creative Beauty

O Lord, what a variety of things you have made! In wisdom you have made them all. The earth is full of your creatures. . . . May the glory of the Lord last forever!
Psalm 104:24, 31

As I look out at our bird habitat in the backyard, yellow, purple, black and white, and red miniature finches flit from branch to branch. Blazing red cardinals, persistent woodpeckers, and chattering blue jays compete for a place at the feeders and suet blocks. Doves fly in and feast for a few minutes on the sunflower seeds scattered on the ground. The variety of winged creatures astounds me, each different and beautiful in its own vibrant way. But that's only in my backyard and with only a few types of one species God made! There are thousands and thousands more. Yet even gazing at this microcosm, I'm struck by the incredible variety and beauty God has created in the world around us. And the same God who hung the stars and moon in the heavens and made these feathered friends in my yard and every other creature on earth shapes and forms each of us humans uniquely for his purposes. Everywhere we look we see evidence of his infinite creativity. In wisdom he has made it all!

LORD, I praise you for the beauty of your creation and for the infinite variety of things you have made! Your Word says that the wonders of creation are sufficient to reveal your attributes and leave us without any excuse for not seeking you. Open my eyes more and more to the evidence of your creative power all around me. May your glory last forever!

TO ME IT SEEMS AS IF WHEN GOD CONCEIVED THE WORLD, THAT WAS POETRY; HE FORMED IT, AND THAT WAS SCULPTURE; HE COLORED IT, AND THAT WAS PAINTING; HE PEOPLED IT WITH LIVING BEINGS, AND THAT WAS GRAND, DIVINE, ETERNAL DRAMA. Emma Stebbins (1816–1876)

The One Year Bible Readings for today are **Judges 19:1–20:48; John 3:22–4:3; Psalm 104:24-35;** and **Proverbs 14:22-24.**

Spread the Good News

The woman left her water jar beside the well and went back to the village and told everyone, "Come and meet a man who told me everything I ever did! Can this be the Messiah?" So the people came streaming from the village to see him.
John 4:28-30

The Samaritan woman was so amazed by Jesus and his revelations about who he was and about the secrets of her heart and life that she forgot her water jar—the very reason she'd come to the well—and rushed back to the village to tell others about the "man" she had met. Up and down the streets she shared the good news about Jesus, for she had seen the Lord, the Messiah! Having received the living water, a perpetual spring within her that gave her eternal life (v. 14), she wanted others to know him too. So the people began streaming from the village to see him, eager to meet this incredible man who can tell people the secrets of their hearts.

Sharing with others what Jesus has done in us and for us stirs up interest in those who don't know him. His revelation in our lives draws to him people who desire to have him work in their lives as he does in ours. With whom could you share the Good News today? Ask the Lord to make you sensitive to his working in the lives of others, and be ready to share the hope that's within you.

LORD, forgive me for times when my excitement over knowing you has waned. I want others to know you and experience your work in their lives. Use me to spread the Good News. I pray that I will be so amazed by what you reveal to me today that I won't hesitate to share my hope with those who don't yet know you.

HOW MANY PEOPLE HAVE YOU MADE HOMESICK FOR GOD? Oswald Chambers (1874–1917)

The One Year Bible Readings for today are **Judges 21:1—Ruth 1:22; John 4:4-42; Psalm 105:1-15;** and **Proverbs 14:25.**

MAY

6

plans

Plans That Never Fail

Then Israel arrived in Egypt; Jacob lived as a foreigner in the land of Ham. And the Lord multiplied the people of Israel until they became too mighty for their enemies. Then he turned the Egyptians against the Israelites, and they plotted against the Lord's servants.

Psalm 105:23-25

When the Egyptians enslaved the Israelites and treated them cruelly, gave the order to slaughter their infant boys, and in every way made their lives miserable, everything seemed hopeless. But God was still in control and had a plan to bring his people out of Egypt with joy. Corrie ten Boom said about her own imprisonment in a Nazi concentration camp that no matter how bad things are on earth, "there is never panic in heaven! You can only hold on to that reality through faith because it seemed then and often seems now, as if the devil is the victor. But God is faithful, and his plans never fail. He knows the future. He knows the way." Whatever you are facing today, you can praise God that he doesn't have problems, only plans. And just as he had a master plan for his people's exodus out of Egypt to the Promised Land, he has a plan for you, and he will not fail to accomplish it!

FATHER, I thank you for the assurance that your plans never fail. When everything around me seems hopeless, remind me of your plan for the Israelites in captivity in Egypt. Help me to see things from your eternal perspective and to hold on to the reality that in spite of the way things look, you are in control. Indeed, you are still on the throne!

GOD IS NEVER IN A PANIC, NOTHING CAN BE DONE THAT HE IS NOT ABSOLUTELY MASTER OF, AND NO ONE IN EARTH OR HEAVEN CAN SHUT A DOOR HE HAS OPENED, NOR OPEN A DOOR HE HAS SHUT. GOD ALTERS THE INEVITABLE WHEN WE GET IN TOUCH WITH HIM. Oswald Chambers (1874–1917)

The One Year Bible Readings for today are **Ruth 2:1–4:22; John 4:43-54; Psalm 105:16-36;** and **Proverbs 14:26-27.**

no other

No Other God Like You

Hannah's song of praise over finally receiving God's long-awaited gift of her son, Samuel, and her decision to dedicate him to God's service were not just ordinary expressions of thanks. Her exultation in the Lord as the Holy and Sovereign One, all powerful and just, rings down through the centuries much the same way Mary's did when she rejoiced at the news that she would bear the Messiah, Jesus. Because he who created the world and rules over all things, who brings both death and life, had answered Hannah's fervent prayers for a child, Hannah praised the Lord with all her heart. She delighted in how he had delivered her from the disgrace she had known as a childless woman. Once weak (v. 4), Hannah was so strengthened that her heart could joyfully release her precious Samuel to the Lord and trust that he would accomplish his good plans in her son's life and in her own.

Hannah prayed: "My heart rejoices in the Lord! Oh, how the Lord has blessed me! Now I have an answer for my enemies, as I delight in your deliverance. No one is holy like the Lord! There is no one besides you; there is no Rock like our God."
1 Samuel 2:1-2

LORD, there is no one like you! No Rock like our God. You accomplished your plan in Hannah's and Samuel's lives in your own perfect time. I trust you to accomplish your plans in my life. Then my heart, too, will overflow in praise for all the ways you have blessed me.

BECAUSE HE POSSESSES UNLIMITED POWER AND IS PERFECTLY IN CONTROL OF ALL THINGS, GOD MAY ALWAYS ACCOMPLISH HIS WISE AND GOOD PLANS FOR YOU. Myrna Alexander

The One Year Bible Readings for today are **1 Samuel 1:1–2:21; John 5:1-23; Psalm 105:37-45;** and **Proverbs 14:28-29.**

MAY

8

listening

A Listening Heart

Then Eli realized it was the Lord who was calling the boy. So he said to Samuel, "Go and lie down again, and if someone calls again, say, 'Yes, Lord, your servant is listening.' " So Samuel went back to bed. And the Lord came and called as before, "Samuel! Samuel!" And Samuel replied, "Yes, your servant is listening."

1 Samuel 3:8-10

Listening does not come as naturally to many of us as it did to young Samuel. In fact, listening isn't what we do best. We much prefer to do the talking! It has been estimated that the average woman spends one-fifth of her life talking and speaks about three thousand words a day. For men, the number is less, but not significantly. Yet if we want miracles in our lives and in our loved ones' lives, if we want God to direct our steps, we need to listen to God's leading and follow it. The good news is that hearing God isn't a special privilege reserved only for pastors, priests, or seminary graduates. It's not just for those who are highly intelligent or especially gifted. You don't even have to be a grown-up to hear God. Even children, such as Samuel was, can hear the voice of the Lord if their hearts are willing, humble, and receptive. God has many things to say to you and wants to bless your life with direction and purpose as you hear his voice and follow. All it takes is a listening heart. Ask God to help you tune in to his Spirit's leading today.

LORD, quiet my heart so that I can hear you. Remove any distractions that would keep me from being open and attentive to what your Spirit might be impressing on my heart and mind. Please make me humble and receptive and willing to answer obediently when you call on me. Your servant is listening.

A MAN PRAYED AND AT FIRST HE THOUGHT PRAYER LIES IN TALKING. BUT HE BECAME MORE AND MORE QUIET UNTIL IN THE END HE REALIZED PRAYER IS LISTENING. Søren Kierkegaard (1813–1855)

The One Year Bible Readings for today are **1 Samuel 2:22–4:22; John 5:24-47; Psalm 106:1-12;** and **Proverbs 14:30-31.**

helper

Our Mighty Helper

When the Philistine rulers heard that all God's people were gathering at Mizpah, they set out to attack and destroy them. But the Israelites begged Samuel to plead for God's help. So Samuel cried out to the Lord, and God responded with an awesome demonstration of his power. His voice thundered from heaven, throwing the Philistines into mass confusion, and God's people experienced a great victory against their enemies that day.

Our modern culture often sees prayer as a magic bullet or as a formula that we can use to get what we want. It is neither. But this we know: God tells us to pray; he gives us his Word to guide our prayers. And as in this account from 1 Samuel and throughout the Bible, when God's people pray, he shows up. That's why at the site of the Israelite victory, Samuel, in praise and thanksgiving to the Lord, erected a monument with the name "Ebenezer," which means "the stone of help." It reminds us to ask God for the help we need today and not to forget to thank him for his answers.

[Samuel] pleaded with the Lord to help Israel, and the Lord answered. Just as Samuel was sacrificing the burnt offering, the Philistines arrived for battle. But the Lord spoke with a mighty voice of thunder from heaven, and the Philistines were thrown into such confusion that the Israelites defeated them.

1 Samuel 7:9-10

DEAR LORD, I praise you because you are a God who hears and answers. Just as you answered and moved on behalf of Israel as they battled their enemies, you move and work today on behalf of your people. Thank you for calling all of your people—young and old, men and women, every denomination and race—to pray and seek your help in these days.

PRAYER MOVES THE ARM WHICH MOVES THE WORLD. James Montgomery

The One Year Bible Readings for today are **1 Samuel 5:1–7:17; John 6:1-21; Psalm 106:13-31;** and **Proverbs 14:32-33.**

MAY

10

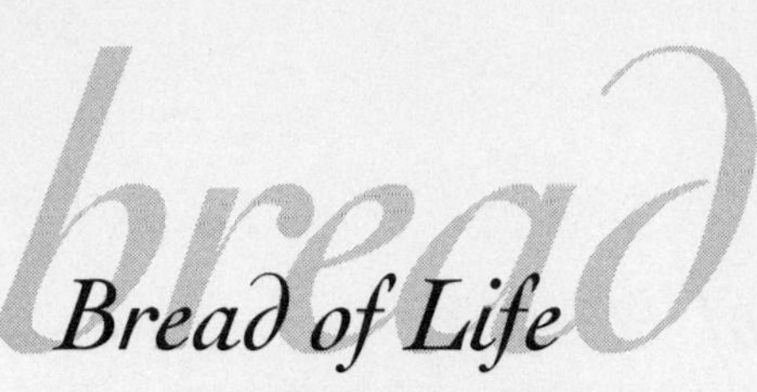

Bread of Life

Jesus replied, "I am the bread of life. No one who comes to me will ever be hungry again. Those who believe in me will never thirst."
John 6:35

Jesus had just fed a multitude of people with only a few fish and five loaves of bread, and the crowds flocked after him. But he knew that they were looking for him because he had met their physical needs, so he told them, "Spend your energy seeking the eternal life that I, the Son of Man, can give you. For God the Father has sent me for that very purpose" (John 6:27). Jesus was pointing them to the spiritual life he offered, but the people were more interested in what Jesus could do for them. They wanted him to give them a miraculous sign before they would believe in him. They still didn't get it! So in this verse he declares himself to be the Bread of Life, the One who came from heaven to give life to the world. He promised that those who believe in him will never hunger or thirst again. It is easy for us to focus on what God can do for us and spend our energies on things that don't truly satisfy. But he has put within each of us a spiritual hunger that only he can fill. Ask God to stir up those yearnings for him today so that you can taste and see that the Lord is good.

BREAD OF LIFE, forgive me for seeking after things that will never really satisfy or fulfill my deepest longings. Forgive me for focusing on what you can do for me materially instead of seeking the rich, true life that comes from you. Cause me to hunger and thirst for you and your life today.

GOD ALONE CAN TRULY SATISFY THE HUNGER OF THE SOUL HE HIMSELF CREATED AND INTO WHICH HE PUT THE HUNGER FOR HIMSELF. Unknown

The One Year Bible Readings for today are **1 Samuel 8:1–9:27; John 6:22-42; Psalm 106:32-48;** and **Proverbs 14:34-35.**

holy one

Holy One of God

Jesus turned to the Twelve and asked, "Are you going to leave, too?" Simon Peter replied, "Lord, to whom would we go? You alone have the words that give eternal life. We believe them, and we know you are the Holy One of God."
John 6:67-69

In John 6, Jesus was teaching a truth that was difficult for the people to accept. Some of those who were considered followers turned away from him because of this teaching. When Jesus asked the Twelve if they were going to leave too, Peter answered, "Lord, to whom would we go? You alone have the words that give eternal life." Peter realized that even though the teaching was difficult, only the words of Christ could give eternal life.

The twelve disciples had a decision to make, and so do we. The Bible presents the truth, and sometimes the truth is hard to understand or accept. The world gives us many options that may seem easier to understand or more pleasant to hear. These options may make it tempting to "leave" rather that to continue on the narrow path. The world is like a magnet that is constantly drawing us to a dead-end road. But we can choose, just as Peter did, to realize that the truth lies in Jesus and that no matter how difficult that truth may appear, he alone has "the words that give eternal life."

FATHER, no matter how difficult the words of the Bible seem to be, help me to make decisions that are in accordance with your Word. Help me, Holy Spirit, to understand how your Word applies to every aspect of my life so that I will not be tempted to turn away as others have done. Remind me daily that you alone have the words that give eternal life.

LET THE BIBLE FILL THE MEMORY, RULE THE HEART AND GUIDE THE FEET.
Henrietta Mears (1890–1963)

The One Year Bible Readings for today are **1 Samuel 10:1–11:15; John 6:43-71; Psalm 107:1-43;** and **Proverbs 15:1-3.**

MAY

12

people

In front of All the People

I will thank you, Lord, in front of all the people. I will sing your praises among the nations. For your unfailing love is higher than the heavens. Your faithfulness reaches to the clouds. Be exalted, O God, above the highest heavens. May your glory shine over all the earth.

Psalm 108:3-5

Identifying with Jesus "in front of all the people" is sometimes quite difficult and often unpopular. Singing praises in church or Sunday school is one thing, but singing his praises among the nations is another issue altogether. The psalmist's declarations of praise can cause each one of us to think about our love for the Lord and the extent to which we will go to identify ourselves with him. God's love is absolutely and completely unfailing, and his faithfulness is so great that if we could measure it, it would reach to the clouds. Do you exalt God above the highest heavens? We serve a wonderful, loving, faithful, glorious God. Let us be like the writer of the psalm—unashamed to thank him in front of all the people and to sing his praises everywhere. May we not be embarrassed to lift up the Lord in every situation and at any time and to do whatever we can to cause his glory to shine over all the earth.

THANK YOU, FATHER, for your unfailing love. I praise you for your faithfulness. Be exalted above the highest heavens. May your glory shine over all the earth. Strengthen me so that I am secure in your love and faithfulness. Help me to thank you and praise you in front of all people and among the nations so that your name will be glorified.

PRAISE GOD FROM WHOM ALL BLESSINGS FLOW;
PRAISE HIM, ALL CREATURES HERE BELOW;
PRAISE HIM ABOVE, YE HEAV'NLY HOST;
PRAISE FATHER, SON, AND HOLY GHOST.

Thomas Ken (1637–1711)

The One Year Bible Readings for today are **1 Samuel 12:1–13:23; John 7:1-30; Psalm 108:1-13;** and **Proverbs 15:4.**

rescuer

Our Rescuer

Perhaps one of the reasons God allows us to go through great trials is so that we might come to the end of our own resources and turn to him. Each difficulty is one more opportunity to depend on the Lord. When we are poor and needy, when we fade or fall or have hearts full of pain, we call on him and find him faithful. And as we cry out to God in prayer and he hears and answers us, we experience his strength and deliverance time after time. "No matter how difficult our circumstances are," Oswald Chambers said, "they are the means of manifesting how wonderfully perfect and extraordinarily pure the Son of God is." When you ask the Lord for help, remember the truth of this psalm and the countless other places in Scripture where God promises he will send help. For the sake of his reputation as a good and faithful God, he will rescue you, lift your life from the pit, and set you on a solid foundation of his faithfulness.

Deal well with me, O Sovereign Lord, for the sake of your own reputation! Rescue me because you are so faithful and good. For I am poor and needy, and my heart is full of pain. I am fading like a shadow at dusk; I am falling like a grasshopper that is brushed aside.
Psalm 109:21-23

HEAVENLY FATHER, thank you for hearing my prayer and rescuing me because you are faithful and good. Forgive me for the times when I have exhausted my meager resources before calling out to you. When I am poor and needy and my heart is full of pain, prompt me to run to you first and to find rest in your faithfulness and goodness. In you, O Lord, I put my trust.

GOD HEARS PRAYER—GOD DELIGHTS TO HEAR PRAYER. HE HAS ALLOWED HIS PEOPLE A THOUSAND TIMES OVER TO BE TRIED, THAT THEY MIGHT BE COMPELLED TO CRY TO HIM, AND LEARN TO KNOW HIM AS THE HEARER OF PRAYER.
Andrew Murray (1828–1917)

The One Year Bible Readings for today are **1 Samuel 14:1-52; John 7:31-53; Psalm 109:1-31;** and **Proverbs 15:5-7.**

MAY

14

obedient

An Obedient Heart

Samuel replied, "What is more pleasing to the Lord: your burnt offerings and sacrifices or your obedience to his voice? Obedience is far better than sacrifice. Listening to him is much better than offering the fat of rams."
1 Samuel 15:22

As the Lord had directed, Saul and the Israelite army attacked and defeated the Amalekites. But instead of killing every person and animal as God had commanded, Saul brought back Agag, the Amalekite king, and the best of their sheep and cattle. Then while Saul was trying to justify his disobedience, Samuel replied with the words in verse 22, truth that is just as important for us today as it was for people in the Old Testament: obeying the voice of the Lord, listening to him, and following his marching orders instead of our own are of far more value to God than the most expensive or grand sacrifice we could offer. When God tells us to go or to call that person or to do this humble task, then as the Nike commercial says, Just do it! Do it God's way. Don't lean on your own understanding or perception of the situation. Don't wait to see the whole blueprint or figure everything out. Follow the light at your feet, and as you are faithful in the small things God asks of you, he will do the great thing.

LORD, work in me a heart of obedience so I can live a life that pleases you. It is so easy to try to rationalize disobedience or attempt to chart my own course. But you are holy and righteous, and you value my obedience above anything else I could ever give you. May my daily sacrifice to you be a humble and obedient heart that delights in your smile.

THERE MUST BE NO DEBATE. THE MOMENT YOU OBEY THE LIGHT, THE SON OF GOD PRESSES THROUGH YOU IN THAT PARTICULAR; BUT IF YOU DEBATE YOU GRIEVE THE SPIRIT OF GOD.
Oswald Chambers (1874–1917)

The One Year Bible Readings for today are **1 Samuel 15:1–16:23; John 8:1-20; Psalm 110:1-7;** and **Proverbs 15:8-10.**

wonders

God's Amazing Wonders

I will thank the Lord with all my heart as I meet with his godly people. How amazing are the deeds of the Lord! All who delight in him should ponder them. Everything he does reveals his glory and majesty. His righteousness never fails. Who can forget the wonders he performs?
Psalm 111:1-4

God wants us to know him and he has chosen to reveal himself through the Bible, through creation, through his intervention in history, and through his work in the lives of people. As this psalm says, everything God does "reveals his glory and majesty." Yet sometimes our spiritual eyes are dim, and we can't see his hand, or we forget the wonders the Lord has performed. When that happens, we neglect to thank the Lord with all our hearts.

What a blessing to have his Word to draw us back again and again to the truth that his deeds are amazing and "his righteousness never fails." As you approach God in prayer today, ask him to help you to see him more clearly, to remember and to ponder his marvelous works of redemption in your life and in the world around you. If your memory of his deeds is dim, take a passage from the Bible and imagine yourself among the Israelites who crossed over the Red Sea or were healed by Jesus. Then with your whole heart thank him for the wonders he has done.

LORD, your deeds are amazing, and everything you do reveals your glory and majesty. Open my eyes to see you in your works so I can thank you with all my heart! Let me never forget the wonders you perform! Help me to take fresh delight in you as I ponder them.

IF WE MISS SEEING GOD IN HIS WORKS, WE DEPRIVE OURSELVES OF THE SIGHT OF A ROYAL DISPLAY OF WISDOM AND POWER SO ELEVATING, SO AWE-INSPIRING AS TO MAKE ALL ATTEMPTS OF DESCRIPTION FUTILE. A. W. Tozer (1897–1963)

The One Year Bible Readings for today are **1 Samuel 17:1–18:4; John 8:21-30; Psalm 111:1-10;** and **Proverbs 15:11.**

MAY

16

flame

Passing the Flame

Happy are those who fear the Lord. Yes, happy are those who delight in doing what he commands. Their children will be successful everywhere; an entire generation of godly people will be blessed. . . . They do not fear bad news; they confidently trust the Lord to care for them.

Psalm 112:1-2, 7

God has given us a mandate to live in such a way that the next generation will know that the Lord is God and that he is worthy of our committing our lives to him. Then an entire generation of godly people will rise up and be blessed. This psalm describes some of the keys to blessing the next generations with the truth. Those who pass on the spiritual baton to the next generation will be people who fear and worship the Lord, who delight in doing his will, and who walk in such an intimate relationship with him that they don't even fear bad times because they are so confident of God's care for them. These godly men and women will not only run the race themselves and live a life of joy and purpose as they delight in doing what God commands, but they will also bless those of the next generation by passing their spiritual legacy to them. What is the best way for you to influence those who will come after you? Fear the Lord today, take delight in obeying him, and trust that he will care for you.

LORD, it's so easy to focus only on the present and forget that what I do today affects the future. May I walk in such obedience and reverence for you that an entire generation of godly people will be blessed. Help me to fear you and delight in doing all that you command. Teach me how to pass on the baton of faith to both my natural and spiritual children so that you, Lord, get all the glory.

IF I AM A CHRISTIAN, I AM NOT SET ON SAVING MY OWN SKIN, BUT ON SEEING THAT THE SALVATION OF GOD COMES THROUGH ME TO OTHERS, AND THE GREAT WAY IS BY INTERCESSION.
Oswald Chambers (1874–1917)

The One Year Bible Readings for today are **1 Samuel 18:5–19:24; John 8:31-59; Psalm 112:1-10;** and **Proverbs 15:12-14.**

MAY

17

happy

A Happy Heart

For the poor, every day brings trouble; for the happy heart, life is a continual feast.
Proverbs 15:15

A person's heart is a major concern of the Lord. God's Word tells us that he doesn't look at the things people look at. We look at the outward appearance, but the Lord looks at the heart; that is, our "thoughts and intentions" (1 Samuel 16:7). Today's verse tells us that a happy, or cheerful, heart makes life "a continual feast." How do we obtain—and maintain—this happy heart? There are many clues throughout the book of Proverbs. We should not let our hearts be anxious or proud because anxiety and pride are deterrents to a cheerful heart (Proverbs 12:25; 16:5). Instead, God calls us to have pure hearts and to keep them on the right path (Proverbs 22:11; 23:19). These are positive steps to achieving a happy heart because when we are being obedient to God's Word and experiencing his smile of approval, our hearts will be lighter, even in difficult times. The Bible gives us many other instructions about how to have "healthy" hearts, but a good place to start is to embrace the truth of Proverbs 15:15 and ask God to show us how to develop hearts that are happy, no matter what challenges we are facing.

FATHER, help me to have a happy heart. Remove the anxiety that sometimes weighs my heart down. Keep my heart from growing proud. Instead, give me a pure heart—a heart that is pleasing to you. Help me to hide your Word in my heart so that I can walk in your ways and enjoy a life that is a continual feast.

WHEN I THINK OF GOD, MY HEART IS SO FULL OF JOY THAT THE NOTES LEAP AND DANCE AS THEY LEAVE MY PEN; AND SINCE GOD HAS GIVEN ME A CHEERFUL HEART, I SERVE HIM WITH A CHEERFUL SPIRIT. Franz Joseph Haydn (1732–1809)

The One Year Bible Readings for today are **1 Samuel 20:1–21:15; John 9:1-41; Psalm 113:1–114:8;** and **Proverbs 15:15-17.**

MAY
18

The Shepherd's Voice

A shepherd enters through the gate. The gatekeeper opens the gate for him, and the sheep hear his voice and come to him. He calls his own sheep by name and leads them out. After he has gathered his own flock, he walks ahead of them, and they follow him because they recognize his voice.
John 10:2-4

This passage from John tells us important things about the shepherd-sheep relationship. The shepherd calls his sheep by name and leads them out; he goes before them, preparing the way and protecting them from harm. When he speaks to them, they follow him because they know his voice. These verses remind us that because sheep are in such an intimate relationship with the shepherd and spend so much time with him, they can discern the difference between their shepherd's voice and that of a stranger and won't be deceived. So it is with us. As we commune more with Jesus, our Good Shepherd, and become familiar with his voice, we will not be deceived by the voice of the enemy; we will not be distracted or derailed by the myriad other voices in the world around us. As the song says, we will hear our shepherd more clearly and follow him more nearly, not just in the extraordinary times but day by day.

LORD, I thank you for making me one of your sheep. What a privilege it is to belong to you! Thank you for going ahead of me and preparing the way for me. You call me by name and speak to my heart and lead me. With all the "voices" clamoring in my world, quiet my mind and heart so that I will recognize your voice and follow only you.

THE CHRISTIAN LIFE ROOTED IN THE SECRET PLACE WHERE GOD MEETS AND WALKS AND TALKS WITH HIS OWN GROWS INTO SUCH A TESTIMONY OF DIVINE POWER THAT ALL MEN WILL FEEL ITS INFLUENCE AND BE TOUCHED BY THE WARMTH OF ITS LOVE. E. M. Bounds (1835–1913)

The One Year Bible Readings for today are **1 Samuel 22:1–23:29; John 10:1-21; Psalm 115:1-18;** and **Proverbs 15:18-19.**

troubled

When I Am Troubled

God has called us to a life of prayer, of constant and ongoing communication with him, and has purposed that we would turn to him in our troubles. That the almighty, all-powerful Lord wants to hear our needs and hurts is great news. But the fact that he not only hears our prayers but also intervenes and delights in showing us his loving-kindness and doing wonderful things in response to our petitions makes prayer a truly amazing thing. Through prayer, everything can change—starting with our own hearts and lives—and even when we feel most helpless or are most troubled, God can infuse the worst situations with his light and grace. When we pray, the impossible becomes possible, and the powers of darkness are dispersed. No wonder Satan tries every scheme to keep us from praying! But because we believe in God and his limitless power, we can take our most honest concerns and feelings to him and know that he will hear us.

I believed in you, so I prayed, "I am deeply troubled, Lord."

Psalm 116:10

LORD, when I am troubled, help me to run to you the way little children run to their fathers when they don't know what to do or where to go. Increase my belief in your fatherly heart and your tenderness toward me, and increase my faith in the power of prayer.

IT IS BY PRAYER THAT WE COUPLE THE POWERS OF HEAVEN TO OUR HELPLESSNESS, THE POWERS WHICH CAN TURN WATER INTO WINE AND REMOVE MOUNTAINS IN OUR OWN LIFE AND IN THE LIVES OF OTHERS, THE POWER WHICH CAN AWAKEN THOSE WHO SLEEP IN SIN AND RAISE UP THE DEAD, THE POWERS WHICH CAN CAPTURE STRONGHOLDS AND MAKE THE IMPOSSIBLE POSSIBLE. Ole Hallesby (1879–1961)

The One Year Bible Readings for today are **1 Samuel 24:1–25:44; John 10:22-42; Psalm 116:1-19;** and **Proverbs 15:20-21.**

MAY
20

waiting

Waiting with Hope

Although Jesus loved Martha, Mary, and Lazarus, he stayed where he was for the next two days and did not go to them. Finally after two days, he said to his disciples, "Let's go to Judea again."
John 11:5-7

Mary and Martha had sent their friend Jesus a message about the critical condition of their brother, Lazarus, and their urgent need for his help: "Lord, the one you love is very sick" (John 11:3). But instead of rushing off to Bethany, Jesus stayed where he was for two days before responding to Mary and Martha's plea. When he did arrive, he raised Lazarus from the dead in a magnificent display of his power.

Just as Mary and Martha struggled when Jesus answered their prayers for Lazarus in a time and way different from what they had expected, we get frustrated when the Lord delays in coming to us and answering our prayers.

As it did for the grieving sisters, two days (or two months or two years) of waiting can seem like an eternity to us. But in the midst of the "delay," God is not inactive. He is teaching us patience, perseverance, and faith and is planning to glorify himself in our circumstances. While we are waiting, he wants to cleanse our hearts and refocus us on Jesus. The Spirit always knows what will glorify God, and we can trust him when we're in the waiting room.

LORD, help me to wait for you in hope and perseverance, knowing that you will come. Remind me that your plan for Lazarus and his sisters did not suffer because of your delay—the delay was part of your plan so that your power would be demonstrated in an even greater way. Grant me patience and faith in the waiting rooms of life yet to be.

GOD OFTEN DELAYS HIS RESPONSE OUT OF LOVE, AS HE WORKS ALL THINGS TOGETHER FOR GOOD.
Jeanne Zornes

The One Year Bible Readings for today are **1 Samuel 26:1–28:25; John 11:1-54; Psalm 117:1-2;** and **Proverbs 15:22-23.**

MAY

21

The Lord Is for Me

Today's verses tell us that the psalmist was in a frightening situation. But in his distress, he cried out to God in prayer. Because of God's presence and strength in response to his plea, the psalmist could look in triumph at those who hated and attacked him. For every difficulty and trial, God has prepared a way. His eyes are on those who trust in him in their distress, and his ears are attentive to their cries. You can know and rest assured that just as God was for David, he is for you! And because the all-powerful Lord who is on your side is your shield and defender, you do not have to be afraid. The Lord is greater than any problem, greater than any fear, greater than any person opposing you. Thank him for his help in past situations when there seemed to be no way out, and trust him and thank him for being "for you" today.

In my distress I prayed to the Lord, and the Lord answered me and rescued me. The Lord is for me, so I will not be afraid. What can mere mortals do to me? Yes, the Lord is for me; he will help me.
Psalm 118:5-7

LORD, thank you for answering me and helping me in my distress. Thank you for being for me! That truth is amazing to me and assures me of your concern for me. Help me to resolve not to be afraid because the Lord of the universe is on my side!

PRAYER OFFERS US A WAY OUT OF OUR FEAR. IT IS ALL A MATTER OF CALLING UPON JESUS' NAME. ONLY IN HIS NAME IS THERE HELP. THE MORE WE CALL UPON HIS NAME, THE MORE WE WILL EXPERIENCE THIS TRUTH.
Mother Basilea Schlink (1904–2001)

The One Year Bible Readings for today are **1 Samuel 29:1–31:13; John 11:55–12:19; Psalm 118:1-18;** and **Proverbs 15:24-26.**

MAY

22

glory

All for God's Glory

[Jesus said,] "All those who want to be my disciples must come and follow me, because my servants must be where I am. And if they follow me, the Father will honor them. Now my soul is deeply troubled. Should I pray, 'Father, save me from what lies ahead'? But that is the very reason why I came! Father, bring glory to your name."

John 12:26-28

Often when our souls are troubled and problems abound, we tend to pray prayers such as, "Lord, fix this situation so I won't have to suffer or have problems! Make everything go smoothly in my life! Please remove the obstacles I'm facing today!" But Jesus, in view of his impending suffering and death, aligned himself with the Father's purposes. While he prayed in Gethsemane, it was only natural for him to ask that if it were possible, he might not need to face the unspeakable torment that was to come. But his greater priority was not his own comfort; it was doing his Father's will and agreeing to what would bring glory to his name.

With Christ as our example, we who follow the Lord are to do the same in our difficulties. We are to align ourselves with God's purposes, commit to seeing them through whatever the cost to us, and enter into Christ's prayer—that God would be glorified in our lives.

LORD, may my highest motivation and desire be that your name would be glorified in every trial and situation I go through. Keep my mind and heart focused on Jesus' example and committed to what you want to accomplish in my life. Holy Spirit, please give me grace to live wholeheartedly for the glory of God's name.

THE POSSIBILITIES OF PRAYER ARE FOUND IN ITS ALLYING ITSELF WITH THE PURPOSES OF GOD, FOR GOD'S PURPOSES AND MAN'S PRAYING ARE THE COMBINATION OF ALL POTENT AND OMNIPOTENT FORCES. E. M. Bounds (1835–1913)

The One Year Bible Readings for today are **2 Samuel 1:1–2:11; John 12:20-50; Psalm 118:19-29;** and **Proverbs 15:27-28.**

follow

Empowered to Follow

The first four verses in Psalm 119 tell us that those who are obedient to God's commands and are wholeheartedly committed to seeking him are happy (some other translations use the word *blessed*), and then verse 5 expresses a prayer for God's help to be among the people who are described here. They will be people of integrity who don't get derailed by the enemy but walk only in God's paths. Just as God charged his people in the psalmist's day to keep his commandments, he charges us with doing the same. But he knew we couldn't do it in our own strength and resources. And so, Peter tells us, "As we know Jesus better, his divine power gives us everything we need for living a godly life" (2 Peter 1:3). He has given us his Spirit to dwell within us, to guide us into all truth, to make us aware and draw us back when we begin to compromise with evil, and to empower us to obey so that our lives and actions can reflect God's principles. In God's strength, we can mirror to the world what we believe.

Happy are people of integrity, who follow the law of the Lord. Happy are those who obey his decrees and search for him with all their hearts. They do not compromise with evil, and they walk only in his paths. You have charged us to keep your commandments carefully. Oh, that my actions would consistently reflect your principles!
Psalm 119:1-5

HOLY SPIRIT, empower me to live in such a way that my actions consistently reflect your principles! As I search for you with all my heart and follow your law, you will make me a person of integrity who knows the happiness that comes from walking in your paths. May all that I do and say honor you.

ALL HEAVEN IS WAITING TO HELP THOSE WHO WILL DISCOVER THE WILL OF GOD AND OBEY IT.
J. Robert Ashcroft (1878–1958)

The One Year Bible Readings for today are **2 Samuel 2:12–3:39; John 13:1-30; Psalm 119:1-16;** and **Proverbs 15:29-30.**

MAY

24

truth

Treasuring Your Truth

Be good to your servant, that I may live and obey your word. Open my eyes to see the wonderful truths in your law. I am but a foreigner here on earth; I need the guidance of your commands. Don't hide them from me! I am overwhelmed continually with a desire for your laws.

Psalm 119:17-20

Have you ever found yourself skimming rapidly over your daily portion of Bible reading to get that task mentally checked off your list? In contrast, the psalmist longed to know the wonderful truths in God's laws and to obey them. He understood his need for God's commands and was consumed with a desire for them. We may not always share the psalmist's hunger and enthusiasm, but we have Psalm 119, where almost every verse describes the greatness of God's Word. It instructs us, encourages us, and shows us the path of life. Much more than just an intellectual challenge, the living words of Scripture are our foundation for prayer and lead us to the Father's heart. If God's Word seems dry and less than "wonderful," maybe it's because you're leaving the Holy Spirit out of your reading time. Ask him to open your spiritual eyes to perceive and understand the wonderful truths in the Word of God. He won't disappoint you!

LORD, Christian brothers and sisters all over the world long to have your Word to read but do not have it. What a privilege to be able to read it anytime I like. Open my eyes, and grant me wisdom to see and understand the wonderful truths in your law! Let me never take your Word for granted. Help me to treasure it and meditate on it day and night.

IF WE WISH TO PRAY WITH CONFIDENCE AND GLADNESS, THEN THE WORDS OF HOLY SCRIPTURE WILL HAVE TO BE THE SOLID BASIS OF OUR PRAYER. . . . THE WORDS WHICH COME FROM GOD BECOME, THEN, THE STEPS ON WHICH WE FIND OUR WAY TO GOD. Dietrich Bonhoeffer (1906–1945)

The One Year Bible Readings for today are **2 Samuel 4:1–6:23; John 13:31–14:14; Psalm 119:17-32;** and **Proverbs 15:31-32.**

peace

A Gift of Peace

[Jesus said,] "I am leaving you with a gift—peace of mind and heart. And the peace I give isn't like the peace the world gives. So don't be troubled or afraid."
John 14:27

Jesus knew that as long as we live on planet Earth, there will be things that can disturb our peace and cause us to be troubled or afraid. All we have to do is turn on the news or open a newspaper to see countless reasons for us to be troubled. Remember the scares related to Y2K, and UFOs, and mad-cow disease? violence, terrorism, and the threat of biochemical warfare? The hormones doctors thought would protect women's hearts have been shown not to do so. Food is tainted with pesticides. It's easy to see that this world and its circumstances won't give us the peace our hearts long for. But we don't have to live in a state of despair. Jesus has left us with a great gift—peace of mind and heart right in the middle of this troubled world. It doesn't come from positive thinking or repeating affirming mantras but from the person of Jesus Christ, who said, "Here on earth you will have many trials and sorrows. But take heart, because I have overcome the world" (John 16:33). We can enter into his peace because he has already provided a way through the Cross.

JESUS, thank you for the peace of mind and heart that you provide for me. In the midst of my circumstances, I want to receive your peace for my life. I love you for overcoming the world through your work on the cross. Help me to keep my eyes fixed firmly on you and to enter into your peace.

A GREAT MANY PEOPLE ARE TRYING TO MAKE PEACE, BUT THAT HAS ALREADY BEEN DONE. GOD HAS NOT LEFT IT FOR US TO DO; ALL WE HAVE TO DO IS TO ENTER INTO IT. D. L. Moody (1837–1899)

The One Year Bible Readings for today are **2 Samuel 7:1–8:18; John 14:15-31; Psalm 119:33-48;** and **Proverbs 15:33.**

MAY

26

bless

Remembering to Bless

One day David began wondering if anyone in Saul's family was still alive, for he had promised Jonathan that he would show kindness to them. He summoned a man named Ziba, who had been one of Saul's servants. "Are you Ziba?" the king asked. "Yes sir, I am," Ziba replied. The king then asked him, "Is anyone still alive from Saul's family? If so, I want to show God's kindness to them in any way I can."

2 Samuel 9:1-3

Have you ever remembered a friendship from long ago and decided to do something to reconnect with that friend? At some point King David remembered a past relationship and a promise he had made to Saul's son Jonathan years before (1 Samuel 20:14-15). After inquiring, he discovered Jonathan's crippled son Mephibosheth was living in Lo-debar. King David had him brought to the palace to his royal table, gave him the inheritance from his grandfather Saul, and showered him with blessings. David restored to Mephibosheth everything that had belonged to Saul and his family. David's whole motivation was to keep his promise to Jonathan to show God's kindness to Jonathan's family in any way he could.

Is there someone from the past, a friend or family member, that you could show God's kindness to? Have you forgotten a promise you made or failed to keep a commitment to pray for someone? We may not have the resources to offer the sort of lavish kindness David showered on Mephibosheth, but one kind act may change a person's life. As someone once said, kindness turns more sinners to Christ than knowledge or zeal ever could!

LORD, bring to my remembrance people I have forgotten and those you would have me intercede for or provide for. When I make a commitment or a promise to someone, please help me to fulfill it quickly so that I don't forget to do it. Remind me often that you never fail to fulfill all of your promises to me!

I EXPECT TO PASS THROUGH LIFE BUT ONCE. IF THEREFORE, THERE BE ANY KINDNESS THAT I CAN SHOW, OR ANY GOOD THING I CAN DO TO ANY FELLOW BEING, LET ME DO IT NOW, AND NOT DEFER OR NEGLECT IT, AS I SHALL NOT PASS THIS WAY AGAIN. Stephen Grellet (1773–1855)

The One Year Bible Readings for today are **2 Samuel 9:1–11:27; John 15:1-27; Psalm 119:49-64;** and **Proverbs 16:1-3.**

mercies

Tender Mercies

I have prayed these verses from Psalm 119 for a friend in the hospital battling leukemia. I have also prayed them for a brokenhearted mother whose son is incarcerated and for an older Christian friend who is hospitalized with severe clinical depression following a stroke. When we pray, *Lord, may your unfailing love comfort those who need it today. Surround them with your tender mercies. And may they feel and experience and believe the love you have toward them,* it is a powerful prayer that God delights to answer, for he is the God of all comfort. He is full of loving-kindness and tender mercies. Do you know someone who is in the midst of a trial, someone who is sick, heartbroken, alone, or in distress and needs to be comforted by the Lord's unfailing love today? What friends or family members need to be surrounded with God's tender mercies? As you pray for your friends and loved ones, you can be confident that there is no pain or suffering too deep for the love and mercy of God to reach.

Now let your unfailing love comfort me, just as you promised me, your servant. Surround me with your tender mercies so I may live, for your law is my delight.
Psalm 119:76-77

LORD, you are the God of all comfort. How grateful I am. I pray that your unfailing love will comfort [insert name(s)] and that your tender mercies will surround [insert name(s)]. These dear ones need your Spirit's tenderness today. May they experience you in the midst of their pain, and please touch them with healing today.

GOD'S MERCY IS BOUNDLESS, FREE, AND THROUGH JESUS CHRIST OUR LORD, AVAILABLE TO US NOW IN OUR PRESENT SITUATION. A. W. Tozer (1897–1963)

The One Year Bible Readings for today are **2 Samuel 12:1-31; John 16:1-33; Psalm 119:65-80;** and **Proverbs 16:4-5.**

MAY

28

unity

A Prayer for Unity

[Jesus said,] "I am praying not only for these disciples but also for all who will ever believe in me because of their testimony. My prayer for all of them is that they will be one, just as you and I are one, Father—that just as you are in me and I am in you, so they will be in us, and the world will believe you sent me."
John 17:20-21

Many Christians believe that chapter 17 of John's Gospel is the most significant collection of words and the most important prayers recorded in human history. Here we see a clear verbal demonstration of the heart of Christ only a few short hours before he poured out his heart physically. In verse 13 Jesus himself tells us that the reason for his praying aloud before his disciples was, "so they would be filled with my joy." In these verses the Lord expressed his prayer for unity in love and purpose, not only for his disciples but also for us and every future believer. Centuries before we were born, the Lord was carrying us to the throne of grace so that we could be one with each other and with him, just as he and the Father are one. We can enter into the prayer of Jesus as we ask God to accomplish this in our lives.

TODAY, LORD, I pray for unity with family members, with other believers, and with all who know you. May we be one with the Father, the Son, and the Holy Spirit. May our unity show the world, Jesus, that you came from the Father, and may others be drawn to you and experience your love.

PRAYER IS THE ONE PRIME, ETERNAL CONDITION BY WHICH THE FATHER IS PLEDGED TO PUT THE SON IN POSSESSION OF THE WORLD. CHRIST PRAYS THROUGH HIS PEOPLE. HAD THERE BEEN IMPORTUNATE, UNIVERSAL AND CONTINUOUS PRAYER BY GOD'S PEOPLE, LONG ERE THIS THE EARTH HAD BEEN POSSESSED FOR CHRIST.
E. M. Bounds (1835–1913)

The One Year Bible Readings for today are **2 Samuel 13:1-39; John 17:1-26; Psalm 119:81-96;** and **Proverbs 16:6-7.**

path

The Path of Life

In this portion of Psalm 119 we can join the psalmist in thanking God for his Word, not only because it gives us understanding and discernment we would otherwise lack but because through it God provides light for every aspect of our lives—relationships, families, careers, ministries. The Word is vital if we are to walk in confidence and faith in Christ. It guides us into discovering God's plan for us and helps us to keep away from false ways of life. The darker the world around us grows, the more important it is to follow God's light and obey his Word. We rarely get a giant searchlight on the future or a panorama of what lies ahead. Instead, God leads us with just the light we need to move forward and make a decision, to take the next step. As we read these verses today, let us commit ourselves to following God's Word as the psalmist did. In it we will find the path of life.

How sweet are your words to my taste; they are sweeter than honey. Your commandments give me understanding; no wonder I hate every false way of life. Your word is a lamp for my feet and a light for my path. I've promised it once, and I'll promise again: I will obey your wonderful laws.
Psalm 119:103-106

LORD, I want to delight in your Word, to obey it, and to commit myself to walking in the light it provides. I praise you that your Word lights the path at my feet so that I don't have to wander in the darkness. Guide me today with your wonderful Word.

IN ALL MY PERPLEXITIES AND DISTRESSES, THE BIBLE HAS NEVER FAILED TO GIVE ME LIGHT AND STRENGTH. Robert E. Lee (1807–1870)

The One Year Bible Readings for today are **2 Samuel 14:1–15:22; John 18:1-24; Psalm 119:97-112; Proverbs 16:8-9.**

MAY

30

hope

Where Is Our Hope?

You are my refuge and my shield; your word is my only source of hope.
Psalm 119:114

As Corrie ten Boom traveled around the world to share a message of forgiveness and love after her release from a Nazi concentration camp after World War II, she met a missionary who was desperately afraid and in despair because Christians were continually suffering persecution and death near her mission base. Corrie advised the missionary to look down on the terrible events around her from on high, from the heavenly realms where Jesus' victory is the greatest reality. But she acknowledged that it is possible to have this kind of perspective only through the Holy Spirit and a renewed vision of the Lord Jesus Christ.

There are times when we can look to the Lord and his Word as our only source of hope. Take a few moments to reflect on where you place your hope. Is it in a person or a hoped-for outcome? financial security? good government? Lift up your eyes to the Lord; place your hope in him and his Word and he will sustain you.

DEAR LORD, how grateful I am that you are my refuge and my shield. Although my perspective is often focused on the circumstances around me, you already know the outcome of your plans for my life. In the midst of difficulties, your Word is my only source of hope. Help me to trust in you and gain an eternal perspective.

SURRENDER TO THE LORD MEANS TURNING AROUND ONE HUNDRED AND EIGHTY DEGREES—THAT MEANS A RENEWED PERSON AND RENEWED VISION. . . . WE ARE NOT READY FOR THE BATTLE UNTIL WE HAVE SEEN THE LORD, FOR JESUS IS THE ANSWER TO ALL PROBLEMS.
Corrie ten Boom (1892–1983)

The One Year Bible Readings for today are **2 Samuel 15:23–16:23; John 18:25–19:22; Psalm 119:113-128;** and **Proverbs 16:10-11.**

MAY
31

thirsty

I'm Thirsty

Jesus knew that everything was now finished, and to fulfill the Scriptures he said, "I am thirsty."
John 19:28

One of the women who lingered at the foot of the cross had once known thirst that ordinary water couldn't quench. She had been an outcast among her peers, and there was no place in society for someone like her. She had a great need, and nothing could fill the emptiness, the void within her. Then came the day when she met Jesus. Although her accusers had already given up on her and would readily have stoned her, Jesus saw her need, and rather than give up on her, he faced her accusers and saved not only her life but her soul as well. From that moment forward, Mary Magdalene was a devoted disciple of Christ, following him even to the foot of a brutal cross. When Jesus cried out in thirst, the soldiers mistook it for weakness of the flesh and thrust sour wine to his lips. What they didn't comprehend is that Jesus' words were a declaration of his completion of his Father's work. He was thirsty because he was being poured out as an offering, not only for the grateful woman who knelt at his feet but also for generations of people to come.

JESUS, you poured out your life like an offering and gave me living water that saved and restored my soul. Help me to take that same living water and extend it to those around me who are thirsty. Please use me to reach out to the abandoned, the scorned, the unlovable, with your sacrificial love.

I HAVE A GREAT NEED FOR CHRIST, I HAVE A GREAT CHRIST FOR MY NEED.
Charles Haddon Spurgeon (1834–1892)

The One Year Bible Readings for today are **2 Samuel 17:1-29; John 19:23-42; Psalm 119:129-152;** and **Proverbs 16:12-13.**

home

Coming Home

I have wandered away like a lost sheep; come and find me, for I have not forgotten your commands.
Psalm 119:176

If we are Christians, each of us, at one time or another, was a lost sheep that the Father found and drew to himself. God wants us, as recipients of his amazing grace, to join him in interceding for other lost sheep—family members, friends, or other people he has brought into our lives. We are to bring them to the throne of grace and ask the Lord to reveal himself to them, to redeem and free them from the entrapment of sin, and to transform them by his love. If they are prodigals who are in the "far country" of an ungodly lifestyle, if they have forgotten God's commands or been deceived by Satan, pray that the Spirit of the Lord will demolish strongholds of pride and unbelief and renew their minds in the truth. Pray that he will bring them out of darkness into his marvelous light.

As you pray for these lost sheep, be confident in God's power to work in their lives, defeat Satan's strategies, and bring them into a full knowledge of Christ Jesus. Give thanks for the fact that God accomplishes this through the finished work of Christ on the cross, and then continue in prayer that God will work out his purposes for these lost sheep.

FATHER, I pray today on behalf of [insert name(s)]. Open their minds and hearts to the truth of your Word. Send the Holy Spirit to release your love and power into their lives, that they may experience your grace, believe your truth, understand their need, turn from their sin, and live forever with you.

GOD WORKS ON THE EARTH THROUGH PRAYER, AND YOU ARE GOING TO HAVE THE AWESOME PRIVILEGE OF PARTNERING WITH GOD TO SEE PEOPLE MEET CHRIST. PEOPLE WILL BE IN HEAVEN BECAUSE OF YOUR PRAYERS. Dutch Sheets

The One Year Bible Readings for today are **2 Samuel 18:1–19:10; John 20:1-31; Psalm 119:153-176;** and **Proverbs 16:14-15.**

different

A Different Way

When Jesus saw that the disciples had fished all night and caught nothing, he was interested in what they were doing. He didn't say, "Stop fishing. Give up. Go home. Try again tomorrow!" Instead, he showed them a different way to go about their pursuit. He gave them a course correction: throw their nets on the other side of the boat. The disciples may have thought, *It's all the same water. How much difference can that make?* But when they followed the new directions Jesus had given them, the nets could hardly hold the bountiful yield.

Perhaps you've been working and working with little fruitfulness to show for your efforts. You may even feel like giving up. But don't do it. Instead, recommit your work to God. Ask him whether he wants you to follow a different strategy. He may have a course correction for you as he did for the disciples. Look for his guidance: he may give it in the midst of your task as he did for the disciples, in the quiet of the early morning, or as you drive down the street. But if you ask him, he will surely give it!

At dawn the disciples saw Jesus standing on the beach, but they couldn't see who he was. He called out, "Friends, have you caught any fish?" "No," they replied. Then he said, "Throw out your net on the right-hand side of the boat, and you'll get plenty of fish!" So they did, and they couldn't draw in the net because there were so many fish in it.
John 21:4-6

LORD, show me the best way to go about the work you've called me to so that I can be more fruitful for you and your kingdom. Thank you for creative ideas and fresh plans I never would think of on my own. I am so grateful that you delight in revealing them to a willing heart. And when you do, may I remember to give you the credit!

PRAYER FITS INTO EVERY PHASE OF OUR EARTHLY EXPERIENCE, AND THEREFORE WE MAY ALWAYS PRAY. YOUR PRESENT NEED, DIFFICULTY, OR TROUBLE MAY BE TAKEN TO GOD IN PRAYER. THERE IS NOTHING IN OUR LIFE IN WHICH OUR HEAVENLY FATHER IS NOT INTERESTED.
Charles Cook

The One Year Bible Readings for today are **2 Samuel 19:11–20:13; John 21:1-25; Psalm 120:1-7;** and **Proverbs 16:16-17.**

JUNE
3

watchcare

The Lord's Watchcare

The Lord himself watches over you! The Lord stands beside you as your protective shade. The sun will not hurt you by day, nor the moon at night. The Lord keeps you from all evil and preserves your life. The Lord keeps watch over you as you come and go, both now and forever.
Psalm 121:5-8

Recently our son left to drive across the country to begin a new chapter of his life as a doctor in the United States Navy. Traveling alone in his packed-to-the-ceiling white minivan, Chris met his wife and new baby at the airport and took up residence in Bethesda, Maryland, later to serve at other military stations and naval hospitals around the nation. I knew that I could not be there to accompany him on the trip or drop by with a pot of soup on the day they began unpacking. But how wonderful to know that the Lord himself was watching over Chris, that almighty God was beside him through the hundreds of miles he drove, and that my son was never alone! He might have gotten sleepy or tired, but God never naps or dozes. He was at Chris's side to protect and guide him and his young family in a bustling, unfamiliar city. How thankful I am that the Lord keeps watch over my son's coming and going, not only on that journey but throughout his life and forever.

Do you know someone who needs the Lord's watchcare? Pray this psalm for that person today and thank God for his divine protection.

LORD, I praise you for watching over and protecting my loved ones! What peace it gives me to know that you never slumber or sleep and that I can confidently entrust those I love to your care and keeping. Bless and keep [insert name(s)]'s coming and going both now and forever.

PRAYER IS THE KEY THAT SHUTS US UP UNDER GOD'S PROTECTION AND SAFEGUARD. Unknown

The One Year Bible Readings for today are **2 Samuel 20:14–21:22; Acts 1:1-26; Psalm 121:1-8;** and **Proverbs 16:18.**

outpouring

Prayer for an Outpouring

It had been seven long weeks of persevering prayer since Jesus had told the apostles to remain in Jerusalem until the Father sent the promised Holy Spirit. The uproar in the city concerning Jesus was increasing, and the pressures were mounting for Christ's followers—even their lives were in jeopardy. Yet they didn't frantically run around Jerusalem seeking help. They didn't start a new building program or hire a church-growth consultant in an attempt to increase their numbers. Instead, they stayed continually in the upstairs room in unified, wholehearted, fervent prayer. It was the plan and purpose of God to pour out his Spirit, but the believers' prayers were the preparation for Pentecost. Through their prayers, God laid the tracks for the demonstration of the Spirit's power that was to come. Down through history we can see the same pattern being repeated: prayer is the preparation for every powerful movement of God's Spirit.

On the day of Pentecost, seven weeks after Jesus' resurrection, the believers were meeting together in one place. Suddenly, there was a sound from heaven like the roaring of a mighty windstorm in the skies above them, and it filled the house where they were meeting.
Acts 2:1-2

LORD, grant us the same unity and fervency in prayer that your followers had in the upper room. We long to see your kingdom expand, your Spirit poured out in power, and the accomplishment of your will and purpose in our time. Give us hearts that take an active role in "laying the tracks" for your Spirit's work in our generation.

NEVER HAS THERE BEEN AN OUTPOURING OF THE DIVINE SPIRIT FROM GOD, WITHOUT A PREVIOUS OUTPOURING OF THE HUMAN SPIRIT TOWARD GOD. A. T. Pierson (1837–1911)

The One Year Bible Readings for today are **2 Samuel 22:1–23:23; Acts 2:1-47; Psalm 122:1-9;** and **Proverbs 16:19-20.**

JUNE

5

clinging

Clinging to God in Prayer

I lift my eyes to you, O God, enthroned in heaven. We look to the Lord our God for his mercy, just as servants keep their eyes on their master, as a slave girl watches her mistress for the slightest signal.
Psalm 123:1-2

This passage gives us a beautiful word picture of focused, single-hearted devotion, of having our attention wholly focused on the Lord of heaven. The psalmist compares his trust in God with the attentiveness of servants or slaves who hang on every word, watching and waiting for even the slightest signal from their master. As I read these verses, I am reminded that some days my eyes are looking to everything else but the Lord. How thankful we can be that even at those times, the blood of Jesus cleanses us as we humbly acknowledge our lack of focus on God and our total dependence on him. It is his Spirit within us looking to the Father that draws our hearts to him in prayer and a partnership with him in his mission on earth. What a good place that is to be! The next time the Spirit reminds you that your vision is "out of focus," remember this picture of the servant, and ask God to draw your attention back to him.

O GOD, enthroned in heaven, I long to have my eyes fixed on you as the psalmist did. Draw me to you, Lord, as I lift my eyes to your throne for your mercy and grace today. Keep me from distractions that would take my eyes from you and make my focus fuzzy. And give me attentiveness to your Holy Spirit's "signals" in my heart and life today.

I DON'T THINK THERE IS ANYONE WHO NEEDS GOD'S HELP AND GRACE AS MUCH AS I DO. SOMETIMES I FEEL SO HELPLESS AND WEAK. I THINK THIS IS WHY GOD USES ME. BECAUSE I CANNOT DEPEND ON MY OWN STRENGTH, I RELY ON HIM TWENTY-FOUR HOURS A DAY. . . . ALL OF US MUST CLING TO GOD THROUGH PRAYER.
Mother Teresa (1910–1997)

The One Year Bible Readings for today are **2 Samuel 23:24–24:25; Acts 3:1-26; Psalm 123:1-4;** and **Proverbs 16:21-23.**

Watching Our Words

Kind words are like honey—sweet to the soul and healthy for the body.
Proverbs 16:24

Oh, the power and force of our words! They can be a soothing balm or a sword that cuts painfully. They can either build others up or tear them down. This proverb calls us to stop and think before we speak and to choose our words wisely so that they will bring health rather than hurt. Just as honey is a life-producing substance, a universal medicine that brings health and energy to the body and sweetness to food, words of kindness are sweet gifts to their hearers. Kind words can bring healing to relationships; even when they are few, they can powerfully encourage others and infuse them with hope while soothing their fear and pain. Gracious words actually promote positive energy and health in their hearers so that they can do their best. Ask God to fill you with kind and nourishing words for all the people you encounter each day—especially those you live or work with who may strain your patience. It is when people are the most irritating and unlovable that they need kind, loving words the most.

LORD, give me kind words—your words of life—with which to bless those around me. Since my words are born in my heart, sweeten my soul with your Spirit, and soften and expand my heart to hold your love for others. May my words be gifts of sweetness to those around me today.

COLD WORDS FREEZE PEOPLE, AND HOT WORDS SCORCH THEM, AND BITTER WORDS MAKE THEM BITTER, AND WRATHFUL WORDS MAKE THEM WRATHFUL. KIND WORDS . . . SOOTHE, QUIET, AND COMFORT THE HEARER. Blaise Pascal (1623–1662)

The One Year Bible Readings for today are **1 Kings 1:1-53; Acts 4:1-37; Psalm 124:1-8;** and **Proverbs 16:24.**

JUNE

7

security

True Security

Those who trust in the Lord are as secure as Mount Zion; they will not be defeated but will endure forever. Just as the mountains surround and protect Jerusalem, so the Lord surrounds and protects his people, both now and forever.

Psalm 125:1-2

What does it mean to trust the Lord? It means looking to him as the source of our security and putting our faith in the grace, love, power, and protection of God when the inevitable pressures of life come. It means knowing as the psalmist did that as the mountains surround and protect the city of Jerusalem, God himself surrounds and shields his people. When we trust the Lord, we don't have to focus on the wicked and what they are doing or might do to us. We don't have to rehash our own woes. Even though there are problems the size of mountains facing us, we can cry out to the Lord who created the mountains and is able to move them. As we focus on him and his truth, he will encourage our hearts and help us to claim the great promise of verse 2: The Lord will surround and protect his people, now and forever.

LORD, I put my trust in you today. You are my security and protection, my shield, my fortress, and my hiding place, and I praise you. When enemies surround me and troubles multiply, help me to remember that you are ever faithful and that you surround and protect me, both now and forever.

IT IS WISE TO BREAK OFF THE CONTEMPLATION OF ENEMIES AND DANGERS BY CRYING OUT TO GOD. PRAYER IS A GOOD INTERRUPTION OF A CATALOGUE OF PERILS. Alexander Maclaren (1826–1910)

The One Year Bible Readings for today are **1 Kings 2:1–3:2; Acts 5:1-42; Psalm 125:1-5;** and **Proverbs 16:25.**

prayer

Giving Ourselves to Prayer

[The apostles said,] "Then we can spend our time in prayer and preaching and teaching the word."
Acts 6:4

With such rapid growth in the numbers of believers, hard feelings and dissension were on the rise in the early church. So the disciples put their heads together and realized that they needed to spend their time and effort teaching and preaching the Word of God and giving themselves to prayer instead of administering a food program or judging disputes. So they did what wise and responsible leaders do: they settled on their highest priority and then delegated remaining important tasks to others.

Missionary and minister Andrew Murray compared the great time, effort, and diligence it takes for a farmer to bring forth a good harvest with the need for us to put time, effort, and diligence into prayer. Rather than relegate it to a tiny segment in our Day-Timers, we need to cultivate an ongoing, wholehearted giving of ourselves to intercession if we are to obtain the blessings God has for us and in the lives of others. Is the highest priority in your life to be diligent in prayer?

LORD, grant me a continual readiness and devotion to prayer. Open my eyes and heart to understand the great privilege you have given me in allowing me free access into your throne room. Give me a heart that is hungry to spend time with you. And as I do, prepare my mind and heart for the work you have for me to do for you and your kingdom.

THE SEED WE SOW ON THE SOIL OF HEAVEN, THE EFFORTS WE PUT FORTH, AND THE INFLUENCE WE SEEK TO EXERT IN THE WORLD ABOVE, HEED OUR WHOLE BEING; WE MUST GIVE OURSELVES TO PRAYER. BUT LET US HOLD FAST THE GREAT CONFIDENCE THAT IN DUE SEASON WE SHALL REAP, IF WE FAINT NOT. Andrew Murray (1828–1917)

The One Year Bible Readings for today are **1 Kings 3:3–4:34; Acts 6:1-15; Psalm 126:1-6;** and **Proverbs 16:26-27.**

JUNE

9

build

Unless the Lord Builds . . .

Unless the Lord builds a house, the work of the builders is useless. Unless the Lord protects a city, guarding it with sentries will do no good. It is useless for you to work so hard from early morning until late at night, anxiously working for food to eat; for God gives rest to his loved ones.
Psalm 127:1-2

This psalm has great application for our ordinary, daily lives. Building a house is symbolic of a task, an enterprise, a career or job. It's what we do when we get up every Monday morning. Solomon, the psalmist, says that if we try to build, work, or guard our "territory" without God as the foundation, all of our efforts are useless and in vain. The blessing of the Lord comes as we use the talents and skills God has given us and trust and rely on him for the outcome. Then our effort won't be in vain; it will bear fruit and blessing—including the blessing of rest.

What is your "building project," the work God has entrusted to you? Is it building a company or a structure? Is it building lives by being a parent, teacher, pastor, or caregiver? Put God at the center of your endeavor, for in him is your blessing and your rest.

LORD, I acknowledge that without dependence and trust in you, all my work is in vain, my effort wasted. I want you to be the foundation of my life, my family, and my vocation so that the work of my hands will bear fruit that honors you. Then I will be able to enjoy the rest that you give.

OF THE BUILDING OF LIFE, GOD IS THE ARCHITECT AND MAN IS THE CONTRACTOR. GOD HAS ONE PLAN AND MAN HAS ANOTHER. IS IT STRANGE THAT THERE ARE CLASHINGS AND COLLISIONS?
Henry Ward Beecher (1813–1887)

The One Year Bible Readings for today are **1 Kings 5:1–6:38; Acts 7:1-29; Psalm 127:1-5;** and **Proverbs 16:28-30.**

JUNE

10

families

A Prayer for Families

These verses paint a picture of a godly family living under the Lord's authority and protection: parents who follow his ways and fear God, a wife who flourishes, children growing up with hope and promise for the future. History shows that when there is peace and order in families, that peace ripples out to the church, the city, the state, and the nation. Unfortunately, this isn't the picture of most homes today. Instead, families are disintegrating on every side; children are troubled; the culture is in a downward moral slide. But thanks be to God, he has an answer! He is the answer for our families. And his heart and desire for families is still the same—to live in simple joy, order, and harmony; to enjoy the fruit of our labor; and to follow his ways. Do you know a family that needs God's help? Pray this psalm as your prayer for them and for your own family today.

LORD, our families need you. Please bless our family and teach us to fear you and follow your ways! May the light from our family bless our church, city, state, and nation. Today I pray for [insert family's name]. They are hurting and need to know you and your plan for them. Draw their hearts to you and give them faith so that they can experience the richness of life you promise to those who fear you.

How happy are those who fear the Lord—all who follow his ways! You will enjoy the fruit of your labor. How happy you will be! How rich your life! Your wife will be like a fruitful vine, flourishing within your home. And look at all those children! There they sit around your table as vigorous and healthy as young olive trees. . . . May you live to enjoy your grandchildren.

Psalm 128:1-3, 6

THE FUTURE OF THE CHURCH AND THE FUTURE OF HUMANITY DEPEND IN GREAT PART ON PARENTS AND ON THE FAMILY LIFE THEY BUILD IN THEIR HOMES. THE FAMILY IS THE TRUE MEASURE OF THE GREATNESS OF A NATION. Pope John Paul II (b. 1920)

The One Year Bible Readings for today are **1 Kings 7:1-51; Acts 7:30-50; Psalm 128:1-6;** and **Proverbs 16:31-33.**

JUNE

11

plan

God Fulfills His Plan

Praise the Lord who has given rest to his people Israel, just as he promised. Not one word has failed of all the wonderful promises he gave through his servant Moses. May the Lord our God be with us as he was with our ancestors; may he never forsake us. May he give us the desire to do his will in everything and to obey all the commands, laws, and regulations that he gave our ancestors.

1 Kings 8:56-58

As we read of God's faithfulness fulfilled in the events of this chapter, these words of Solomon spring forth from our hearts as well: "Praise the Lord who has given rest to his people Israel, just as he promised!" When the ark of the covenant came to rest in its place between the wings of the cherubim, signifying the completion of the temple in which God would dwell, "a cloud filled the Temple of the Lord" (v. 10). God's presence was so glorious that the priests couldn't continue their work but could only bow before him in worship. It was as if God was saying, "It is done. The temple I planned has been built. And I am here to dwell with you!" Thus Solomon was able to make the requests that followed: "May he never forsake us. May he give us the desire to do his will." He could make these requests with such heartfelt fervor because of his trust in the covenant-keeping God who fulfills his purposes. If we truly grasp the majesty of what God did during Solomon's reign, we can thank him in faith that he will fulfill his purposes in our lives as well.

BLESSED BE THE LORD, who keeps his covenant and fulfills his purposes! Please give me the desire to do your will in everything. Thank you, Father, for the promise that in your infinite faithfulness you will fulfill your purpose in my life just as you fulfilled all of your promises to Moses. Not one of them failed, and neither will your promises to me.

IN SPITE OF ALL APPEARANCES TO THE CONTRARY, GOD HAS A PLAN FOR THIS BANKRUPT WORLD . . . THIS EARTH OF OURS, HE STILL WANTS AS A THEATRE FOR HIS GRACE AND GLORIOUS DIRECTION. Helmut Thielicke (1908–1986)

The One Year Bible Readings for today are **1 Kings 8:1-66; Acts 7:51–8:13; Psalm 129:1-8;** and **Proverbs 17:1.**

JUNE

12

glory

The Glory of God

This passage is a source of great encouragement that God desires to glorify his name through his people to the whole world. The grandeur of the kingdom of Solomon and his incredible wisdom gave widespread testimony to the greatness and majesty of the God of Israel. The whole earth was talking about the glory of Solomon. People from every country traveled just to see what the Lord had done and to hear the wisdom God had given this king. And when the Queen of Sheba arrived in Jerusalem, she didn't believe Solomon's reputation until she saw it with her own eyes. "Truly I had not heard the half of it!" she said (1 Kings 10:7). The king's wisdom and grandeur so far exceeded what this pagan queen expected that even she was drawn into praise to God. Just as Solomon's reputation brought glory to the name of the Lord and made the whole world aware of God's greatness, we can live in such a way that God's name will be honored.

"The Lord your God is great indeed! He delights in you and has placed you on the throne of Israel. Because the Lord loves Israel with an eternal love, he has made you king so you can rule with justice and righteousness." . . . People from every nation came to visit [Solomon] and to hear the wisdom God had given him.

1 Kings 10:9, 24

LORD, glorify yourself in my life so that others might see you and be drawn to you. I have no palaces, jewels, or servants, and I don't have the wisdom of Solomon, but I have you dwelling in my heart! Enable me by your Spirit to live each day in a way that causes others to marvel at your greatness.

IN COMMANDING US TO GLORIFY HIM, GOD IS INVITING US TO ENJOY HIM. C. S. Lewis (1898–1963)

The One Year Bible Readings for today are **1 Kings 9:1–10:29; Acts 8:14-40; Psalm 130:1-8;** and **Proverbs 17:2-3.**

JUNE

13

turning

Freshly Turning to the Lord

Thus, Solomon did what was evil in the Lord's sight; he refused to follow the Lord completely. . . . The Lord was very angry with Solomon, for his heart had turned away from the Lord, the God of Israel, who had appeared to him twice.

1 Kings 11:6, 9

When we reflect on the marvelous interaction Solomon had with God, the great gifts God had given him and the great deeds described in previous chapters, this passage is sobering indeed. It reminds us that if a man as wise as Solomon can turn his heart away from God, then we, too, are vulnerable. Just as Solomon's devotion was turned from the one true God to false gods through the women he loved, our hearts' focus can be diverted from Jesus by things in this world that distract us, entrap us, and constantly vie for our attention. Yet we don't have to live in fear that we'll fail as Solomon did because God never calls us to live more than one day at a time. His grace is sufficient to keep us as we freshly turn to him. That is the good news! Today and each day is a new start, where God is waiting with open arms for you to draw near to him.

LORD, I am turning freshly to you today. I want to stay close to you and not turn my heart away as Solomon did. Keep me and strengthen me to follow you all the days of my life. I am dependent on you, Lord. I know that you are able.

RELYING ON GOD HAS TO BEGIN ALL OVER AGAIN EVERY DAY AS IF NOTHING HAD YET BEEN DONE.
C. S. Lewis (1898–1963)

The One Year Bible Readings for today are **1 Kings 11:1–12:19; Acts 9:1-25; Psalm 131:1-3;** and **Proverbs 17:4-5.**

encourager

Barnabas, an Encourager

Barnabas had the God-given ability to see and understand what the Lord was doing around him. Just as Joshua and Caleb saw the potential in the land God had promised to give to his people, Barnabas saw with spiritual eyes something of God's potential in Saul, a former enemy who had zealously persecuted believers before he met Christ on the road to Damascus. When the other believers feared Saul, rejected his ministry, and pointed their fingers at him, Barnabas spoke up in Saul's defense and declared what God had deposited in him. He continued to be a peacemaker and a bridge between Saul and the apostles, and eventually the believers embraced Saul and welcomed him into their fellowship. Thus, God's kingdom would be extended throughout Judea and the world. Are you like Barnabas—an encourager? If you're willing, you could be just the person God uses to help someone in trouble. You could be the bridge of divine grace in another's spiritual journey.

When Saul arrived in Jerusalem, he tried to meet with the believers, but they were all afraid of him. . . . Then Barnabas brought him to the apostles and told them how Saul had seen the Lord on the way to Damascus. Barnabas also told them what the Lord had said to Saul and how he boldly preached in the name of Jesus in Damascus.

Acts 9:26-27

LORD, I want to be an encourager like Barnabas. Help me to see others with your eyes. Give me the vision to see the potential you've deposited in them. Fill me with courage to stand with those who are in trouble and need my help or defense. Make me a bridge of encouragement from your heart to the hearts of others.

EVERY TIME WE ENCOURAGE SOMEONE WE GIVE THEM A TRANSFUSION OF COURAGE.
Charles R. Swindoll (b. 1934)

The One Year Bible Readings for today are **1 Kings 12:20–13:34; Acts 9:26-43; Psalm 132:1-18;** and **Proverbs 17:6.**

JUNE
15

Tuning In to God

The next day as Cornelius's messengers were nearing the city, Peter went up to the flat roof to pray. It was about noon, and he was hungry. But while lunch was being prepared, he fell into a trance.
Acts 10:9-10

God never stops communicating his will to his people, and in this particular situation, he had a historic, world-changing message for Peter and the apostles—a message that would extend God's kingdom to the Gentiles and ultimately, to all the nations of the earth. Peter received this revelation because he was in the habit of setting aside time to seek God. He was a busy leader with huge ministry responsibilities, and yet he found time to pray. As Peter was in a position of prayer, he was able to hear the Lord's voice and agenda: God revealed in a vision that the Good News of Jesus Christ was not just for the Jews but for all people who would believe in his name. Who knows what God will reveal in our time as we tune in to his Spirit through prayer and position our hearts and minds to hear him?

LORD, I can't expect to hear your messages to me if I'm not often in your presence, and yet it is such a privilege to be there! Open my eyes and ears to what is on your heart today. And although sometimes what you want to say to me is hard to understand—as it was for Peter—give me a heart of obedience to what you want to impress on me.

PRAYER OPENS THE WAY FOR GOD HIMSELF TO DO HIS WORK IN AND THROUGH US.
Andrew Murray (1828–1917)

The One Year Bible Readings for today are **1 Kings 14:1–15:24; Acts 10:1-23; Psalm 133:1-3;** and **Proverbs 17:7-8.**

provision

Thanks for God's Provision

She did as Elijah said, and she and Elijah and her son continued to eat from her supply of flour and oil for many days. For no matter how much they used, there was always enough left in the containers, just as the Lord had promised through Elijah.

1 Kings 17:15-16

The adventures of Elijah and the widow of Zarephath in 1 Kings 17 show us that God is a God who cares for our physical needs, who keeps his promises, and whose provision is always sufficient. God had sent ravens with bread and meat to Elijah to sustain him, but eventually Kerith Brook had dried up so there was no water, and severe famine had ravaged the land. The widow to whom God sent Elijah also faced desperate and uncertain times. She had no bread and was down to her last handful of flour and a bit of oil. But God wasn't panicked. He had a plan and gave Elijah and the woman instructions that would lead not just to survival for a day but to miraculous provision day after day throughout the famine. As they followed his plan, there was always enough left—just as the Lord had promised. Are you willing to follow God's leading even when circumstances seem overwhelming and his instructions go against your own instincts?

FATHER, thank you for your constant care and for your plan in uncertain times. It's so easy to panic and do what seems most reasonable to me rather than to trust you and follow your leading in those times. Give me the assurance that your way is best, and remind me of your amazing provision for Elijah and the widow because they followed your way instead of their own.

THERE IS NEVER PANIC IN HEAVEN! YOU CAN ONLY HOLD ON TO THAT REALITY THROUGH FAITH BECAUSE IT SEEMED THEN, AND OFTEN SEEMS NOW, AS IF THE DEVIL IS THE VICTOR. BUT GOD IS FAITHFUL, AND HIS PLANS NEVER FAIL! HE KNOWS THE FUTURE. HE KNOWS THE WAY.
Corrie ten Boom (1892–1983)

The One Year Bible Readings for today are **1 Kings 15:25–17:24; Acts 10:24-48; Psalm 134:1-3;** and **Proverbs 17:9-11.**

JUNE

17

acts

A God Who Acts

[Elijah prayed,] "O Lord, answer me! Answer me so these people will know that you, O Lord, are God and that you have brought them back to yourself." Immediately the fire of the Lord flashed down from heaven and burned up the young bull, the wood, the stones, and the dust. It even licked up all the water in the ditch! And when the people saw it, they fell on their faces and cried out, "The Lord is God! The Lord is God!"

1 Kings 18:37-39

At the showdown at Mount Carmel, Elijah pitted the Baal gods against the Lord God, and no matter what the 450 prophets of Baal did—dance wildly, cut themselves, and shout for hours for Baal to answer—there was "no reply, no voice, no answer" (v. 29). But when Elijah placed himself before the Lord and did what God showed him to do by rebuilding the altar and praying, God heard and answered in a mighty way. He revealed himself by sending fire from heaven that consumed the sacrifice and everything surrounding it, even the water. And the people returned to him.

Our God is not a "God at a distance" as a popular song and modern culture often depicts him. He is not like the impotent false gods who had no reply, no voice, and no answer. The Lord is a God who not only hears and speaks but who answers and acts on behalf of those who seek him.

LORD, you are the one true God and I praise you! Thank you for going to such great lengths to demonstrate your power and to bring people back to you. Those great lengths led your only Son to the cross because of your love for those who are blind to your glory and power. Show yourself powerful in my life.

WE CANNOT CREATE THE WIND OR SET IT IN MOTION, BUT WE CAN SET OUR SAILS TO CATCH IT WHEN IT COMES; WE CANNOT MAKE THE ELECTRICITY, BUT WE CAN STRETCH THE WIRE ALONG UPON WHICH IT IS TO RUN AND DO ITS WORK; WE CANNOT IN A WORD, CONTROL THE SPIRIT, BUT WE CAN SO PLACE OURSELVES BEFORE THE LORD, AND SO DO THE THINGS HE HAS BIDDEN US TO DO THAT WE WILL COME UNDER THE INFLUENCE AND POWER OF HIS MIGHTY BREATH.
The Independent

The One Year Bible Readings for today are **1 Kings 18:1-46; Acts 11:1-30; Psalm 135:1-21;** and **Proverbs 17:12-13.**

power

Wonder-Working Power

[Herod] arrested Peter during the Passover celebration and imprisoned him, placing him under the guard of four squads of four soldiers each. . . . But while Peter was in prison, the church prayed very earnestly for him.
Acts 12:3-5

If any story in the New Testament shows the power of corporate prayer, the account of Peter's dramatic release from prison does! While he was clamped down in chains and surrounded by guards to prevent his escape, the believers who were assembled at John Mark's house prayed fervently and persistently for him. They didn't expect, however, God's miraculous deliverance to come so fast or in such an amazing way. In fact, so incredulous were they when he appeared to Rhoda at the door, that they thought it must be Peter's angel and initially didn't even let him in.

Do you know people who are held captive in a prison of their own making? a situation in your own life that needs fervent prayer? Let this story encourage your heart that the Lord is able to break chains, open closed doors, and deliver. And your prayers joined with those of other believers are the very conduits through which God releases his power.

LORD, thank you for your wonder-working power! I once was locked in a prison of darkness to your truth and light. Thank you for shining the light of your truth into my heart and freeing me from sin. Please use me to share the truth about your great power with others who need to know true freedom in Christ.

PRAYER IS THE EASIEST AND HARDEST OF ALL THINGS; . . . ITS RESULTS LIE OUTSIDE THE RANGE OF HUMAN POSSIBILITIES; THEY ARE LIMITED ONLY BY THE OMNIPOTENCE OF GOD.
E. M. Bounds (1835–1913)

The One Year Bible Readings for today are **1 Kings 19:1-21; Acts 12:1-23; Psalm 136:1-26;** and **Proverbs 17:14-15.**

JUNE

19

ministry

Important Ministry

One day as these men were worshiping the Lord and fasting, the Holy Spirit said, "Dedicate Barnabas and Saul for the special work I have for them." So after more fasting and prayer, the men laid their hands on them and sent them on their way.
Acts 13:2-3

Many of us get so enthusiastically wrapped up in the work of the Lord that we forget the God we serve. So busy do we become in ministering to others that we don't take time to minister to the Lord himself. But as the account in today's verses shows, the Holy Spirit's divine direction to send out Paul and Barnabas to spread the gospel in Asia Minor came to men who were worshiping and fasting. Ministering to the Lord bears deeply significant fruit in our lives as well.

Perhaps today you have a full schedule of activities and responsibilities: tasks you need to perform and deadlines you need to meet, children who need your care, people who need ministry or encouragement or the skills you can provide. But don't neglect the most important ministry of all—ministering to the Lord. As you take time to adore and worship him, you will be better equipped for those other tasks, and you will be in a position to receive God's direction for your life as well.

LORD, I worship and adore you. Let me not become so consumed with the good things that I want to do for others and you that I neglect the best thing—bowing before you in worship and praise and seeking your direction for my life daily in prayer. Draw me into daily worship and communion with you.

GOD WANTS WORSHIPPERS BEFORE WORKERS; INDEED THE ONLY ACCEPTABLE WORKERS ARE THOSE WHO HAVE LEARNED THE LOST ART OF WORSHIP. A. W. Tozer (1897–1963)

The One Year Bible Readings for today are **1 Kings 20:1–21:29; Acts 12:24–13:15; Psalm 137:1-9;** and **Proverbs 17:16.**

JUNE
20

promises

Precious Promises

When David Livingstone had to pass through the most dangerous country of the fierce native chief Mburuma and decide whether to furtively sneak through at night or go by day and risk being killed, he staked his life on the promise of Jesus' presence in Matthew 28:19-20: "Go and make disciples of all the nations. . . . And be sure of this: I am with you always, even to the end of the age." He wrote in his journal, "[I]t is the word of a Gentleman of the most sacred and strictest honor, so there's an end on it!" Livingstone knew that God backs up his promises with all the honor of his name, so he proceeded in broad daylight, trusting in his Savior's promise. God fulfilled his Word, and Livingstone made the crossing safely because the Lord Jesus was beside him, just as he said he would be. God's promises are just as true and alive today for those who will pray them, trust them, stand on them, and walk in them.

I bow before your holy Temple as I worship. I will give thanks to your name for your unfailing love and faithfulness, because your promises are backed by all the honor of your name.
Psalm 138:2

THANK YOU, FATHER, for backing your promises by all the honor of your name. It is a mighty and powerful and trustworthy name! I give thanks to you for your unfailing love and faithfulness. Help me to move forward under your direction in the light of your unfailing and precious promises.

GOD MAKES A PROMISE; FAITH BELIEVES IT, HOPE ANTICIPATES IT, PATIENCE QUIETLY AWAITS IT.
Unknown

The One Year Bible Readings for today are **1 Kings 22:1-53; Acts 13:16-41; Psalm 138:1-8;** and **Proverbs 17:17-18.**

JUNE
21

appointed

Appointed to Eternal Life

[The Lord said,] "I have made you a light to the Gentiles, to bring salvation to the farthest corners of the earth." When the Gentiles heard this, they were very glad and thanked the Lord for his message; and all who were appointed to eternal life became believers.
Acts 13:47-48

When I read this verse, I am reminded that there are people all around us whom God is pursuing. It may be the teenager down the street, a lonely coworker, a weary single parent, or even someone standing next to you in line at the bank. The world is full of men and women who have been crying out to God in the quiet desperation of their hearts or in the darkness of a long night. God has been working in their lives and stirring a desire for him. He wants to use us to be a light to them and bring them the good news of hope in Jesus Christ. Ask that his Spirit would show you those in your neighborhood or workplace who need to be the recipients of your prayers. He will help you to build relationships with them and be a vessel through whom God can share his love.

LORD, show me those in my neighborhood, my circle of friends, and my family that you want me to pray for and build relationships with. They may be the very people you have appointed to eternal life. Equip me to be a light to those who don't know you and to love them for Christ's sake.

JESUS WANTS US TO SEE THAT NEIGHBOR NEXT DOOR OR THE PEOPLE SITTING NEXT TO US ON A PLANE OR IN A CLASSROOM ARE NOT INTERRUPTIONS TO OUR SCHEDULE. THEY ARE THERE BY DIVINE APPOINTMENT. JESUS WANTS YOU TO SEE THEIR NEEDS, THEIR LONELINESS, THEIR LONGINGS, AND HE WANTS TO GIVE US THE COURAGE TO REACH OUT TO THEM.
Rebecca Manley Pippert

The One Year Bible Readings for today are **2 Kings 1:1–2:25; Acts 13:42–14:7; Psalm 139:1-24;** and **Proverbs 17:19-21.**

cheerful

A Cheerful Heart

A cheerful heart is good medicine, but a broken spirit saps a person's strength.
Proverbs 17:22

This verse describes the positive benefits to our physical bodies when the inner person of the heart is happy. It also describes the opposite effect: when we are depressed or sad for an extended length of time, it is detrimental to our physical health and strength. When I pondered this verse on a not-so-happy day, it made me think, "Why am I *not* cheerful? Where has my joy gone?" Nine times out of ten I have been fretting about circumstances—which may not be all that happy— instead of focusing on my relationship with Jesus. Life isn't always a feast of pleasant experiences. We can't control the ways our days unfold or muster up a cheerful heart on our own, but we *can* pour our energies into knowing and loving Jesus, the source of all joy, and lifting his name high in good times and bad. When he and his kingdom are our focus, he provides what we need in those other situations and circumstances (Matthew 6:33), and he fills us with true cheerfulness, hope, and joy.

LORD, I want to have a cheerful heart, not a broken spirit. Help me to focus today on you and not on the circumstances I see around me. As you help me to do that by your Spirit, I will know and experience your true joy in my heart and life.

HAPPINESS IS CAUSED BY THINGS THAT HAPPEN AROUND ME AND CIRCUMSTANCES WILL MAR IT; BUT JOY FLOWS RIGHT ON THROUGH TROUBLE; JOY FLOWS ON THROUGH THE DARK. . . . IT IS AN UNCEASING FOUNTAIN BUBBLING UP IN THE HEART. D. L. Moody (1837–1899)

The One Year Bible Readings for today are **2 Kings 3:1–4:17; Acts 14:8-28; Psalm 140:1-13;** and **Proverbs 17:22.**

JUNE

23

count on

A God We Can Count On

O Lord, I am calling to you. Please hurry! Listen when I cry to you for help! . . . Take control of what I say, O Lord, and keep my lips sealed. Don't let me lust for evil things; don't let me participate in acts of wickedness. Don't let me share in the delicacies of those who do evil.
Psalm 141:1-4

In this psalm David not only called on the Lord for protection from the enemies that were hunting him down; he also cried out to God and counted on him to do a deep work within his own heart. He needed God to set a guard over his lips and prevent wrong speech, to preserve his heart, to deliver him from lust and evil desires that would lead to wicked acts, and to so work within David that he would welcome reproof from godly people. He knew he couldn't depend on his flesh and human effort. They are too weak and too easily led astray. He relied instead on God's heart-changing power to be at work within him. As David prayed, we also can—and must—freshly call on the Lord to be at work in our hearts, and then we can rest in and count on his faithfulness to transform us from the inside out.

LORD, I praise you that you are a God I can count on to keep me! Left to myself, I am not strong enough to walk in your paths. Deliver me from choosing my own way instead of yours. Strengthen my heart, and thank you for working within me according to your purposes!

IF GOD MAINTAINS SUN AND PLANETS IN BRIGHT AND ORDERED BEAUTY, HE CAN KEEP US.
F. B. Meyer (1847–1929)

The One Year Bible Readings for today are **2 Kings 4:18–5:27; Acts 15:1-35; Psalm 141:1-10;** and **Proverbs 17:23.**

strength

God's Strength Is Greater

The Aramean army was advancing. Enemy horses, troops, and chariots were everywhere, surrounding the city with the express purpose of seizing Elisha. No wonder his servant was petrified when he woke up to the sight of a massive army bearing down on them. When the servant cried out to his master, Elisha shared how he perceived in spirit the might of the Lord, which was far greater than the forces opposing them. And when Elisha prayed for God to open his servant's eyes so that he, too, can see what Elisha has seen, immediately he perceives the horses and chariots of fire protecting them.

The Lord is ready to open our eyes afresh for each new situation and to show us his vast resources. His strength and might are far greater than the enemy's, but we, like the servant, see "through a glass darkly," and we need for God to open our spiritual eyes.

LORD, grant me the light this day to see in the unseen realm how your strength is greater than any foe that threatens to assail me. Open my eyes, Lord! Remind me of your awesome power and unlimited resources, and then let me take courage because you are fighting for me!

"Ah, my lord, what will we do now?" [Elisha's servant] cried out to Elisha. "Don't be afraid!" Elisha told him. "For there are more on our side than on theirs!" Then Elisha prayed, "O Lord, open his eyes and let him see!" The Lord opened his servant's eyes, and when he looked up, he saw that the hillside around Elisha was filled with horses and chariots of fire.
2 Kings 6:15-17

SO LET IT BE IN GOD'S OWN MIGHT
WE GIRD US FOR THE COMING FIGHT,
AND, STRONG IN HIM WHOSE CAUSE IS OURS,
IN CONFLICT WITH UNHOLY POWERS,
WE GRASP THE WEAPONS HE HAS GIVEN,
THE LIGHT AND TRUTH AND LOVE OF HEAVEN.
John Greenleaf Whittier (1807–1892)

The One Year Bible Readings for today are **2 Kings 6:1–7:20; Acts 15:36–16:15; Psalm 142:1-7;** and **Proverbs 17:24-25.**

praise

The Power of Praise

Around midnight, Paul and Silas were praying and singing hymns to God, and the other prisoners were listening. Suddenly, there was a great earthquake, and the prison was shaken to its foundations. All the doors flew open, and the chains of every prisoner fell off!
Acts 16:25-26

Paul and Silas's praise lifted their eyes from their dire circumstances in a filthy prison to the God who was able to deliver them. They had been stripped and beaten and then thrown into the inner prison with their feet fastened into stocks. It would have been natural for these two disciples to be fearful or to just give up. But instead, they prayed and sang hymns to God! The other prisoners heard their praise—the throne of God heard their worship. The Lord delivered them with a mighty earthquake that rocked the prison to its core, causing the doors to open and the prisoners' chains to fall off.

Are you shaken by your own circumstances? Is your inclination to be fearful or to give up? Start praising God and sing hymns and choruses to him. Our praise not only helps to lift our fear and depression; it also ushers in God's powerful intervention on our behalf.

LORD, I praise you for your mighty power at work in our lives. I magnify your name, for there is none like you! When I look at my circumstances and am tempted to "throw in the towel" and give up, remind me of the example of Paul and Silas and how you intervened for them. Then put words of praise in my mouth. You are my hope in the midst of trouble!

YOUR PRAISE AND THANKSGIVING CAN HELP FORM A HIGHWAY—A SMOOTH, LEVEL ROAD—ON WHICH THE LORD CAN RIDE FORTH UNHINDERED TO DELIVER AND BLESS. Ruth Myers

The One Year Bible Readings for today are **2 Kings 8:1–9:13; Acts 16:16-40; Psalm 143:1-12;** and **Proverbs 17:26.**

All about God

God

We humans just naturally tend to be self-absorbed, so it is easy to get things all turned around and think that the Christian life is all about me—all about *my* disciplines and *my* effort, all about *my* problems and what *I* can do to solve them. But this wonderful psalm is one that pulls us back to the center, back to the truth: it's all about *God,* not about me! It's about God's strength and skill, not my puny efforts. It's about God's shelter and deliverance and protection, not my efforts to watch out for myself. As we use these verses to praise the Lord who is our rock, our loving ally, our fortress and tower of safety, our deliverer and shield, we will find our rest and refuge in him and learn that his overcoming power is sufficient for whatever happens to me today.

Bless the Lord, who is my rock. He gives me strength for war and skill for battle. He is my loving ally and my fortress, my tower of safety, my deliverer. He stands before me as a shield, and I take refuge in him.
Psalm 144:1-2

FATHER, I don't know what is going to happen in the next twenty-four hours, but I know that you will give me the strength I need to handle it and to deal with whatever challenges I may face. I bless you, Lord! Give me your peace as I look to you for everything I need.

PRAYER IS THE EVIDENCE THAT I AM SPIRITUALLY CONCENTRATED ON GOD.
Oswald Chambers (1874–1917)

The One Year Bible Readings for today are **2 Kings 9:14–10:31; Acts 17:1-34; Psalm 144:1-15;** and **Proverbs 17:27-28.**

JUNE
27

helper

The Lord Our Helper

The Lord is faithful in all he says; he is gracious in all he does. The Lord helps the fallen and lifts up those bent beneath their loads.
Psalm 145:13-14

Have you ever felt bent beneath your load? Has life become a grind? Are you burdened with so many responsibilities and so much work that you can't see any way to get it all done, and even if you did, a new pile of demands would be waiting for you tomorrow? Or perhaps you are bent beneath a load of worry for unsaved children or have fallen because the burdens you were carrying were so heavy. What good news it is that God takes delight in helping the fallen. He wants to lift us up when we're bent beneath our own personal load! Whatever burden you are carrying today, give it to God, and ask him to lift your heart and show you his faithfulness. Then you can join with the psalmist in proclaiming, "The Lord is kind and merciful. . . . He showers compassion on all his creation" (Psalm 145:8-9).

LORD JESUS, thank you for lifting our burdens when we are bent beneath our loads. I look to you for help. Thank you for your faithfulness and for helping the fallen. Lift me up by your Spirit, I pray, so that I can praise your kindness and mercy with the psalmist.

TO PRAY IS TO LET JESUS INTO OUR LIVES. HE KNOCKS AND SEEKS ADMITTANCE, NOT ONLY IN THE SOLEMN HOURS OF SECRET PRAYER; HE KNOCKS IN THE MIDST OF YOUR DAILY WORK, YOUR DAILY STRUGGLES, YOUR DAILY "GRIND." THAT IS WHERE YOU NEED HIM THE MOST.
Ole Hallesby (1879–1961)

The One Year Bible Readings for today are **2 Kings 10:32–12:21; Acts 18:1-22; Psalm 145:1-21;** and **Proverbs 18:1.**

rescues

A God Who Rescues

Jehoahaz, king of Israel, lived an evil life. He committed all the sins of Jeroboam and continued leading the nation into the sin of idolatry. So the Lord had turned the people of Israel over to be oppressed by the Arameans. But even though Jehoahaz had been a failure and disobedient to God as a king, when he sought the Lord's help, God heard. And seeing the terrible oppression Israel was living under, he intervened. He raised up a deliverer and savior (a foreshadowing of Christ), one who rescued them from tyranny, and Israel once again lived in safety and peace.

If God will do this for an evil king and an idolatrous nation when they call out to him, how much more will he hear and respond to the prayers of his children, who are reconciled to him because of the sacrifice of our savior, Jesus.

LORD, I thank you that your ear is open to the cry of your children and that you will act on our behalf. With that knowledge, we don't ever have to hesitate to cry out to you for your help and intervention in our lives. What a wonderful Father you are!

PRAYER IS WEAKNESS LEANING ON OMNIPOTENCE.
W. S. Bowden

Jehoahaz prayed for the Lord's help, and the Lord heard his prayer. The Lord could see how terribly the king of Aram was oppressing Israel. So the Lord raised up a deliverer to rescue the Israelites from the tyranny of the Arameans. Then Israel lived in safety again as they had in former days.
2 Kings 13:4-5

The One Year Bible Readings for today are **2 Kings 13:1–14:29; Acts 18:23–19:12; Psalm 146:1-10;** and **Proverbs 18:2-3.**

JUNE
29

delights

What God Delights In

The strength of a horse does not impress him; how puny in his sight is the strength of a man. Rather, the Lord's delight is in those who honor him, those who put their hope in his unfailing love.
Psalm 147:10-11

In this psalm we discover an important secret about relating to the Lord. Our great and mighty God, who has absolute power over everything in heaven and on earth, is not impressed with powerful people. Those who are strong and mighty in their own strength don't get God's attention. Instead, it is the brokenhearted and humble he notices and supports (vv. 3, 6).

He chooses to work not through those who are strong but through those who are weak. And most of all, we don't earn his approval by being great or strong. He delights in those who reverently honor him and put their hope and trust in his unfailing love and mercy, not in their own ability. Today, if you've put your hope in anyone or anything else, ask the Lord to forgive you. But don't stop there. Ask his Spirit to so work in your life that your primary goal becomes honoring and pleasing God.

DEAR LORD, there have been times—even many—when I have relied on someone or something other than you. Forgive me. Those things are "puny" compared to the strength that you give to us when we acknowledge our own weakness and dependence on you. Help me to put my trust in you, and show me the way to a life that honors you. I hope in your unfailing love.

GOD BEING WHO AND WHAT HE IS, AND WE BEING WHO AND WHAT WE ARE, THE ONLY THINKABLE RELATION BETWEEN US IS ONE OF FULL LORDSHIP ON HIS PART AND COMPLETE SUBMISSION ON OURS. WE OWE HIM EVERY HONOR THAT IT IS IN OUR POWER TO GIVE HIM. A. W. Tozer (1897–1963)

The One Year Bible Readings for today are **2 Kings 15:1–16:20; Acts 19:13-41; Psalm 147:1-20;** and **Proverbs 18:4-5.**

praise

The Spirit of Praise

This psalm is an expression of corporate praise at its highest: angels, stars and skies, mountains and hills, wild animals, kings and rulers, all people everywhere, even old men and children—all are commanded to praise the name of the Lord. Why? Because each of these are expressions of his grandeur and glory! Because every created thing in heaven and on earth exists because God spoke them into existence and sustains them by the word of his power! This is the spirit of praise that we will all be ushered into when every knee will bow at Christ's second coming. That is a wondrous thought, but this psalm is also a call to us today to get caught up in the spirit of praise, which is continually going on in heaven. Read this psalm aloud to God and ask the Spirit to give you great freedom in praising him today.

Let them all praise the name of the Lord. For his name is very great; his glory towers over the earth and heaven!
Psalm 148:13

LORD, I join all heaven in praise to you. Lift me up to that realm where the focus is concentrated on you alone. Your glory towers over the earth and heaven! Your name is great. May my heart and voice offer you the praise your glory deserves!

IN PRAISE MY SOUL ASCENDS TO SELF-FORGETTING ADORATION, SEEING AND PRAISING ONLY THE MAJESTY AND POWER OF GOD, HIS GRACE AND REDEMPTION. Ole Hallesby (1879–1961)

The One Year Bible Readings for today are **2 Kings 17:1–18:12; Acts 20:1-38; Psalm 148:1-14;** and **Proverbs 18:6-7.**

Running for Cover

When King Hezekiah heard their report, he tore his clothes and put on sackcloth and went into the Temple of the Lord to pray. And he sent Eliakim the palace administrator, Shebna the court secretary, and the leading priests, all dressed in sackcloth, to the prophet Isaiah son of Amoz. They told him, "This is what King Hezekiah says: This is a day of trouble, insult, and disgrace. . . . Oh, pray for those of us who are left!"

2 Kings 19:1-4

What did King Hezekiah do when the going got tough? He ran for cover—prayer cover, that is! Not only did he go to the temple to pray, but he also sent his own dream team of sorts to beg the prophet Isaiah to pray for him and his people. It's not always easy to ask for help, is it? Our tendency is to wring our hands with worry by day and to toss and turn by night. Or, fearing others might think less of us if we admit our desperate need for help, we smile and say, "Fine, thank you," when they ask how we are. Neither response is good for our souls. One eats away at our peace, and the other robs us of the support we crave. Whether we're kings or common people, we all need to be covered with a blanket of prayer. Like King Hezekiah, let's be quick to admit our needs to God and to those who will faithfully pray for us.

OH, FATHER, help me to remember to run to you when I need help. Help me to swallow my pride and ask others to pray for me when my circumstances seem overwhelming—or even before they get to that point. And thank you, God, for the peace that you give when we run to you.

THE GREATEST OF ALL DISORDERS IS TO THINK WE ARE WHOLE AND NEED NO HELP.
Thomas Wilson (1663–1735)

The One Year Bible Readings for today are **2 Kings 18:13–19:37; Acts 21:1-17; Psalm 149:1-9;** and **Proverbs 18:8.**

When Words Won't Come

Have you ever been so upset about something that you couldn't even find the words to pray? Hezekiah was. News of his impending death was more than he could handle. When he tried to talk to God about it, his emotions got the best of him. He was too choked up for the words to flow, so his tears gushed out instead. But look what happened: God heard. God saw. God responded.

Isn't it great to know prayers don't have to be pretty or polished to get God's attention? Oftentimes we feel we must be articulate for our prayers to be powerful. But prayer is not an English assignment, and God doesn't grade us on our vocabulary and grammar. God hears us even when our words are inaudible. Why? Because he sees beyond our words and into our very hearts. He knows our pain before our first tears fall. And what's even more incredible is that his love compels him to respond.

Find comfort today in knowing that even when your tears drown out your words, God still hears. God still sees. God still responds.

GOD, sometimes I just can't get my words to say what my heart feels. Thank you for reminding me that you hear me even when I can't speak. Thank you for seeing beyond my words and for understanding how I feel even better than I do. Most of all, God, thank you for caring enough to respond when you know I'm hurting.

PRAYER IS A CONDITION OF MIND, AN ATTITUDE OF HEART, WHICH GOD RECOGNIZES AS PRAYER WHETHER IT MANIFESTS ITSELF IN QUIET THINKING, IN SIGHING OR IN AUDIBLE WORDS.
Ole Hallesby (1879–1961)

When Hezekiah heard this, he turned his face to the wall and prayed to the Lord, "Remember, O Lord, how I have always tried to be faithful to you and do what is pleasing in your sight." Then he broke down and wept bitterly. But before Isaiah had left the middle courtyard, this message came to him from the Lord: "Go back to Hezekiah, the leader of my people. Tell him, 'This is what the Lord, the God of your ancestor David, says: I have heard your prayer and seen your tears. I will heal you, and three days from now you will get out of bed and go to the Temple of the Lord.' "
2 Kings 20:2-5

The One Year Bible Readings for today are **2 Kings 20:1–22:2; Acts 21:18-36; Psalm 150:1-6;** and **Proverbs 18:9-10.**

JULY

3

The Joy of Following God

Oh, the joys of those who do not follow the advice of the wicked, or stand around with sinners, or join in with scoffers. But they delight in doing everything the Lord wants; day and night they think about his law.

Psalm 1:1-2

Awful advice, crushing consequences, and a raunchy reputation—that's what you can get when you follow worldly counsel and people. What do you get when you follow God? Joy! There is delight in doing what God wants because it is only then that we are doing what we were created to do. We are accomplishing our purpose. We are following the counsel of an all-wise, all-knowing God and experiencing the countless benefits that come with that: We're not harming anyone and being eaten alive with guilt. We're not continually embarrassing ourselves (and those who love us) with our behavior. But how in the world can we do *everything* the Lord wants? By surrendering to him and immersing ourselves in his Word, we will begin to delight in doing what he has planned. Thinking about his law day and night is what brings true joy not only to *our* hearts but also to God's.

GOD, more than anything, I want to make you happy. I want to do and be all that you planned when you created me. It's your counsel I want to follow, your side I want to be on, and your behavior I most want to imitate. Help me to continually think of you and the words you wrote so that I might experience your joy. May you smile when you think of me.

JOY IS THE MOST INFALLIBLE SIGN OF THE PRESENCE OF GOD. Léon Henri Marie Bloy (1846–1917)

The One Year Bible Readings for today are **2 Kings 22:3–23:30; Acts 21:37–22:16; Psalm 1:1-6;** and **Proverbs 18:11-12.**

facts

Getting the Facts

What a shame, what folly, to give advice before listening to the facts!
Proverbs 18:13

This proverb tells us how important it is to listen to the facts *before* giving advice—and how easy it is to give advice *before* listening. We are not alone in this dilemma. The Bible gives examples of times when people attempted to take action before they had all the facts. Paul was nearly flogged because the magistrates didn't know that he was a Roman citizen (see Acts 22). The jailer in Acts 16 almost took his own life because he didn't know that no prisoners had escaped during the earthquake that freed Paul and Silas. On the other hand, Jesus continually gave facts to his disciples so that they would be able to give accurate advice. You and I can do a great deal of harm when we jump to conclusions and give advice before we listen to the facts. Advisors must have adequate information if the advice they give is to be useful. Be sure you listen to the facts and to the one speaking before you offer advice. Not doing so, as this verse says, is shame and folly.

LORD, let the advice I give be based on facts, not on feelings or false representation. Keep me from jumping to conclusions and becoming involved in folly. Let my words be consistent with your Word. Help me to be an advisor who listens to the facts and gives godly counsel.

NATURE HAS GIVEN MEN ONE TONGUE BUT TWO EARS, THAT WE MAY HEAR FROM OTHERS TWICE AS MUCH AS WE SPEAK. Epictetus (ca. 50–120)

The One Year Bible Readings for today are **2 Kings 23:31–25:30; Acts 22:17–23:10; Psalm 2:1-12;** and **Proverbs 18:13.**

JULY
5

knowing

Knowing God

You, O Lord, are a shield around me, my glory, and the one who lifts my head high. I cried out to the Lord, and he answered me from his holy mountain. I lay down and slept. I woke up in safety, for the Lord was watching over me. . . . Victory comes from you, O Lord. May your blessings rest on your people.
Psalm 3:3-5, 8

At times the world paints a distorted picture of the Lord. In fact, misrepresentation occurs more often than not. In order for us to get a clear picture of God, we must read the Bible. In his Word, we are able to get an accurate representation of who he is and of how he operates. For instance, in this one passage from Psalm 3 we learn the following:

- The Lord is our shield. He protects us, defends us, and guards us.
- The Lord is the One who lifts our heads high. We do not have to be ashamed as we follow him.
- He answers us when we cry out and watches over us when we sleep. What comfort there is in knowing that he is ever present.
- Victory and blessings come from him.

These are true statements about the Lord and his character on which our confidence can rest. As we internalize these and other truths about God that we find throughout the Scriptures, we gain a deeper knowledge of who he is and how he operates. The Word helps us to know him better and better.

FATHER, help me to take the time to read and learn of you from your Word. Show me your true self—who you are and how you operate. Help me, Father, to be assured of your protection and watchful eye. Open my heart to your truth so that I can know and trust you more.

LIFE'S MAJOR PURSUIT IS NOT KNOWING SELF . . . BUT KNOWING GOD. . . . UNLESS GOD IS THE MAJOR PURSUIT OF OUR LIVES, ALL OTHER PURSUITS ARE DEAD-END STREETS, INCLUDING TRYING TO KNOW OURSELVES. Charles R. Swindoll (b. 1934)

The One Year Bible Readings for today are **1 Chronicles 1:1–2:17; Acts 23:11-35; Psalm 3:1-8;** and **Proverbs 18:14-15.**

fear

Banishing Fear

You have given me greater joy than those who have abundant harvests of grain and wine. I will lie down in peace and sleep, for you alone, O Lord, will keep me safe.
Psalm 4:7-8

The September 11 hijackings and terrorist assaults were a shock and a tragedy for our nation. The magnitude of the attacks cut to the soul of Americans, bringing trauma and panic. The following summer, multiple children were abducted, some from their own homes . . . their own bedrooms. It would seem that the safety of the people of our country has been under attack. In many people's lives, fear has taken the place of peace and safety. Moms, dads, grandparents, and youth wonder, *How can I ever feel safe and secure again?*

Just as the psalmist reminds us in these verses that true joy is not based on our having an "abundant harvest of grain or wine" because joy comes from the Lord, peace and safety come from him as well. When we allow fear to govern our lives, it not only paralyzes us and undermines our faith, it also robs us of many things, including a peaceful night's sleep. Just as joy comes from the Lord, peaceful sleep is a benefit and by-product of trusting in him.

HEAVENLY FATHER, wrap your arms around me and drive out any fear. When I'm afraid, help me to run to you. Thank you for keeping me safe and for providing me with the ability to lie down in peaceful sleep. Help me to always keep my mind focused on you—the source of my joy and peace.

THE BETTER YOU BECOME ACQUAINTED WITH GOD, THE LESS TENSIONS YOU FEEL AND THE MORE PEACE YOU POSSESS. Charles L. Allen (b. 1913)

The One Year Bible Readings for today are **1 Chronicles 2:18–4:4; Acts 24:1-27; Psalm 4:1-8;** and **Proverbs 18:16-18.**

JULY

7

prayer

A Simple Prayer

There was a man named Jabez who was more distinguished than any of his brothers. His mother named him Jabez because his birth had been so painful. He was the one who prayed to the God of Israel, "Oh, that you would bless me and extend my lands! Please be with me in all that I do, and keep me from all trouble and pain!" And God granted him his request.

1 Chronicles 4:9-10

What a powerful prayer and witness God put in the book of 1 Chronicles. Each of us can identify with one or more of the requests Jabez made. He asked for God's blessing and the extension of his lands. He prayed for God to be close to him. And he asked that no trouble or pain enter his life. If God had chosen to grant any one of those requests, Jabez would have been a blessed man. But God gave an answer for each of these petitions and in doing so, fulfilled his plans for this man.

We can learn many things from Jabez and his prayer. Perhaps one of the most important is the fact that Jabez prayed; he asked. He sought God's blessing. It is essential that we pray—that we talk with God. A simple prayer to God changed the life of Jabez dramatically. We have the same accessibility to the same heavenly Father who granted Jabez his request.

THANK YOU, FATHER, for putting Jabez and his prayer in the Bible. Thank you for loving me and for being just as accessible to me as you were to Jabez. Let me never take the privilege of prayer for granted. And thank you for hearing my simple prayers.

PRAYER IS MEN COOPERATING WITH GOD IN BRINGING FROM HEAVEN TO EARTH HIS WONDROUSLY GOOD PLANS FOR US.
Catherine Marshall (1914–1983)

The One Year Bible Readings for today are **1 Chronicles 4:5–5:17; Acts 25:1-27; Psalm 5:1-12;** and **Proverbs 18:19.**

Satisfying Words

Words satisfy the soul as food satisfies the stomach; the right words on a person's lips bring satisfaction. Those who love to talk will experience the consequences, for the tongue can kill or nourish life.
Proverbs 18:20-21

We all know how refreshing it is to hear words of life, hope, and encouragement. They can help our performance and brighten our attitudes. The right word at the right time can bring us renewed vigor for a task and can challenge us to improve. Young or old, people blossom under the influence of encouraging words. Too often, however, we do not hear encouraging words. Worse yet, sometimes we do not *speak* encouraging words.

Our tongues have the ability to kill or to nourish life. That is a tremendous amount of power and responsibility. The right words bring satisfaction to both the person listening and the person speaking. We have the choice whether or not to encourage—to allow our words to nourish life—or to discourage with our words and crush someone's spirit. We cannot make that choice for another person, nor can we control what comes from the lips of someone else. Everyone must choose for themselves. But these verses tell us that the God-pleasing choice is obvious: choose the "right words" that can bring satisfaction.

HEAVENLY FATHER, please give me the right words to speak, words that will satisfy the soul of every listener. Let my words encourage and not discourage those who hear me speak. Help my tongue to nourish life and not to kill. And perhaps most important of all, help me to encourage others to be encouragers.

SING THEM OVER AGAIN TO ME,
WONDERFUL WORDS OF LIFE.

Philip P. Bliss (1838–1876)

The One Year Bible Readings for today are **1 Chronicles 5:18–6:81; Acts 26:1-32; Psalm 6:1-10;** and **Proverbs 18:20-21.**

JULY

9

opening

Opening Our Minds and Hearts

End the wickedness of the ungodly, but help all those who obey you. For you look deep within the mind and heart, O righteous God. God is my shield, saving those whose hearts are true and right. . . . I will thank the Lord because he is just; I will sing praise to the name of the Lord Most High.
Psalm 7:9-10, 17

Have you ever imagined someone looking deep within your mind and heart? The thought may actually be a little frightening. We don't typically open our minds and hearts to others. Often we imagine that the thoughts and memories buried there are hidden from everyone else. We determine that no one will ever know what is truly in our hearts or what we are thinking unless we choose to allow it. This kind of thinking is not completely accurate. The psalmist reveals the actual truth. The truth is that God not only looks into our hearts and minds, but he looks *deep within*. We might as well extend an open invitation to the Lord to search us and know us, for he is already capable of this. Our willingness to volunteer for this access to our private thoughts and to the matters of our heart can help us to keep our hearts and minds pure and true and right. God looks deep within. Welcome this intimacy with him.

FATHER, I invite you into the innermost parts of my heart and mind. Look deep within me. Help me to make daily decisions to keep the door of my heart and mind open to you. Help me to embrace your entrance and searching and to welcome and delight in your presence in every area of my life.

GOD KNOWS US THROUGH AND THROUGH. NOT THE MOST SECRET THOUGHT, WHICH WE MOST HIDE FROM OURSELVES, IS HIDDEN FROM HIM. AS THEN WE COME TO KNOW OURSELVES THROUGH AND THROUGH, WE COME TO SEE OURSELVES MORE AS GOD SEES US, AND THEN WE CATCH SOME LITTLE GLIMPSE OF HIS DESIGNS WITH US, EACH CHECK TO OUR DESIRES.
Edward Bouberie Pusey (1800–1882)

The One Year Bible Readings for today are **1 Chronicles 7:1–8:40; Acts 27:1-20; Psalm 7:1-17;** and **Proverbs 18:22.**

awesome

Awesome God

God and only God can be described with such powerful images as those recorded in this psalm. The majesty and brilliance of our God fills the earth. The glory of God is higher than the heavens. Even children and infants give him praise. He set the sky, the moon and the stars, and all the galaxies in place. He is truly an awesome God! When we consider these images and descriptions, it stretches our minds to realize that God, the almighty Creator, actually considers us. Who are we? "Mortals" and "mere humans," the psalmist says. And not only does God *consider* us, but he has placed us only a little lower than himself. And he has crowned us with glory and honor and put us in charge of caring for the earth. There is no doubt that these acts of our heavenly Father should produce words of praise from our lips— praise to him and for him. "O Lord, our Lord, the majesty of your name fills the earth!"

LORD, we praise you for who you are. Your glory is higher than the heavens. Your majesty fills the earth. We worship and adore you. Help us to walk as your children, giving honor and glory to you and never losing sight of your power or your love. You are our Lord.

ON EARTH JOIN ALL YE CREATURES TO EXTOL HIM FIRST, HIM LAST, HIM MIDST, AND WITHOUT END.
John Milton (1608–1674)

O Lord, our Lord, the majesty of your name fills the earth! Your glory is higher than the heavens. You have taught children and nursing infants to give you praise. They silence your enemies who were seeking revenge. When I look at the night sky and see the work of your fingers—the moon and the stars you have set in place—what are mortals that you should think of us, mere humans that you should care for us? For you made us only a little lower than God, and you crowned us with glory and honor.
Psalm 8:1-5

The One Year Bible Readings for today are **1 Chronicles 9:1–10:14; Acts 27:21-44; Psalm 8:1-9;** and **Proverbs 18:23-24.**

JULY

11

refuge

A Shelter and Refuge

The Lord is a shelter for the oppressed, a refuge in times of trouble. Those who know your name trust in you, for you, O Lord, have never abandoned anyone who searches for you.
Psalm 9:9-10

Oppression and trouble are not pleasant things to encounter. Nevertheless, we do experience both of them in our lives. Oppression pushes us down and hinders our ability to grow and to be all we were meant to be. Trouble harasses and inconveniences us and causes worry to creep into our lives. Oppression and trouble try their best to keep us from enjoying our days. A small dose of either can send us into a tailspin. We need a solution—a solution that can give us hope—a solution that can come against oppression and give us protection in times of trouble.

The psalmist declares that the Lord is the solution. Knowing his name means understanding, declaring, proclaiming, and confessing who God is and what he does. It means discovering more and more the grandeur, the glory, and the unshakable foundation of his character. As we know his name, trust him more fully, and search for him more diligently, oppression and trouble lose their effectiveness. The Lord is our shelter and refuge. He has never abandoned anyone who sought him, and he will never abandon us!

FATHER, I want to know your name! Guide me as I purpose to increase my knowledge of you. Help me to understand the importance of loving you, trusting you, and seeking you. When oppression and trouble come my way, shelter me and be my refuge, for I know that you have never abandoned anyone who searches for you.

WE MUST TRUST GOD. WE MUST TRUST NOT ONLY THAT HE DOES WHAT IS BEST, BUT THAT HE KNOWS WHAT IS AHEAD. Max Lucado (b. 1955)

The One Year Bible Readings for today are **1 Chronicles 11:1–12:18; Acts 28:1-31; Psalm 9:1-12;** and **Proverbs 19:1-3.**

agenda

Seeking God's Agenda

Instead of making plans and asking God to bless them, David sought the Lord. Although he was a great leader who had enjoyed many successive victories, he took time to seek the Lord about how to proceed when facing his enemy. When he had soundly defeated the Philistines, he didn't attack the same way again just because it worked the first time. Each attempted victory had a different plan.

Often, however, *we* devise a plan or follow a plan that worked five years ago and then ask God to support it. But that is altogether different from seeking God's agenda and his will for a current battle or a new problem as David did—to inquire and ask God's direction before we proceed with a plan. Whether you are dealing with a job or family issue, a puzzling dilemma, or a financial challenge, ask God what to do today. And just as the Lord answered David, he will show you the way.

LORD, I ask you concerning [insert situation] that I'm facing today; what should I do? I don't want to run ahead of your plan. I want to follow David's example and seek your wisdom first. Only then can I be sure that I will be following your plan. Guide my actions by your wisdom and truth.

ALL HEAVEN IS WAITING TO HELP THOSE WHO WILL DISCOVER THE WILL OF GOD AND DO IT.
J. Robert Ashcroft (1878–1958)

The Philistines had arrived in the valley of Rephaim and raided it. So David asked God, "Should I go out to fight the Philistines? Will you hand them over to me?" The Lord replied, "Yes, go ahead. I will give you the victory." . . . But after a while, the Philistines returned and raided the valley again. And once again David asked God what to do. "Do not attack them straight on," God replied. "Instead, circle around behind them and attack them near the balsam trees."
1 Chronicles 14:9-10, 13-14

The One Year Bible Readings for today are **1 Chronicles 12:19–14:17; Romans 1:1-17; Psalm 9:13-20;** and **Proverbs 19:4-5.**

JULY

13

seek

Hide and Seek

O Lord, why do you stand so far away? Why do you hide when I need you the most?
Psalm 10:1

The psalmist's question is not an uncommon one to ask when our lives turn upside down. It is difficult to grasp the idea that a loving God might hide away while chaos seems to be reigning. The psalmist was honest with God. He didn't conceal his fears or the feeling that he was alone in his battle. Yet he also encouraged himself with these words: "You hear, O Lord, the desire of the afflicted; you encourage them, and you listen to their cry" (Psalm 10:17, NIV). This assurance was birthed out of past experiences when God heard him in his time of need and responded.

Sometimes we are frustrated or overwhelmed when we cannot fix the battles that threaten us or our loved ones. Honesty with God is not a lack of faith but rather an admittance that we are powerless to turn the situation around. The good news is that producing strength and beauty out of darkness is God's specialty. When we seek him in the hard times, we find that he is not far away and that he is faithful.

ABBA, FATHER, sometimes I feel abandoned when I can't fix my circumstances. Please help me to trust you, to place this situation in your hands, for you can see this battle from a perspective that I do not have. Lord, though I feel weak, I know that I am strong as I lean on your strength rather than my own.

YOU SAY, "BUT HE HAS NOT ANSWERED." HE HAS, HE IS SO NEAR TO YOU THAT HIS SILENCE IS THE ANSWER. HIS SILENCE IS BIG WITH TERRIFIC MEANING THAT YOU CANNOT UNDERSTAND YET BUT PRESENTLY YOU WILL.
Oswald Chambers (1874–1917)

The One Year Bible Readings for today are **1 Chronicles 15:1–16:36; Romans 1:18-32; Psalm 10:1-15;** and **Proverbs 19:6-7.**

SUCCESS

Seesaw Success

King David went in and sat before the Lord and prayed, "Who am I, O Lord God, and what is my family, that you have brought me this far?"
1 Chronicles 17:16

When two children climb onto a seesaw, there is only one rule: to go up, you have to go down. True humility is the ability to look up, no matter how high the mountaintop on which you stand. Just as children work in tandem to soar high in the sky on a seesaw, God lifts us to higher places when we push our pride, our ambition, our thoughts of grandeur down and lift his name for all to see. King David was a shepherd boy when God plucked him from the green pastures to rule a kingdom. It must have been a heady experience to have riches, servants, and power at his fingertips. Yet David never lost sight of the fact that God was the resource behind all his triumphs. Even amidst the afterglow of a successful battle, David humbled himself and lifted the name of God high above his own. He had grasped the secret that he was a great ruler because of the might of the one, true King.

GOD, your ways are higher than mine. You have plans for me that I cannot even fathom. Yet it is easy to bask in my successes and forget that it is you who have blessed me. Lord, let me tell someone today about the goodness of God. Help me to lift your name high for all to see.

HUMILITY IS RECOGNIZING THAT GOD AND OTHERS ARE RESPONSIBLE FOR THE ACHIEVEMENTS IN MY LIFE. Bill Gothard (b. 1934)

The One Year Bible Readings for today are **1 Chronicles 16:37–18:17; Romans 2:1-24; Psalm 10:16-18;** and **Proverbs 19:8-9.**

JULY

15

price

The Price Is Never Right

People with good sense restrain their anger; they earn esteem by overlooking wrongs.
Proverbs 19:11

When we place an item on a scale, it is the moment of truth, whether we are measuring fruit, a bouncing baby, precious metals, or our own body weight. The scales measure loss or gain with unflinching accuracy. How do we weigh the value of self-control? It might be measured by calculating the losses. What is the cost when we unleash anger without restraint? Self-control is the act of hesitating and counting the cost before we speak a word or carry out an action.

How many times have we fallen at the Savior's feet and asked him to cover our shortcomings with his grace? Each time he has forgiven us and brought us back into fellowship with him. Counting other's wrongs seems natural—until we measure them against our own failures and the unconditional love we have been granted in Christ.

Weighing an unruly temper against self-control is much the same as measuring scrap aluminum against gold. One is cutting and worth little; the other is of great value.

GOD, help me to forgive others in light of the unconditional love I have found in you. Help me to see past my anger and to resolve disagreements with wisdom and grace. Help me to measure my words and actions before I speak or act. When others wrong me, may I remember all the times you reached down and covered my wrongs with your mercy, and may I be filled with your love for them.

DON'T GET ANGRY AT THE PERSON WHO ACTS IN WAYS THAT DISPLEASE YOU. GIVE HIM THE SMILE HE LACKS. SPREAD THE SUNSHINE OF GOD'S LIMITLESS LOVE. Joni Eareckson Tada (b. 1949)

The One Year Bible Readings for today are **1 Chronicles 19:1–21:30; Romans 2:25–3:8; Psalm 11:1-7;** and **Proverbs 19:10-12.**

I Have Good News!

All have sinned; all fall short of God's glorious standard. Yet now God in his gracious kindness declares us not guilty. He has done this through Christ Jesus, who has freed us by taking away our sins.
Romans 3:23-24

As the song "Amazing Grace" resounded in the sanctuary, a woman on the front pew wept with joy. It seemed only yesterday that she had sat in a prison cell, shaking as her body suffered from withdrawal. She remembered crying out to a God she didn't know, hoping that someone would hear her prayers. In that dark hour God sent women from a local church to tell her the good news that Christ could heal her and take away her sins. One year later she was not only free from the four walls of prison, but God had healed her of a ten-year addiction.

When the women entered the prison that first day, they felt shy, inadequate, and unsure in that environment but confident in God. And they were God's answer to the prisoner's prayers. Many times we feel inadequate to reach out to others. We make the gospel cumbersome or complicated and fear sharing it. Yet it is a simple message: God in his grace has declared us not guilty. We are free from sin through Jesus Christ. We encounter many every day who are crying out to a God they do not know, hoping someone will hear their prayers. Let's share the Good News!

SAVIOR, every day people who are hurting and lost surround me. Help me to share the good news that you are the Christ and that you have set us free! Lord, if there are those in my life who are crying out to you, open my spiritual eyes that I might see, and give me the courage to share the gospel message with them.

JESUS CHRIST IS GOD'S EVERYTHING FOR MAN'S TOTAL NEED. Richard Halverson (1916–1995)

The One Year Bible Readings for today are **1 Chronicles 22:1–23:32; Romans 3:9-31; Psalm 12:1-8;** and **Proverbs 19:13-14.**

JULY

17

hymns

Battle Hymns

I trust in your unfailing love. I will rejoice because you have rescued me. I will sing to the Lord because he has been so good to me.

Psalm 13:5-6

In the early verses of Psalm 13, the psalmist called out to God and heard nothing in reply. What could he count on to carry him through that bleak moment? He reached deep within and pulled out memories of the times God had rescued him in the past, times he had his back against the wall and had seen the hand of God move. Times he had felt abandoned and later discovered that God had been working behind the scenes in ways that were miraculous? It was those memories that allowed him to sing of God's goodness in the midst of overwhelming circumstances. The psalmist's experience is much like a soldier crouched behind a barrier, gunshots and fire exploding around him, unaware that the general sits on a higher plain, mapping out the enemy's next move. It is only when the smoke has cleared and the general's plan is revealed that the soldier understands that he was never alone. Sometimes we may wonder where God is when we are in the middle of a battle, but it is the memory of past victories that allows us to sing while we wait for him to rescue us.

LORD, I can't help but praise you when I remember all the times you have rescued me in the past. There were times when I felt alone and realized only later that you were there all along. I see your handiwork in those valleys as you gently guided me when I stumbled, held my hand, and lifted me to the mountaintops once again. Help me to trust you for what I am facing today.

IT IS THE TRIAL OF OUR FAITH THAT IS PRECIOUS. IF WE GO THROUGH THE TRIAL, THERE IS SO MUCH WEALTH LAID UP IN OUR HEAVENLY BANK ACCOUNT TO DRAW UPON WHEN THE NEXT TEST COMES. Oswald Chambers (1874–1917)

The One Year Bible Readings for today are **1 Chronicles 24:1–26:11; Romans 4:1-12; Psalm 13:1-6;** and **Proverbs 19:15-16.**

JULY

18

Beyond Mere Words

It is a recurring theme through both the Old and New Testaments: God cares about the needs of the poor. In the Old Testament he reminds Israel through the counsel of the prophets to remember the needy, the orphan, and the widow. In the New Testament Jesus showed the disciples that the crowd could better grasp spiritual food when their need for physical food had been met. Jesus set aside the disciples' concern and pulled little children onto his lap. He ignored the cultural prejudice of his day to offer living water to the woman at the well. Each of those acts demonstrated a love that went beyond mere words.

If you help the poor, you are lending to the Lord—and he will repay you!
Proverbs 19:17

A sermon means very little to those who are physically hungry and offers scant warmth to the one suffering in the cold, but a hand extended in compassion and love speaks volumes. One lost man once said, "Don't tell me that you care about my soul. Show me that you care, and I will respond." Are you demonstrating God's love and compassion through your actions?

LORD, I recognize that your heart beats with compassion for the poor, the fatherless, and the widow. To those who are cold, let me offer what they need to be warm. To those who are hungry, let me sacrifice so that they and their children might have food. Help me to see beyond the comfort of my own world and reach out with actions that show your love.

IF WE HAVE GOT THE TRUE LOVE OF GOD SHED ABROAD IN OUR HEARTS, WE WILL SHOW IT IN OUR LIVES. WE WILL NOT HAVE TO GO UP AND DOWN THE EARTH PROCLAIMING IT. WE WILL SHOW IT IN EVERYTHING WE SAY OR DO. D. L. Moody (1837–1899)

The One Year Bible Readings for today are **1 Chronicles 26:12–27:34; Romans 4:13–5:5; Psalm 14:1-7;** and **Proverbs 19:17.**

JULY
19

rejoice

A Reason to Rejoice

Since we were restored to friendship with God by the death of his Son while we were still his enemies, we will certainly be delivered from eternal punishment by his life. So now we can rejoice in our wonderful new relationship with God—all because of what our Lord Jesus Christ has done for us in making us friends of God.

Romans 5:10-11

This passage reminds us that our reason to rejoice is not only that our future salvation is assured, that we've been delivered from eternal punishment, or that Christ died for us while we were still his enemies. Certainly that would be reason enough! But we also rejoice because in the present, right here on earth in the midst of where we are—today, tomorrow, and all the days we are alive—we can enjoy a wonderful new relationship with our heavenly Father. This is not a distant relationship but a close, intimate one. We are blessed with this intimacy because the finished work of Christ removed every barrier standing between the Lord and us and restored our relationship so that we could be friends of God. We did nothing to accomplish this; we receive it because of what Christ did. Think of it—friends of the Almighty! If nothing else is going well today, we still have great reason to rejoice.

I rejoice in my relationship with you, Father—all because of what Jesus Christ has done for me. Having an intimate relationship with Jesus, the friend of sinners, allows me to have an eternal perspective about everything else that happens to me today. I praise you for the joy such a friendship brings.

THE WHOLE MEANING OF PRAYER IS THAT WE MAY KNOW GOD. Oswald Chambers (1874–1917)

The One Year Bible Readings for today are **1 Chronicles 28:1–29:30; Romans 5:6-21; Psalm 15:1-5;** and **Proverbs 19:18-19.**

master

Master? Master!

Now you are free from sin, your old master, and you have become slaves to your new master, righteousness.
Romans 6:18

The word *slavery* conjures up images of drudgery, menial tasks, and the forfeiture of self. It reminds us of people bent to the will of another, suffering abuse at the hands of those who have complete power over them. Why then would the apostle Paul describe both sin and righteousness in such terms? Paul knew what it was like to live in bondage to sin. Yet he had also watched as his new master tore off his chains. Sin offered to destroy his purpose. Yet Jesus reached out to him when Paul was blinded and humbled on the road to Damascus and set him on a different path—the path of life and freedom. Sin enticed Paul with pride and promises of power. Yet Jesus freed him from the confines of his self-made prison to embrace the destiny God intended for him from the beginning. Having served both masters, Paul had learned the secret and couldn't wait to share it: When we bow at the feet of Jesus, he is the only master who truly sets us free!

JESUS, I kneel at your feet again today. I ask that you be the master of my heart, of my thoughts, of my ambitions, of my time, of my life. Thank you for being such a gracious, kind, and merciful God. It is in offering my life to you that I find abundant life. It is by serving you that I find true freedom!

FREEDOM DOES NOT MEAN I AM ABLE TO DO WHATEVER I WANT TO DO. THAT'S THE WORST KIND OF BONDAGE. FREEDOM MEANS I HAVE BEEN SET FREE TO BECOME ALL THAT GOD WANTS ME TO BE, TO ACHIEVE ALL THAT GOD WANTS ME TO ACHIEVE, TO ENJOY ALL THAT GOD WANTS ME TO ENJOY.
Warren W. Wiersbe (b. 1929)

The One Year Bible Readings for today are **2 Chronicles 1:1–3:17; Romans 6:1-23; Psalm 16:1-11;** and **Proverbs 19:20-21.**

JULY

21

shine

Let It Shine

Solomon then cast ten gold lampstands according to the specifications that had been given and put them in the Temple. Five were placed against the south wall, and five were placed against the north wall.
2 Chronicles 4:7

The lampstands in the temple were merely golden ornaments until the priests poured the oil, trimmed the wicks, and lit the lampstands for the first time. Then light flooded the Holy Place and illuminated the temple. A hush came over the priests as the glory of God hovered over the temple and then filled the Holy of Holies. Thousands upon thousands stood outside—dancing, singing, and cheering as they celebrated the arrival of Jehovah to the place where he would dwell among his people. Today we who are Christians are the lampstands in a nation looking for spiritual truth. Christianity can be reduced to just one more religion, a mere ornament among the many religions the world offers, or it can burn brightly as the presence of the living God inhabits our homes, our families, and our daily lives. Like a million points of light, the body of Christ can show the way to a living God.

LIVING GOD, fan the flames of my passion for you so that others will see your light inside of me. Let the fire that burns be a steady flame, not one that flickers in winds of change or consumes with damaging heat. Let it be a light that shows the way to you.

LORD, MAKE MY LIFE A WINDOW FOR YOUR LIGHT TO SHINE THROUGH AND A MIRROR TO REFLECT YOUR LOVE TO ALL I MEET. Robert H. Schuller (b. 1929)

The One Year Bible Readings for today are **2 Chronicles 4:1–6:11; Romans 7:1-13; Psalm 17:1-15;** and **Proverbs 19:22-23.**

JULY

22

control

Spirit-Controlled Life

Those who are dominated by the sinful nature think about sinful things, but those who are controlled by the Holy Spirit think about things that please the Spirit. If your sinful nature controls your mind, there is death. But if the Holy Spirit controls your mind, there is life and peace.

Romans 8:5-6

There are so many forces in the world that aim to control our minds: the media, trends and advertising, secular philosophy, and materialism. Yet none of these brings us real life. Through computers, television, malls, and music, the enemy comes in like a flood to distract us, capture our minds, and dominate our thoughts. There's also our own sinful nature, which today's verses say will lead to death if we give over the controls of our life to it. But the good news is in the last part of verse 6: "If the Holy Spirit controls your mind, there is life and peace." Yielding our minds and thoughts to Christ Jesus will result in a spirit of calmness, a quiet confidence that he is in control no matter what is happening in the world around us. When the Spirit controls us, we are able to think about things that please God and, as this verse describes, he will allow our hearts to experience life and peace.

LORD, I want your Holy Spirit to control my mind, heart, and thoughts so that I can experience life and peace. I yield my mind to you today. Direct my thoughts. Cause me to think about things that please you. Guard my mind from being controlled by anything that is contrary to your ways. Thank you for setting me free from sin and death through the power of your life-giving Spirit!

HOLY SPIRIT, THINK THROUGH ME UNTIL YOUR IDEAS BECOME MY IDEAS. Amy Carmichael (1867–1951)

The One Year Bible Readings for today are **2 Chronicles 6:12–8:10; Romans 7:14–8:8; Psalm 18:1-15;** and **Proverbs 19:24-25.**

JULY

23

father

Father, Dear Father

You should not be like cowering, fearful slaves. You should behave instead like God's very own children, adopted into his family—calling him "Father, dear Father." For his Holy Spirit speaks to us deep in our hearts and tells us that we are God's children.

Romans 8:15-16

"God's very own children, adopted into his family." What an amazing thought, especially for those of us who are fatherless or have been abandoned or abused by our earthly fathers. We tend to see God through the filter of the dad we've known in our growing-up years. If our father was loving, affectionate, and accepting, we picture our heavenly Father the same way. But if our earthly father was harsh, critical, or unloving, it's doubtful we'll want to jump into God's lap or rest in his love. Our view of God may cause us to run from him or to close off our hearts. But God tells us to call him "Father, dear Father," not to cower or withdraw like fearful slaves but to behave like children who are dearly loved.

Think about your relationship with your earthly father or mother and about how it colored your perspective of God. If you don't see him as "Father, dear Father," bring your view of him to the throne of grace, and ask the Holy Spirit to clear your vision of him so that you can experience his true daddy-love for you.

FATHER, here's how I've seen you: [describe how you see God]. I bring to your altar that view and everything I think about you that is incorrect or contrary to your Word. Cleanse me of faulty perspectives, and renew my vision of you as my patient, merciful Father who loves me tenderly and who will never leave me or forsake me.

THE HIGHEST SCIENCE, THE LOFTIEST SPECULATION, THE MIGHTIEST PHILOSOPHY WHICH CAN EVER ENGAGE THE ATTENTION OF A CHILD OF GOD IS THE NAME, THE PERSON, THE WORK, THE DOINGS, AND THE EXISTENCE OF THE GREAT GOD WHOM HE CALLS HIS FATHER.

Charles Haddon Spurgeon (1834–1892)

The One Year Bible Readings for today are **2 Chronicles 8:11–10:19; Romans 8:9-25; Psalm 18:16-36;** and **Proverbs 19:26.**

resource

A Great Prayer Resource

Have you ever just not known how or what to pray? Perhaps you have run out of words, or a situation has left you speechless or in so much pain that all you can do is groan. In Romans 8:26 Paul explains a prayer resource we may not realize we have or do not take advantage of: the Holy Spirit. When circumstances or pain leave us without words to pray, we can yield to God's Spirit. This means that we do not pray out of our own understanding or try to figure out what to pray but we rest in the fact that he knows our heart and he knows the situation. Verse 27 says that the Father who knows all hearts also knows what the Spirit is saying on our behalf in the most baffling or distressing times. He makes prayers out of our tears, our sighs, and our groanings. What a wonderful thing to know that the Holy Spirit is interceding and, even beyond that, *pleading* for us believers *in harmony with God's will*. In addition, Jesus, at the right hand of the Father in heaven, the place of highest honor—*is praying for us!*

The Holy Spirit helps us in our distress. For we don't even know what we should pray for, nor how we should pray. But the Holy Spirit prays for us with groanings that cannot be expressed in words. And the Father who knows all hearts knows what the Spirit is saying, for the Spirit pleads for us believers in harmony with God's own will.
Romans 8:26-27

THANK YOU, HOLY SPIRIT, for praying through us in perfect agreement with God's will and, with Jesus, interceding for us at the throne of God. When we don't know the words to say or have no words at all, you carry our sighs, groans, and tears into God's presence for us. What amazing grace!

THIS IS THE GOD-GIVEN REVELATION: THAT WHEN WE ARE BORN AGAIN OF THE SPIRIT OF GOD AND INDWELT BY THE HOLY SPIRIT, HE INTERCEDES FOR US WITH A TENDERNESS AND AN UNDERSTANDING AKIN TO THE LORD JESUS CHRIST AND AKIN TO GOD, THAT IS, HE EXPRESSES THE UNUTTERABLE FOR US. Oswald Chambers (1874–1917)

The One Year Bible Readings for today are **2 Chronicles 11:1–13:22; Romans 8:26-39; Psalm 18:37-50;** and **Proverbs 19:27-29.**

JULY

25

foxhole

Foxhole Prayers

Asa cried out to the Lord his God, "O Lord, no one but you can help the powerless against the mighty! Help us, O Lord our God, for we trust in you alone. It is in your name that we have come against this vast horde. O Lord, you are our God; do not let mere men prevail against you!"
2 Chronicles 14:11

A foxhole prayer is born when a person dives into prayer out of fear or desperation, when all the usual trusted resources have failed and prayer is a last resort. Asa was surrounded by a million warriors, but his cry to God was not a foxhole prayer. It was an affirmation of his faith nurtured during times of peace. Though Asa had inherited riches and power from his father, he had learned that it was the Lord who was his provider. He called on him to help him live in trust each day. When our lives are uncomplicated, it is easy to rely on our own strength and to forget that it is God who gives us our very breath. When the hard times come, and they do come for all of us, it is our daily trust in him that will allow us to call out to our Savior in confidence.

GREAT PROVIDER, help me exercise my faith daily that I might instinctively look to you during the peaceful times as well as in the storms of life. Help me to see how you show up in even the smallest details of my life. Thank you for times of peace and for your strength during times of chaos.

ALL I HAVE SEEN TEACHES ME TO TRUST THE CREATOR FOR ALL I HAVE NOT SEEN.
Ralph Waldo Emerson (1803–1882)

The One Year Bible Readings for today are **2 Chronicles 14:1–16:14; Romans 9:1-24; Psalm 19:1-14;** and **Proverbs 20:1.**

presence

A Prayer for God's Presence

When David was in trouble, he didn't just think about how nice it would be if God showed up and helped him out. He didn't just put his request on a prayer chain or whisper a polite little prayer: "God, if you're not too busy, I'd like some help when you get a chance." No, he *cried out*—meaning literally that he *shouted* or *pleaded loudly and fervently for God's help,* believing that the Lord would hear and respond to his cries—and he did.

There are times when we also need to cry out to God, storming his sanctuary for much-needed help. Crying out to the Lord brings us his help, protection, and victory. Whatever you are facing, lift your voice aloud, and proclaim God's ability to hear you, to respond to your cry, to sustain you and help you, and to fulfill his plans for you. If someone you know comes to mind as you read this psalm, personalize this plea for him or her: "May the Lord hear and answer all *your* prayers! May we shout for joy when we hear of your victory!"

In times of trouble, may the Lord respond to your cry. May the God of Israel keep you safe from all harm. May he send you help from his sanctuary. . . . May he grant your heart's desire and fulfill all your plans. May we shout for joy when we hear of your victory, flying banners to honor our God. May the Lord answer all your prayers.
Psalm 20:1-2, 4-5

GOD, I cry out to you today about [name the situation] or for [person's name]. I am so concerned about [your concern]. Hear from heaven and answer! Grant my heart's desire! Send help from your sanctuary! Rescue by your great power! Thank you for hearing and responding to the cries of your people.

WHEN LIFE KNOCKS YOU TO YOUR KNEES, YOU'RE IN POSITION TO PRAY. Unknown

The One Year Bible Readings for today are **2 Chronicles 17:1–18:34; Romans 9:25–10:13; Psalm 20:1-9;** and **Proverbs 20:2-3.**

JULY
27

dependence

Daily Dependence

Jehoshaphat was a good king, following the ways of his father, Asa. He did what was pleasing in the Lord's sight. During his reign, however, he failed to remove all the pagan shrines, and the people never fully committed themselves to following the God of their ancestors.
2 Chronicles 20:32-33

Jehoshaphat's father, Asa, was a stubborn man who refused to admit his failures because of sin. When God's angel confronted him, Asa went into a rage, rationalizing his mistakes instead of recognizing them and moving on in repentance. When his son, Jehoshaphat, came to the throne, he learned from his father's mistakes, at least in some aspects. When the people needed religious education or there was a threat of war, Jehoshaphat turned to God for guidance and made the right choices. He relied on the Lord for the big stuff, when the odds were clearly against him. However, when it came to depending on God for guidance about everyday plans and actions, Jehoshaphat failed. We can repeat Jehoshaphat's error when we relegate God to the background in the mundane, daily stuff or the "easy" decisions of life. God wants us to give him not only the major problems and decisions we face but also the "small stuff" of life, the things we are most often fooled into believing we can control. Although you may not be facing anything major today, have you paused long enough to give your day—including the small stuff—to God?

LORD, let me not neglect spending time with you and take for granted the love and provisions you have daily for my life. Keep me from making the same mistakes Jehoshaphat made. I need your guidance just as much in the "easy" days as I do when I'm facing difficulties. I desire to prayerfully come to you, trusting in your control and sufficiency for each day.

LET GOD HAVE YOUR LIFE. HE CAN DO MORE WITH IT THAN YOU CAN. D. L. Moody (1837–1899)

The One Year Bible Readings for today are **2 Chronicles 19:1–20:37; Romans 10:14–11:12; Psalm 21:1-13;** and **Proverbs 20:4-6.**

JULY
28

honesty

Honesty with God

When someone asks, "How are you?" do you ever reply, "Oh, just great," when really you are doing anything but great? At times we talk to God that way, telling him what we think he wants to hear but not sharing our true selves. The psalmist didn't operate like that with the Lord. He told it like it was: *I'm a worm. I'm despised. I'm mocked. I'm desperate. I need you.* He even told God he felt distant and ignored by him. These may sound like brash things to say to the almighty God, but David was honest with the Lord, and God honored that honesty; he rescued David and blessed him. A great transformation, new intimacy with the Lord and rest in our souls will come into our lives when we are totally honest with God. Are you discouraged? Tell God honestly about it. Do you not even feel like praying? God receives you just as you are and stands ready to forgive, empower, and bless you as you draw near to him.

I am a worm and not a man. I am scorned and despised by all! Everyone who sees me mocks me. They sneer and shake their heads, saying, "Is this the one who relies on the Lord? Then let the Lord save him! If the Lord loves him so much, let the Lord rescue him!"

Psalm 22:6-8

FATHER, help me to be just as candid as a child when I come to you, to honestly express what I think, what I feel, and what I need. Give me confidence that you accept my honesty just as any loving father accepts his child's honest expressions of feelings or needs.

HONESTY IS A VITAL ELEMENT OF TRUE PRAYER. . . . PRAYER WILL INCREASE IN POWER AND REALITY AS WE REPUDIATE ALL PRETENSE AND LEARN TO BE UTTERLY HONEST BEFORE GOD AS WELL AS BEFORE MEN. A. W. Tozer (1897–1963)

The One Year Bible Readings for today are **2 Chronicles 21:1–23:21; Romans 11:13-36; Psalm 22:1-18;** and **Proverbs 20:7.**

JULY

29

sacrifice

A Living Sacrifice

Dear brothers and sisters, I plead with you to give your bodies to God. Let them be a living and holy sacrifice—the kind he will accept. When you think of what he has done for you, is this too much to ask? Don't copy the behavior and customs of this world, but let God transform you into a new person by changing the way you think. Then you will know what God wants you to do, and you will know how good and pleasing and perfect his will really is.

Romans 12:1-2

Perhaps one of the most powerful and life-changing prayers we can pray is the prayer of surrender we read about in this verse: "Lord, I offer myself to you as a living sacrifice." When we yield all of ourselves to God, he works and loves and thinks through us to accomplish his purposes, which are far more than we could ask or imagine. We experience enormous joy as God does his works through us. If we try to live life in our own strength, we become empty and depleted. But when we're continually offering ourselves to the Lord, he continually fills us with his spirit of love, joy, peace, and patience.

Verse 2 is also an important part of the equation: we are to couple that surrender to God with seeking his transforming work in us. He makes us into new people from the inside out by changing the way we think as our minds are renewed with his Word. As this happens, we will know increasingly that good, pleasing, and complete will of God for our lives.

LORD, I don't know what this day will hold, but I give myself to you as a living sacrifice. Renew and transform my mind with your truth. Make me a new person, and show me what you want me to do—the good work you've designed me to do, that task to accomplish, the one person you want me to minister to or encourage today. And may you get all the glory!

TO PRAY IS TO CHANGE. PRAYER IS THE CENTRAL AVENUE GOD USES TO TRANSFORM US.
Richard J. Foster (b. 1943)

The One Year Bible Readings for today are **2 Chronicles 24:1–25:28; Romans 12:1-21; Psalm 22:19-31;** and **Proverbs 20:8-10.**

JULY
30

voice

A Familiar Voice

In the eastern tradition, a shepherd walks at the head of the flock. This is much different from the western tradition of driving the sheep from behind. The shepherd calls the flock out of the pen in the early morning to lead them to pools or wells of water where they can quench their thirst. He then guides them to green pastures, taking them around the rocky places where they might stumble. He assists the tiny and fragile sheep by lifting them with the crook of his staff. He runs his hand over the sheep as they enter the pen, counting them and ensuring that they have returned from the pasture unharmed. Then the shepherd settles in for the night to watch for predators. How awesome that Jesus is our shepherd. He will lead us to living water and guide us along the right path even when the way is rocky. He carries us when we stumble and watches over us during the dark nights of our lives, making us feel secure. All that he asks is that we respond to his voice and follow him.

The Lord is my shepherd; I have everything I need. He lets me rest in green meadows; he leads me beside peaceful streams. He renews my strength. He guides me along right paths, bringing honor to his name.
Psalm 23:1-3

It is comforting to know that I am not alone in the journey called life. God, I thank you that you are ever vigilant, watching over me, meeting with me in the morning, and abiding with me through the night. May I always respond to your voice and stay close to you. I gladly follow you as you call my name!

LORD, HELP ME TO REMEMBER THAT NOTHING IS GOING TO HAPPEN TODAY THAT YOU AND I CANNOT HANDLE. Unknown

The One Year Bible Readings for today are **2 Chronicles 26:1–28:27; Romans 13:1-14; Psalm 23:1-6;** and **Proverbs 20:11.**

JULY

31

blanket

A Warm Blanket

Let us aim for harmony in the church and try to build each other up.
Romans 14:19

Yarn can be used as a cat toy or something to tie around a finger to remind us to buy milk. That same yarn, when placed in skilled hands, can become a colorful crocheted blanket or knitted sweater. When blue yarn and yellow yarn are placed side by side, they may seem like a mismatch. Yet knitted together they can be a work of art. A single strand is pulled apart easily, but combined strands are strong. A skein of yarn does little to bring warmth, but turned into a crocheted coverlet, that skein can warm the shoulders of those who are cold. Just as a field of flowers may wave with various shapes and hues of colors, the body of Christ is sprinkled with differences. When we stand side by side, our differences may seem like a mismatch, but the common ground is a love for God and a desire to please him. When we come together in unity, the church is strengthened and we can bring beauty and warmth into the lives of others.

LORD, help me to recognize that you are the master artist. You have created us the way a painter fashions a masterpiece. The differences I have stumbled over may be the very things you needed to create a work of art that can minister to a diverse and hurting world.

THERE CAN BE NO UNITY, NO DELIGHT OF LOVE, NO HARMONY, NO GOOD BEING, WHERE THERE IS BUT ONE. TWO AT LEAST ARE NEEDED FOR ONENESS. George Macdonald (1824–1905)

The One Year Bible Readings for today are **2 Chronicles 29:1-36; Romans 14:1-23; Psalm 24:1-10;** and **Proverbs 20:12.**

storm

Soaring through the Storm

Show me the path where I should walk, O Lord; point out the right road for me to follow. Lead me by your truth and teach me, for you are the God who saves me. All day long I put my hope in you.
Psalm 25:4-5

Have you ever been on an airplane as it flew through a thunderstorm? All around you, you see and hear the storm's beating rain and the wind whipping against the cabin wall. Looks of worry and panic cloud passengers' faces, and they wonder, *When will we ever get to the other side of this storm?* They long to see the sun, and even before the plane has landed, a few of them may have begun forming a line to get off. On such a turbulent flight we can dramatically experience the light and peace after a storm almost instantly. Peace replaces anxiety in just a moment as we break through a cloud and see the sun and its radiance just on the other side of the storm.

As God's children we do not need to wait until our personal storms have passed in order to see and experience the light and peace of the Son. The Word of God, his truth, not only sustains us in the storms of life but also opens our eyes to see the Son, the radiance of God's glory, while we are soaring through them.

DEAR LORD, I want to know your will. I'm willing to do your will, and I'll wait, in hope, for your truth to lead me in it. No matter what storms of life I may face, I will keep my eyes on the brightness of your Son—the radiance of your glory!

GOD IS THE LIGHT IN MY DARKNESS, THE VOICE IN MY SILENCE. Helen Keller (1880–1968)

The One Year Bible Readings for today are **2 Chronicles 30:1–31:21; Romans 15:1-22; Psalm 25:1-15;** and **Proverbs 20:13-15.**

AUGUST
2

grace

A Picture of God's Grace

Manasseh led the people of Judah and Jerusalem to do even more evil than the pagan nations whom the Lord had destroyed when the Israelites entered the land. . . . So the Lord sent the Assyrian armies, and they took Manasseh prisoner. They put a ring through his nose, bound him in bronze chains, and led him away to Babylon. But while in deep distress, Manasseh sought the Lord his God and cried out humbly to the God of his ancestors. And when he prayed, the Lord listened to him and was moved by his request for help.
2 Chronicles 33:9-13

Manasseh not only practiced evil himself; he led the whole nation of Judah and the people of Jerusalem to do even more evil than the pagan nations had thought of. He practiced witchcraft and sorcery, burned his own sons at a pagan altar, and to top it all off, defiled the temple of God by placing an idol of the sex goddess Asherah there. That was the last straw for God. After giving numerous warnings, the Lord caused Manasseh to be captured by the Assyrians and led away to Babylon like an animal. Now if anyone didn't deserve God's help, it was Manasseh. But in his captivity he cried out to God in humility and repentance, and the Lord not only listened but let Manasseh go back to Jerusalem and restored his kingdom. Manasseh forever after knew that the Lord alone is God.

For any of us who may have fallen away from God, either in open rebellion or in taking subtle steps off his path, this passage is a picture of God's loving grace and desire to forgive and restore. He wants us to humble ourselves before him, and he will heal and redeem our lives.

LORD, how amazing your grace, forgiveness, and restoration are! I praise you for your mercy and loving-kindness offered so freely to me. I want to follow you, but when I stray from your paths, help me to humbly cry out to you as Manasseh did, and let me know the joy of your forgiveness and healing.

THE MOST MARVELOUS INGREDIENT IN THE FORGIVENESS OF GOD IS THAT HE ALSO FORGETS, THE ONE THING A HUMAN BEING CAN NEVER DO.
Oswald Chambers (1874–1917)

The One Year Bible Readings for today are **2 Chronicles 32:1–33:13; Romans 15:23–16:9; Psalm 25:16-22;** and **Proverbs 20:16-18.**

seeing

Seeing Clearly

Imagine driving down a winding mountain road through thick fog without your headlights on. As you inch forward, you strain to see the road through the gloom in hopes of not making a wrong move and careening off the mountain. It's a frightening picture, isn't it? Yet we sometimes travel the road of life in the same way, moving forward with our own agenda and relationships but without the light of God's Word and prayer to guide us. In Paul's final words to the Romans in this chapter, he advises them to stay away from false teachers and smooth-talking people, to steer clear of evil, and to follow the truth. How can they do this? The same way we do today: by asking God to help us see clearly what is right and by being obedient to the Lord. The good news is that we aren't left to accomplish such a daunting task on our own. Jesus Christ, as the One who lights up the world at large also lights our own personal paths as well. He gave us his Word to help us live "innocent of any wrong" and gives us his Spirit to lead us into all truth.

Everyone knows that you are obedient to the Lord. This makes me very happy. I want you to see clearly what is right and to stay innocent of any wrong.
Romans 16:19

DEAR FATHER, how I long to travel life's road seeing clearly and living innocent of wrong. Help me to depend completely on the light of your Son, Jesus, who helps me see the path you have for me and through the truth of your Word leads me gently on it.

GOD WANTS US TO FEEL THAT OUR WAY THROUGH LIFE IS ROUGH AND PERPLEXING, SO THAT WE MAY LEARN THANKFULLY TO LEAN ON HIM. THEREFORE, HE TAKES STEPS TO DRIVE US OUT OF SELF-CONFIDENCE TO TRUST IN HIMSELF.
J. I. Packer (b. 1926)

The One Year Bible Readings for today are **2 Chronicles 33:14–34:33; Romans 16:10-27; Psalm 26:1-12;** and **Proverbs 20:19.**

fear

No Fear

The Lord is my light and my salvation—so why should I be afraid? The Lord protects me from danger—so why should I tremble? When evil people come to destroy me, when my enemies and foes attack me, they will stumble and fall. Though a mighty army surrounds me, my heart will know no fear. Even if they attack me, I remain confident.
Psalm 27:1-3

Fear is a powerful thing. It can push its way into so many areas of our lives. We all know someone who fears death or illness, pain and suffering, defeat, accidents, or failure. In fact, you may have some of those—and perhaps many others—on your own list of things you fear. Fear can undermine our faith, paralyze our progress, and blur the vision we have received from God. Fear is capable of robbing us of joy and peace.

David claimed that his heart would "know no fear." And the reason for this confidence was that the Lord was his light, his salvation, and his protector. This psalm is a reminder to all of us. Why should we be afraid? Why should we tremble? We can have the same confidence and assurance that David did if the Lord is our light and our salvation. It is he who protects us from danger.

FATHER, help me to see the truth in your Word. You are my light and my salvation. You are my protector from danger and from evil. Help me, Father, to draw close to you and to rest in the confidence I have in you. Help me to defeat fear in my life as I trust in you.

ONLY HE WHO CAN SAY, "THE LORD IS THE STRENGTH OF MY LIFE," CAN SAY, "OF WHOM SHALL I BE AFRAID?" Alexander Maclaren (1826–1910)

The One Year Bible Readings for today are **2 Chronicles 35:1–36:23; 1 Corinthians 1:1-17; Psalm 27:1-6;** and **Proverbs 20:20-21.**

Draw Near

near

When the Lord calls us to draw near to his throne of grace, to pray or wait on him, how often we respond, *Lord, I'm busy. I have so much to do today. I don't have time for prayer.* When his Spirit whispers someone's name to our hearts and nudges us to intercede for that person or make a phone call, we think, *I'll do that later when I've got everything done or get caught up on my sleep.* Our intentions may be good, but then in the crush of tasks and activities, we forget prayer.

My heart has heard you say, "Come and talk with me." And my heart responds, "Lord, I am coming."
Psalm 27:8

A life ruled by to-do lists and Day-Timers instead of by God's Spirit robs us of the intimacy with him that he wants us to experience. But when we respond, "Yes, Lord, I am coming!" to God's gentle whispers, we are open to the life-giving power of the Lord's Spirit and his grace, and help flows not only into our own life but also into the lives of others as we pray on their behalf.

LORD, give me such a desire for you that I will run to you right away when you say, "Come." Help me to be willing to lay aside my to-do lists and to come into your presence and talk with you. Tune my ears to your voice, and make my heart sensitive to your nudgings.

GOD OFTEN VISITS US, BUT MOST OF THE TIME WE ARE NOT AT HOME. Danish proverb

The One Year Bible Readings for today are **Ezra 1:1–2:70; 1 Corinthians 1:18–2:5; Psalm 27:7-14;** and **Proverbs 20:22-23.**

AUGUST
6

hears

He Hears!

Praise the Lord! For he has heard my cry for mercy. The Lord is my strength, my shield from every danger. I trust in him with all my heart. He helps me, and my heart is filled with joy. I burst out in songs of thanksgiving.
Psalm 28:6-7

This psalm encourages us to lift our hearts in gratitude and praise to God because he has heard our cries. And because he has heard, our hearts are helped even before the situation changes. Because we live in a high-tech world, we have become accustomed to instant messages and immediate replies to our e-mails. Caller ID, call waiting, pagers, and cell phones encourage an almost certain "no waiting period" for conversation, and speed-dial links allow us to connect even more quickly. However, many times when we pray, we don't hear a booming voice instantly reply from heaven, "Message has been sent and received." We may have poured out our requests but seen nothing change in the circumstances. Yet deep inside we can know that God has heard us. Even when we do not have the *feeling* of being heard, we still have the *fact*. We have God's word on it: The Lord "has heard my cry for mercy."

FATHER, thank you for hearing my prayers . . . always! Even when my situation remains the same, grant me grace to trust you and to thank you for your listening ear and your gracious help. Because of your mercy, I will sing songs of thanksgiving to you. Because of your help, may my heart be filled with joy!

O LORD! THAT LENDS ME LIFE,
LEND ME A HEART REPLETE WITH THANKFULNESS!
William Shakespeare (1564–1616)

The One Year Bible Readings for today are **Ezra 3:1–4:23; 1 Corinthians 2:6–3:4; Psalm 28:1-9;** and **Proverbs 20:24-25.**

voice

The Voice of the Lord

Our God has a powerful voice. He "approaches with the noise of thunder" (Psalm 50:3). He spoke, and the world was created. He spoke, and there appeared light and all creatures, great and small. And just as he created everything by his word, he also controls everything by his word. His voice is not weak or easily drowned out; it thunders over the loudest ocean or the raging storm. It is so powerful that it splits the mighty cedars and strips the forests of their foliage. Throughout the Bible we see him speaking in many different ways: through angels, through visions and dreams, through a mighty storm, and through a gentle whisper to our hearts. But are we listening, or have we forgotten how? Do we know only how to talk to God? If we want to see miracles in our lives and in our loved ones' lives, if we want to become all God created us to be, we must *listen* and follow what the Lord says. For he is still speaking today, and his voice is powerful!

The voice of the Lord echoes above the sea. The God of glory thunders. The Lord thunders over the mighty sea. The voice of the Lord is powerful; the voice of the Lord is full of majesty. The voice of the Lord splits the mighty cedars. . . . The voice of the Lord twists mighty oaks and strips the forests bare.
Psalm 29:3-5, 9

LORD, I'm thankful that you aren't silent, that your voice thunders over the whole earth. But it's easy to become distracted and fail to listen for your leading. Remove anything that is clogging my spiritual ears so that I might hear your powerful voice. And make me willing and quick to obey.

GOD THE FATHER IS BOTH FAR AWAY AND NEAR AT HAND; HIS VOICE IS, AT ONCE, DEAFENING IN ITS THUNDEROUSNESS, AND TOO STILL AND SMALL TO BE EASILY AUDIBLE. Malcolm Muggeridge (1903–1990)

The One Year Bible Readings for today are **Ezra 4:24–6:22; 1 Corinthians 3:5-23; Psalm 29:1-11;** and **Proverbs 20:26-27.**

AUGUST

8

help

Help!

O Lord my God, I cried out to you for help, and you restored my health. You brought me up from the grave, O Lord. You kept me from falling into the pit of death.

Psalm 30:2-3

The cry for help. . . . How many times is it directed toward the wrong things? People often look for help in riches and wealth. They may place their trust in power and prestige. They seek after fame, fortune, and fantasy in the hope that in these things they will find what they desire. Some work at preserving their youth in an attempt to gain hope and help. But the truth is that *things* will not provide the kind of lasting help and satisfaction that most people desire. The positive influence of these *things* is fleeting at best and may, in fact, not even be a positive influence at all. There is only One who can bring the help that will keep us from the pit of death.

Let us cry out to the Lord for help, just as the psalmist did. God is the One whose love is unending. He is the One with limitless resources. God is the One with ultimate power. Call out to the One who is more than capable of providing whatever help and hope you need.

HEAVENLY FATHER, forgive me for looking for help in all the wrong places. Thank you for your constant love and your desire to be my help. And thank you for extending your help to me today! Only your love will not fail. Only you can satisfy. Only you can give hope that does not disappoint us.

TO PRAY IS NOTHING MORE INVOLVED THAN TO OPEN THE DOOR, GIVING JESUS ACCESS TO OUR NEEDS AND PERMITTING HIM TO EXERCISE HIS OWN POWER IN DEALING WITH THEM.
Ole Hallesby (1879–1961)

The One Year Bible Readings for today are **Ezra 7:1–8:20; 1 Corinthians 4:1-21; Psalm 30:1-12;** and **Proverbs 20:28-30.**

AUGUST

9

power

The Power of His Hands

I entrust my spirit into your hand.
Psalm 31:5

The word *entrust* means "to confide, to commit, to leave with." What surrender this brief prayer expresses. It was spoken not only by the psalmist David but also by Stephen, the first martyr, as he was being stoned and by Jesus as he hung on the cross. Each of these men yielded their very lives into the hands of almighty God, for they knew his hands are the instruments of his power—his personal and active involvement. God the Father beckons us also to come to him and to entrust our hopes and dreams, our possessions, our families, and our careers to his control. He calls us to commit every worry or burden to his care, and he graciously summons us, through the shed blood of his Son, to leave even our lives in his powerful hands. And he has provided prayer as our means of doing this. When we "let go and let God," we will begin to experience his power transforming our lives more and more into the image of his Son, Jesus.

OH, FATHER, I entrust my spirit, my very life, into your hands this day. You are mighty beyond my ability to imagine, and you have made the way for me to do so . . . through the blood of Jesus. How I praise you for prayer, for through it I can let go and give over control of my life to you!

TRUST INVOLVES LETTING GO AND KNOWING GOD WILL CATCH YOU. James C. Dobson (b. 1936)

The One Year Bible Readings for today are **Ezra 8:21–9:15; 1 Corinthians 5:1-13; Psalm 31:1-8;** and **Proverbs 21:1-2.**

AUGUST
10

integrity

Walking in Integrity

The Lord is more pleased when we do what is just and right than when we give him sacrifices.
Proverbs 21:3

Are you grieved when you see corruption in the business world and in the culture at large? Almost weekly the newspapers reveal another instance of a widespread lack of integrity on the part of an individual or a corporation. Fewer and fewer people, it seems, think it's important to do what is right simply because it is right. But God has an answer, a way for us to escape the corruption of this present age by the power of his life within us. It is through the one perfect sacrifice—the death and resurrection of Jesus—that we can come humbly to the Father, receive his wisdom, and trust his Spirit to guide us in doing what is right and just.

What choices are you facing today in your marriage or family, in your business or financial life? Because the Lord loves you so much, he has provided his written Word, prayer, and the transforming work of his Spirit to enable you to live justly and walk humbly with him, for this pleases him.

DEAR LORD, in all the decisions and choices that I face each day, help me to walk in obedience to you and, thus, in honesty and integrity. Empower me by your Spirit to do what is just and right so that I'm living a life that pleases you and reflects your character.

GOD DOES NOT SUPPLY US WITH CHARACTER, HE GIVES US THE LIFE OF HIS SON, AND WE CAN EITHER IGNORE HIM AND REFUSE TO OBEY HIM, OR WE CAN SO OBEY HIM, SO BRING EVERY THOUGHT AND IMAGINATION INTO CAPTIVITY, THAT THE LIFE OF JESUS IS MANIFESTED IN OUR MORTAL FLESH.
Oswald Chambers (1874–1917)

The One Year Bible Readings for today are **Ezra 10:1-44; 1 Corinthians 6:1-20; Psalm 31:9-18;** and **Proverbs 21:3.**

spirit

Stirred by His Spirit

When Nehemiah, cup-bearer to King Artaxerxes of Persia, heard of the suffering and disgrace of the Jews in Jerusalem, the burned-down gates and its desecrated walls, he mourned for days, fasting and crying out to God. The Lord had purposed to rebuild the walls, but it was Nehemiah he stirred to stand in the gap. Totally identifying with his people's sin and need, he was drawn to repentance and intercession—and then he put feet to his prayers as he returned to Jerusalem to lead the rebuilding effort. We, too, can be part of God's rebuilding effort. We can be part of God's answer to the suffering and evils of this world as we enter into prayer for what God has impressed on us and then are willing to be part of the restoration. What situation in the community, city, or nation grieves your heart? That grief may be God's way of stirring you, just as he did Nehemiah, to join in fulfilling his purposes on the earth.

I said, "O Lord, God of heaven, the great and awesome God who keeps his covenant of unfailing love with those who love him and obey his commands, listen to my prayer! Look down and see me praying night and day for your people Israel. I confess that we have sinned against you. Yes, even my own family and I have sinned!"

Nehemiah 1:5-6

OH, GOD, I want my heart to be gripped by the things that grip your heart for your purposes and your people. Make me sensitive to the stirring of your Spirit and the sound of your voice! And when I have sought your will and direction, make me joyfully eager to participate in your plan.

GOD WANTS TO COME TO HIS WORLD, BUT HE WANTS TO COME TO IT THROUGH MAN. THIS IS THE MYSTERY OF OUR EXISTENCE, THE SUPERHUMAN CHANCE OF MANKIND. Martin Buber (1878–1965)

The One Year Bible Readings for today are **Nehemiah 1:1–3:14; 1 Corinthians 7:1-24; Psalm 31:19-24;** and **Proverbs 21:4.**

AUGUST

12

A Path Lit by His Presence

The Lord says, "I will guide you along the best pathway for your life. I will advise you and watch over you. Do not be like a senseless horse or mule that needs a bit and bridle to keep it under control."

Psalm 32:8-9

In this passage God declares his desire and intention to *guide* us, to *advise* us, and to *watch over* his children. He promises not only his loving protection but also a path that is lit by his very presence and word so we won't be confused about which way to go. Of course, just as young people can reject their fathers' advice and guidance, just as a horse can resist its master's leading, we can reject the "best pathway" that God has marked out for us and instead choose to go our own way. We do that by following the world's way instead of God's way. We might ignore his guidance by neglecting time with him, by being too busy to read his Word, or by looking everywhere for answers to our dilemmas except to the Shepherd, who will always steer us in the right direction. As you meditate on these verses, let them gently lead you to the Lord for the guidance you need today.

FATHER, guard me from being like the senseless horse who pushes against your control. I want you to guide me on the best pathway for my life day by day. Thank you for your assurance of direction and protection and especially for your promise that your unfailing love surrounds those who trust you.

BEFORE US IS A FUTURE ALL UNKNOWN, A PATH UNTROD; BESIDE US IS A FRIEND WELL LOVED AND KNOWN—THAT FRIEND IS GOD. Unknown

The One Year Bible Readings for today are **Nehemiah 3:15–5:13; 1 Corinthians 7:25-40; Psalm 32:1-11;** and **Proverbs 21:5-7.**

Sing with Joy

This psalm is chock-full of reasons to sing songs of joy to the Lord and to praise him no matter what we are facing: because his Word holds true and everything he does is worthy of our trust. Because his unfailing love fills the earth. Because with just a word from God the heavens and earth were created. Because his plans stand firm forever. And in spite of the enemy's schemes or even the actions of powerful nations, God's intentions for you and for his kingdom can never be shaken.

But what if today you don't feel like singing songs of joy? What if painful or difficult circumstances have stolen your joy? Frustrations assail you; burdens or responsibilities weigh your heart down so that the last thing you want to do is sing with joy. Ask God for the grace to praise him; ask him to open your spiritual eyes so that you stand in awe of him, for "it is fitting to praise him"!

LORD, open my eyes to see your unfailing love and goodness. Renew my trust in your Word. With a word you brought into existence the stars in the heavens and held the seas in place. Nothing can thwart your plans. Fill my heart with songs of joy. You are worthy of my unending praise!

Let the godly sing with joy to the Lord, for it is fitting to praise him. Praise the Lord with melodies on the lyre; make music for him on the ten-stringed harp. Sing new songs of praise to him; play skillfully on the harp and sing with joy. For the word of the Lord holds true, and everything he does is worthy of our trust He loves whatever is just and good, and his unfailing love fills the earth.

Psalm 33:1-5

JOY IS AN UNCEASING FOUNTAIN BUBBLING UP IN THE HEART; A SECRET SPRING THE WORLD CAN'T SEE AND DOESN'T KNOW ANYTHING ABOUT. THE LORD GIVES HIS PEOPLE PERPETUAL JOY WHEN THEY WALK IN OBEDIENCE TO HIM.

D. L. Moody (1837–1899)

The One Year Bible Readings for today are **Nehemiah 5:14–7:73a; 1 Corinthians 8:1-13; Psalm 33:1-11;** and **Proverbs 21:8-10.**

AUGUST

14

The Lord Alone Will Save

Don't count on your warhorse to give you victory—for all its strength, it cannot save you. . . . We depend on the Lord alone to save us. Only he can help us, protecting us like a shield.

Psalm 33:17, 20

As important as a warhorse was to a soldier's confidence in battle, this passage describes dependence on the strength of a horse instead of on the strength of the Lord as vain and false hope, even deception. A "warhorse" in our lives might be a person, a plan, a strategy, or a technique that we rely on to assist us in gaining victory or working out a problem. We all face different battles that cause us to turn to someone else for defense or help. We may even spend hours talking, thinking through, and planning with people of spiritual, mental, emotional, or legal strength to help give us victory, especially when we've been treated unjustly. God doesn't tell us, "Don't have a warhorse." He says, "Don't count on your warhorse." In other words, we are to depend on the strength of the Lord to save us in the battles we face and not on the intricate preparations we make or the influence or intelligence of someone else. We need to be prepared, but once we have done that, we can rest in the knowledge we have done the best we can and now the victory truly lies with God.

DEAR LORD, thank you for being my victor, for fighting my battles for me. When I start fretting over battle plans, help me to depend on you to protect and save me. My confidence does not lie in horses but in the living God. Help me to place my trust in your strength and not in the strength of another.

THE TRIUMPHANT CHRISTIAN DOES NOT FIGHT FOR VICTORY; HE CELEBRATES A VICTORY ALREADY WON. Reginald Wallis

The One Year Bible Readings for today are **Nehemiah 7:73b–9:21; 1 Corinthians 9:1-18; Psalm 33:12-22;** and **Proverbs 21:11-12.**

AUGUST
15

Oh, the Joys!

Those who look to him for help will be radiant with joy. . . . Oh, the joys of those who trust in him!

Psalm 34:5, 8

Twice in these short verses we see the word *joy* being connected with the act of trusting. This joy indwells and encompasses God's people and leads them to say, "Oh, the joys . . . !" even in the midst of suffering, frustration, or trouble.

Perhaps, like me, you've met people who seem to have a special radiance about them in their words, in their actions, or simply in their very presence. We walk away from them not only with curiosity about how they live in such luminous joy but also with a desire to know and experience that joy for ourselves. So, how can we radiate this kind of joy in the Lord? By looking for evidences of God's hand at work throughout the day, by seeking to know more of him, and by meditating on the wonder of his works instead of on the hassles and trials of this life. Once our perspective has shifted, we begin to wait expectantly for him to show himself as trustworthy. We will find our fulfillment in him and be filled with joy.

DEAR LORD, help me to look to you and to trust in you today. There is great joy to be found in living with my eyes fixed on you. Help me to do that so that my life will be radiant with your joy. May others be drawn to you because of the joy you have put in my heart. Oh, the joys of trusting in Jesus!

JOY HAS SOMETHING WITHIN ITSELF THAT IS BEYOND HAPPINESS AND SORROW. THIS SOMETHING IS CALLED BLESSEDNESS. . . . IT MAKES THE JOY OF LIFE POSSIBLE IN PLEASURE AND PAIN, IN HAPPINESS AND UNHAPPINESS, IN ECSTASY AND SORROW. WHERE THERE IS JOY, THERE IS FULFILLMENT. AND WHERE THERE IS FULFILLMENT, THERE IS JOY. Paul Tillich (1886–1965)

The One Year Bible Readings for today are **Nehemiah 9:22–10:39; 1 Corinthians 9:19–10:13; Psalm 34:1-10;** and **Proverbs 21:13.**

AUGUST

16

peace

Elbow Grease of Peace

Do any of you want to live a life that is long and good? Then watch your tongue! Keep your lips from telling lies! Turn away from evil and do good. Work hard at living in peace with others.
Psalm 34:12-14

This psalm spells out how to live a life of longevity and goodness. Who wouldn't want such a life?! Among the list of instructions the psalmist gives, he specifically tells us to "work hard at living in peace with others." We work hard at so many things—careers, projects, activities, event-planning, scheduling, housework, yard work—and all of them seem to demand our very best. However, the Lord says we are to work just as hard at living in peace with others, to aim for harmony in our relationships as his Spirit of peace lives through us and touches the lives of others. All of this begins with prayer. As you pray for peace with others, God's Spirit may lead you to forgive, cooperate, serve, give, or just listen. As you do, you will be sowing seeds that eventually will reap a harvest of peace. Is there a relationship in your life that is not peaceful? One that is marked more by tension or conflict than by love? Ask the Lord today what you need to do or pray so that you may live in peace with that person.

LORD, my desire is to live in peace with others. Please open my eyes to see how you are directing me so that peace can flow through me and into the lives of others. Show me where I may have contributed to conflict or tensions with others, and help me to humbly seek forgiveness and sow seeds of peace for the future.

SOWING SEEDS OF PEACE IS LIKE SOWING BEANS. YOU DON'T KNOW WHY IT WORKS; YOU JUST KNOW IT DOES. SEEDS ARE PLANTED, AND TOPSOILS OF HURT ARE SHOVED AWAY. Max Lucado (b. 1955)

The One Year Bible Readings for today are **Nehemiah 11:1–12:26; 1 Corinthians 10:14-33; Psalm 34:11-22;** and **Proverbs 21:14-16.**

compare

Who Can Compare?

I will praise him from the bottom of my heart: "Lord, who can compare with you? Who else rescues the weak and helpless from the strong? Who else protects the poor and needy from those who want to rob them?"
Psalm 35:10

Once again David's enemies were on the attack, trying to destroy him not only with spears or javelins but with slander and accusations. In the earlier verses of Psalm 35 he honestly expresses his fears concerning his foes and cries out to God to rescue him and to defeat those who are opposing him. But then David picks up his best weapon of all—worship. As he praises the Lord from the depths of his heart, his attitude goes from discouragement to hope, from desperation to devotion.

When we praise God from the bottom of our hearts, we, too, are consumed with hope in the Lord, who rescues the weak and helpless, protects the poor and needy, and who will do more than we could ask or think on our behalf. His Spirit can open the eyes of our understanding to see, know, and proclaim, "Lord, who can compare with you?" Truly nothing compares with the love, mercy, and saving power of our God.

OH, LORD, MY GOD, how worthy of praise you are! I praise you from the bottom of my heart. I lift my voice to proclaim who you are, your character, your mighty deeds, your willingness to rescue those who cannot help themselves. I am one of those, Lord, and so I give you praise. Lord, who can compare with you?

MOST OF THE VERSES WRITTEN ABOUT PRAISE IN GOD'S WORD WERE PENNED BY MEN AND WOMEN WHO FACED CRUSHING HEARTACHES, INJUSTICE, TREACHERY, SLANDER, AND SCORES OF OTHER INTOLERABLE SITUATIONS.
Joni Eareckson Tada (b. 1949)

The One Year Bible Readings for today are **Nehemiah 12:27–13:31; 1 Corinthians 11:1-16; Psalm 35:1-16;** and **Proverbs 21:17-18.**

AUGUST

18

hearts

Changer of Hearts

It is better to live alone in the desert than with a crabby, complaining wife.
Proverbs 21:19

Whether we are male or female, most of us have days when others could describe us as crabby and complaining. A "bad-off day" one of my high school students used to call it, a day when things seem impossible and most of all, when it feels impossible for me to handle it all. On days like these, our attitude's down, and everything—and everyone—irritates us. Maybe the cause is missed sleep, a stack of unpaid bills, cabin fever because the kids are sick, or weariness about the tenth gray day without any sunshine.

Whatever is causing our crabbiness and complaining, there is an antidote: turn from our bad attitude to the One who can bring a turnaround, not just in our day but in us. God is the great changer of hearts, the lifter of attitudes. As I give him the things that darken my day, he can be the sunshine in my soul. When I turn to him and pray, he delights in lifting my heart heaviness and giving me a spirit of gratefulness.

LORD, just as I am, I come to you. Thank you for receiving me and loving me just as much when I'm feeling down as when I'm having a good day. Help me to remember that this is a day you have made. Change my heart so that instead of complaining, I'm able to thank you for all that you are and all you have done for me.

WHEN HE SAYS TO YOUR DISTURBED, DISTRACTED, RESTLESS SOUL OR MIND, "COME UNTO ME," HE IS SAYING, COME OUT OF THE STRIFE AND DOUBT AND STRUGGLE OF WHAT IS AT THE MOMENT WHERE YOU STAND, INTO THAT WHICH WAS AND IS AND IS TO BE—THE ETERNAL, THE ESSENTIAL, THE ABSOLUTE. Phillips Brooks (1835–1893)

The One Year Bible Readings for today are **Esther 1:1–3:15; 1 Corinthians 11:17-34; Psalm 35:17-28;** and **Proverbs 21:19-20.**

fasting

Prayer with Fasting

Esther's response when she faced impending doom for herself, her family, and all the Jewish people, was to fast and pray and to call the people to fasting and prayer as well before she went in to appeal to the king.

When difficult times come, when we face our own particular desperate situations, what do we do? Seeking God with prayer and fasting should never be our last resort; it's the first place to start. Our actions when we fast, as Esther did, demonstrate to God, "Lord, more than I want food, TV, creature comforts, or anything else, I want you and am looking for your way of dealing with this." As the Jews earnestly sought God in this way, he gave Esther a plan that brought about a mighty deliverance for her and for God's people. When we add to our prayers the discipline of fasting, God will open our hearts to his strategies and will show us things we never would have known in the natural scheme of things. And because we are drawing near to him in this way, we will enter into closer intimacy with him through his Spirit.

Go and gather together all the Jews of Susa and fast for me. Do not eat or drink for three days, night or day. My maids and I will do the same. And then, though it is against the law, I will go in to see the king. If I must die, I am willing to die.
Esther 4:16

LORD, show me when your Spirit is calling me to put everything else aside in order to seek you, and give me grace to respond to that call. Give me the discipline I need to be able to follow through, and the faith to know that you are able to deliver in whatever circumstances I find myself. Make my heart obedient, as Esther's was, in seeking you above my daily bread.

BEAR UP THE HANDS THAT HANG DOWN, BY FAITH AND PRAYER; SUPPORT THE TOTTERING KNEES. HAVE YOU ANY DAYS OF FASTING AND PRAYER? STORM THE THRONE OF GRACE AND PERSEVERE THEREIN, AND MERCY WILL COME DOWN.
John Wesley (1703–1791)

The One Year Bible Readings for today are **Esther 4:1–7:10; 1 Corinthians 12:1-26; Psalm 36:1-12;** and **Proverbs 21:21-22.**

AUGUST

20

delight

He Is Our Delight

Take delight in the Lord, and he will give you your heart's desires.
Psalm 37:4

So often my prayers center on what I want the Lord to do: I intercede for critically ill people battling cancer. There's a great need in a missionary family in Thailand, so I petition daily for God's help on their behalf. A friend is on bed rest during a fragile pregnancy. On the home front we may want our children to do better in school, our job situation or marriage to improve, relief from stress, or myriad other desires. All of these are valid requests, which if answered in the way we hope, would delight us. But this verse calls us to a different prayer focus: to stop and center our heart on the Lord and make him our delight. And the promised result? "He will give you your heart's desires."

To delight means to take great pleasure or to find joy and satisfaction in something. If it's hard for you to find your greatest pleasure and delight in God, take heart. Though it's impossible for us to do that in our own strength, the Father has provided a way: his Spirit graciously reveals Jesus to us and causes us to fall more and more in love with him. Then we find great delight in him and in his presence.

LORD, I want to delight in you! Center my heart in knowing you more and loving you more day by day. Help me to discover that there is fullness of joy in your presence and to take great delight in my relationship with you. May my heart desire you above everything else.

JOY IN GOD IS BOTH THE ROOT AND THE FRUIT OF FAITH. . . . CHRIST HIMSELF HAS BECOME A TREASURE CHEST OF HOLY JOY. THE TREE OF FAITH GROWS ONLY IN THE HEART THAT CRAVES THE SUPREME GIFT THAT CHRIST DIED TO GIVE; NOT HEALTH, NOT WEALTH, NOT PRESTIGE, BUT GOD! John Piper (b. 1946)

The One Year Bible Readings for today are **Esther 8:1–10:3; 1 Corinthians 12:27–13:13; Psalm 37:1-11;** and **Proverbs 21:23-24.**

giver

The Giver of Gifts

Since you are so eager to have spiritual gifts, ask God for those that will be of real help to the whole church.
1 Corinthians 14:12

In this passage from 1 Corinthians, Paul teaches on the marvelous variety of spiritual gifts: how God has uniquely designed each of us and decided which gifts we will have, how the Holy Spirit distributes these gifts, and how different and yet very important each spiritual gift is. Whether it is the gift of teaching, leading, faith, miracles, or helping others, he reminds us that God's Spirit is the source behind every gift. However, it's easy, isn't it, to look around at those who seem so gifted in teaching, leading, singing, running a company, or excelling in hospitality and wonder where we were when the gifts were handed out. But in this verse God encourages us to ask him to give us the spiritual gifts that will be of most help to the body of Christ. With his grace, we can receive, cultivate, and use our spiritual gifts. And when there is fruitfulness or success, we can boast not in our own abilities or talents but in God, who created and distributed all of the gifts for his purposes. To God be the glory!

LORD, I ask you to give me the spiritual gifts that you know will be of real help to the whole church and will fulfill your purpose and destiny for my life. Thank you for creating me with particular interests and talents. Help me to see opportunities to use them to serve others and to glorify you.

THESE ARE GIFTS FROM GOD ARRANGED BY INFINITE WISDOM, NOTES THAT MAKE UP THE SCORES OF CREATION'S LOFTIEST SYMPHONY, THREADS THAT COMPOSE THE MASTER TAPESTRY OF THE UNIVERSE. A. W. Tozer (1897–1963)

The One Year Bible Readings for today are **Job 1:1–3:26; 1 Corinthians 14:1-17; Psalm 37:12-29;** and **Proverbs 21:25-26.**

AUGUST
22

engraving

The Engraving of His Word

They fill their hearts with God's law, so they will never slip from his path.
Psalm 37:31

As we see the day approaching when Christ will return in glory, this psalm grows from being instructional or insightful—which is important, of course—to being *vital* in our spiritual lives. The Holy Spirit's daily engraving of his Word on our hearts is imperative if we are to continue walking on the steep path through the narrow gate that leads to life.

A wood burner literally engraves or burns its mark down into the grain of the wood, leaving a permanent imprint. So should the law of God be engraved in our hearts. When we read and meditate on his Word with teachable hearts, the Holy Spirit will engrave his truths into our lives so that it, too, leaves a permanent imprint of God and his love for us. Although we veer at times from its counsel, the love and grace of the Father will lead us back to that truth that he has etched so deeply into our hearts.

LORD, help me to fill my heart with your law so that I may never slip from your path. Engrave your truths into my heart and mind so that your love and mercy are forever imprinted in my life. Keep my feet on the path that leads to life so that I am prepared for your glorious return.

ONE OF THE HIGHEST AND NOBLEST FUNCTIONS OF MAN'S MIND IS TO LISTEN TO GOD'S WORD, AND SO TO READ HIS MIND AND THINK HIS THOUGHTS AFTER HIM. John R. W. Stott (b. 1921)

The One Year Bible Readings for today are **Job 4:1–7:21; 1 Corinthians 14:18-40; Psalm 37:30-40;** and **Proverbs 21:27.**

AUGUST
23

He Hears Our Every Sigh

You know what I long for, Lord; you hear my every sigh.
Psalm 38:9

In the midst of this sorrowful psalm is hidden a wonderful truth: although God has chastened David for his sin and caused him to endure the painful physical and spiritual consequences brought on by his foolishness and sin, yet God heard David's every sigh and knew that he was longing for healing, restoration, and help. The Lord didn't turn a deaf ear to his cries just because David had made a huge mistake. And he doesn't distance himself from us because of our failures either. What an amazing and loving truth: our Creator Father knows exactly what we long for with tears. He knows the meaning and feeling behind our every sigh. We can't take a breath in our loneliness, disappointment, or grief without our caring heavenly Father's hearing it and being there to help us and bring restoration. What a wonderful motivation for taking everything to the Lord in prayer!

DEAR FATHER, thank you for knowing what I long for and for hearing my every sigh. And thank you for not turning away from me when I make a foolish mistake. What a loving and merciful Father you are! Today I want to give you my deepest desires, for you are near, you are here.

PRECIOUS, LORD! BEYOND EXPRESSING,
ARE THY BEAUTIES ALL DIVINE;
GLORY, HONOR, POWER, AND BLESSING,
BE HENCEFORTH FOREVER THINE.

Charles Haddon Spurgeon (1834–1892)

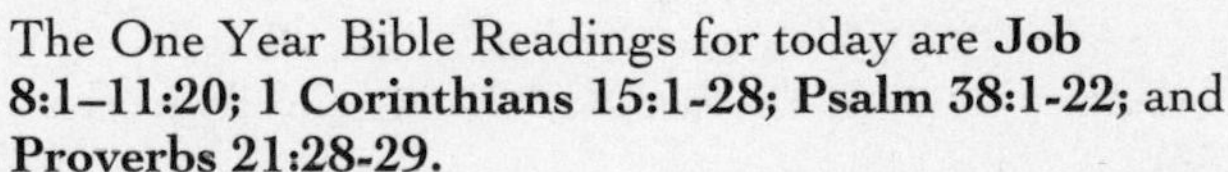
The One Year Bible Readings for today are **Job 8:1–11:20; 1 Corinthians 15:1-28; Psalm 38:1-22;** and **Proverbs 21:28-29.**

AUGUST

24

tongue

Curbing the Tongue

I said to myself, "I will watch what I do and not sin in what I say. I will curb my tongue when the ungodly are around me." But as I stood there in silence—not even speaking of good things—the turmoil within me grew to the bursting point. My thoughts grew hot within me and began to burn, igniting a fire of words. . . . Lord, where do I put my hope? My only hope is in you. Rescue me from my rebellion.

Psalm 39:1-3, 7-8

David knew the importance of curbing his tongue. Yet even with this knowledge he struggled not to lash out and speak or act in a sinful manner toward those he described as ungodly. How often do we find ourselves in a similar situation? The cutting comeback is on the tip of our tongues. The fiery defense is only a breath away. We fight to keep our words from flying at our enemies. This struggle is natural and, obviously, is nothing new.

So what is the answer? Do we count to ten or take a deep breath? Those aren't bad ideas, and they can help, but David had an answer that is much more likely to provide success in this battle with our tongues. David put his hope in God and cried out to him, "Rescue me from my rebellion." And indeed, only God can set us free from the turmoil within us. Only God can rescue us from our own sin.

FATHER, rescue me from my rebellion. I put my hope in you and only in you. Give me the desire and the power to curb my tongue and to control what I say and do. Help me, Lord, to extinguish the anger and to keep silent when the ungodly are around. Keep my angry thoughts from igniting a fire of words. You alone can do this.

THE TONGUE IS THE AMBASSADOR OF THE HEART.
John Lyly (ca. 1554–1606)

The One Year Bible Readings for today are **Job 12:1–15:35; 1 Corinthians 15:29-58; Psalm 39:1-13;** and **Proverbs 21:30-31.**

waiting

Waiting on God

While the kind of waiting this psalm describes is somewhat foreign to our twenty-first-century demand for quick responses, quick solutions, and quick results, it is truly a key to effective prayer. We may tend to think of waiting as passive—sitting and doing nothing until someone or something changes—or as a waste of time (we want to be busy accomplishing things). But in this passage waiting is very active; it's continuing to pray that God will work and staying on the lookout for him to put forth his power. To wait with the kind of hopeful expectation and confidence David showed, we must know the One we are waiting for—not a "slow" God but a patient one. Not a God who is uninvolved but the One whose holy presence is closer to us than our own breath. He is the Lord who in a heartbeat can lift us out of the pit of despair, steady us, and fill us with a brand-new song. This is the God we wait on, and he rewards those who wait for him.

I waited patiently for the Lord to help me, and he turned to me and heard my cry. He lifted me out of the pit of despair, out of the mud and the mire. He set my feet on solid ground and steadied me as I walked along. He has given me a new song to sing, a hymn of praise to our God.

Psalm 40:1-3

LORD, I look to you to work within me a spirit of patient waiting. Grant me hope and expectation as I watch for you to display your grace in my life. Keep me from losing heart or becoming impatient, and cause me to continue to pray as I wait to see your powerful hand at work.

IT IS BY THE PRESENCE OF GOD, AS HE CAN IN CHRIST BY HIS HOLY SPIRIT MAKE HIMSELF KNOWN, AND KEEP THE SOUL UNDER ITS COVERING AND SHADOW, THAT WILL AWAKEN AND STRENGTHEN THE TRUE WAITING SPIRIT. LET US BE STILL AND WAIT AND WORSHIP UNTIL WE KNOW HOW NEAR HE IS, AND THEN SAY, "ON THEE DO I WAIT." Andrew Murray (1828–1917)

The One Year Bible Readings for today are **Job 16:1–19:29; 1 Corinthians 16:1-24; Psalm 40:1-10;** and **Proverbs 22:1.**

AUGUST

26

comfort

Conduits of Comfort

All praise to the God and Father of our Lord Jesus Christ. He is the source of every mercy and the God who comforts us. He comforts us in all our troubles so that we can comfort others. When others are troubled, we will be able to give them the same comfort God has given us.
2 Corinthians 1:3-4

Comfort is a powerful word that means "to strengthen, aid, encourage, give hope, alleviate grief, lift one's spirit from loneliness or pain." When Paul wrote on comfort in his second letter to the Corinthian Christians, he wasn't speaking of it in some hypothetical or theoretical way. Paul had experienced profound suffering and trouble, and he had received great comfort and encouragement from God and from God's people. Paul wanted the believers of that age and all those who followed to know that their suffering is never in vain. He was conveying the truth that the comfort we receive is part of God's great plan to strengthen and help those who are in need. While the source of all comfort is God himself, the Father of our Lord Jesus Christ, he gives us the privilege of being conduits of his comfort to those we meet.

Has God brought comfort and hope to you when you were distressed by waves of trials? Has someone's prayer support lifted you up in a time of illness or brokenness? God does not intend for that comfort to stagnate in our hearts once we receive it. He wants us to dispense it to a hurting world.

LORD, thank you for the times you have comforted me. I know that you have comforted me so that I can do the same for others. This world is full of people who are hurting. Make me sensitive to those I meet who need your touch of comfort. Keep me an open vessel through which your life, love, and comfort can flow.

GOD DOES NOT COMFORT US TO MAKE US COMFORTABLE, BUT TO MAKE US COMFORTERS.
John Henry Jowett (1864–1923)

The One Year Bible Readings for today are **Job 20:1–22:30; 2 Corinthians 1:1-11; Psalm 40:11-17;** and **Proverbs 22:2-4.**

AUGUST
27

promises

God's Promises

Paul preached uncompromisingly of Jesus Christ, who is the fulfillment of all God's promises to Abraham, Moses, David, and to his people throughout the Old Testament. Peace, provision, salvation, deliverance, forgiveness—Jesus is the divine affirmation to all of God's promises. Knowing that his promises are true gives us strength, encouragement, and a solid foundation for our prayers. Understanding that God has the power to do what he has promised and that he never breaks his promises gives us confidence as we come to his throne of grace. Meditating on his promises reminds us of his faithfulness to all generations. But God doesn't want us only to think on his great and precious promises or merely to thank him for his promises. He wants us to turn them into prayers and petitions, to ask him to continue to fulfill his promises, for they reflect his will and purpose for our lives and for his church.

He is the one whom Timothy, Silas, and I preached to you, and he is the divine Yes—God's affirmation. For all of God's promises have been fulfilled in him. That is why we say "Amen" when we give glory to God through Christ.

2 Corinthians 1:19-20

THANK YOU, LORD, for your great and precious promises! Thank you for reminding us that Jesus is the "divine Yes," the affirmation of all your promises. Help me to sense and experience your love behind every promise as I trust in you. And help me to pray with confidence because I know that not one of your promises will ever fail.

THOUGH THE BIBLE BE CROWDED WITH GOLDEN PROMISES FROM BOARD TO BOARD, YET WILL THEY BE INOPERATIVE UNTIL WE TURN THEM INTO PRAYER. F. B. Meyer (1847–1929)

The One Year Bible Readings for today are **Job 23:1–27:23; 2 Corinthians 1:12–2:11; Psalm 41:1-13;** and **Proverbs 22:5-6.**

AUGUST
28

where

Where Is God?

As the deer pants for streams of water, so I long for you, O God. I thirst for God, the living God. When can I come and stand before him? Day and night, I have only tears for food, while my enemies continually taunt me, saying, "Where is this God of yours?" . . . Why am I discouraged? Why so sad? I will put my hope in God! I will praise him again—my Savior and my God!

Psalm 42:1-3, 11

Where is God when we're in the emergency room with a severely injured loved one? Where was God in the bombing of the Murrah Federal Building in Oklahoma City in 1995? Where was God in the terrorist attacks of September 11, 2001? When trouble or tragedy strikes, we long for God, the living God. Who can tell us where God is? His Word tells us over and over: he is in the one who visits those in prison; he is in those who give food to the hungry; he is in the comfort of a loving arm extended around those who are hurting. He is in the prayers of a mother for her sick child. He is in the rescuers who work to save lives and in the missionaries who leave family and friends and personal comforts to share the gospel with those in darkness. He is demonstrated best, though, at the Cross, where he gave his only Son, Jesus Christ, for our sakes that we might have hope for this life and for eternity.

LORD, I praise you that you are Emmanuel—God with us—in everything we experience as we walk through this broken, hurting world. Help me to be your hands and feet today, your words of comfort and encouragement to those who need to know "where you are" in their times of deep need.

THE PRESENCE OF GOD IS A FACT OF LIFE. ST. PAUL RIGHTLY SAID OF GOD, "IN HIM WE LIVE, AND MOVE, AND HAVE OUR BEING." JESUS SAID, "THE KINGDOM OF GOD IS WITHIN YOU." WE MAY, BY DEFYING THE PURPOSE OF GOD, INSULATE OURSELVES FROM THAT PRESENCE. WE MAY, BY UNREPENTED SIN, CUT OFF THE SENSE OF GOD BECAUSE WE ARE CLOUDED BY A SENSE OF GUILT. WE MAY, THROUGH NO FAULT OF OUR OWN, BE UNABLE TO SENSE THE GOD WHO IS ALL ABOUT US. BUT THE FACT REMAINS THAT HE IS WITH US ALL THE TIME. J. B. Phillips (1906–1982)

The One Year Bible Readings for today are **Job 28:1–30:31; 2 Corinthians 2:12-17; Psalm 42:1-11;** and **Proverbs 22:7.**

AUGUST
29

confidence

God Confidence

It is not that we think we can do anything of lasting value by ourselves. Our only power and success come from God.
2 Corinthians 3:5

If anyone might have felt adequate or qualified, it was the apostle Paul. With his impressive credentials and the breadth of his ministry and influence, he could have come up with a lot to be confident about. But he states in this verse that his adequacy and competency didn't come from his own human resources but from God's. He knew that God was his only source of power and authority. Nothing worthwhile came from Paul himself. God alone made him adequate as a servant of the new covenant.

Are you feeling inadequate today? Is there a task or responsibility that is weighing heavily on you? This verse is a call to dependency filled with hope. God has ordained our dependence on him. He designed us to function best with him, not apart from him. Those challenges and assignments that are beyond our abilities and make us feel inadequate aren't intended to make us fear but rather to drive us to the Lord who *is* adequate so that we will develop a God-confidence that cannot be shaken.

LORD, thank you for the areas in which I feel inadequate or struggle, because those draw me to you. I am able to accomplish what you ask of me only through your power. Thank you for your Word because in it I learn that you are my adequacy! You are my sufficiency! May my confidence always be in you through Christ Jesus. Then you will receive praise.

IT IS NOT MY ABILITY, BUT MY RESPONSE TO GOD'S ABILITY, THAT COUNTS. Corrie ten Boom (1892–1983)

The One Year Bible Readings for today are **Job 31:1–33:33; 2 Corinthians 3:1-18; Psalm 43:1-5;** and **Proverbs 22:8-9.**

AUGUST

30

power

His Glorious Power

This precious treasure — this light and power that now shine within us — is held in perishable containers, that is, in our weak bodies. So everyone can see that our glorious power is from God and is not our own. We are pressed on every side by troubles, but we are not crushed and broken. We are perplexed, but we don't give up and quit. We are hunted down, but God never abandons us. We get knocked down, but we get up again and keep going.

2 Corinthians 4:7-9

Paul's life was a clear and unmistakable demonstration of the power of God held in a jar of clay. He wasn't exempt from difficulties because he was the Lord's servant; in fact, the overwhelming circumstances, troubles, and mental anguish that accompanied them served to display the glorious message of Christ and to reveal the power of God in Paul's life. In today's passage he reveals to us the secret that God has designed us as earthen vessels and that the treasure of his light and power and glory is held in our perishable, weak bodies. Why? So that everyone will know that this power and greatness is from God—not from us—but from God. That is why we can say with Paul that though we may get knocked down, we get up again and keep going. We may suffer, but we won't be crushed. We may be perplexed or frustrated, but we are never driven to despair, all because of the treasure of Jesus, who dwells within us by his Spirit.

LORD, thank you for designing me to be a clay jar with an amazing treasure inside. And though the circumstances of life may press me down, you never abandon me. May others see your power and light through my life. May you truly be glorified in my weakness, in this earthen vessel that I am.

GOD DOES NOT EXPECT US TO IMITATE JESUS CHRIST. HE EXPECTS US TO ALLOW THE LIFE OF JESUS TO BE MANIFESTED.
Oswald Chambers (1874–1917)

The One Year Bible Readings for today are **Job 34:1–36:33; 2 Corinthians 4:1-12; Psalm 44:1-8;** and **Proverbs 22:10-12.**

afflictions

Our Light Afflictions

Some people would argue that the concept Paul presents in these verses is a cop-out, an "opiate." Indeed, if we are trying to avoid the pressures of life and secure some future pleasure, they might be right. However, if we are fixing our eyes on the eternal God and he is transforming us into his likeness, that's another story!

Our challenge is to learn to see Jesus as he is. Paul tells us to leave our worldly understanding behind and to lay hold of the true, eternal Treasure, Jesus himself. Jesus told the Samaritan woman, "God is Spirit," and therefore, spiritually discerned, and his disciples, "On that day you will realize that I am in my Father, and you are in me, and I am in you" (John 14:20, NIV). "That day" was after his resurrection, and it is *now*. Our present troubles are designed to turn our attention away from the temporal and toward the eternal, that we might live in God's glory, now and forever!

LORD JESUS, focus my eyes clearly on the eternal, for that puts my present troubles into a proper perspective. Help me to see you as you are, to perceive you with my spirit, not just with my mind, and to realize that you are in me and I am in you! What glory!

Our present troubles are quite small and won't last very long. Yet they produce for us an immeasurably great glory that will last forever! So we don't look at the troubles we can see right now; rather, we look forward to what we have not yet seen. For the troubles we see will soon be over, but the joys to come will last forever.
2 Corinthians 4:17-18

GOD [IS] SPEAKING TO JOB OUT OF THE WHIRLWIND, AND SAYING, "IN THE SUNSHINE AND THE WARMTH YOU CANNOT MEET ME; BUT IN THE HURRICANE AND THE DARKNESS WHEN WAVE AFTER WAVE HAS SWEPT DOWN AND ACROSS THE SOUL, YOU SHALL SEE MY FORM AND KNOW THAT YOUR REDEEMER LIVES."
Frederick William Robertson (1816–1853)

The One Year Bible Readings for today are **Job 37:1–39:30; 2 Corinthians 4:13–5:10; Psalm 44:9-26;** and **Proverbs 22:13.**

reality

A New Reality

We have stopped evaluating others by what the world thinks about them. Once I mistakenly thought of Christ that way, as though he were merely a human being. How differently I think about him now!
2 Corinthians 5:16

When the Lord first awakens us by his grace to receive the life he has provided for us in Jesus, we tend to comprehend the things of the Spirit through the reference base we have acquired over the years. The trouble is, we cannot grasp spiritual things through natural processes. Our lives were once concerned only with the elements of this physical world, but now we realize that eternal life supersedes our momentary pilgrimage on this planet. In Romans 12, Paul admonished the believers not to be conformed to this world but to be transformed by the renewing of their minds, that they might begin to live out the life that God had called them to. In today's verse, he is helping us understand that this whole principle applies to everything. He challenges us to learn to live in a superseding reality, relating to everything and everybody from this new perspective. We can be thankful that God is the author of this renewed insight in us and he will bring it to completion.

THANK YOU, LORD, for the grace that gives me spiritual sight to see things that no physical eye can see. Help me to work together with you in this whole process as you transform me into your likeness by the power of your Spirit. May I come to grasp your light, which is the substance behind the shadows.

GOD DOES NOT DO ANYTHING WITH US, ONLY THROUGH US. Oswald Chambers (1874–1917)

The One Year Bible Readings for today are **Job 40:1–42:17; 2 Corinthians 5:11-21; Psalm 45:1-17;** and **Proverbs 22:14.**

fortress

God Is Our Fortress

God is our refuge and strength, always ready to help in times of trouble. So we will not fear, even if earthquakes come and the mountains crumble into the sea.
Psalm 46:1-2

What is the source of the psalmist's calmness and of our encouragement in times of trouble? These verses don't say that our lack of fear during earthquakes and tumultuous happenings when everything around us crumbles is related to the fact that *we* are strong or mighty or invincible. Instead it is because of *who God is*—our refuge and strength, the One who is always present with us and is standing ready to help in times of trouble. The fact that the Lord Almighty is here among us and is our fortress is reason enough not to panic when everything around us that can be shaken shakes. The circumstances of our lives may change, our nation or world may be in an uproar, but our position within the safety of God's love and protection remains a constant . . . for he delights in us, cares for us, and is always ready to help. Do times of trouble come in the lives of saints? Most definitely. Will God be there to protect and strengthen us? In today's psalm he has promised to do just that . . . and he always keeps his promises.

LORD, when everything in my life seems to be on the verge of crumbling and falling apart, help me to experience you as my refuge and strength, my firm foundation. You are the mountain mover, but you also hold creation steady in the palm of your hand. Guide me as I entrust my "mountains" to you, my solid, ever faithful Father.

IN SPITE OF ALL APPEARANCES TO THE CONTRARY, GOD HAS A PLAN FOR THIS BANKRUPT WORLD. HE STILL HAS SOMETHING IN STORE FOR IT. THIS DARK, SATANIC EARTH, DROWNED IN BLOOD AND TEARS, THIS EARTH OF OURS, HE STILL WANTS AS A THEATER FOR HIS GRACE AND GLORIOUS DIRECTION. Helmut Thielicke (1908–1986)

The One Year Bible Readings for today are **Ecclesiastes 1:1–3:22; 2 Corinthians 6:1-13; Psalm 46:1-11;** and **Proverbs 22:15.**

SEPTEMBER

3

Empty Words

There is ruin in a flood of empty words. Fear God instead. . . . The more words you speak, the less they mean. So why overdo it?

Ecclesiastes 5:7; 6:11

I am a person of many words. So when I read these verses from Ecclesiastes, I am convicted of sometimes "overdoing it" when it comes to talking. I may speak words quickly without thinking first or without praying about the situation. Sometimes my words give more information than the hearer needs to know. Often the flood of words comes because I'm worried or concerned about something. But the instruction to "fear God instead" doesn't mean to just shut up the flow of words or be silent. It means to understand that God is the first place to turn, that we can take our thoughts, worries, and concerns to him in prayer and pour them out to him rather than continue to rehash a situation with others. Then the words that we speak will not cause ruin. As we yield our conversation to God and ask the Holy Spirit to inspire and guide our words, they will not be empty or spoken in vain; instead, they will be full of life.

LORD, forgive me for speaking empty words without thinking first and for times when I talk too much and say too little. I want my words to be full of life, to be of help and value to others, and to reflect your love and grace. Teach me to turn first to you and pour out my concerns and thoughts. Then your Spirit will give me right words to speak.

WORDS. DO YOU FULLY UNDERSTAND THEIR POWER? CAN ANY OF US REALLY GRASP THE MIGHTY FORCE BEHIND THE THINGS WE SAY? DO WE STOP AND THINK BEFORE WE SPEAK, CONSIDERING THE POTENCY OF THE PHRASES WE UTTER? Joni Eareckson Tada (b. 1949)

The One Year Bible Readings for today are **Ecclesiastes 4:1–6:12; 2 Corinthians 6:14–7:7; Psalm 47:1-9;** and **Proverbs 22:16.**

wise

Words of the Wise

What a wondrously encouraging thought that God desires to write his ways and words on our hearts. How amazing it is to think that the God we serve, the One who commands the winds and the waves and the whole universe, also commits himself to being our personal instructor and guide! We have only to apply our hearts to his instruction, to present ourselves before him. He not only takes the initiative but also promises to teach us. How do we "apply our hearts"? By doing our part to read the Bible regularly and to meditate on his unchanging principles. By learning to listen to those who are wise, that is, those who know and live by God's truth and have grown in the wisdom and knowledge of God. Then we won't have to muster up deeper trust in God. We won't have to strive for wisdom—because, as this verse tells us, God himself will teach us and lead us to a wholehearted trust in him.

Listen to the words of the wise; apply your heart to my instruction. For it is good to keep these sayings deep within yourself, always ready on your lips. I am teaching you today—yes, you—so you will trust in the Lord.
Proverbs 22:17-19

THANK YOU, FATHER, for your desire and willingness to teach me today. You call me to rest in the fact that you take responsibility for instructing me, just as a loving earthly father instructs his own children. Plant your truth deep within me so that your name will always be on my lips. As I apply my heart and mind to your Word, bring me into a deeper trust in you.

THE SACRED PAGE IS NOT MEANT TO BE THE END, BUT ONLY THE MEANS TOWARD THE END, WHICH IS KNOWING GOD HIMSELF. A. W. Tozer (1897–1963)

The One Year Bible Readings for today are **Ecclesiastes 7:1–9:18; 2 Corinthians 7:8-16; Psalm 48:1-14;** and **Proverbs 22:17-19.**

today

Today

If you wait for perfect conditions, you will never get anything done.
Ecclesiastes 11:4

There is a place in the future that we often speak of. We call it "one day," the time when we will accomplish those things we've always longed to do. The time when we've lost the weight we wanted to and had our joy restored. The time when we will give generously to those in need or work within the ministry that excites our hearts. We'll do great things for God when our finances prosper or when time is not so short—one day! Yet there are two places we cannot go. We cannot travel back into the past or propel ourselves into the future. All we have is today. When we give of our time or finances in proportion with what we have at hand at the present time, God sees the heart of the giver, not the gift. It is he who multiplies and blesses that gift—just as he did when he fed a multitude with a little boy's meager lunch of loaves and fishes. What has God asked us to do today? When we are faithful in small things, big things can take place in the kingdom of God.

MIGHTY GOD, though my efforts may seem insignificant compared with those of others, I pray that I will be faithful in the small things you give me to do so that one day I will be faithful with an abundance of time or finances or gifts. Thank you for blessing that faithfulness and producing results far greater than anything I could do by myself.

DO LITTLE THINGS AS IF THEY WERE GREAT BECAUSE OF THE MAJESTY OF THE LORD JESUS CHRIST WHO DWELLS IN YOU; AND DO GREAT THINGS AS IF THEY WERE LITTLE AND EASY BECAUSE OF HIS OMNIPOTENCE.
Blaise Pascal (1623–1662)

The One Year Bible Readings for today are **Ecclesiastes 10:1–12:14; 2 Corinthians 8:1-15; Psalm 49:1-20;** and **Proverbs 22:20-21.**

thanksgiving

A Sacrifice of Thanksgiving

[God said,] "I don't need the bulls you sacrifice; I don't need the blood of goats. What I want instead is your true thanks to God; I want you to fulfill your vows to the Most High. Trust me in your times of trouble, and I will rescue you, and you will give me glory."
Psalm 50:13-15

What does God want from us? Does he want an outward show or performance, attendance at a host of church meetings, or sacrificial giving of a certain amount of money to his work? Does he want feigned obedience or responses of certain words? No, he says in these verses that in our times of trouble he wants simple, heartfelt thanks and trust in him. Maybe you aren't feeling thankful today because your prayers haven't yet been answered. Perhaps you haven't seen the provision of money you need, or someone you love hasn't turned from a life of sin. How can we give thanks to God in light of unresolved difficulties that discourage us and weigh us down? How can we praise him when the cup looks empty? God knows how wearying these troubles are to us, and he finds it a sweet gift when in our brokenness we choose to give thanks to him and acknowledge that he will rescue us. That is precisely when our thanks becomes a sacrifice that his Word says truly honors him (v. 23) and gives him glory.

LORD, thank you for not being interested in outward displays but in the condition of my heart. I want to offer that sweet sacrifice of thanksgiving. Help me to turn to you in times of trouble, to trust you, and even then to be thankful. For in this way I will bring you glory.

THOU HAST GIVEN SO MUCH TO ME
GIVE ONE THING MORE—A GRATEFUL HEART:
NOT THANKFUL WHEN IT PLEASETH ME,
AS IF THY BLESSINGS HAD SPARE DAYS,
BUT SUCH A HEART WHOSE PULSE MAY BE
THY PRAISE.

George Herbert (1593–1633)

The One Year Bible Readings for today are **Song of Songs 1:1–4:16; 2 Corinthians 8:16-24; Psalm 50:1-23;** and **Proverbs 22:22-23.**

The ONE YEAR BIBLE

truth

New Testament Truth

Create in me a clean heart, O God. Renew a right spirit within me. . . . Restore to me again the joy of your salvation.
Psalm 51:10, 12

The Hebrew word for "create" is *bara;* it means "to create something out of nothing." When we read in Genesis 1:1 that God created the heavens and the earth, the word translated "created" is the same *bara,* reflecting the supernatural creative dynamism by which God brings something out of nothing. This was David's prayer. He wanted God to perform a heart transplant, an out-with-the-old, in-with-the-new procedure. He desired a completely new heart, one that had never existed before. David wasn't praying simply to have the old heart restored; he wanted it regenerated. He wanted a "new nature." Therefore, David took his sin and guilt and his desire for a brand-new beginning to the Father and asked him to restore his joy.

As with David, when we sin, we lose the joy of the salvation God gives us. Yet the Lord loves nothing more than to create in us a clean heart and to restore that joy *daily*. This was the purpose of the cross. To make a way for us to know constant fellowship with the Father through new mercies and grace each morning and to live in the bright and beautiful joy of his salvation.

FATHER, how blessed I am to have the chance to live each day with a brand-new heart . . . a pure heart . . . a supernaturally regenerated heart full of the breath of your Spirit. Create in me a clean heart, and restore to me the joy of your salvation.

A HEART IN EVERY THOUGHT RENEWED
AND FULL OF LOVE DIVINE,
PERFECT AND RIGHT AND PURE AND GOOD,
A COPY, LORD, OF THINE.

Charles Wesley (1707–1788)

The One Year Bible Readings for today are **Song of Songs 5:1–8:14; 2 Corinthians 9:1-15; Psalm 51:1-19;** and **Proverbs 22:24-25.**

weapons

Wonderful Weapons

The title for today's devotional sounds full of irony, doesn't it . . . weapons that are *wonderful?* When we think of war, by no means do we think of any aspect of it as being marvelous, outstanding, or remarkable, especially in regards to the weapons ordinarily used to inflict injury or death. However, "God's mighty weapons" bestow *blessing* instead of injury, and *life* instead of death, for his weapons are the Word of God, the blood of the Lamb, and prayer. When we intercede for others or are under spiritual attack ourselves, the strongholds may seem invincible, or you may feel overpowered and already defeated by the enemy. This is when we must stop and take a deep breath of truth: "We use God's mighty weapons . . . to knock down the Devil's strongholds."

God's mighty weapons of war will destroy the Devil's strongholds, whether they be strongholds of intellectualism, pride, unbelief, or addiction. The newest believer or weakest saint who wars with spiritual weapons can pierce the darkness of difficulty. Through the blood of the Lamb and through proclaiming the truth of God's Word in prayer, we will see God's victory.

We are human, but we don't wage war with human plans and methods. We use God's mighty weapons, not mere worldly weapons, to knock down the Devil's strongholds.

2 Corinthians 10:3-4

LORD, thank you for your weapons of warfare, which are mighty, invincible, and supernatural. Teach me to wield them as I stand against the enemy. Strengthen me as I intercede for others. I pray that you will demolish the devil's dark strongholds and establish your kingdom of light and truth.

THE PRAYER OF THE FEEBLEST SAINT ON EARTH WHO LIVES IN THE SPIRIT AND KEEPS RIGHT WITH GOD IS A TERROR TO SATAN. THE VERY POWERS OF DARKNESS ARE PARALYZED BY PRAYER. . . . NO WONDER SATAN TRIES TO KEEP OUR MINDS FUSSY IN ACTIVE WORK TILL WE CANNOT THINK IN PRAYER. Oswald Chambers (1874–1917)

The One Year Bible Readings for today are **Isaiah 1:1–2:22; 2 Corinthians 10:1-18; Psalm 52:1-9;** and **Proverbs 22:26-27.**

SEPTEMBER

9

surprised

Beware of Being Surprised!

I am not surprised! Even Satan can disguise himself as an angel of light.
2 Corinthians 11:14

"Surprise!" Usually we use this expression in the context of something exciting and wondrous or in the unveiling of something amazing. Yet today's Scripture verse uses the word *surprised* to mean, "I am not . . . overwhelmed, puzzled, or shocked." Paul was clearly stating his inability to be caught off guard by Satan and his deceptive ways of twisting and tainting the truth. "An angel of light" refers to the fact that Satan can appear disguised as a messenger of truth, but there is no truth in him. Just as bank employees learn to detect counterfeit bills by painstakingly poring over authentic ones, we learn to perceive the enemy by acquainting ourselves deeply with the ways of our Father. So beware of being surprised! Be alert and on guard. Arm yourself with God's Word, and learn his ways so that in the day or hour when you are a target for Satan's deception, you will not fall for his trickery but will instead see and know the truth.

How precious and perfect are your Word and your ways, O Lord. I pray that my relationship with you through the shed blood of Christ will be strong and that your Word will grow deep in my heart. Then the enemy's deceptions will not take me by surprise. I will recognize him for who he is, the father of lies.

THE DEVIL NEVER SLEEPS, AND YOUR FLESH IS VERY MUCH ALIVE. PREPARE YOURSELF FOR BATTLE. SURROUNDING YOU ARE ENEMIES THAT NEVER REST. Thomas à Kempis (ca. 1380–1471)

The One Year Bible Readings for today are **Isaiah 3:1–5:30; 2 Corinthians 11:1-15; Psalm 53:1-6; Psalm 22:28-29.**

Something New

[God said,] "Ask me for a sign, Ahaz, to prove that I will crush your enemies as I have promised." . . . But the king refused.
Isaiah 7:11-12

King Ahaz and his people were terrified at the presence of their enemies and the imminent invasion by an army far too great for them to successfully resist. But God's plan was to teach them a lesson, one that we can also learn from today. It is our natural tendency to seek outward, tangible signs as indications of God's direction and as a basis for our faith in him. However, God intends to nurture in us a faith and a trust that do not require external support. The kind of faith God wants us to have is one that rests on the character of the Cross and thus paves the way for God's supreme intervention. He's not trying to build something new in us. He wants us to see and grow in the light of what he has already put in us through Jesus!

ETERNAL FATHER, forgive me for seeking outward signs rather than being drawn into closer communion with you. Though heaven and earth may pass away, you are the same yesterday, today, and forever, and I am yours. Nothing can change that. May you take pleasure in me and be glorified as I trust—not test—you.

TRUST GOD WHERE YOU CANNOT TRACE HIM. DO NOT TRY TO PENETRATE THE CLOUD HE BRINGS OVER YOU; RATHER LOOK TO THE BOW THAT IS ON IT. THE MYSTERY IS GOD'S; THE PROMISE IS YOURS. John MacDuff (1818–1895)

The One Year Bible Readings for today are **Isaiah 6:1–7:25; 2 Corinthians 11:16-33; Psalm 54:1-7; Proverbs 23:1-3.**

SEPTEMBER

rest

Finding Rest in Him

Please listen and answer me, for I am overwhelmed by my troubles. . . . Oh, how I wish I had wings like a dove; then I would fly away and rest!
Psalm 55:2, 6

Have you ever been so burdened by stress that you wished you could just get on a plane and fly away? Most of us at one time or other have had troubles so overwhelming, situations so burdensome and heavy, that we, like the psalmist, have wished we could fly away like a bird and be at rest. We may imagine a getaway to a quiet beach or the mountains, a place free from stress and problems and endless responsibilities. We dream of a turnaround in a pressing situation so that we won't have that to worry about anymore. But God offers a kind of rest that is different from what our own minds would conceive. God offers us rest in the *midst* of our distress. It is the only true rest—an inner rest that comes from abandoning ourselves to the Lord and entrusting to him whatever troubles or problems are overwhelming us. Instead of flying away, run straight into the arms of God, and rest in his care and love for you today.

OH, LORD, I do want my problems solved and my troubles removed, but from the crushing weight of my burdens, I turn my eyes to you. I entrust this perplexity to you. Enable me to find my rest in you, to discover a place of deeper abandonment and security in your everlasting love. You are my only rock. You are my only rest.

HOW SHALL WE REST IN GOD? BY GIVING OURSELVES WHOLLY TO HIM. Jean Nicolas Grou (1731–1803)

The One Year Bible Readings for today are **Isaiah 8:1–9:21; 2 Corinthians 12:1-10; Psalm 55:1-23;** and **Proverbs 23:4-5.**

SEPTEMBER

12

fears

Beyond Our Fears

When I am afraid, I put my trust in you. O God, I praise your word. I trust in God, so why should I be afraid?
Psalm 56:3-4

Have you ever found yourself in such a frightening situation that it pushed your "panic button"? Some people face that kind of fear because of a dreadful circumstance. Others may fear failure, rejection, illness, or death. Children often fear the dark and want their parents to hold their hand as they walk into a dark room.

Whatever you fear, you don't have to handle it alone by working harder, trying to control things, living in denial, or worst of all, backing away from God and his promises. Instead, these Scripture verses tell us we can turn to God when we are afraid. As we honestly admit what we're afraid of, our fear can actually draw us closer to the Lord than we ever thought possible. Reading God's promises in the Bible gives us assurance that we are not alone in this fearful place. God has promised to be with you in every situation and to never leave you, so you can put your trust in him. He is the source of our courage and security. He can turn your fear into faith.

LORD, you have said that when I'm afraid, at the very point of my anxiety, I can put my trust in you and experience your protection. I thank you for your Word that promises your presence with me. You are my heavenly Father, so please hold my hand in dark and frightening circumstances, and help me to trust you and walk close to you today.

YOUR FEAR IS A HANDLE FOR LAYING HOLD ON GOD. WHEN YOU STOP RUNNING AND FACE YOUR FEAR HEAD ON WITH FAITH, YOU FIND GOD. IT IS HIS PRESENCE AND POWER THAT MOVE US BEYOND OUR FEARS—PAST, PRESENT, AND FUTURE.
Bruce Larson

The One Year Bible Readings for today are **Isaiah 10:1–11:16; 2 Corinthians 12:11-21; Psalm 56:1-13;** and **Proverbs 23:6-8.**

SEPTEMBER
13

plan

God's Sovereign Plan

The Lord Almighty has sworn this oath: "It will all happen as I have planned. It will come about according to my purposes. . . . I have a plan for the whole earth, for my mighty power reaches throughout the world. The Lord Almighty has spoken—who can change his plans? When his hand moves, who can stop him?"
Isaiah 14:24-27

When our plans are upended or our dreams are shattered, when we feel as if we have lost it all, these verses in Isaiah encourage us to turn to the Lord, whose plans cannot be frustrated. Even when we have seen *our* plans and dreams go astray or crumble, God still has a plan for the whole world—and for us. How comforting to remember that *nothing* can change God's plans! His purposes always stand. His hand stretches out and moves in the earth, and no one can turn it back or stop him.

In the face of the worst tragedy or disaster, remember that God has a sovereign plan for the whole earth, for our nation, for every nation of the world, and for each one of us individually. That is why we can cry out to God in confidence, knowing that he will fulfill his purposes for each of us, for our families, and for our world.

How I praise you, FATHER, for your sovereignty, your eternal unshakable stability, and for your perfect wisdom and purpose. In the face of my broken dreams or disappointed plans, how thankful I am for your Word. In it I find deep and wonderful encouragement that nothing can thwart your purposes. And I know you will accomplish your perfect plans for my life.

GOD'S PLANS, LIKE LILIES PURE AND WHITE, UNFOLD. WE MUST NOT TEAR THE CLOSESHUT LEAVES APART. TIME WILL REVEAL THE CALYXES OF GOLD. Mary Riley Smith (1842–1927)

The One Year Bible Readings for today are **Isaiah 12:1–14:32; 2 Corinthians 13:1-13; Psalm 57:1-11;** and **Proverbs 23:9-11.**

approval

Seeking Approval

Obviously, I'm not trying to be a people pleaser! No, I am trying to please God. If I were still trying to please people, I would not be Christ's servant.
Galatians 1:10

Paul knew that if he was going to be a real servant of Christ, he could not tiptoe around the message that the people of Galatia needed to hear. They were in much danger of being led astray by false teaching, and he did not make apologies for his bluntness or straightforwardness in steering them back to the truth. Paul knew that he was dealing with life-and-death issues because the Judaizers' perversion of the gospel of Christ was spreading like wildfire throughout Galatia. "I am trying to please God," he proclaimed. He was clear on who his real audience was: God. Is our focus on pleasing people or on pleasing God? What dilemmas, situations, concerns, or people do you face that tempt you not to speak out in boldness or not to live in a way that will bring God the greatest honor and glory? Just as Paul did, we can exchange being a people pleaser for a much higher calling—being a servant of Christ!

LORD, I desire to live as Christ's servant and not as a people pleaser. I realize that I cannot seek the approval of others as I live for you. It is your approval alone that I seek, the approval that really counts. Help me to speak and act in boldness and love as I serve you.

TEACH US, GOOD LORD, TO SERVE THEE AS THOU
DESERVEST;
TO GIVE AND NOT TO COUNT THE COST;
TO FIGHT AND NOT TO HEED THE WOUNDS;
TO TOIL AND NOT TO SEEK FOR REST;
TO LABOR AND NOT TO ASK FOR ANY REWARD,
SAVE THAT OF KNOWING THAT WE DO THY WILL.
AMEN.

Saint Ignatius of Loyola

The One Year Bible Readings for today are **Isaiah 15:1–18:7; Galatians 1:1-24; Psalm 58:1-11;** and **Proverbs 23:12.**

SEPTEMBER
15

morning

Morning Joy

As for me, I will sing about your power. I will shout with joy each morning because of your unfailing love. For you have been my refuge, a place of safety in the day of distress.
Psalm 59:16

David always seemed to find something to sing about. No matter how perilous his situation, no matter how many enemies were chasing him, he had a song of praise for his King. He lived with an awareness that it was God who saved him in his day of distress when his life was threatened. It was God—and God alone—who kept him safe. He knew his place of refuge was in the powerful arms of God. That is why he wanted to sing.

How fitting and marvelous it is for us to greet each new day with a song in our hearts because of God's unfailing love in our lives, because each day is a gift from him. We can remember the things he has gotten us through and his promised presence for every day of our life. Realizing anew God's grace and love stirs such emotion in our spirits that songs of praise may seem to burst forth and lead us to rest in the powerful arms of God in times of distress. What a way to start the day—joyfully resting in the mighty arms of God!

LORD, "morning by morning new mercies I see." I want to begin today to sing about your power and to bless your name each morning. Thank you for being my place of safety in the day of distress. I praise you for this new day. May I rest in your powerful arms today and sing of your mercies once again tomorrow.

YOU DON'T LEARN TO PRAISE IN A DAY, ESPECIALLY SINCE YOU MAY HAVE BEEN COMPLAINING FOR YEARS! NEW HABITS TAKE TIME TO DEVELOP. BUT YOU CAN BEGIN TODAY, AND PRACTICE TOMORROW, AND THE NEXT DAY, UNTIL IT BECOMES PART OF YOU. Erwin W. Lutzer (b. 1941)

The One Year Bible Readings for today are **Isaiah 19:1–21:17; Galatians 2:1-16; Psalm 59:1-17;** and **Proverbs 23:13-14.**

living

Christ Living in Me

I myself no longer live, but Christ lives in me. So I live my life in this earthly body by trusting in the Son of God, who loved me and gave himself for me.
Galatians 2:20

Have you known the frustration of trying to put your selfish nature to death? It's about as easy as putting out a fire with gasoline! In ourselves we cannot destroy the old ways any more than we can make ourselves righteous. And therein lies the key: only the living presence of the Holy Spirit *in* us can accomplish these things. Our lives in our earthly bodies must be captured by the revelation of God's unconditional love for us, demonstrated in the life, sacrifice, and resurrection of Jesus. This love is not merely a future hope. It is a present reality—now! Just as light displaces darkness, Christ in us will displace what needs to die as we focus our attentions on him. He will use our circumstances to bring us to the point where we are teachable and ready to truly learn to put our trust in him. That is the time when we can begin to fight our selfish nature—through the power of Christ living in us.

OH, LORD, thank you for loving me and giving yourself for me. Thank you for your desire to live through me and enable me to live for you. May the truth of your Word give me the vision to trust you with all that I am so that all you are may dwell in me.

FEED ON CHRIST, AND THEN GO AND LIVE YOUR LIFE, AND IT IS CHRIST IN YOU THAT LIVES YOUR LIFE, THAT HELPS THE POOR, THAT TELLS THE TRUTH, THAT FIGHTS THE BATTLE, AND THAT WINS THE CROWN. Phillips Brooks (1835–1893)

The One Year Bible Readings for today are **Isaiah 22:1–24:23; Galatians 2:17–3:9; Psalm 60:1-12;** and **Proverbs 23:15-16.**

SEPTEMBER
17

peace

A Promised Peace

You will keep in perfect peace all who trust in you, whose thoughts are fixed on you!
Isaiah 26:3

In this verse God's promised peace has two conditions: First, it is for those who trust in him, which means to commit ourselves to the Lord, lean on him, and hope confidently in him. Second, it is for those who fix their thoughts on God. We are often preoccupied and have our minds focused on many other things. Some of us seem to have a tape in our minds that keeps replaying a list of responsibilities, tasks and scheduled activities, problems and burdens, and the tragedies and fearful things going on in the world around us. But when we fix our minds and thoughts on the character and attributes of the Lord our God, we have something different playing in our minds: the reminder that God is our everlasting rock, our refuge in times of trouble, the Lord Almighty who holds the whole world and each of us individually in his hands. With God as our focus and with our faith firmly fixed on him, we can experience the truth of today's verse: he will keep us in perfect and constant peace no matter what happens. It's a promise.

LORD, I am hearing that "list" replaying in my head, and I need your peace for today. I ask you to help me to do these things: to lean on you, to meditate on your character and attributes, and to trust you with all my heart. Thank you for your promise that your perfect peace will guard my heart and mind.

IN CHRIST WE ARE RELAXED AND AT PEACE IN THE MIDST OF THE CONFUSIONS, BEWILDERMENTS, AND PERPLEXITIES OF THIS LIFE. THE STORM RAGES, BUT OUR HEARTS ARE AT REST. WE HAVE FOUND PEACE—AT LAST! Billy Graham (b. 1918)

The One Year Bible Readings for today are **Isaiah 25:1–28:13; Galatians 3:10-22; Psalm 61:1-8;** and **Proverbs 23:17-18.**

friend

Intimate Friend

O my people, trust in him at all times. Pour out your heart to him, for God is our refuge.
Psalm 62:8

This verse is an open invitation to be honest and deeply real with the Lord. It calls us to take our masks off and pour out our true thoughts and feelings to God, to be there before him telling it like it is, not how we think things should be. How freeing it is to realize that we can be totally honest with God and express our sadness or joy, our fears, our faults and weaknesses, our pain, desires and dreams, and to know that the contents of our hearts are really safe with God, our refuge. This verse also reminds us that although the specific patterns or formats for prayer are excellent principles for individual or corporate prayer times, we don't have to follow them in order for God to hear us, nor do we have to hide our negative emotions and attitudes just so we'll look good. God already knows all that we are feeling and struggling with, so we can come to him just as we are and pour out our hearts "at all times." He invites us in the midst of conflicts, stresses, responsibilities, and frustration to seek him as our closest confidante, our intimate friend.

How thankful I am for the confidence and security that you long to hear from me and to comfort me. You know and understand all the thoughts of my heart better than I do myself, and you invite me to pour out my heart to you now. And so I will. . . .

THE SPIRIT OF PRAYER MAKES US SO INTIMATE WITH GOD THAT WE SCARCELY PASS THROUGH AN EXPERIENCE BEFORE WE SPEAK TO HIM ABOUT IT, EITHER IN SUPPLICATION, IN SIGHING, IN POURING OUT OUR WOES BEFORE HIM, IN FERVENT REQUESTS, OR IN THANKSGIVING AND ADORATION.
Ole Hallesby (1879–1961)

The One Year Bible Readings for today are **Isaiah 28:14–30:11; Galatians 3:23–4:31; Psalm 62:1-12;** and **Proverbs 23:19-21.**

SEPTEMBER

19

confidence

Quiet Confidence

The Sovereign Lord . . . says, "Only in returning to me and waiting for me will you be saved. In quietness and confidence is your strength."
Isaiah 30:15

This verse describes the revealed heart of God toward humanity: "Return to me" was always God's heart toward his people even when they were in rebellion and were rejecting his call to come under the shelter of his wings. Despite the hardened condition of the people's hearts at the time Isaiah penned these verses, God declared this to be his desire—to receive the penitent, to extend salvation to them, and to grant them rest, quietness, and strength. What a shining promise to us today! Wherever we are in life, whatever mess we have made of things, or however bleak the outlook, God calls to us, "Return to me!" He knows that only in him can we find true rest for our souls as we live in this hectic world. He calls us to repentance so that we can experience his salvation. He calls to us to be quiet, still, and confident in him so that we can experience his strength.

OH, LORD, thank you for always calling me to return to you. My desire is to walk in harmony with you. But sometimes I become distant from you. Even then, I know that you haven't distanced yourself from me. You are ever waiting for me to return, to repent, and to find rest in you.

IS NOT PRAYER PRECISELY OF ITSELF PEACE, SILENCE, STRENGTH, SINCE IT IS A WAY OF BEING WITH GOD? Jacques Ellul (1912–1994)

The One Year Bible Readings for today are **Isaiah 30:12–33:9; Galatians 5:1-12; Psalm 63:1-11;** and **Proverbs 23:22.**

fruit

Spiritual Fruit

When the Holy Spirit controls our lives, he will produce this kind of fruit in us: love, joy, peace, patience, kindness, goodness, faithfulness, gentleness, and self-control.

Galatians 5:22-23

Suppose you wanted to start an apple orchard. In early spring you carefully cut dozens of twigs from an apple tree and stick them in the ground twenty feet apart. You water and fertilize and watch and wait. But in the fall, you have no apples to pick. Why? Because those twigs could not mature and bear fruit once they were not rooted in the tree they came from. The same is true with spiritual fruit. It is only when we belong to Christ and stay close to him that his Spirit lives in us and produces the virtues, or "fruit," listed in today's verse.

Self-effort won't produce this fruit. Good intentions won't produce love, joy, peace, patience, or kindness. Instead, as we yield ourselves to Christ, his Spirit lives and moves freely through us and touches others through our lives. We express his gentleness as we respond to children, his great patience as we encounter difficult people. We demonstrate his faithfulness as we keep commitments, and we share his goodness and kindness as we bless others.

LORD, teach me to yield to the control of the Holy Spirit. How I realize that none of the virtues reside within my flesh. But this understanding is a gift from you that enables me to humble myself before you and rely wholly on your Spirit rising up within me. Do so, Lord, and may the fruit you produce draw others to you!

I HAVE A GLOVE HERE IN MY HAND. THE GLOVE CANNOT DO ANYTHING BY ITSELF, BUT WHEN MY HAND IS IN IT, IT CAN DO MANY THINGS. TRUE, IT IS NOT THE GLOVE, BUT MY HAND IN THE GLOVE THAT ACTS. WE ARE GLOVES. IT IS THE HOLY SPIRIT IN US WHO IS THE HAND, WHO DOES THE JOB. WE HAVE TO MAKE ROOM FOR THE HAND SO THAT EVERY FINGER IS FILLED. Corrie ten Boom (1892–1983)

The One Year Bible Readings for today are **Isaiah 33:10–36:22; Galatians 5:13-26; Psalm 64:1-10;** and **Proverbs 23:23.**

SEPTEMBER
21

heart

Don't Lose Heart

Don't get tired of doing what is good. Don't get discouraged and give up, for we will reap a harvest of blessing at the appropriate time. Whenever we have the opportunity, we should do good to everyone, especially to our Christian brothers and sisters.

Galatians 6:9-10

How can we not get discouraged when we deal with overwhelming tasks and challenges and the brokenness, opposition, and evil in the world around us? How can we not faint or give up but keep doing good to everyone, even those who are difficult? Paul tells us here that we can successfully keep running our race with endurance and not burn out in doing what's right only by fixing our eyes on Jesus. Our faith, our ability to be a blessing and to do good to our brothers and sisters or to accomplish anything at all of lasting value depends on Christ from start to finish. When we lift our eyes to the all-powerful, all-loving God, we can commit our way to him and receive his assurance that in God's time we will reap what he has richly prepared for us—a harvest of blessing—as we daily draw fresh strength from his inexhaustible supply to keep on running in his footsteps.

LORD, thank you for teaching me in my weariness or in times when I lose heart that I can do nothing apart from you. You are my life, my strength, my salvation. I give myself to you and ask that the power of your life will restore my joy and renew my vision to keep doing your will and doing good to those around me.

WHEN WE HAVE EXHAUSTED OUR STORE OF
ENDURANCE,
WHEN OUR STRENGTH HAS FAILED ERE THE DAY IS
HALF DONE,
WHEN WE REACH THE END OF OUR HOARDED
RESOURCES,
OUR FATHER'S FULL GIVING IS ONLY BEGUN.

Annie Johnson Flint (1862–1932)

The One Year Bible Readings for today are **Isaiah 37:1–38:22; Galatians 6:1-18; Psalm 65:1-13;** and **Proverbs 23:24.**

plan

God's Eternal Plan

This is one of the greatest prayers Paul prayed for the early church, and it's an important prayer for us to pray today: that we would know God intimately, that our hearts would be flooded with light so that we can understand the bright future God promises, and that we would see how great his power is for us believers. Just as Paul knew this revelation wouldn't happen apart from God's Holy Spirit, we can't perceive these things with just our own intellect because they are spiritual truths, not intellectual truths. These verses encourage us to ask the Lord to give us good spiritual eyesight and insight about the character of God, the hope he has given us for both this life and the life to come, and the incredible dynamic power available to us through his Spirit. This is a prayer to pray often, not only for yourself but for all those you love and want to see walk with the Lord. As we pray God's Word, we pave the way for his will and purpose to be fulfilled in our lives.

FATHER, I am awed to think that from eternity past you have planned and provided a way to share your riches, your grace, your power, and your very nature with me through the sacrifice of Jesus on my behalf. Do, Lord, open my eyes, and flood my heart with vision to behold this incredible truth.

IF WE WISH TO PRAY WITH CONFIDENCE AND GLADNESS, THEN THE WORDS OF HOLY SCRIPTURE WILL HAVE TO BE THE SOLID BASE OF OUR PRAYER. FOR HERE WE KNOW THAT JESUS CHRIST, THE WORD OF GOD, TEACHES US TO PRAY. THE WORDS WHICH COME FROM GOD BECOME, THEN, THE STEPS ON WHICH WE FIND OUR WAY TO GOD.
Dietrich Bonhoeffer (1906–1945)

[I am] asking God, the glorious Father of our Lord Jesus Christ, to give you spiritual wisdom and understanding, so that you might grow in your knowledge of God. I pray that your hearts will be flooded with light so that you can understand the wonderful future he has promised to those he called. I want you to realize what a rich and glorious inheritance he has given to his people. I pray that you will begin to understand the incredible greatness of his power for us who believe him.
Ephesians 1:17-19

The One Year Bible Readings for today are **Isaiah 39:1–41:16; Ephesians 1:1-23; Psalm 66:1-20;** and **Proverbs 23:25-28.**

SEPTEMBER

23

trials

When Trials Come

When you go through deep waters and great trouble, I will be with you. When you go through rivers of difficulty, you will not drown! When you walk through the fire of oppression, you will not be burned up; the flames will not consume you.
Isaiah 43:2

Two important words are repeated over and over again in this passage: *when* and *through*. As children of God, each of us will experience times of trouble, trials, and testing. There will be seasons when our circumstances are frightening or painful. Sometimes we will face not just one problem but waves of difficulties. This is why the Lord says, "when," not "if," the waters rise, the rivers flood, and the fires burn. Yet in these verses the Lord also gives us reassurance that he will get us "through." No matter how deep the waters, you will get to the other side. No matter how intense the fiery trials, you will experience victory because he is "the Lord, your God, . . . your Savior" (v. 3). Use these verses from Isaiah to remind yourself that God is not only able to keep and protect you when you encounter rivers of difficulty but that he has committed himself to carrying you through them.

LORD, thank you for your promises of deliverance and protection. Because you've said, "I will be with you," what have I to fear? Help me to trust in you, not only in the small details or battles of life, but also in times of great trouble. You are my Lord, my God, my Savior.

CHRISTIAN! PRAY FOR GRACE TO SEE IN EVERY TROUBLE, SMALL OR GREAT, THE FATHER'S FINGER POINTING TO JESUS, AND SAYING, ABIDE IN HIM.
Andrew Murray (1828–1917)

The One Year Bible Readings for today are **Isaiah 41:17–43:13; Ephesians 2:1-22; Psalm 67:1-7;** and **Proverbs 23:29-35.**

love

The Depth of God's Love

May your roots go down deep into the soil of God's marvelous love. And may you have the power to understand, as all God's people should, how wide, how long, how high, and how deep his love really is. May you experience the love of Christ, though it is so great you will never fully understand it.
Ephesians 3:17-19

This prayer is not asking God for more head knowledge about his love but that we would *understand and comprehend it*—that it would really sink in and go from being head knowledge to heart knowledge about how very much he loves us. Most of all, it asks that we would *experience for ourselves* the love of Christ. Knowledge isn't enough. Great speeches or sermons won't suffice, neither will hearing what the Lord did in someone else's life. It takes God's Spirit imparting power to each of us to fathom the depth and length and width, the incomparable nature, of God's amazing love for us in Christ Jesus. Just as Paul was praying earnestly for the Ephesian Christians, we are to ask that our roots would go down deep into the soil of God's marvelous love. And as we continually pray this life-transforming prayer, we will drink deeply of God's love. When we receive and experience the love of Christ in our own hearts, his love can flow through us to others.

LORD JESUS, I want to understand and experience your love in a deeper way than I ever have before. May your love be my anchor as your Spirit causes my roots to sink deeper in you. Grant me the power to understand the limitless extent of your love. Be the center of my life and reveal yourself to me today!

WE MUST DAILY COME AND DRINK AT THE FOUNTAIN OF DIVINE LOVE. HEREIN LIES THE PURPOSE OF ALL PRAYER. Margaret Therkelsen

The One Year Bible Readings for today are **Isaiah 43:14–45:10; Ephesians 3:1-21; Psalm 68:1-18;** and **Proverbs 24:1-2.**

SEPTEMBER
25

care

Everlasting Care

Listen to me, all you who are left in Israel. I created you and have cared for you since before you were born. I will be your God throughout your lifetime—until your hair is white with age. I made you, and I will care for you. I will carry you along and save you.
Isaiah 46:3-4

God is speaking to the faithful remnant of his people, first exhorting them, "Listen to me," because he has something important to say. Then after he has their—and our—attention, he reminds us of his faithfulness in the past and assures us of his care and salvation for our future—even into old age. From the time we were conceived and born into this world to the very end of our lives, our creator, who knitted us together in our mother's womb, the same eternal, unchanging One who created the heavens and the earth, is the One who has been caring for us all along, through the hands of parents and others who have loved, nurtured, and taught us. And it is he who will sustain us—throughout our childhood and youth, in our active years of working or parenting, and into the elder years when our hair is white with age and we can no longer care for ourselves but are dependent on the care of others. Our heavenly Father is our God of everlasting care.

LORD, help me to realize that you are everlastingly my Father, intimately acquainted with me and with every moment of my entire lifetime. Help me to rely on you through every season of my life and to rest in the knowledge that even when I am old, you will still be caring for me.

GOD HAS GIVEN TO MAN A SHORT TIME HERE UPON EARTH, AND YET UPON THIS SHORT TIME ETERNITY DEPENDS. Jeremy Taylor (1613–1667)

The One Year Bible Readings for today are **Isaiah 45:11–48:11; Ephesians 4:1-16; Psalm 68:19-35;** and **Proverbs 24:3-4.**

grace

Words That Give Grace

Don't use foul or abusive language. Let everything you say be good and helpful, so that your words will be an encouragement to those who hear them.
Ephesians 4:29

When Paul wrote to the believers in Ephesus in chapter 4, he instructed them about how to live differently from the way the ungodly do: don't steal, work honestly, give generously, etc. In this verse, however, he teaches about the importance of the words they speak, a message just as applicable to believers in the twenty-first century as to those early Christians. For most of us, "foul or abusive language" isn't what trips us up. Instead, it's the critical, judgmental, unloving, harsh, or subtly sarcastic words that slip out from time to time and tear down the people around us (especially those we are closest to). Paul holds us to a higher standard: speak only words that are encouraging and words that build others up. In a moment of conflict, irritation, or frustration, less-than-helpful words can so easily slip out of our mouths. Oh, how we need the Holy Spirit to work Christ's gentleness and love in our hearts so that the words we speak will truly be words that give grace.

LORD, may my heart and words today be full of encouragement and may they give grace to others. Work your gentleness and patience in me so that I won't be so quick to respond in ways that don't honor you. "May the words of my mouth and the thoughts of my heart be pleasing to you, O Lord, my rock and my redeemer."

OH GOD, STAY WITH ME; LET NO WORD CROSS MY LIPS THAT IS NOT YOUR WORD, NO THOUGHTS ENTER MY MIND THAT ARE NOT YOUR THOUGHTS.
Malcolm Muggeridge (1903–1990)

The One Year Bible Readings for today are **Isaiah 48:12–50:11; Ephesians 4:17-32; Psalm 69:1-18;** and **Proverbs 24:5-6.**

SEPTEMBER
27

welcome

Welcome, Holy Spirit

Don't be drunk with wine, because that will ruin your life. Instead, let the Holy Spirit fill and control you. Then you will sing psalms and hymns and spiritual songs among yourselves, making music to the Lord in your hearts. And you will always give thanks for everything to God the Father in the name of our Lord Jesus Christ.
Ephesians 5:18-20

In order to live filled with the Holy Spirit, there is only one prerequisite: acceptance, belief, and trust in Jesus Christ as our Savior and our Lord. However, we experience the manifestation of the Spirit's power and of Christ in our lives as we daily yield ourselves to his control. In the original text, verse 19 reads, "Speaking to ourselves." This means making a conscious choice to praise the Lord and to center our lives on Christ. In doing so, we are laying down the welcome mat to his Holy Spirit's presence in our hearts and lives. Each day we can celebrate God's goodness and faithfulness. Take a few minutes to meditate on the numerous ways he has blessed you and your family. Ask to be filled with his Spirit, and don't forget to give thanks to him. There is no better way to live than to spend our days extolling him with his praise always on our lips (Psalm 34:1, NIV).

FATHER, I welcome your Holy Spirit to fill me and have full control of my life. Thank you for your precious empowering Spirit and all you have done in my life. If I were to stop and really begin counting all the ways you have blessed me, my heart would overflow with praise to you. Oh, Holy Spirit, fill my heart with that kind of gratitude and praise.

THE GREAT REASON WHY THE HOLY SPIRIT WAS GIVEN FROM HEAVEN WAS TO MAKE CHRIST'S PRESENCE MANIFEST TO US.
Andrew Murray (1828–1917)

The One Year Bible Readings for today are **Isaiah 51:1–53:12; Ephesians 5:1-33; Psalm 69:19-36;** and **Proverbs 24:7.**

SEPTEMBER

28

praying

Praying in the Spirit

Pray at all times and on every occasion in the power of the Holy Spirit.
Ephesians 6:18

Do you ever get sick and tired of praying? We're all guilty of it, but in this verse we see how to get out of that prayer rut. Continual, effectual prayer is not, and cannot be, an exercise of our flesh; . . . it is the exercise of the Spirit within us. In Romans 8:26, Paul gives us additional insight into this essential matter when he points out that "the Holy Spirit prays for us with groanings that cannot be expressed in words." We typically find ourselves trying to project our prayers and petitions through space to some far-off place where God dwells and where we have a mansion awaiting our arrival. But Paul tells us in Ephesians that God is joining us "together as part of this dwelling where God lives by his Spirit" (2:22). Our eternal destiny is to corporately and individually be the place where the Spirit dwells and through which he intercedes. God is using every circumstance to help us grasp this truth and to learn to let the "rivers of living water" flow through us.

OH, GOD, teach me to know the presence of your Spirit within me and to walk and live in continual awareness of it. May you freely live your life in me, express your heart through me, and pray through me. I know that I can't accomplish any of this through my own efforts, but with you, nothing is impossible!

THE SPIRIT OF PRAYER WILL NOT ONLY SHOW YOU THE TRUE MEANING AND PURPOSE OF PRAYER; HE WILL ALSO LIFT YOU IN ALL YOUR HELPLESSNESS UP TO THE VERY HEART OF GOD WHERE YOU WILL BE WARMED BY HIS LOVE, SO THAT YOU CAN BEGIN TO PRAY ACCORDING TO HIS WILL, ASKING FOR NOTHING EXCEPT THOSE THINGS WHICH ARE IN HARMONY WITH HIS PLANS AND PURPOSES.
Ole Hallesby (1879–1961)

The One Year Bible Readings for today are **Isaiah 54:1–57:14; Ephesians 6:1-24; Psalm 70:1-5;** and **Proverbs 24:8.**

SEPTEMBER

29

heart

God's Heart for You

The high and lofty one who inhabits eternity, the Holy One, says this: "I live in that high and holy place with those whose spirits are contrite and humble. I refresh the humble and give new courage to those with repentant hearts."
Isaiah 57:15

This verse gives us a beautiful picture of God's relationship with his people. He is high and holy, the glorious, exalted One. He reigns over all in heaven and on earth. The Lord Almighty needs no house, for his dwelling place is all eternity. And yet he chooses to dwell with—literally to abide and make his home in—those who are anything but "high and holy" and who know it. Rather they are those whose spirits are humble, contrite, open, and teachable. Instead of being like the Pharisee in Luke 18, who thanked God that he wasn't like the unjust or other unsavory people, they are like the tax gatherer who cried out for God's mercy. They know how unworthy they are of God's love and mercy. But God's holy and loving heart is moved by individuals who humble themselves and acknowledge their weakness and dependence on him. Then he refreshes, revives, and gives new courage to these repentant souls. How gracious our God is!

OH, GOD, you are high and lifted up, glorious and exalted! And I am not. I bow before you and ask you to develop in me a heart of humility. Your Word says that you will not despise a repentant heart, and so I ask you to work that in me today. Thank you for meeting me right where I am and for bringing renewed courage for my life.

BETWEEN THE HUMBLE AND CONTRITE HEART AND THE MAJESTY OF HEAVEN, THERE ARE NO BARRIERS; THE ONLY PASSWORD IS PRAYER.
Hosea Ballou (1771–1852)

The One Year Bible Readings for today are **Isaiah 57:15–59:21; Philippians 1:1-26; Psalm 71:1-24; Proverbs 24:9-10.**

humble

Humble Hearts

In this passage Paul was exhorting the believers at Philippi to demonstrate in practical ways the unity that belonged to them in Christ Jesus, a unity not wrought by human means but by the Holy Spirit within them. Don't live out of selfish motives but out of love, pouring yourself out as Jesus did, he urged them. Care more about pleasing God than about making a good impression on others.

Our natural human tendency is toward selfishness instead of sacrifice and service, but in a world that rewards self-promotion and puts celebrities on pedestals, God calls us in these verses to assume a lowly place—as Jesus did when he came to earth to serve, not to be served. This King of kings and Lord of all lords made himself nothing and didn't cling to his rights as God but obediently humbled himself even to the point of dying on the cross. And he is calling us to join his family of servants, to bend over the fallen and lift their load, to be his hands and feet, and to call others to come to his side.

HOLY SPIRIT, work in me a desire to please you rather than to impress people. Forgive me for my selfishness and for focusing on my life, my needs, my problems. Help me to care more about others and their needs and to have a servant's heart so that you can do your work through me.

IN GOD'S FAMILY THERE IS TO BE ONE GREAT BODY OF PEOPLE: SERVANTS. IN FACT, THAT'S THE WAY TO THE TOP IN HIS KINGDOM.
Charles R. Swindoll (b. 1934)

Don't be selfish; don't live to make a good impression on others. Be humble, thinking of others as better than yourself. Don't think only about your own affairs, but be interested in others, too, and what they are doing. Your attitude should be the same that Christ Jesus had. Though he was God, he did not demand and cling to his rights as God. He made himself nothing; he took the humble position of a slave and appeared in human form.
Philippians 2:3-7

The One Year Bible Readings for today are **Isaiah 60:1–62:5; Philippians 1:27–2:18; Psalm 72:1-20;** and **Proverbs 24:11-12.**

OCTOBER

1

coming

The Coming Down of the Lord

Oh, that you would burst from the heavens and come down! How the mountains would quake in your presence! As fire causes wood to burn and water to boil, your coming would make the nations tremble. . . . When you came down long ago, you did awesome things beyond our highest expectations. And oh, how the mountains quaked! For since the world began, no ear has heard, and no eye has seen a God like you, who works for those who wait for him!

Isaiah 64:1-4

When almighty God "comes down," he comes in awesome, majestic ways. So often, when we least expect to experience or hear from God, that is when he surprises us with his presence and his voice. That is when a breakthrough in a situation happens; the darkness lifts, and we see the light of day. Sometimes because of impatience or discouragement, we wonder if God is able to help us, and we no longer expect him to "come down." But this passage from Isaiah encourages us not to lose the expectancy of his moving in our lives. It urges us to wait for God and calls us to remember that it is through his mercy, forgiveness, compassion, and the shed blood of his Son that we are even allowed to stand in awe of him who causes mountains to quake and nations to tremble. Before time began, no one has even imagined or seen a God like our God, who works on behalf of those who wait for him.

LORD, I stand in awe of you! I thank you for doing such awesome things, for working beyond my highest expectations. And you continue to do them for those who wait for you. Help me to wait for you with hope. Fill me with a holy expectancy of your coming, and glorify yourself through my life.

IN MY HEART I DO HAVE A FEAR. . . . I LONG TO GROW MORE GODLY WITH EACH PASSING DAY. CALL IT "THE FEAR OF THE LORD," BEING IN AWE OF HIM AND SCARED TO DEATH OF ANY SIN THAT WOULD MAR MY LIFE AT THIS POINT. Anne Ortlund

The One Year Bible Readings for today are **Isaiah 62:6–65:25; Philippians 2:19–3:3; Psalm 73:1-28;** and **Proverbs 24:13-14.**

goal

Focused on the Goal

World-class sports stars such as cyclist Lance Armstrong, tennis champion Venus Williams, and golfer Tiger Woods have been the subjects of research by people who are trying to determine why they win championships against other athletes who have just as much talent and skill. What is their secret? It's not just that they set aside distractions and make personal sacrifices in order to practice and hone their skills. It was their ability to stay *focused under stress.* This verse tells us what the supreme and heavenly prize is and what our focus should be: it's not winning the Tour de France or Wimbledon, not the U.S. Open or an Olympic gold medal. It's the greatest prize of all—knowing Christ Jesus and following him as he calls us upward from glory to glory. Let us forget the past, ask for the endurance and strength to finish the race, and focus all our energies on this one thing, this eternal prize!

No, dear brothers and sisters, I am still not all I should be, but I am focusing all my energies on this one thing: Forgetting the past and looking forward to what lies ahead, I strain to reach the end of the race and receive the prize for which God, through Christ Jesus, is calling us up to heaven.
Philippians 3:13-14

LORD, help me to keep my eye on the goal, where you are beckoning me upward and onward to Jesus. Keep me from being distracted by the past—my sins and wrong choices have been washed in the blood of Christ. Therefore, grant me grace and strength not to turn back, and even under great stress help me to keep my eyes on the eternal prize—unending life in your glorious presence!

NOT IN THE ACHIEVEMENT, BUT IN THE ENDURANCE OF THE HUMAN SOUL DOES IT SHOW ITS DIVINE GRANDEUR AND ITS ALLIANCE WITH THE INFINITE GOD. Edwin Hubbel Chapin (1814–1880)

The One Year Bible Readings for today are **Isaiah 66:1-24; Philippians 3:4-21; Psalm 74:1-23;** and **Proverbs 24:15-16.**

OCTOBER

3

peace

Experiencing God's Peace

Don't worry about anything; instead, pray about everything. Tell God what you need, and thank him for all he has done. If you do this, you will experience God's peace, which is far more wonderful than the human mind can understand. His peace will guard your hearts and minds as you live in Christ Jesus.
Philippians 4:6-7

This pattern given in Philippians 4, of taking our worries to God and centering our thoughts on him and all he has done is an important secret of prayer. We all have different "panic buttons," or experiences that cause our hearts and minds to race, our confidence and strength to waver. Your panic button may relate to your children's safety, your finances, your health, or an uncertain employment future. Whatever they are, these needs and burdens are actually meant to draw us to God in prayer. If we open our hearts and invite Jesus into our need and put our focus on him, he will quiet our anxious thoughts and bring us a sense of calm. His peace, which is far more wonderful than our human minds can comprehend, then brings comfort and order to our hearts. In the midst of this anxiety-ridden, fear-filled world we live in, the Lord wants to reveal himself as the God who calms our fears and turns our worries into wonder at what a great God he is.

HOLY SPIRIT, here is my worry. Here is my need. I give them to you, and ask you to calm my anxious heart and quiet my racing thoughts. Center them on Jesus Christ and on his power and sufficiency today. Because I belong to you, I know that your peace will guard my heart and mind.

THE ONLY WAY IN WHICH WE CAN GATHER AND KEEP COLLECTED OUR DISTRACTED MINDS AND OUR ROAMING THOUGHTS IS TO CENTER THEM ABOUT JESUS CHRIST. . . . LET CHRIST LAY HOLD OF, ATTRACT, CAPTIVATE AND GATHER ABOUT HIMSELF ALL OUR INTERESTS. THEN OUR SESSIONS OF PRAYER WILL BECOME REAL MEETINGS WITH GOD . . . AND THE PEACE OF GOD WILL DESCEND WITH HEALING AND BLESSING UPON MY DISTRACTED SOUL. Ole Hallesby (1879–1961)

The One Year Bible Readings for today are **Jeremiah 1:1–2:30; Philippians 4:1-23; Psalm 75:1-10;** and **Proverbs 24:17-20.**

Ask Big

Paul is asking God for a great deal on behalf of the Colossian Christians: for spiritual wisdom to understand the very ways and purposes of God so that their lives will always please and honor him; for strength so to walk in patience and endurance; and for not just a survival mentality but for hearts filled with joy and thankfulness no matter what happens. These are lofty requests—almost more than we could hope for. Yet since this is indeed God's will, stated clearly in his Word for not only the first-century Christians but all believers, we can begin to see the depths of what God intends and desires to grant through prayer. So ask—ask big! Ask for the whole package of wisdom, understanding, and the strength of his glorious power expressed in these verses. Ask that you will be filled with *so much joy* that you will continually thank God, who has made us to share in his wonderful and eternal inheritance.

OH, LORD, thank you for providing a way for me to be illuminated with the understanding of your will and for desiring that I fully grasp your purposes in my life! Fill me with spiritual wisdom. Strengthen me with your glorious power so that I will have all the patience and endurance I need, and fill me with your joy so that I will constantly be offering thanks to you.

JOY IS THAT DEEP SETTLED CONFIDENCE THAT GOD IS IN CONTROL OF EVERY AREA OF MY LIFE.
Paul Sailhamer

We ask God to give you a complete understanding of what he wants to do in your lives, and we ask him to make you wise with spiritual wisdom. . . . We also pray that you will be strengthened with his glorious power so that you will have all the patience and endurance you need. May you be filled with joy, always thanking the Father, who has enabled you to share the inheritance that belongs to God's holy people, who live in the light.
Colossians 1:9-12

The One Year Bible Readings for today are **Jeremiah 2:31–4:18; Colossians 1:1-17; Psalm 76:1-12;** and **Proverbs 24:21-22.**

OCTOBER

5

Christ in You

This is the secret: Christ lives in you, and this is your assurance that you will share in his glory.

Colossians 1:27

Here is the heart of Christianity, which distinguishes it from every other religion in the world. It is not simply some universal spirit of goodness dwelling in humanity that we must strive to realize. Nor is it a set of rules and regulations that will bring us into union with our creator. The only hope and assurance we have of that eternal life, that object of the human quest, is what God himself has given us in Christ.

If we have accepted the gift of our Maker, forgiveness of sin and new life through Jesus Christ, we can begin to live each day in intimate fellowship with him. That goal is no longer unattainable or hindered by our human weakness. It is an accomplished reality. Because of Christ, God's dwelling place is not somewhere on the other side of the cosmos. He inhabits the spirits of those who have been "born of God," and continually calls to us, "Come unto me."

DEAR GOD, as I walk through this day, may I be aware of the fact that Jesus is actually living in me by his Spirit. I don't begin to understand how that can be, but help me to realize that your presence in me is a reality and my only life and hope. In that knowledge, grant me the freedom to enjoy this time together with you.

TRUE PEACE IS FOUND BY MAN IN THE DEPTHS OF HIS OWN HEART, THE DWELLING PLACE OF GOD.
Johann Tauler (ca. 1300–1361)

The One Year Bible Readings for today are **Jeremiah 4:19–6:15; Colossians 1:18–2:7; Psalm 77:1-20;** and **Proverbs 24:23-25.**

complete

Complete in Christ

In Christ the fullness of God lives in a human body, and you are complete through your union with Christ.
Colossians 2:9-10

This verse expresses the uniqueness of "God's one and only Son" (John 3:18, NIV). The Messiah was not merely a prophet on whom the Spirit of God occasionally settled. Even in the beginning, Jesus was "with God, and he was God" (John 1:1). If he were anything less, Christianity would be just another human attempt to bring peace on earth. The fullness of God—everything that God is—lives in Jesus, and Jesus lives in us, and we are complete in him. Think about that!

When we struggle with our daily cares and lose sight of our purpose in life, we usually begin to feel that much is lacking in us. And that's true! As a matter of fact, that's exactly why God takes us through the tribulations of life. It is when we think we've got it all together that we tend to be the farthest from God. But if we recognize and acknowledge our genuine need of him, we will find that in him we are complete.

LORD JESUS, you are so completely great and awesome! How can it be that you have chosen to live in me? And yet you have. Help me to trust you, knowing that you are in control and that you are using everything that happens in my life to show me that in you I am complete and lack nothing.

HOLY HAS THE SAME ROOT AS *WHOLLY*, IT MEANS COMPLETE. A MAN IS NOT COMPLETE IN SPIRITUAL STATURE IF ALL HIS MIND, HEART, SOUL, AND STRENGTH ARE NOT GIVEN TO GOD. R. J. Stewart

The One Year Bible Readings for today are **Jeremiah 6:16–8:7; Colossians 2:8-23; Psalm 78:1-31;** and **Proverbs 24:26.**

OCTOBER

7

heavenly

Be Heavenly Minded

Since you have been raised to new life with Christ, set your sights on the realities of heaven, where Christ sits at God's right hand in the place of honor and power. Let heaven fill your thoughts. Do not think only about things down here on earth. For you died when Christ died, and your real life is hidden with Christ in God.
Colossians 3:1-3

In his letter to the Christians in Rome, Paul admonishes us, "Don't copy the behavior and customs of this world, but let God transform you into a new person by changing the way you think" (Romans 12:2). In today's verses, he gives us an important step in that process of transformation. Our inherent tendency is to direct our lives on this earth according to what we perceive with our five senses. The fact is, if we have embraced Christ, our attachment to this physical world is no longer the defining element of our existence. Jesus himself is.

The present reality of his love for us and our new life in him must become the primary focus of our attention if we hope to escape the clutches of darkness of this present world. No religious activity can set us free, no matter how transcendent it might be. The realities of heaven become the substance of our lives only when we set our sights on him in whom our life is hidden.

LORD, help me to see with new eyes today. Instead of the troubles of my life in this world, may I focus my vision on you, the author and finisher of my faith, the lover and keeper of my soul. Help me to trust in the realities of your kingdom more than I trust what I can experience with my physical body.

A MAN WITH THE VISION OF GOD IS NOT DEVOTED SIMPLY TO A CAUSE OR A PARTICULAR ISSUE BUT TO GOD HIMSELF. Oswald Chambers (1874–1917)

The One Year Bible Readings for today are **Jeremiah 8:8–9:26; Colossians 3:1-17; Psalm 78:32-55;** and **Proverbs 24:27.**

work

The Greatest Work

Epaphras, from your city, a servant of Christ Jesus, sends you his greetings. He always prays earnestly for you, asking God to make you strong and perfect, fully confident of the whole will of God.
Colossians 4:12

As Epaphras prayed for his fellow Colossian Christians to stand firm in everything God wanted them to do in order to become mature believers, he didn't utter a casual prayer now and then. Paul tells us in this verse that Epaphras prayed earnestly, which means that he was "always wrestling in prayer" (NIV). It implies an act of agonizing in prayer. In today's world we see thirty-minute solutions on network television programs. Because of the level of technology we have at our disposal, we have come to expect quick responses or results, and we want prayer to be as light and easy as possible. The saints of old understood the truth this verse expresses: prayer is work. It is easy to fall into thinking that the most vital work into which we can invest our energy and time is our career, our ministry, or the tasks of running an organization, supporting a political cause, or managing a household. But prayer is the most important work of all, and it's worth our effort, our time, our persistence, and our wholehearted passion.

LORD, grant me the same strength of heart and perseverance that Epaphras had, to pray earnestly and faithfully and even forcefully for my children, both natural and spiritual, and for other believers you have ordained as my circle of prayer. Make us strong and complete and help us to live fully confident of your will.

WE ARE TO LABOR AT PRAYER AS A MAN LABORS AT HIS DAILY WORK. WE ARE TO PUT FORTH OUR ENERGY IN THIS WORK UNTIL WE ARE WEARY.
George H. C. MacGregor

The One Year Bible Readings for today are **Jeremiah 10:1–11:23; Colossians 3:18–4:18; Psalm 78:56-72;** and **Proverbs 24:28-29.**

OCTOBER

9

legacy

A Legacy of Prayer

We always thank God for all of you and pray for you constantly.
1 Thessalonians 1:2

Some people have the resources to leave a large sum of money to their loved ones when they die. Others will leave a great legacy through hospitals and university buildings named after them. A few will leave vast real estate holdings or thriving family businesses. But this verse expresses the greatest legacy we can leave to our children, our grandchildren, and other loved ones: it's the legacy of prayer. Your prayers for your family and those God calls you to intercede for are never in vain! As you live a life of intercession, God will hear your prayers. He will bless the ones you are praying for and fulfill his plans for their lives. But the blessing won't stop when you leave this earthly body for heaven. Your prayers will continue to have an impact. You can give your children and loved ones many gifts in this life and be a positive influence, but the greatest influence, the greatest gift you can give them, is through your prayers.

FATHER, I thank you for the gift of prayer and for my children, grandchildren, other family members, and friends. I intercede today on behalf of [insert name(s)]. Bless them, draw them into a closer relationship with you, and help me to be faithful in praying for them constantly, as long as I have breath!

AROUND US IS A WORLD LOST IN SIN, ABOVE US IS A GOD WILLING AND ABLE TO SAVE; IT IS OURS TO BUILD THE BRIDGE THAT LINKS HEAVEN AND EARTH, AND PRAYER IS THE MIGHTY INSTRUMENT THAT DOES THE WORK. IF WE DO OUR PART, GOD WILL DO HIS. E. M. Bounds (1835–1913)

The One Year Bible Readings for today are **Jeremiah 12:1–14:10; 1 Thessalonians 1:1–2:8; Psalm 79:1-13;** and **Proverbs 24:30-34.**

OCTOBER
10

hunger

A Hunger for His Word

Your words are what sustain me. They bring me great joy and are my heart's delight, for I bear your name, O Lord God Almighty.
Jeremiah 15:16

Depending on people's eating habits and the version of the Bible they are using, they might misunderstand the meaning of this verse. The *New International Version* translates the first sentence, "When your words came, I ate them." The Hebrew word translated "ate" means "to devour," "to eat up," or "to consume." God is instructing us in this verse to approach his Word with a hearty appetite . . . a burning hunger. His words, our manna, are there for us to feast on every day. But as with Jeremiah, we must choose each day to meditate on his instructions and promises, for it is only in reading and following God's Word that we find true joy. When we daily rely on the nutrition of God's words, we will say as the psalmist did, "The laws of the Lord . . . are sweeter than honey, even honey dripping from the comb" (Psalm 19:9-10). We will be sustained by his Word day by day and will experience joy. If you don't have this kind of hunger and dependence on God's Word, ask him to make this a reality in your life.

LORD, thank you for your holy and powerful Word! Build in me a deeper hunger for it and reliance on it day by day. Lead me as I consume your instructions, promises and testimonies. Through them you will sustain me, and they will be my joy and my heart's delight.

ONE OF THE HIGHEST AND NOBLEST FUNCTIONS OF MAN'S MIND IS TO LISTEN TO GOD'S WORD, AND SO TO READ HIS MIND AND THINK HIS THOUGHTS AFTER HIM. John R. W. Stott (b. 1921)

The One Year Bible Readings for today are **Jeremiah 14:11–16:15; 1 Thessalonians 2:9–3:13; Psalm 80:1-19;** and **Proverbs 25:1-5.**

OCTOBER

Deep Roots

Cursed are those who put their trust in mere humans and turn their hearts away from the Lord. . . . But blessed are those who trust in the Lord and have made the Lord their hope and confidence. They are like trees planted along a riverbank, with roots that reach deep into the water. Such trees are not bothered by the heat or worried by long months of drought. Their leaves stay green, and they go right on producing delicious fruit.
Jeremiah 17:5-8

What a stark contrast Jeremiah describes in these verses between those who trust in God and those who trust in human beings and have turned away from God. Instead of thriving and prospering, people who look to mere humans for help and rescue live unproductive, dry lives, like a stunted shrub languishing in the desert for lack of water.

But those whose hearts trust in God, those for whom the Lord is their hope and confidence, will be blessed. Like a tree planted by water, the heat and hard times don't destroy them because their roots are sunk deep into God's resources and life. Even in months of drought, even into old age, they will stay green and keep producing, not just any fruit—but delicious fruit. Though their bodies may decline in physical strength or grow more fragile with advancing age, yet God's Spirit will renew their inner strength day by day. As they are rooted in Christ's inexhaustible supply, they will continue to be productive and bring glory to God as long as they live.

LORD, I put my trust in you. You are my hope and my confidence. Let me never turn from you. As my roots go deep into you, thank you for your promise to bring forth fruit—delicious fruit—in my life and to make my soul prosperous even in the long, dry spells.

A MAN WITHOUT PRAYER IS LIKE A TREE WITHOUT ROOTS. Pope Pius XII (1876–1958)

The One Year Bible Readings for today are **Jeremiah 16:16–18:23; 1 Thessalonians 4:1–5:3; Psalm 81:1-16;** and **Proverbs 25:6-8.**

Spiritual Lessons

Always be joyful. Keep on praying. No matter what happens, always be thankful, for this is God's will for you who belong to Christ Jesus. Do not stifle the Holy Spirit.

1 Thessalonians 5:16-19

When spiritual directives such as Paul gives us here confront us—always be joyful, always be thankful no matter what happens—our natural response is, "That's impossible!" We tend to feel inadequate and unable to please God. How can we rejoice in tragedy, pray when we are otherwise occupied, or be thankful in times of adversity? The key is in Paul's next words: "Do not stifle the Holy Spirit."

The purpose of our existence is not simply to be "good" people. God has laid hold of and redeemed us for the purpose of forming us into his likeness as we walk through the experiences of this life with him. We are to become a dwelling place for his Spirit. Our challenge is learning to let him do the impossible through us! He is using everything in our lives to teach us that apart from him we can do nothing but through his Spirit we can do all things, even rejoice always, pray without ceasing, and give thanks in everything.

LORD, help me to understand that you are truly causing all things to work together for my good this very day. I want to be obedient to what your Word asks of me. I cannot do this on my own. But in your Spirit's power, I can do what you tell me to do. May you be my joy, and enable me to be aware of your presence with me continually in Jesus.

PRAY AND NEVER FAINT, IS THE MOTTO CHRIST GIVES US FOR PRAYING. IT IS THE TEST OF OUR FAITH, AND THE MORE SEVERE THE TRIAL AND THE LONGER THE WAITING, THE MORE GLORIOUS THE RESULTS. E. M. Bounds (1835–1913)

The One Year Bible Readings for today are **Jeremiah 19:1–21:14; 1 Thessalonians 5:4-28; Psalm 82:1-8;** and **Proverbs 25:9-10.**

OCTOBER

13

worthy

Who Is Worthy?

We keep on praying for you, that our God will make you worthy of the life to which he called you. And we pray that God, by his power, will fulfill all your good intentions and faithful deeds. Then everyone will give honor to the name of our Lord Jesus because of you.

2 Thessalonians 1:11-12

All of us have experienced feelings of inadequacy and unworthiness in areas of our lives. As Christians, our insecurities often keep us from coming boldly into God's presence to receive his power for service. Paul knew the Thessalonians were feeling unworthy in their present calling to suffering and persecution. He wanted to encourage them by clarifying that God himself would make them worthy (1:5). To what life has God called you? Preaching or teaching God's Word? Caring for young children? Serving God in the business world or taking the gospel to a foreign land? Whatever our calling, our best intentions and good deeds will accomplish nothing of eternal value apart from the power of the Holy Spirit. It's when we die to our own abilities and surrender our work to God that he infuses our feeble efforts with his power. When we seek the Lord humbly in prayer, admit our inadequacy, and ask for his grace and sufficiency, he will divinely enable us to fulfill our calling. He and he alone can make us worthy of the life to which he has called us.

THANK YOU, LORD, that my effectiveness in your calling doesn't depend on my abilities. In your grace, impart your power to me so that I may live the life to which you have called me. Make me a vessel of your glory so that those who see my works will look past me and be drawn to you.

"HAVE YOU, O GOD, SEEN YOURSELF IN WHAT I SAID, THOUGHT, AND DID TODAY? DID I CARE FOR OTHERS THE WAY YOU WOULD HAVE?" THROUGH THESE QUESTIONS I FIND THE ANSWERS TO THE GREATEST OF ALL LIFE'S QUESTIONS: DID I FULFILL MY DESTINY TODAY? DID I GLORIFY GOD?
John Hannah

The One Year Bible Readings for today are **Jeremiah 22:1–23:20; 2 Thessalonians 1:1-12; Psalm 83:1-18;** and **Proverbs 25:11-14.**

OCTOBER

14

joy

Paths of Joy

Happy are those who are strong in the Lord, who set their minds on a pilgrimage to Jerusalem. . . . For the Lord God is our light and protector. He gives us grace and glory. No good thing will the Lord withhold from those who do what is right.

Psalm 84:5, 11

Psalm 84 reflects a longing for the presence of God. But the psalmist knows that he doesn't have to wait until heaven to find happiness. Those who have set their minds on Christ can walk each day in paths of joy.

But what if we're in the "Valley of Weeping" (v. 6)? What if the diagnosis is cancer? What if our children make horrible choices? What if we lose our job? What will sustain us in our darkest days?

Our hope is not in a distant city with streets of gold. Our hope is in the omnipresent Lord God, who travels with us each step of our journey. He is the One who sheds light on our dark path and protects us from evil. His grace and glory make our wilderness a place of refreshing springs with pools of blessings. Because he will not withhold from us any good thing, we can have peace in his faithfulness to supply all we need.

In our prayers for our daily needs, let us not lose sight of the One who sojourns with us. Let us set our minds on the goal: to live every day strengthened in the glorious light of his presence.

LORD, forgive me for my nearsightedness that keeps me focused on worldly cares. Please give me an eternal perspective on all that happens to me today. Set my mind and my heart on you so that I can embrace your presence moment by moment. You, O Lord, are my strength and my hope.

OH, WHAT A LIFE OF WONDERFUL JOY, ADVENTURE, AND EVER-DEEPENING LOVE THE GOOD SHEPHERD LEADS US ALL TO! AS WE FOLLOW HIM ALONG THE PATH OF LIFE, LET US LEAVE HIM TO CHOOSE EVERY STEP OF THE WAY, AS WE LIVE IN HIS RADIANT PRESENCE AND ARE EVER LED TO STILL HIGHER PLACES.

Hannah Hurnard (1905–1990)

The One Year Bible Readings for today are **23:21–25:38; 2 Thessalonians 2:1-17; Psalm 84:1-12;** and **Proverbs 25:15.**

OCTOBER

15

gospel

Spreading the Gospel

Dear brothers and sisters, I ask you to pray for us. Pray first that the Lord's message will spread rapidly and be honored wherever it goes, just as when it came to you.

2 Thessalonians 3:1

The apostle Paul was a great communicator with exemplary credentials. But as great a communicator of the gospel as he was, he did not believe that he could spread God's Word in his own strength. He knew he desperately needed the power of the Holy Spirit, which is released through prayer and through the intercession of others, to accomplish what God had called him to do.

Today there is still a great need to pray for the spread of the gospel! There are millions of people who are living in darkness and have not heard the good news of salvation through Jesus. There are unreached people groups who do not have the Bible in their native languages. And there are evangelists, pastors, and missionaries all around the world with a passion to spread God's Word who need to be upheld in intercession. When we are faithful to pray, those people will be empowered, the Lord's message will spread and his name will be honored.

LORD, show me the "Pauls" I need to be faithful to support in prayer as they spread your truth throughout our city, our nation, and the world. Strengthen the hearts of those who preach the gospel. Equip them in every way to do your will, and may your name and message be honored wherever they go.

IT IS IN THE PATHS OF INTERCESSORY PRAYER THAT WE ENTER THE RICHEST FIELDS OF SPIRITUAL GROWTH AND GATHER PRICELESS RICHES. TO PRAY FOR OTHERS IS OF DIVINE APPOINTMENT, AND IT REPRESENTS THE HIGHEST FORM OF CHRISTIAN SERVICE. E. M. Bounds (1835–1913)

The One Year Bible Readings for today are **Jeremiah 26:1–27:22; 2 Thessalonians 3:1-18; Psalm 85:1-13;** and **Proverbs 25:16.**

future

Our Future and Hope

"I know the plans I have for you," says the Lord. "They are plans for good and not for disaster, to give you a future and a hope. In those days when you pray, I will listen. If you look for me in earnest, you will find me when you seek me."
Jeremiah 29:11-13

What an encouraging word this must have been to the Israelites, who had just learned that they would be exiled to Babylon for seventy years. When chaos and confusion were rampant, when their lives had been turned upside down, this word of hope came to guide them through their years of captivity. When our lives don't make sense and our futures look hopeless, the profound truth in these verses gives us a new perspective. God says, *"I know* the plans I have for you" [italics added]. He's not hoping he can conjure something up, nor is he wringing his hands and wondering what went wrong. His eternal plans for you and for me were established before the foundation of the world, and nothing can derail them.

What is the condition for God's plans being fulfilled in our lives? This passage tells us to seek him earnestly—not halfheartedly, not occasionally, but with all of our hearts. Through earnest prayer we can expect to see his good plans for our future and our hope. In the process, we can also expect to find God.

LORD, thank you that you have planned a future and a hope for my life. Because of your power and your faithfulness, I know that nothing in my life is outside your control. Help me to fully and willingly submit to your will for my future. Draw me to look for you earnestly and to pray wholeheartedly. May my hope be grounded in your unchanging character.

HAVE YOU BEEN ASKING GOD WHAT HE IS GOING TO DO? HE WILL NEVER TELL YOU. GOD DOES NOT TELL YOU WHAT HE IS GOING TO DO; HE REVEALS TO YOU WHO HE IS. Oswald Chambers (1874–1917)

The One Year Bible Readings for today are **Jeremiah 28:1–29:32; 1 Timothy 1:1-23; Psalm 86:1-17;** and **Proverbs 25:17.**

OCTOBER

17

enemies

Lord, Bless My Enemies

I urge you, first of all, to pray for all people. As you make your requests, plead for God's mercy upon them, and give thanks. Pray this way for kings and all others who are in authority.
1 Timothy 2:1-2

Paul knows that nothing of eternal significance happens without prayer, so he urges young Timothy, "Pray for all people," and he gets specific about who "all" is in verse 2: kings and those in authority. If I had been Timothy, I would have protested, "Paul, those in authority threw you into prison. And Nero is capturing our brothers and sisters, covering them with tar, and using them as human torches to light his gardens. Surely you don't expect me to plead for mercy and give thanks for these enemies of the Cross!"

Does Paul really expect us to beg God's mercy for those who ruthlessly inflict pain on us? Paul fully understood God's great mercy and patience with him, "the worst of sinners" (1:16, NIV). If we truly grasp the mercy and patience God has graciously given us, it's easier to pray for mercy for our enemies. God's mercy causes people to turn from evil and come to repentance. His mercy brings unlikely people to salvation (1:16). We can even thank God for our enemies because we know he uses everything—even them—to accomplish his good purposes.

GRACIOUS FATHER, thank you for your mercy that brought me to salvation. Thank you for using my enemies to drive me to my knees and to root out pride and produce humility. I pray for your mercy on the enemies of your Cross, mercy that will lead them to repentance and salvation. Thank you that in your mercy you use all things to fulfill your eternal purposes.

TRULY, ENEMIES HAVE CUT ME LOOSE FROM THE WORLD AND HAVE STRETCHED OUT MY HANDS TO THE HEM OF YOUR GARMENT. BLESS MY ENEMIES, O LORD. EVEN I BLESS THEM AND DO NOT CURSE THEM. St. Nikolai of Zicha and Ochrid (1880–?)

The One Year Bible Readings for today are **Jeremiah 30:1–31:26; 1 Timothy 2:1-15; Psalm 87:1-7;** and **Proverbs 25:18-19.**

hard

Is Anything Too Hard?

This message came to Jeremiah from the Lord: "I am the Lord, the God of all the peoples of the world. Is anything too hard for me?"
Jeremiah 32:26-27

Have you lived with a difficult situation that remained unchanged no matter how fervently you prayed? If so, you may have begun to doubt God's ability to intervene. Have you wondered if your problems were beyond God's power to help your difficult marriage? out-of-control finances? failing health? a wayward child? God's Word to Jeremiah is a powerful declaration of who God is and what he is able to do. He is the one true God, the sovereign ruler over all the earth. The rhetorical question "Is anything too hard for me?" is actually a statement of God's supreme power in all circumstances. If anything were too difficult for him, he would not be God. If God is not sovereign over all, he is not sovereign at all!

Because nothing is too hard for God, we can rest assured that nothing in our lives is outside of God's purposeful control. We may not understand why God hasn't answered our prayers as we wish, but we do know that greater difficulties are opportunities to draw closer to him. We can have peace in all circumstances when we have absolute confidence that nothing is too hard for God.

THANK YOU, LORD, that nothing in my life is beyond your reach; nothing is too large or difficult for your powerful hand. Help me to remember that you display your power best in my impossible situations. Give me greater understanding of who you are so that my trust in you will be complete.

NO PRAYER IS TOO HARD FOR HIM TO ANSWER, NO NEED TOO GREAT FOR HIM TO SUPPLY, NO PASSION TOO STRONG FOR HIM TO SUBDUE; NO TEMPTATION TOO POWERFUL FOR HIM TO DELIVER FROM, NO MISERY TOO DEEP FOR HIM TO RELIEVE.
Arthur Pink (1889–1952)

The One Year Bible Readings for today are **Jeremiah 31:27–32:44; 1 Timothy 3:1-16; Psalm 88:1-18;** and **Proverbs 25:20-22.**

OCTOBER

19

example

Be an Example

Don't let anyone think less of you because you are young. Be an example to all believers in what you teach, in the way you live, in your love, your faith, and your purity.

1 Timothy 4:12

The early church was suffering persecution and desperately needed strong spiritual leaders. Evidently some thought Timothy was too young to be a serious candidate for ministry. But Paul encouraged Timothy to keep focused on the spiritual gift he had received when the elders laid hands on him (4:14). He knew that if Timothy lived what he taught and modeled a life of love, faith, and purity, he would demonstrate to the critics that he was indeed following God's call. When we do what God is leading us to do, we may face criticism, or others may question our qualifications for ministry. We may become discouraged by careless comments about our weaknesses and begin to doubt God's ability to work through us.

By humbly acknowledging our weaknesses and at the same time recognizing that God has equipped us to serve him effectively, we can continue in faith to minister. As our lives increase in godliness, demonstrated through love, faith, and purity, it will become evident to others that we are following God's will.

LORD, I am thankful that your opinion of me is more important than anyone else's opinion. The work you accomplish through me is equally effective whether in my gifts or in my weaknesses since my weaknesses cause greater dependence on you. Help me not to shy away from using the gifts you have given me, and make me an example of your love, faith, and purity.

A LIFE LIVED LISTENING TO THE DECISIVE CALL OF GOD IS A LIFE LIVED BEFORE ONE AUDIENCE THAT TRUMPS ALL OTHERS—THE AUDIENCE OF ONE.
Os Guinness

The One Year Bible Readings for today are **Jeremiah 33:1–34:22; 1 Timothy 4:1-16; Psalm 89:1-13;** and **Proverbs 25:23-24.**

worship

Call to Worship

We were created to worship God. It is the reason for our existence both here on earth and throughout eternity. Sometimes our concept of worship is going to church one hour each week. But God desires continual fellowship with us and wants us to live a lifestyle characterized by worship. How is that possible? When we go about our day delighting in the things God delights in, finding our greatest satisfaction and joy in him, honoring him in all we do, and ascribing to the Lord the glory due his name—we are worshiping God. Whether our days are filled with washing diapers and dirty dishes, sitting at a computer, or teaching seminary students, we can experience worship as a lifestyle. When we fulfill God's call with joyful obedience and do our work to the glory of God, that is true worship. Outward expressions of worship such as kneeling, bowing, praying, and lifting hands may enhance our worship experience, but true worship emanates from our hearts. Let us respond joyfully to God's call to worship. We will be blessed beyond measure as we walk all day long in the light of his presence!

Happy are those who hear the joyful call to worship, for they will walk in the light of your presence, Lord. They rejoice all day long in your wonderful reputation. They exult in your righteousness.
Psalm 89:15-16

LORD, what a privilege it is to worship you! Purify my heart and my thoughts so that I can learn to worship you continually. Help me to perform all of my duties today in joyful obedience to you so that even my work becomes authentic worship. You are great and greatly to be praised.

BY PRACTICING GOD'S PRESENCE AND CONTINUOUSLY LOOKING AT HIM, THE SOUL FAMILIARIZES ITSELF WITH HIM TO THE EXTENT THAT IT PASSES ALMOST ITS WHOLE LIFE IN CONTINUAL ACTS OF LOVE, PRAISE, CONFIDENCE, THANKSGIVING, OFFERING, AND PETITION.
Brother Lawrence of the Resurrection (1605–1691)

The One Year Bible Readings for today are **Jeremiah 35:1–36:32; 1 Timothy 5:1-25; Psalm 89:14-37;** and **Proverbs 25:25-27.**

OCTOBER

21

fight

Fight the Good Fight

Fight the good fight for what we believe. Hold tightly to the eternal life that God has given you, which you have confessed so well before many witnesses.

1 Timothy 6:12

In Paul's final instructions to Timothy, he wants to impress on his young disciple the need to hold fast, stay the course, fight the good fight. Paul knows that the road ahead of Timothy will not be easy. Wherever the gospel is preached, there will be battles; there will be persecution. But Paul knows the greatest battle is not with flesh and blood. It's against the evil rulers and authorities of the unseen world.

The battle is over "what we believe," and those who persevere will win the prize of eternal life promised to those who confess Jesus as Lord.

Does the battle around you continue to rage no matter how hard you fight? Have your enemies gained the upper hand? Have you grown weary or lost sight of the prize? God did not call us to fight our battles alone. When we seek God in prayer and acknowledge our weakness and weariness, he will fight the battle for us. Someday we will stand at the gates of heaven and gaze in wonder at the prize in front of us, and the battles behind us will become a fading memory.

HEAVENLY FATHER, help me not grow weary in the battles I face but continually seek you to fight the good fight on my behalf. Give me faithfulness and perseverance. Thank you for your promise of eternal life in your presence.

AND THOUGH THIS WORLD, WITH DEVILS FILLED,
SHOULD THREATEN TO UNDO US,
WE WILL NOT FEAR, FOR GOD HAS WILLED
HIS TRUTH TO TRIUMPH THROUGH US.
THE PRINCE OF DARKNESS GRIM, WE TREMBLE NOT FOR HIM—
HIS RAGE WE CAN ENDURE, FOR LO! HIS DOOM IS SURE:
ONE LITTLE WORD SHALL FELL HIM.

Martin Luther (1483–1546)

The One Year Bible Readings for today are **Jeremiah 37:1–38:28; 1 Timothy 6:1-21; Psalm 89:38-52;** and **Proverbs 25:28.**

OCTOBER
22

morning

Good Morning!

Satisfy us in the morning with your unfailing love, so we may sing for joy to the end of our lives.
Psalm 90:14

What morning routine do you most depend on to get your day off to a good start? A warm shower? Your first cup of coffee? Revising your to-do list?

Moses, the author of Psalm 90, wasn't anticipating a refreshing shower when he pulled back his tent flap to face another day in the hot, barren wilderness. His to-do list usually had one thing on it: walk until God says stop.

Moses began each day with something many of us are missing: an unwavering assurance of God's unfailing love. His confidence in God's love and care was all he needed to face each day in the wilderness.

We have the same promise that Moses had. Nothing we do or say will alter the passionate love God pours out on us. In our waking moments, before our minds become cluttered with concerns, before our feet hit the floor, we can pray, "Lord, satisfy me today with your unfailing love." When God's love becomes our greatest source of satisfaction, joy will carry us through our daily stresses, and God will put a song in our hearts . . . "to the end of our lives."

LOVING FATHER, thank you for your promise of unfailing love. Impress on my heart a deeper awareness of your love and care for me. Give me eyes to see all the ways you express that to me throughout this day. Forgive me for seeking satisfaction in material possessions, family, friends, and work. I pray that you will become my greatest source of satisfaction and joy.

YOUR RELATIONSHIP WITH GOD OUGHT TO BRING YOU MORE JOY, SATISFACTION, AND PLEASURE THAN ANY OTHER RELATIONSHIP, ACTIVITY, OR MATERIAL POSSESSION YOU HAVE.
Henry Blackaby (b. 1935)

The One Year Bible Readings for today are **Jeremiah 39:1–41:18; 2 Timothy 1:1-18; Psalm 90:1–91:16;** and **Proverbs 26:1-2.**

OCTOBER
23

heritage

A Rich Heritage

Timothy, my dear son, be strong with the special favor God gives you in Christ Jesus. You have heard me teach many things that have been confirmed by many reliable witnesses. Teach these great truths to trustworthy people who are able to pass them on to others.
2 Timothy 2:1-2

God had only one plan for propagating the gospel of Jesus Christ to the ends of the earth: word of mouth. One person who experienced God's favor in Christ Jesus would pass that truth on to other trustworthy people.

If someone has passed on a heritage of faith that led you to salvation, then you have indeed experienced God's favor. Who first opened the pages of Scripture to you? Who did the Holy Spirit use to bring you to salvation? Who discipled you in the truths of the Christian faith? All of us who have come to a saving knowledge of Jesus Christ came to faith through the faithful witness of trustworthy brothers and sisters in Christ.

It has been said that Christianity is always just one generation away from extinction. We have the wonderful privilege of passing on to the next generation the truth that someone entrusted to us. God may be calling you to invest time and truth in a young child, a coworker, a relative, or someone else's teenager. Trust the Holy Spirit to give you the heart and wisdom to pass on your rich heritage of faith to another trustworthy person.

LORD, thank you for the blessed privilege of being used by your Holy Spirit in the lives of others. Prepare the hearts of those to whom you are calling me to witness. Give me boldness mingled with love, and let me not miss or shy away from any opportunity to pass on to others the great truths that have changed my life.

AS IMAGE-BEARER AND REPRESENTATIVE OF GOD ON EARTH, REDEEMED MAN HAS BY HIS PRAYERS TO DETERMINE THE HISTORY OF THIS EARTH.
Andrew Murray (1828–1917)

The One Year Bible Readings for today are **Jeremiah 42:1–44:23; 2 Timothy 2:1-21; Psalm 92:1–93:5;** and **Proverbs 26:3-5.**

scripture

The Power of Scripture

Beginning our quiet time with God without our Bibles open is like trying to read in the dark—we'll have only limited, dim understanding instead of the bright illumination of God's Word. Without the knowledge of Scripture we are not only at a loss about how to pray in agreement with the Holy Spirit, but we are also impaired in our ability to receive God's response to us.

Someone once said, "When I pray, I speak to God; when I read the Bible, God speaks to me." We could add, "When I pray Scripture, I pray the words of God!" When God's Word guides our prayers, they become a lively interchange of speaking and listening.

Do you desire God's wisdom for decisions? Do you need power to live and walk by the Spirit? Would you like to see God's intervention in the lives of others? Take your Bible with you into your prayer closet. Through it the Spirit will guide you in how to pray, and he will prepare and equip you for every good thing God wants you to do.

All Scripture is inspired by God and is useful to teach us what is true and to make us realize what is wrong in our lives. It straightens us out and teaches us to do what is right. It is God's way of preparing us in every way, fully equipped for every good thing God wants us to do.
2 Timothy 3:16-17

THANK YOU, LORD, for not leaving us to walk in darkness and for giving us the light of your Word to guide us. Help me to cherish the wonderful gift I have in your holy Scriptures and to receive its teaching and instruction for my life. Guide my prayers through the inspiration of your Word.

PRAYER AND THE WORD ARE INSEPARABLY LINKED TOGETHER: POWER IN THE USE OF EITHER DEPENDS UPON THE PRESENCE OF THE OTHER.
Andrew Murray (1828–1917)

The One Year Bible Readings for today are **Jeremiah 44:24–47:7; 2 Timothy 2:22–3:17; Psalm 94:1-23;** and **Proverbs 26:6-8.**

OCTOBER
25

praise

True Praise

Sing to the Lord; bless his name. Each day proclaim the good news that he saves. Publish his glorious deeds among the nations. Tell everyone about the amazing things he does.
Psalm 96:2-3

Scripture speaks often of the importance of praise. Praise lifts us out of ourselves and redirects our attention to our Father in heaven. It's easy to proclaim God's greatness when he has stretched out his hand of blessing. But if things are not going well and the stresses of life press in from all sides, can we still praise God? Praise that exudes from us in the warm light of summer but disappears in the cold darkness of winter is not true praise. True praise is grounded in faith in who God is, not just in what he does. When we focus on God's character and attributes, we gain an eternal perspective on life, and praise becomes our natural response.

If almighty God has come to dwell inside you and has written your name in the Lamb's Book of Life, "sing to the Lord; bless his name." If you've been delivered from the curse of sin and death, "proclaim the good news that he saves." When you experience answered prayers, "publish his glorious deeds." And as you see evidence of God's grace, mercy, and loving-kindness in your life, "Tell everyone about the amazing things he does!"

LORD, thank you for giving me the gift of praise. Help me to sing to you and bless your name every day. Give me a joyful heart to tell others about the amazing things you do. Please continue to reveal more of yourself to me so that I might praise you more and more.

O FOR AN ENLARGED MIND, RIGHTLY TO CONCEIVE HIS DIVINE MAJESTY. NEXT, FOR THE GIFT OF UTTERANCE TO CLOTHE THE THOUGHT IN FITTING LANGUAGE. THEN, FOR A VOICE LIKE MANY WATERS, TO SOUND FORTH THE NOBLE STRAIN. ALAS! AS YET WE ARE HUMBLED AT OUR FAILURES TO PRAISE THE LORD AS WE WOULD LIKE.
Charles Haddon Spurgeon (1834–1892)

The One Year Bible Readings for today are **Jeremiah 48:1–49:22; 2 Timothy 4:1-22; Psalm 95:1–96:13;** and **Proverbs 26:9-12.**

OCTOBER
26

freedom

Our Freedom in Christ

If you have ever won a spiritual battle, experienced victory over temptation, or been delivered from an addiction, you know the joy of being set free. Freedom is exhilarating, but the joy of victory is often tainted by the threat of losing our freedom again. Maintaining our freedom can be just as daunting as gaining it. God's words of hope for Israel in Jeremiah 50 can guide us in our prayers for gaining and maintaining our freedom. God describes what will happen when he delivers his people after seventy long years of captivity. Israel and Judah will experience unity, weep tears of repentance, and seek the Lord and his counsel for their trip home. These elements are crucial when we can ask the Lord to accomplish these things for us in order to gain freedom.

But the key to *maintaining* our freedom is found in verse 5: "They will bind themselves to the Lord with an eternal covenant that will never again be broken." If we stay connected to the Lord, his power will give us the strength to resist the places, people, thoughts, and sins that led us into captivity in the first place.

"Then the people of Israel and Judah will join together," says the Lord, "weeping and seeking the Lord their God. They will ask the way to Jerusalem and will start back home again. They will bind themselves to the Lord with an eternal covenant that will never again be broken."
Jeremiah 50:4-5

LORD, thank you for the gift of freedom you bought for me on the cross. Thank you that in Christ I no longer walk as a slave. Guard my steps and my thoughts from places that will snare me again, and use me to help others walk in your freedom.

REMEMBER, WE NEVER FIND FREEDOM FROM BONDAGE IN INDEPENDENCE. WE FIND IT BY TAKING THE SAME HANDCUFFS THAT ONCE BOUND US TO SIN AND BINDING OURSELVES TO THE WRIST OF CHRIST. Beth Moore

The One Year Bible Readings for today are **Jeremiah 49:23–50:46; Titus 1:1-16; Psalm 97:1–98:9;** and **Proverbs 26:13-16.**

OCTOBER

27

lifestyle

A Godly Lifestyle

Similarly, teach the older women to live in a way that is appropriate for someone serving the Lord. . . . These older women must train the younger women to love their husbands and their children, to live wisely and be pure, to take care of their homes, to do good.
Titus 2:3-5

This passage exhorts those who are older to lead by example and to mentor others in living a godly lifestyle. But you don't have to be a senior citizen to be a Titus 2 man or woman! If you have been married a few years, you could mentor an engaged couple or disciple a college student. If you are experienced in finances or business, your wisdom would be valuable to a young person. If you have older children, you could encourage a young mother in child rearing and homemaking, help with her kids, and be an example of a godly mother.

This kind of lifestyle is useful for two reasons: being faithful in our ministry with home and family brings honor to God, and mentoring others builds up the body of Christ, which also honors him. But merely having good intentions about showing others how to live won't do it. We need the grace of God to equip us and then to show us how to pass on what we know to others. Do you know someone who could benefit from your experience—both practically and spiritually? Begin to build a relationship with that person today.

LORD, I want to be a person who with strong faith, love, and patience helps others younger than myself live godly lives. Since I can do nothing apart from you, I ask for your grace and the power of your Holy Spirit to fill me and teach me how to be a Titus 2 person, a shining example who mentors others in living a life that honors and glorifies you.

A GOOD EXAMPLE IS THE BEST SERMON.
Sir Thomas Fuller (1608–1661)

The One Year Bible Readings for today are **Jeremiah 51:1-53; Titus 2:1-15; Psalm 99:1-9;** and **Proverbs 26:17.**

OCTOBER
28

thanks

Give Thanks

Enter his gates with thanksgiving; go into his courts with praise. Give thanks to him and bless his name. For the Lord is good. His unfailing love continues forever, and his faithfulness continues to each generation.
Psalm 100:4-5

This psalm is a song of thanksgiving that God's people used in the temple along with the sacrifices of praise they offered. The psalmist tells us to come into God's presence with grateful hearts and expressions of thanksgiving because he is a good God—all the time—even when we are in difficult circumstances or think our prayers have not been answered yet. We express our gratitude because he is the creator of everything and we are his possession; and because his unfailing love continues forever and his faithfulness endures to every new generation. Perhaps Scripture reminds us so often, as in this psalm, to come to God with thanksgiving because we are so apt to forget his goodness and what he has already done for us or because we simply forget to say thank you. Today as you pray, begin by numbering some of the many blessings God has given you, and then thank him and bless his name. Enter his presence with words of praise on your lips and in your heart.

LORD, transform my heart and give me an attitude of gratefulness. Open my eyes to see your hand in every area of my life. When I have forgotten your goodness, remind me of what an awesome God you are and the myriad things I have to be thankful for. I thank you for your goodness, love, and faithfulness to me that you have shown in these ways you have blessed my life: ____________________, ____________________, ____________________.

THE MOST IMPORTANT PRAYER IN THE WORLD IS JUST TWO WORDS LONG: "THANK YOU."
Meister Eckhart (ca. 1260–ca. 1327)

The One Year Bible Readings for today are **Jeremiah 51:54–52:34; Titus 3:1-15; Psalm 100:1-5;** and **Proverbs 26:18-19.**

OCTOBER

29

children

Pray for the Children

Rise during the night and cry out. Pour out your hearts like water to the Lord. Lift up your hands to him in prayer. Plead for your children as they faint with hunger in the streets.
Lamentations 2:19

When Jerusalem was devastated by the enemy and the people lay in hopelessness, Jeremiah called to them, "Pour out your hearts like water to the Lord." This meant a call to earnest prayer, prayer with tears (water), especially on behalf of the starving children. He exhorted them that instead of fainting in despair, they should turn to God as their only hope and cry out to him, not stopping but praying all night if necessary. Children in our own country may not experience the same level of hunger in the physical sense, but millions are starving spiritually. At the school right down the street from your house there are children who are dying spiritually, starving for the truth, with no one to show them the way. Pray for these children. Pray for their parents to come to know Christ, for mothers to rise up in intercession for every school. Pray for Christian teachers to fill our classrooms and for a great awakening to happen throughout our land.

LORD, give me a burden for lost children in my neighborhood, city, and nation, even for the children of other nations, and increase my faith to intercede for them. Bring others near to pray with me for this generation of children and young people. I ask that you would raise up workers so that children who are starving physically, emotionally, or spiritually, would find all their needs met in you.

WE MUST HAVE PRAYING MOTHERS TO GIVE THEM BIRTH, PRAYING HOMES TO INFLUENCE THEIR LIVES, AND PRAYING SURROUNDINGS TO IMPRESS THEIR MINDS AND TO LAY THE FOUNDATION FOR PRAYING LIVES. PRAYING SAMUELS COME FROM PRAYING HANNAHS. E. M. Bounds (1835–1913)

The One Year Bible Readings for today are **Lamentations 1:1–2:22; Philemon 1-25; Psalm 101:1-8;** and **Proverbs 26:20.**

timing

His Timing Is Perfect

The Lord is wonderfully good to those who wait for him and seek him. So it is good to wait quietly for salvation from the Lord.
Lamentations 3:25-26

In a fast-moving culture such as ours, in which time is measured in nanoseconds and sound bites, waiting in traffic or in the doctor's office longer than we had planned can mess up our schedule. We can become irritated when things don't happen according to our packed agenda. And we can become just as frustrated with God when he doesn't seem to answer our prayers as soon as we'd hoped or move in a needy situation according to our timetable. Sometimes we pray and give our requests to God and then turn and run out of the prayer closet before we have taken time to be aware of his answer. But this passage tells us the great benefit of learning to wait on the Lord—both waiting for his timing and just waiting in his presence, spending moments being quiet and waiting to hear his "still, small voice." God is wonderfully good to those who wait for him and continue to seek him.

LORD, quiet my heart and mind so that I am willing to wait on you, not with grumbling and frustration but with hope and assurance that you do everything in your perfect timing. Give me patience, and help me to look for your answers to the requests I make of you. And increase my faith that you are working, even when I must wait for your answer.

WAITING ON GOD EXERCISES YOUR GIFT OF GRACE AND TESTS YOUR FAITH. THEREFORE CONTINUE TO WAIT IN HOPE, FOR ALTHOUGH THE PROMISE MAY LINGER, IT WILL NEVER COME TOO LATE.
Charles Haddon Spurgeon (1834–1892)

The One Year Bible Readings for today are **Lamentations 3:1-66; Hebrews 1:1-14; Psalm 102:1-28;** and **Proverbs 26:21-22.**

OCTOBER

31

same

The Same Forever

Lord, you remain the same forever! Your throne continues from generation to generation.
Lamentations 5:19

In the midst of the ongoing upheaval in the world around us, the ravages of war on the nation of Judah that the prophet has lamented in this verse, the enormous changes we see as the result of war, terrorist attacks, cultural shifts, climate upheaval, or natural disasters, have you ever wondered, where is God? The answer to that question is that he is still on his throne and reigning over all heaven and earth. He is not shocked, surprised, panicked, or disturbed by what happens in the world. Nothing can thwart his plans. How encouraging and comforting to remember that in an ever-changing world, God does not change. His mercy is as fresh today as it was the day we first believed. His grace is just as available today as it was the day he allowed his Son to die on the cross so that all who trusted him would not perish but have everlasting life (John 3:16). No matter what happens, we have hope because our hope is in him, not in what we can see around us. He reigns from generation to generation, and he is working out his purposes perfectly!

ALMIGHTY, UNCHANGING GOD who sits above the centuries, I praise you for your faithfulness and unfailing love. You remain the same forever. You reign over all the heavens and earth! You are the reason we hope!

WHAT PEACE IT BRINGS TO THE CHRISTIAN'S HEART TO REALIZE THAT OUR HEAVENLY FATHER NEVER DIFFERS FROM HIMSELF. . . . TODAY, THIS MOMENT, HE FEELS TOWARD HIS CREATURES, TOWARD BABIES, TOWARD THE SICK, THE FALLEN, THE SINFUL, EXACTLY AS HE DID WHEN HE SENT HIS ONLY BEGOTTEN SON INTO THE WORLD TO DIE FOR MANKIND. A. W. Tozer (1897–1963)

The One Year Bible Readings for today are **Lamentations 4:1–5:22; Hebrews 2:1-18; Psalm 103:1-22;** and **Proverbs 26:23.**

courage

Keep Up Your Courage

We are God's household, if we keep up our courage and remain confident in our hope in Christ. That is why the Holy Spirit says, "Today you must listen to his voice."
Hebrews 3:6-7

This passage calls us to a deeper faith and joyful confidence based on our hope in Christ. Just as their unbelief kept the first generation of Israelites from entering the land God had promised and prepared for them, when we go through testing, trials, or wilderness seasons, our hearts can turn away from God through unbelief. We may continue going through all the outward motions, going to church and attending meetings, but inwardly discouragement sets in and our confidence fails. We wonder if the Lord really cares. We begin to doubt his love and try to live life in our own strength instead of depending on him. As we tune out God's voice, we tune in the world's. That is why the writer of Hebrews exhorts us to keep up courage, to listen to God's voice, and to remain confident because of our hope in Christ. God doesn't leave us to our own devices to muster up this confidence; he stands ready to fill us anew with hope and courage whenever we ask.

FATHER, thank you for making me a part of your household. I ask you, Holy Spirit, to fill me and renew my confidence in Christ Jesus, in his finished work on the cross, and in his glorious coming again. Strengthen me to keep up my courage today, and empower me to believe your Word, to listen attentively to your voice, and to remain confident because my hope is in Christ.

THE RESURRECTION OF JESUS CHRIST IS OUR HOPE TODAY. IT IS OUR ASSURANCE THAT WE HAVE A LIVING SAVIOR TO HELP US LIVE AS WE SHOULD NOW, AND THAT WHEN, IN THE END, WE SET FORTH ON THAT LAST GREAT JOURNEY, WE SHALL NOT TRAVEL AN UNCHARTED COURSE, BUT RATHER WE SHALL GO ON A PLANNED VOYAGE—LIFE TO DEATH TO ETERNAL LIVING. Raymond MacKendree

The One Year Bible Readings for today are **Ezekiel 1:1–3:15; Hebrews 3:1-19; Psalm 104:1-23;** and **Proverbs 26:24-26.**

NOVEMBER

2

throne

The Throne of Grace

This High Priest of ours understands our weaknesses, for he faced all of the same temptations we do, yet he did not sin. So let us come boldly to the throne of our gracious God. There we will receive his mercy, and we will find grace to help us when we need it.
Hebrews 4:15-16

This passage of Hebrews contains one of the most vital truths in the New Testament concerning Christ and those who believe in him. It also contains one of the greatest promises and invitations in the Bible: come boldly to the throne of grace and receive mercy and grace in our time of need. Why? Not because we're good or we deserve it but because Jesus is in his place at the right hand of the Father and is our great High Priest. That's why we have constant access to God's grace; that's why we can take all our needs and problems to him in prayer—because he is right now at God's throne beckoning us to come for the grace and mercy he is so ready to give! He isn't oblivious to the reality of our humanness; in fact, he understands our weaknesses. There is help when we most need it, mercy and strength when we're weak, sufficient grace for anything we will ever face—if only we will come to the throne of our gracious God, ask, and receive. Come to him today!

LORD JESUS, thank you for facing the same temptations and problems we do and for fully understanding our weaknesses. Thank you for pouring out your life on the cross, for rising again and reigning at the right hand of the Father. Your throne is a place of grace for your children, where we can receive your mercy and help when we most need it. I come, Lord, to you, and ask. . . .

THE ONLY HAVEN OF SAFETY IS IN THE MERCY OF GOD, AS MANIFESTED IN CHRIST, IN WHOM EVERY PART OF OUR SALVATION IS COMPLETE.
John Calvin (1509–1564)

The One Year Bible Readings for today are **Ezekiel 3:16–6:14; Hebrews 4:1-16; Psalm 104:24-35;** and **Proverbs 26:27.**

searching

Searching for God

Give thanks to the Lord and proclaim his greatness. Let the whole world know what he has done. Sing to him; yes, sing his praises. Tell everyone about his miracles. Exult in his holy name; O worshipers of the Lord, rejoice! Search for the Lord and for his strength, and keep on searching.
Psalm 105:1-4

The psalmist calls us in these verses to praise God, give him thanks, proclaim his greatness, and let the whole world know what he has done, but he also calls us to search for the Lord and his strength and to keep on searching. To search means to look carefully and thoroughly in an effort to find something important. The original Hebrew text has the idea of seeking with our whole hearts continually, regularly, daily, and then depending on his strength for all the challenges we face in living as his followers instead of in our own strength.

In response to our searching, the Lord loves to reveal himself to us and then manifest his strength in our lives. He has not hidden his character from his people; over and over throughout the Bible, through his Son, Jesus, and through his Spirit and creation, he has revealed his heart, his glory, and his nature that we might know him. Those who seek God and give their time to searching for him and knowing him will find all their needs met in him.

LORD, I give thanks to you and proclaim your greatness! I want to tell everyone what you have done. Thank you for the many promises in your Word that you will come and strengthen me and reveal yourself so that I can know you more intimately. Cause me to seek you with all my heart, to search for you daily and throughout my life, and to depend on your strength for each day.

OUR GOD LOVES TO COME; HE WANTS TO COME FORTH IN US, TO RISE UP IN US IN ALL HIS BEAUTY.
Margaret Therkelsen

The One Year Bible Readings for today are **Ezekiel 7:1–9:11; Hebrews 5:1-14; Psalm 105:1-15;** and **Proverbs 26:28.**

NOVEMBER

4

anchor

The Anchor of Our Souls

God also bound himself with an oath, so that those who received the promise could be perfectly sure that he would never change his mind. So God has given us both his promise and his oath. These two things are unchangeable because it is impossible for God to lie. Therefore, we who have fled to him for refuge can take new courage, for we can hold on to his promise with confidence. This confidence is like a strong and trustworthy anchor for our souls.

Hebrews 6:17-19

Following the terrorist attacks of September 11, sniper attacks the following year, bombings, school violence, upheaval in the stock market, and the downfall of once-solid major corporations, surveys showed the majority of Americans had lost their sense of security. As human beings, we long for security. The more the world seems out of control, the greater our need for an anchor, for something to hold on to and trust in. But our security and anchor aren't going to come from the government, from the economy, or from any other circumstances. Today's verses tell us that God has provided a rock-solid, strong, and trustworthy anchor for our souls. That anchor is our hope in Christ and our confidence in God's promises to us. Just as God's covenant with Abraham enabled him to persevere and gave him the courage to wait patiently for what God had promised, we can wait for the fulfillment of all God has promised us as we meditate on his Word and put our faith in Jesus.

LORD, thank you for providing something to hold on to when everything in this world seems to be shaking. My hope in Jesus is an anchor for my soul and will keep me steady in all the storms of life. Thank you for the promise that those who flee to you for refuge can take new courage because your promises are true and you never break your word!

THROUGH THIS DARK AND STORMY NIGHT
FAITH BEHOLDS A FEEBLE LIGHT
UP THE BLACKNESS STREAKING;
KNOWING GOD'S OWN TIME IS BEST,
IN A PATIENT HOPE I REST
FOR THE FULL DAY-BREAKING!

John Greenleaf Whittier (1807–1892)

The One Year Bible Readings for today are **Ezekiel 10:1–11:25; Hebrews 6:1-20; Psalm 105:16-36;** and **Proverbs 27:1-2.**

provider

The Great Provider

This is a song of God's provision. While Psalm 105 summarizes the vast history of the people of Israel and their amazing deliverance from Egypt, it also paints a panorama of God's provision. The Lord protected with the cloud and directed with the fire. He fed them with manna and quail and provided water enough to form a river when they were thirsty. He was faithful to them every step of their wandering through the wilderness. All of this happened so that they would follow God's principles and obey his laws, verse 45 says. These verses remind me that the same God who gave the cloud as a covering and fire to light the darkness and brought the Israelites out with joy, is our God who longs to protect us, direct us, and empower us. The same Lord who gave his people manna and quail from heaven and water from a rock wants to provide for us today, regardless of what our needs are, so that we will follow him and obey him. Pray your way through this great psalm. Speak its verses aloud to God, and thank him for his provision in the past, the present, and the future.

The Lord spread out a cloud above them as a covering and gave them a great fire to light the darkness. They asked for meat, and he sent them quail; he gave them manna—bread from heaven. He opened up a rock, and water gushed out to form a river through the dry and barren land.

Psalm 105:39-41

OH, LORD, my provider, I praise you. Thank you for your Word, which reminds me of your faithful provision to your people through history. Thank you for all the ways you have provided for my needs, physically, spiritually, emotionally, and relationally. Help me to respond with thanksgiving and with obedience to your principles and your will.

THE LORD MY PASTURE SHALL PREPARE,
AND FEED ME WITH A SHEPHERD'S CARE;
HIS PRESENCE SHALL MY WANTS SUPPLY,
AND GUARD ME WITH A WATCHFUL EYE.

Joseph Addison (1672–1719)

The One Year Bible Readings for today are **Ezekiel 12:1–14:11; Hebrews 7:1-17; Psalm 105:37-45;** and **Proverbs 27:3.**

NOVEMBER

6

thanks

Give Thanks

Praise the Lord! Give thanks to the Lord, for he is good! His faithful love endures forever. Who can list the glorious miracles of the Lord? Who can ever praise him half enough?
Psalm 106:1-2

Psalm 106 is a prayer of remembrance. David recalls how although he and his ancestors had sinned and forgotten the Lord's many acts of kindness to them, yet God saved them and rescued them from their enemies. They continued to go astray, but time after time God delivered them because of his faithful love and goodness.

Reading this psalm reminded me to stop and thank God and list his glorious miracles in my journal, regardless of what I am concerned about today. Imagine how God might enjoy it if, instead of one day, we set aside the whole month of November to focus on expressing our gratefulness! As I looked at my prayer lists for the last month and thanked God for each step of progress, each thing he had done in the hearts and lives of those I'd prayed for, I was astounded, and my heart was refreshed by a new sense of his greatness and glory. Let me encourage you to write down what God has done either individually or with your family. Then thank him aloud, for "who can ever praise him half enough?"

LORD, you have given me so much. You have blessed me with salvation so that I could enjoy abundant life here on earth and eternally in heaven. Help me to praise you not only on a special, appointed Thanksgiving day but regularly and continually. May I, like David, begin and punctuate my prayers with praise and thanksgiving! Your faithful love endures forever. I can never praise you half enough.

FROM DAVID LEARN TO GIVE THANKS FOR EVERYTHING. EVERY FURROW IN THE BOOK OF PSALMS IS SOWN WITH THE SEEDS OF THANKSGIVING.
Jeremy Taylor (1613–1667)

The One Year Bible Readings for today are **Ezekiel 14:12–16:41; Hebrews 7:18-28; Psalm 106:1-12;** and **Proverbs 27:4-6.**

covenant

A New Covenant

This is a great passage of freedom—the good news that God has made a new covenant with his people. The old covenant failed because it is beyond our human ability to keep God's laws. Therefore, God undertook to supply his own Spirit to live within us. He writes his laws in our minds so we will understand them. He writes his words on our hearts so that we will obey them. He frees us from striving to fulfill the letter of the law and draws us into intimate communion with him. This new covenant through our rebirth in Christ Jesus provides a brand new relationship: "everyone, from the least to the greatest" might know him (v. 11). When we realize that God takes the initiative to work within us by his Spirit what is pleasing to him, we can rest from our futile attempt to live the Christian life in our own strength. This is such great news—it doesn't depend on me! God has forgiven us, cleansed us through the blood of Christ, and given us his Spirit, and he will complete his work in us as we trust in him.

This is the new covenant I will make with the people of Israel on that day, says the Lord: I will put my laws in their minds so they will understand them, and I will write them on their hearts so they will obey them. I will be their God, and they will be my people.
Hebrews 8:10

LORD, thank you for the incredible freedom and rest it brings me to realize that through the new covenant in Christ Jesus I can obey you. Thank you for lifting me to intimacy with you through Jesus. Empower me to cling to you, and write your words on my heart. Open the eyes of my heart to see your great work in those who believe.

[IF WE WERE TO GRASP] THE FULL KNOWLEDGE OF WHAT GOD DESIRES TO DO FOR [US]; THE ASSURANCE THAT IT WILL BE DONE BY AN ALMIGHTY POWER; THE BEING DRAWN TO GOD HIMSELF IN PERSONAL SURRENDER, AND DEPENDENCE, AND WAITING TO HAVE IT DONE; ALL THIS WOULD MAKE THE COVENANT THE VERY GATE OF HEAVEN. Andrew Murray (1828–1917)

The One Year Bible Readings for today are **Ezekiel 16:42–17:24; Hebrews 8:1-13; Psalm 106:13-31;** and **Proverbs 27:7-9.**

NOVEMBER

8

veil

The Veil Was Torn

Only the high priest goes into the Most Holy Place, and only once a year, and always with blood, which he offers to God to cover his own sins and the sins the people have committed in ignorance. By these regulations the Holy Spirit revealed that the Most Holy Place was not open to the people.
Hebrews 9:7-8

In the Old Testament, people couldn't just walk into the Holy Place to ask for God's help or mercy. The priests ministered there daily, but only the High Priest—and only on the Day of Atonement—could go into God's presence in the Most Holy Place, to offer a blood sacrifice for his own sins and the people's sins and intercede for them. Even then, he had a rope tied around his foot so that if God struck him dead, the other priests could pull his body out.

When Jesus was crucified, he entered the Most Holy Place once and for all by shedding his own blood as the perfect sacrifice for our sins. When he died, the thick veil separating the people from the Most Holy Place was torn. Think of it! Because of Jesus, we have unlimited access to the Lord. We don't have to wait for a once-a-year meeting with God. We don't have to ask someone else to go to the Lord on our behalf. We can enter his throne room anytime night or day. Go freely into God's presence and thank him for his great gift of Jesus and this wonderful accessibility through prayer.

With all my heart I thank you, Jesus, for being the perfect sacrifice for my sins and the sins of the whole world. When your blood was presented on the heavenly mercy seat and you offered up your Spirit, the veil of the temple was forever rent, providing me access into the very presence of the Father. How I thank you. Lord, I come, I come. . . .

GOD HIDES NOTHING. HIS VERY WORK FROM THE BEGINNING IS REVELATION—A CASTING ASIDE OF VEIL AFTER VEIL, A SHOWING UNTO MEN OF TRUTH AFTER TRUTH. ON AND ON FROM FACT DIVINE HE ADVANCES, UNTIL AT LENGTH IN HIS SON JESUS HE UNVEILS HIS VERY FACE. George Macdonald (1824–1905)

The One Year Bible Readings for today are **Ezekiel 18:1–19:14; Hebrews 9:1-10; Psalm 106:32-48;** and **Proverbs 27:10.**

wits' end

At Our Wits' End

Four times in this psalm, we see God's amazing response when his people, in desperation, cried out to him for deliverance. Some wandered in the wilderness (v. 4). Some rebelled and were chained and broken by hard labor (v. 12). Some were in distress because of their sins and were at the brink of death (vv. 17-18). Some went off in trading ships and were tossed by a storm (vv. 23-25). But when they cried to the Lord in their trouble, in his unshakable faithfulness and great love he heard their cries and rescued them. He led those in the wilderness to a city where they could live. He snapped the chains of those bound by hard labor and slavery. He snatched those near death from the doors of destruction and sent his Word to heal them. And he stilled the storm, saving those tossed on the sea and bringing them safely into harbor. What a tremendous encouragement to us today. Regardless of how we've messed up, regardless of whether our distress is of our own making or not, when we humble ourselves and cry to the Lord, he will unquestionably hear and marvelously rescue.

Some wandered in the desert, lost and homeless. Hungry and thirsty, they nearly died. "Lord, help!" they cried in their trouble, and he rescued them from their distress. He led them straight to safety, to a city where they could live. Let them praise the Lord for his great love and for all his wonderful deeds to them.

Psalm 107:4-8

FATHER, help us to be wise and take all this to heart so that we will be able to see in the history of your people and in our own history yet to be written "the faithful love of the Lord" (v. 43). Help us lift up our eyes and see the incredible things you do in response to our wholehearted cries for help. At our wits' end, Lord, you glorify yourself!

WHEN WE HAVE NOTHING LEFT BUT GOD, THEN WE BECOME AWARE THAT GOD IS ENOUGH.
Agnes Maude Royden (1876–1956)

The One Year Bible Readings for today are **Ezekiel 20:1-49; Hebrews 9:11-28; Psalm 107:1-43;** and **Proverbs 27:11.**

NOVEMBER

10

wake

Wake Up!

My heart is confident in you, O God; no wonder I can sing your praises! Wake up, my soul! Wake up, O harp and lyre! I will waken the dawn with my song.

Psalm 108:1-2

Many times I have read, "I will waken the dawn with my song," and have longed to do this very thing. But as a young mother up all night with three sick little ones, as a mother of teenagers keeping late hours studying, and more recently as a grandmother helping to care for a fourteen-month-old while his mom was in the hospital, how can I wake up early to spend time with God? Only by asking him for the energy, the desire, and the power to do so: *Lord, cause me to hear your voice calling to me each day. Open my heart to respond to your Spirit.* Yes, we are weak, frail, and often tired, but God promises his strength in our weakness. This is not simply a matter of waking up at a certain hour to fulfill our Christian duty and have our devotions; it is a cry to passionately, consistently seek the Lord before the day crushes in with all its responsibilities. Even before we raise our heads off the pillow, we can express our love to the Lord and commit the day to him. Ask for the help of his Spirit, and look to him to work it out.

THANK YOU, LORD, for always calling me to draw near to you. That is my desire, so I look to you to work within me the power and energy to rise morning by morning to meet you. My heart is confident in you, O God. No wonder I can sing your praises! This day, before the duties of the day rush in, I give myself to you and say, "Arise, my soul!"

THE SUN DOES NO CHOOSING. GOD CHOOSES—EVERY MORNING SO FAR—TO MAKE IT RISE. YET THE LORD OF THE UNIVERSE ASKS ME TO CHOOSE TO FOLLOW HIM—TO PARTICIPATE, AS CHRIST DID, IN THE FLOWING ACTION WHICH IS HIS WILL.
Elisabeth Elliot

The One Year Bible Readings for today are **Ezekiel 21:1–22:31; Hebrews 10:1-17; Psalm 108:1-13;** and **Proverbs 27:12.**

hope

Hold to Hope

Every time I read this passage I am spurred on to vigorously pass God's encouragement on to others. So many things in our world can discourage, dampen enthusiasm, and drain away one's energy. Everyone needs regular doses of encouragement to counteract these negatives and to know they are loved and cared for; most of all, they need to know the One who will always be there for them (1 John 4:4) and is their greatest encourager (2 Thessalonians 2:16-17). The writer of Hebrews is also talking about giving *spiritual* encouragement. He instructs us to hold tightly to the hope we say we have and to encourage one another's faith. He tells us to encourage one another to outbursts of love and good deeds and not to neglect meeting together. Your words will inspire confidence in God and show love and support. They will inflate the deflated and lift up the weary. And those whose hearts are failing or are distant from Christ and his body will be drawn closer to his heart because of you. Ask God to show you who needs encouragement today: a weary single mom, a lonely senior citizen, a stressed-out teen, or a neighbor next door.

Without wavering, let us hold tightly to the hope we say we have, for God can be trusted to keep his promise. Think of ways to encourage one another to outbursts of love and good deeds. And let us not neglect our meeting together, as some people do, but encourage and warn each other, especially now that the day of his coming back again is drawing near.
Hebrews 10:23-25

FATHER, empower me to hold tightly to my hope so that I can encourage those around me. Who needs inspiration to love and good deeds today? Who could I gently encourage to gather with me and other believers to worship you and pray? Use me to give others assurance and hope. Give me creative ideas that will spur others to an outburst of love and good deeds! And I will give you all the glory.

TAKE WITH YOU WORDS, STRONG WORDS OF COURAGE: WORDS THAT HAVE WINGS! . . . TALL WORDS, WORDS THAT REACH UP, AND GROWING WORDS, WITH DEEP LIFE WITHIN THEM. Jo Petty

The One Year Bible Readings for today are **Ezekiel 23:1-49; Hebrews 10:18-39; Psalm 109:1-31;** and **Proverbs 27:13.**

NOVEMBER

12

increase

Increase My Faith

You see, it is impossible to please God without faith. Anyone who wants to come to him must believe that there is a God and that he rewards those who sincerely seek him.
Hebrews 11:6

This verse highlights the two essential elements of prayer: faith in God's existence and faith that he cares enough to listen, answer, and move on behalf of those who seek him. Each of the men and women in the Hebrews 11 "Hall of Faith" who saw the invisible and believed God could do the impossible, pleased God and received great rewards because of their confidence and faith in him. By faith Enoch was taken up to heaven without dying. Noah's family was saved; Abraham, Isaac, and Jacob left their homes and followed God; Sarah bore a son in her old age. What did this faith look like? Although their circumstances were different, it was faith in what God said, faith in who God is, faith that God would show them the way into a future they couldn't see. But in believing, they would see what they had believed. This is a faith we can build our lives on, and without it, we can't please God at all. Pray earnestly that through the Holy Spirit, your faith in God will grow.

LORD, increase my faith so that I can trust you even when the way is dark and uncertain. As I pray, empower and strengthen me to believe that you are who you say you are in your Word and that you will respond and reward those who seek you. I want to live by faith in the Son of God, who loved me and gave his life for me!

FAITH NEVER KNOWS WHERE IT IS BEING LED. BUT IT LOVES AND KNOWS THE ONE WHO IS LEADING.
Oswald Chambers (1874–1917)

The One Year Bible Readings for today are **Ezekiel 24:1–26:21; Hebrews 11:1-16; Psalm 110:1-7;** and **Proverbs 27:14.**

NOVEMBER

13

focus

Keeping Our Focus

Instead of listening to the voices of Pharaoh and the naysayers among his own people, Moses turned to God and kept right on going in the direction the Lord led. Instead of fixing his eyes on the treasures of Egypt, he looked ahead and understood the infinitely great value of the things that are not seen and was willing to suffer rather than stay in Pharaoh's court and prosper. Moses kept his eyes on God. He left the power and prestige of Egypt and chose God's people and promises though it meant difficulty, because he was focused on one thing: obeying God's voice. That single-minded, wholehearted focus kept him unafraid of the terrible wrath of Pharaoh. It was the source of his confidence and strength as he led the Israelites out of bondage and through the Red Sea. So it is with us: keeping our eyes on the One who is invisible instead of on the overwhelming problems or difficult people in our paths, we can keep going wherever God leads us. And as we are fixed on him, we perceive the realities of the unseen and find the key to walking by faith, not by sight.

He thought it was better to suffer for the sake of the Messiah than to own the treasures of Egypt, for he was looking ahead to the great reward that God would give him. It was by faith that Moses left the land of Egypt. He was not afraid of the king. Moses kept right on going because he kept his eyes on the one who is invisible.
Hebrews 11:26-27

LORD, help me today to keep my eyes on you who are invisible. Fill me with faith and focus like Moses had so that I will not be afraid and can keep following wherever you lead. I desire to be obedient to your call on my life. Help me to walk by faith and not by sight and to understand the greater value of things unseen.

RELINQUISHMENT OF BURDENS AND FEARS BEGINS WHERE ADORATION AND WORSHIP OF GOD BECOME THE OCCUPATION OF THE SOUL.
Frances J. Roberts

The One Year Bible Readings for today are **Ezekiel 27:1–28:26; Hebrews 11:17-31; Psalm 111:1-10;** and **Proverbs 27:15-16.**

NOVEMBER

14

blessing

The Way of Blessing

Happy are those who fear the Lord. Yes, happy are those who delight in doing what he commands. Their children will be successful everywhere; an entire generation of godly people will be blessed. . . . When darkness overtakes the godly, light will come bursting in.
Psalm 112:1-2, 4

This psalm tells us two essentials for happiness: to fear God and to delight in following—not just reading or hearing—his commands. For those who fear, who have an attitude of deep humility and acknowledge God's majesty with a healthy awe and respect, there are specific blessings: prosperity, light even in dark times, honor from God, and even emotional stability to the point of not being afraid of the future, of bad news, or even of wicked people. As we fear God and delight in living according to his principles, he opens the way of blessing.

Spend time contemplating the awesome majesty and splendor of the creator and sustainer of the universe, who has spared nothing to reveal his Father's heart. Recommit yourself to him and to living according to his ways. Ask for the empowering of his Spirit to delight in doing what God commands.

LORD, reveal yourself to me in your sovereign majesty and fill me with awe and humility before you. Develop in me a healthy fear of you and a desire to not just read your Word but to commit myself to follow all that you command. Thank you for your promise of blessing for those who fear and obey you and that as I continue to follow you, an entire generation will be blessed.

THERE IS A VIRTUOUS FEAR WHICH IS THE EFFECT OF FAITH, AND A VICIOUS FEAR WHICH IS THE PRODUCT OF DOUBT AND MISTRUST. THE FORMER LEADS TO HOPE AS RELYING ON GOD, IN WHOM WE BELIEVE, THE LATTER INCLINES TO DESPAIR. . . . PERSONS OF THE ONE CHARACTER FEAR TO LOSE GOD; THOSE OF THE OTHER CHARACTER FEAR TO FIND HIM. Blaise Pascal (1623–1662)

The One Year Bible Readings for today are **Ezekiel 29:1–30:26; Hebrews 11:32–12:13; Psalm 112:1-10;** and **Proverbs 27:17.**

praise

Purposing to Praise

This psalm is a call to praise the Lord at all times and places in the world. What a God we serve! Although he is enthroned in heaven, high above the nations, he comes down to earth to provide comfort and save the oppressed. God is worthy of our praise. Do you find it difficult to praise God today? Do you just not feel thankful? Tell him about your feelings, your problems, and even your difficulty in praising him. Ask him for the grace to praise him in the midst of your circumstances. Read this psalm aloud as your sacrifice of praise. There is praise in heaven all the time, and when we purpose to reach beyond our problems to enter into that praise, God's grace is there to usher us in. We can experience being lifted above our problems because of the vital force that praise is. As you praise God from your heart, he will direct your eyes from the troubles on earth to the glory and sufficiency of our King and Lord, and you will gain God's eternal perspective to face the difficulties in your life.

Praise the Lord! Yes, give praise, O servants of the Lord. Praise the name of the Lord! Blessed be the name of the Lord forever and ever. Everywhere—from east to west—praise the name of the Lord. For the Lord is high above the nations; his glory is far greater than the heavens.
Psalm 113:1-4

I GIVE YOU PRAISE, LORD, for you are high above the nations and your glory is beyond anything else in earth or heaven. I lift up your mighty name and praise you for who you are. Grant me grace to worship you from my heart. Add my praise to those always going on in heaven. Blessed be the name of the Lord forever and ever. Praise the name of the Lord!

TO GIVE THANKS WHEN YOU DON'T FEEL LIKE IT IS NOT HYPOCRISY; IT'S OBEDIENCE. Dr. Jack Mitchell

The One Year Bible Readings for today are **Ezekiel 31:1–32:32; Hebrews 12:14-29; Psalm 113:1–114:8;** and **Proverbs 27:18-20.**

NOVEMBER

16

equipped

Fully Equipped

May the God of peace, who brought again from the dead our Lord Jesus, equip you with all you need for doing his will. May he produce in you, through the power of Jesus Christ, all that is pleasing to him. Jesus is the great Shepherd of the sheep by an everlasting covenant, signed with his blood. To him be glory forever and ever. Amen.

Hebrews 13:20-21

Paul has just asked the Hebrew Christians to pray that he and his followers will have good consciences and live honorably in all they do. Then he promises that he will pray for them, especially that they will be obedient to the will of God. He asks God to bless them with peace, hope in Christ, and everything they need to live out the destiny he has called them to through the power of Jesus Christ.

Paul's prayer for the Hebrew Christians can be a wonderful prayer for us to pray for ourselves and for those for whom we intercede: that God will prepare and equip us with everything we need for doing his will and that he will so work within us that our lives will be pleasing to him. None of this happens apart from the resurrection power of Jesus. Only Christ working in us by the indwelling Holy Spirit and the Word of God can produce a life that pleases the Lord. So let this prayer be the cry of your heart.

LORD, strengthen and equip me with every good thing so that I can do your will. Prepare me for what you're preparing for me. And open my heart wider to the working of your Spirit so that my life—inside and outside—will honor you. Produce in me, through the power of Jesus Christ, all that is pleasing to you.

GRANT ME GRACE, O MERCIFUL GOD, TO DESIRE ARDENTLY ALL THAT IS PLEASING TO THEE, TO EXAMINE IT PRUDENTLY, TO ACKNOWLEDGE IT TRUTHFULLY, AND TO ACCOMPLISH IT PERFECTLY, FOR THE PRAISE AND GLORY OF THY NAME. AMEN.
Saint Thomas Aquinas (1225–1274)

The One Year Bible Readings for today are **Ezekiel 33:1–34:31; Hebrews 13:1-25; Psalm 115:1-18;** and **Proverbs 27:21-22.**

listens

He Bends Down and Listens

This verse expresses one of the greatest truths and blessings of the Christian life: God hears us. In fact, this awesome, almighty God not only hears us but he also brings us into the outworking of his will on the earth through our prayers. He loves us enough to bend down and listen. In the original language the word for *listens* means that he inclines or strains his ears to hear us when we pray. He wants us to tell him our needs, our hurts, and our desires. And he doesn't stop with hearing. He answers our prayers and petitions. He intervenes in the affairs of men. He acts on behalf of those who ask for his help. He has initiated and established this avenue of our asking to be the means by which he shows himself mighty and fulfills his will. He hears! That is reason enough to love the Lord and to continue to pray as long as we have breath.

I love the Lord because he hears and answers my prayers. Because he bends down and listens, I will pray as long as I have breath!

Psalm 116:1-2

LORD, thank you for the incredible privilege of prayer. How amazing it is that you bend down and listen to me, that you hear and answer my prayers. Thank you for the privilege of being a partner with you as you fulfill your purposes, and thank you for showing yourself mighty as I pray. Empower me to pray as long as I breathe!

SPEAK TO HIM, THOU, FOR HE HEARS,
AND SPIRIT WITH SPIRIT CAN MEET—
CLOSER IS HE THAN BREATHING,
AND NEARER THAN HANDS AND FEET.

Alfred Lord Tennyson (1809–1892)

The One Year Bible Readings for today are **Ezekiel 35:1–36:38; James 1:1-18; Psalm 116:1-19;** and **Proverbs 27:23-27.**

NOVEMBER
18

anger

Slow to Anger

My dear brothers and sisters, be quick to listen, slow to speak, and slow to get angry. Your anger can never make things right in God's sight.
James 1:19-20

This verse is worth praying often because our human tendency is to do just the opposite. On my own I can be too quick to say what's on my mind, neglect listening to others, and be easily angered. But when we give vent to our anger, we rarely act lovingly or make things right. Instead, we wind up hurting people's feelings and regretting our words.

The Lord calls us to a better way of handling relationships, and he will give us the power and grace we need to live this way. We need only to ask him and spend time with him so that his nature can grow within us and we can draw deeply from his limitless supply of goodness and love. Then we will have confidence that God is working in the midst of our difficult situation or relationship and will be able to entrust it to him. Spend a few moments being still in God's presence, and ask him to reveal times or places where you're tempted to speak too quickly or to respond in anger instead of turning to him for grace to respond the way he wants you to.

LORD, thank you for being slow to anger and full of mercy and patience. Forgive my quick or angry reactions. Help me today to be quick to listen, slow to speak, and slow to get angry, as you are. Work in me by your Holy Spirit. Help me to pour out to you the things that grieve and frustrate me and to rely on you to work in difficult situations in ways I can't.

DON'T GET ANGRY AT THE PERSON WHO ACTS IN WAYS THAT DISPLEASE YOU. GIVE HIM THE SMILE HE LACKS. SPREAD THE SUNSHINE OF YOUR LORD'S LIMITLESS LOVE. Joni Eareckson Tada (b. 1949)

The One Year Bible Readings for today are **Ezekiel 37:1–38:23; James 1:19–2:17; Psalm 117:1-2;** and **Proverbs 28:1.**

NOVEMBER
19

wisdom

Wisdom from Heaven

The wisdom that comes from heaven is first of all pure. It is also peace loving, gentle at all times, and willing to yield to others. It is full of mercy and good deeds. It shows no partiality and is always sincere.
James 3:17

In this passage James contrasts human wisdom with heavenly wisdom. Bragging about good deeds or trying to look better than others, he says, isn't wisdom, and neither is doing anything else motivated by selfishness or envy. The wisdom that comes from God is 180 degrees different: pure, peaceable, and gentle—at all times. It is easily entreated, shows no partiality, and is always sincere. Those with godly wisdom are merciful and willing to yield to others, and they produce good fruit in their relationships.

How can we ever attain this? First, by realizing that we were never meant to tackle life with our own human wisdom. Real wisdom, the kind we desperately need, belongs only to God, so we need to ask him for it and, even more, we need to grow in wisdom by learning to function in unity with God. Then we begin to see things from his viewpoint. As we acknowledge our need for his wisdom and ask him for it, he will give it (James 1:5). Do you have a decision to make or a challenging situation at work or in your family? Seek God's wisdom today.

THANK YOU, LORD, for your wisdom that is peace-loving, gentle, merciful, and willing to yield to others. Thank you for the provision of your wisdom day by day as I abide in you. Show me what to do in the difficult situations I am facing today. I need your heavenly view of things. Thank you for making your divine wisdom available to me through your indwelling Holy Spirit!

WISDOM IS SEEING LIFE FROM GOD'S PERSPECTIVE.
Bill Gothard (b. 1934)

The One Year Bible Readings for today are **Ezekiel 39:1–40:27; James 2:18–3:18; Psalm 118:1-18;** and **Proverbs 28:2.**

NOVEMBER

20

rejoice

Rejoice and Be Glad

This is the day the Lord has made. We will rejoice and be glad in it.
Psalm 118:24

Some days we wake up with anything but a rejoicing spirit. We may not feel up to par physically. The sun may not have come out for a few days. Our life situation may be stressful; burdens may weigh heavily on our hearts. We may have experienced a loss. Unanswered prayers may be stacked as high as our pile of unpaid bills. Still, God has given us this day, and he calls us to rejoice in it. No matter what else is going on, God is still God, the Father, the Creator, who rules from his throne and declares his glory in every blade of grass, every bird that sings, every sunrise. Think of it—every day is new! His mercies are new. He has made us new creations in Christ Jesus and has given us a world full of his beauty. This day is another day to love our family and friends. It is another day to serve God, another day for him to extend his kingdom through us. It is another day of opportunity to trust him and see him work even in the problems and difficulties we face.

LORD, this is the day you have made, a place of new beginnings for me. You display your glory in all of creation. Help me to see your goodness and lift up my head and rejoice. No matter what happens during the next twenty-four hours, help me rejoice and be glad in the day you have made! And help me to see even my problems as one more opportunity to depend on you.

THERE IS NOT ONE BLADE OF GRASS, THERE IS NO COLOR IN THIS WORLD THAT IS NOT INTENDED TO MAKE US REJOICE. John Calvin (1509–1564)

The One Year Bible Readings for today are **Ezekiel 40:28–41:26; James 4:1-17; Psalm 118:19-29;** and **Proverbs 28:3-5.**

NOVEMBER
21

praying

Keep On Praying

Are any among you suffering? They should keep on praying about it. And those who have reason to be thankful should continually sing praises to the Lord.
James 5:13

This verse shares a key principle for effective intercession: "keep on praying" until the breakthrough comes.

The actual building of the dam usually takes many months, and then the water begins accumulating behind the dam. Drop by drop and day by day the water level rises, yet on the other side of the dam it's not apparent that anything is happening. Then when the water level finally reaches the right height, the sluice gates are opened wide. Water begins to turn the generators, and incredible power is released.

Whether we are suffering from physical illness, financial problems, or broken relationships, sometimes it looks as if things will never change. This verse encourages us to press on. Keep praying until you have accumulated a great mass of prayer. Gather others to intercede for you. The breakthrough may be just around the corner.

LORD, I want to be a faithful follower who doesn't stop praying because of delay, discouragement, or weariness. You won't delay one day or one moment longer than is needed for you to accomplish your purposes. Empower me to "keep on praying" until the answers come and to continually be thankful and bless your name.

PRAYER MUST OFTEN BE 'HEAPED UP' UNTIL GOD SEES THAT ITS MEASURE IS FULL. THEN THE ANSWER COMES. JUST AS EACH OF TEN THOUSAND SEEDS IS A PART OF THE FINAL HARVEST, FREQUENTLY REPEATED, PERSEVERING PRAYER IS NECESSARY TO ACQUIRE A DESIRED BLESSING. . . . REAL FAITH CAN NEVER BE DISAPPOINTED. IT KNOWS THAT TO EXERCISE ITS POWER, IT MUST BE GATHERED UP, JUST LIKE WATER, UNTIL THE STREAM CAN COME DOWN IN FULL FORCE.
Andrew Murray (1828–1917)

The One Year Bible Readings for today are **Ezekiel 42:1–43:27; James 5:1-20; Psalm 119:1-16;** and **Proverbs 28:6-7.**

NOVEMBER

22

mercy

Boundless Mercy

All honor to the God and Father of our Lord Jesus Christ, for it is by his boundless mercy that God has given us the privilege of being born again. Now we live with a wonderful expectation because Jesus Christ rose again from the dead. For God has reserved a priceless inheritance for his children.

1 Peter 1:3-4

These verses in 1 Peter are a prayer of thanksgiving to God for the marvelous gift of new birth we believers have because of the resurrection of Jesus Christ. Not only do we have our new lives on earth to be grateful for, but we are born again to a living, eternal hope. God's nature transforms our natures on the earth and gives us purpose, meaning, and hope not only for this life but for the one to come. We have a "wonderful expectation" of our future in heaven and a priceless inheritance because we are his children and heirs. This inheritance isn't like those we receive on earth. God watches over it, and it is "beyond the reach of change or decay." Take time to meditate on the Lord's boundless mercy and the priceless inheritance he has reserved for you, all because Christ rose from the dead. Ask him to increase your expectation that the best is yet to be.

FATHER, I bless you and praise you for the hope, expectation, and inheritance you have provided by the resurrection of your Son, our Savior. I praise you for the boundless mercy that gave me the privilege of being born again to a living hope. Thank you for giving me life with a wonderful expectation because you have reserved a priceless inheritance for me and for all your children.

TRUE FAITH IS NEVER FOUND ALONE; IT IS ACCOMPANIED BY EXPECTATION.
C. S. Lewis (1898–1963)

The One Year Bible Readings for today are **Ezekiel 44:1–45:12; 1 Peter 1:1-12; Psalm 119:17-32;** and **Proverbs 28:8-10.**

chosen

Chosen of God

You are a chosen people. You are a kingdom of priests, God's holy nation, his very own possession. This is so you can show others the goodness of God, for he called you out of the darkness into his wonderful light.
1 Peter 2:9

This is a wonderful word of encouragement, and it reflects the great destiny of every believer. We who once were not a people are now the people of God, greatly prized and loved, his own possession. Thus we have a high calling: to be his ambassadors, proclaiming his attributes and living lives that demonstrate his goodness so that others can see and experience his gracious, boundless love. Because God called us "out of the darkness into his wonderful light," we are to be witnesses to the watching world, not just with our words but also with our actions—the way we run our businesses, treat our neighbors, and nurture our children. How we need the Spirit to make us more like Jesus so that others will want to know him because of what they see in us! Ask God to help you surrender more of yourself to him that he might release more of his light in you. May he help you to show his goodness in your home, at your workplace, and wherever you go.

HOLY SPIRIT, thank you for bringing me out of darkness into your wonderful light because of your mercy. Thank you for making us your people, your very own possession. Help me to continually yield to you so that the life and character of Christ will be formed in me. Then others may see your goodness and will be drawn to you.

GOD IS PREPARING YOU AS HIS CHOSEN ARROW. AS YET YOUR SHAFT IS HIDDEN IN HIS QUIVER, IN THE SHADOWS . . . BUT AT THE PRECISE MOMENT AT WHICH IT WILL TELL WITH THE GREATEST EFFECT, HE WILL REACH FOR YOU AND LAUNCH YOU TO THAT PLACE OF HIS APPOINTMENT.
Charles R. Swindoll (b. 1934)

The One Year Bible Readings for today are **Ezekiel 45:13–46:24; 1 Peter 1:13–2:10; Psalm 119:33-48;** and **Proverbs 28:11.**

NOVEMBER

24

heirs

Heirs of Life

You [wives] should be known for the beauty that comes from within, the unfading beauty of a gentle and quiet spirit, which is so precious to God. . . . In the same way, you husbands must give honor to your wives. Treat her with understanding as you live together. She may be weaker than you are, but she is your equal partner in God's gift of new life. If you don't treat her as you should, your prayers will not be heard.

1 Peter 3:4, 7

This passage encourages husbands and wives to nurture and cherish what God has put within them and to relate to each other as "equal partners in God's gift of new life." We can infer that the perspective of being "equal partners" facilitates prayer because we see the contrasting idea in these verses: when husbands demonstrate a lack of respect and understanding toward their wives, God will not hear their prayers. That's why Peter exhorts wives to respect their husbands and cultivate an inner beauty characterized not by showy outward adornment but by a gentle and quiet spirit. And he instructs husbands to honor their wives as equals and live with them in an understanding way so their prayers don't get derailed. When we lose sight of who we and our spouses are in Christ, we can humbly ask God's forgiveness and begin again to live in grace and forgiveness toward each other as the partners God has called us to be.

Ask the Lord to reveal to you anything in your own marriage that may be derailing harmony or hindering your prayers. Pray for a new perspective of your spouse as your partner in God's gift of new life.

LORD, we need your empowering grace in our marriage! Help us to nurture and cherish the wonderful new life within each of us, to honor and respect each other, and to glorify your Son in our lives together. Teach us your way of compassion, understanding, love, and forgiveness, and remove every hindrance to our prayer lives.

UNLESS HUSBAND AND WIFE ARE HEIRS TOGETHER OF THE GRACE OF LIFE, AND TREAT EACH OTHER AS BECOMETH SAINTS, HOW CAN THEY EXPECT THEIR PRAYERS TO HAVE ANY WEIGHT WITH GOD?
Herbert Lockyer

The One Year Bible Readings for today are **Ezekiel 47:1–48:35; 1 Peter 2:11–3:7; Psalm 119:49-64;** and **Proverbs 28:12-13.**

NOVEMBER
25

revelation

God of Revelation

In a very crucial time Daniel didn't lean on his own understanding and knowledge. Neither did he panic when the king ordered that Daniel along with all the king's wise men would be killed because they had failed to interpret his dream. Instead, Daniel asked the king for more time, went home, and urged his three friends to join him in prayer. Together they asked God to show them his mercy by revealing the secret of the king's dream. Daniel's prayer of praise and thanksgiving is a reminder to us that God reveals "deep and mysterious things"—things that are unseeable and unknowable and unsearchable to the natural mind—to those who seek him and ask for his wisdom instead of trying to figure things out on their own. What area of your life do you feel most baffled about? Where do you need wisdom the most—in your parenting, your business, in relationships or ministry? Praise God today for being the source of all wisdom, light, and strength and the One who can reveal to you just what you need.

LORD, I praise your name. You are the God who "has all wisdom and power," the One who guides world events. You give "wisdom to the wise," and you know what is "hidden in darkness" and all mysteries. I pray for your wisdom and strength in this situation today. . . .

GOD REVEALS HIMSELF UNFAILINGLY TO THE THOUGHTFUL SEEKER. Honoré de Balzac (1799–1850)

Praise the name of God forever and ever, for he alone has all wisdom and power. . . . He reveals deep and mysterious things and knows what lies hidden in darkness, though he himself is surrounded by light. I thank and praise you, God of my ancestors, for you have given me wisdom and strength. You have told me what we asked of you and revealed to us what the king demanded.
Daniel 2:20, 22-23

The One Year Bible Readings for today are **Daniel 1:1–2:23; 1 Peter 3:8–4:6; Psalm 119:65-80;** and **Proverbs 28:14.**

NOVEMBER

26

love

The Love That Covers

Most important of all, continue to show deep love for each other, for love covers a multitude of sins.

1 Peter 4:8

Do you have days when you are not showing others the "deep love" that Peter talks about? I do. In fact, there are times when—in spite of my best intentions—my love runs dry, even for people I really care about. Such is the sad truth of the human condition. Apart from the Creator, it is impossible to love in the way the he designed us: as vessels of his love. We will eventually run out of our own natural love for our spouses, children, or friends. But at that point we have a great opportunity to draw on the unfailing, everlasting love of God. It is a constant, renewable resource available to us twenty-four hours a day.

What about you? Maybe your husband's decisions have caused you pain. Perhaps you are sleep-deprived and under extreme stress. Maybe someone has said hurtful things about you. Think for a few minutes about the relationship you find most difficult or the person you find hardest to love. Pray for God's Spirit to pour into your heart the love that covers a multitude of sins.

LORD, I admit my lack of love and my desperate need for your unfailing love toward [insert name]. Help me to yield to your Spirit and experience deeper intimacy with you and your love for me. Then may your love so fill me that others around me feel splashes from the overflow. And in those relationships that are the toughest, grant me your love—which covers a multitude of sins.

THE SPRINGS OF LOVE ARE IN GOD, NOT IN US. IT IS ABSURD TO LOOK FOR THE LOVE OF GOD IN OUR HEARTS NATURALLY, IT IS ONLY THERE WHEN IT HAS BEEN SHED ABROAD IN OUR HEARTS BY THE HOLY SPIRIT. Oswald Chambers (1874–1917)

The One Year Bible Readings for today are **Daniel 2:24–3:30; 1 Peter 4:7–5:14; Psalm 119:81-96;** and **Proverbs 28:15-16.**

value

The Value of the Word

How sweet are your words to my taste; they are sweeter than honey. Your commandments give me understanding; no wonder I hate every false way of life.
Psalm 119:103-104

In this prayer we can join the psalmist as he expresses thankfulness for God's words. His words nourish us, give us understanding, and keep us from deceptive ways. No wonder they are better than the choicest food! The Word of our Lord provides the fuel for our spiritual growth and health and gives us the guidance we need for each step of the journey. Almost every verse of Psalm 119 speaks of this overarching theme—the great value of the revealed Word of God. It calls us to come back to the Scriptures and to approach reading them as a delight, not as a duty. It reminds us what a gift it is to know what God says and to be able to follow that path that leads to eternal life instead of the false path that leads to destruction. Ask his Spirit to increase your enjoyment of the Scriptures and to open your eyes to his wonderful ways. Pray that you will hunger for his Word more than for your favorite food so that with Moses you can say, "These instructions are not mere words—they are your life!" (Deuteronomy 32:47).

FATHER, thank you for your Word, which is my very life! It gives me the understanding I need to stay on the right path and live a life that honors you. Fill me with delight in the Scriptures, and increase my appreciation of them as each year passes. Keep me from distraction when I sit down to read, and may I never take for granted the great privilege of knowing what you have said.

GOD DID NOT WRITE A BOOK AND SEND IT BY MESSENGER TO BE READ AT A DISTANCE BY UNAIDED MINDS. HE SPOKE A BOOK AND LIVES IN HIS SPOKEN WORDS, CONSTANTLY SPEAKING HIS WORDS AND CAUSING THE POWER OF THEM TO PERSIST ACROSS THE YEARS. A. W. Tozer (1897–1963)

The One Year Bible Readings for today are **Daniel 4:1-37; 2 Peter 1:1-21; Psalm 119:97-112;** and **Proverbs 28:17-18.**

NOVEMBER

28

Straining to See

My eyes strain to see your deliverance, to see the truth of your promise fulfilled. I am your servant; deal with me in unfailing love, and teach me your principles.
Psalm 119:123-124

Have you ever strained to see God's deliverance? We yearn to see his promises fulfilled. We long for his answer. Perhaps you desire to see your son turn from an empty lifestyle and crown Jesus as Lord. You may long for God to restore health to someone for whom you've been praying or to open the doors to joy in your marriage. The Bible is full of people who strained to see God's deliverance and his promises fulfilled. There were twenty-five years between God's promise of a son to Abraham and Sarah and the fulfillment of that promise. Hannah agonized and waited for the son she longed for until God gave her Samuel. Joseph waited through long periods of struggle until God finally fulfilled the dream he had given him years before.

There can be periods of waiting for us as well—not as long, we hope, as the one Abraham experienced! In those waiting times, our faith is sorely tested. We get impatient. We are given to doubt and despair. But in that very weakness and testing, we can look to God to deal lovingly with us and give us trust and patience as we wait on him.

LORD, my eyes strain to see your deliverance and to see the truth of your promises fulfilled! Strengthen me in those places where I get weary of waiting. In your loving-kindness, renew my flagging trust in you. Deal with me in your unfailing love and compassion, and teach me day by day to trust in you and your principles even while I am in the waiting rooms of life.

O LORD MY GOD! . . . WE UNDERSTAND NATURE'S SEASONS; WE KNOW HOW TO WAIT FOR THE FRUIT WE LONG FOR. FILL US WITH THE ASSURANCE THAT YOU WON'T DELAY ONE MOMENT LONGER THAN IS NECESSARY, AND THAT OUR FAITH WILL HASTEN THE ANSWER. Andrew Murray (1828–1917)

The One Year Bible Readings for today are **Daniel 5:1-31; 2 Peter 2:1-22; Psalm 119:113-128;** and **Proverbs 28:19-20.**

devotion

Devotion in Prayer

When Daniel learned that the law had been signed, he went home and knelt down as usual in his upstairs room, with its windows open toward Jerusalem. He prayed three times a day, just as he had always done, giving thanks to his God.

Daniel 6:10

As a result of Daniel's simple act of continuing devotion to God, the entire course of a nation and human history was altered. It was not his eloquence, his physical strength, or his vocation that had such an impact on the world. No, God used the most basic exercise of the human spirit—turning to him in prayer—to accomplish what no army could ever hope to achieve. We often make the mistake of thinking that "ministry" is something God expects us to do for him. However, the work of God is to believe in the One whom the Father has sent. Jesus calls to us, "Come to me." It is our continued prayer, faithful "abiding" in Christ, and growth in intimacy with him in the face of the adversities on earth that will result in our victory and the world's deliverance. Flesh begets flesh. Only the Holy Spirit can produce the fruit that will glorify the Father in the Son.

FATHER, help me to trust in you this day and to recognize your intimate presence with me and in me. Give me devotion and tenacity in prayer, the kind Daniel had. May I abide in constant communion with you, even while I'm working to do all that is before me with excellence, and may I ever heed your call to "come."

THE POTENCY OF PRAYER HATH SUBDUED THE STRENGTH OF FIRE; IT HAS BRIDLED THE RAGE OF LIONS, HUSHED ANARCHY TO REST, EXTINGUISHED WARS, APPEASED THE ELEMENTS, EXPELLED DEMONS, BURST THE CHAINS OF DEATH, EXPANDED THE GATES OF HEAVEN, ASSUAGED DISEASES, REPELLED FRAUDS, RESCUED CITIES FROM DESTRUCTION, STAYED THE SUN IN ITS COURSE, AND ARRESTED THE PROGRESS OF THE THUNDERBOLT. Saint John Chrysostom (ca. 347–407)

The One Year Bible Readings for today are **Daniel 6:1-28; 2 Peter 3:1-18; Psalm 119:129-152;** and **Proverbs 28:21-22.**

NOVEMBER

30

treasure

Great Treasure

See how I love your commandments, Lord. Give back my life because of your unfailing love. All your words are true; all your just laws will stand forever. Powerful people harass me without cause, but my heart trembles only at your word. I rejoice in your word like one who finds a great treasure.

Psalm 119:159-162

Each day we are confronted by people who harass us or by challenges that will be either stumbling blocks or stepping stones depending on our response to them. While it should be the goal of every Christian to engage each situation with the very heart of Jesus, it is important to understand that we achieve this objective primarily by letting the Word of God dwell richly in us. The Holy Spirit has always lived in and worked through the Word of God. And while the Old Testament people sought to make their ways righteous by observing the law and keeping God's commandments, we now have the joy of Jesus, the physical manifestation of his Word, living within us in his Spirit. That is why we rejoice in his Word like one who finds a treasure. It is his Word in our hearts and minds that provides the Spirit a vehicle through which to bring his will to bear on earth as it is in heaven.

LORD, thank you for the treasure of your Word. "All your words are true," and "all your just laws will stand forever." Grant me an insatiable hunger for your Word. May my heart tremble at its truths. May I always rejoice in it, and may it be alive and powerful in me.

THE BIBLE IS ALIVE, IT SPEAKS TO ME; IT HAS FEET, IT RUNS AFTER ME; IT HAS HANDS, IT LAYS HOLD ON ME. Martin Luther (1483–1546)

The One Year Bible Readings for today are **Daniel 7:1-28; 1 John 1:1-10; Psalm 119:153-176;** and **Proverbs 28:23-24.**

song

The Pilgrim's Song

I took my troubles to the Lord; I cried out to him, and he answered my prayer. Rescue me, O Lord, from liars and from all deceitful people.
Psalm 120:1-2

Psalm 120 is sometimes called a pilgrim song because it was sung as the Israelites were going up to Jerusalem to celebrate the annual feasts. In this particular song the pilgrims' trouble involved deceitful people who constantly harassed them and lied about them. They had suffered among the "scoundrels of Meshech" (v. 5), their own people who should have been peaceful but wanted only war. As the psalmist cried out to God for deliverance and poured out his pain, he felt confident that God was answering his prayers. God was his center, and prayer his first resource. He had taken his troubles to the right place, so even before anything had changed in the situation, he could thank God for answering his prayer. We may not be on our way to Jerusalem, but as believers we, too, are pilgrims and sojourners in this world and will face opposition. We may encounter harassment and trouble beyond our ability to handle. Others may lie about us or betray us, as David experienced, but this passage assures us that when we take all our troubles to God and cry out to him, he *will answer* our prayer.

FATHER, I thank you that there is no trouble beyond your help. When I bring my problems to you, when I cry out to you, you are always there, listening, answering, and working in my life. Though I may be harassed or distressed, you are my sure refuge. You are my strong tower, and I run to you and am safe. Thank you for hearing and answering my prayers!

IT IS THE ANSWER TO PRAYER WHICH MAKES PRAYING A POWER FOR GOD AND FOR MAN, AND MAKES PRAYING REAL AND DIVINE.
E. M. Bounds (1835–1913)

The One Year Bible Readings for today are **Daniel 8:1-27; 1 John 2:1-17; Psalm 120:1-7;** and **Proverbs 28:25-26.**

DECEMBER

2

alone

We Are Not Alone

I look up to the mountains—does my help come from there? My help comes from the Lord, who made the heavens and the earth! He will not let you stumble and fall; the one who watches over you will not sleep. Indeed, he who watches over Israel never tires and never sleeps.
Psalm 121:1-4

Like the psalmist who journeyed to Jerusalem, our strength and help don't come from the mountains but from the One who made them. He who created us is able to sustain us. He enables us to finish whatever journey we're on, even if there is weariness, sickness, or trouble along the way. He who guards us *never* falls asleep on the job. He is up all night protecting his own, guarding our lives.

My mother called this the traveler's psalm because it assures us that no matter where we are, whether we journey by car, airplane, train, or on foot, whether we are awake or asleep, we are not alone. She prayed this psalm aloud whenever she embarked on a trip. As she proclaimed God's watchful care over her comings and goings, her heart, which had often been anxious, calmed. As she reminded herself of the One who stood beside her, watched over her, prepared the way before her, kept her from all evil and preserved her life (v. 7), she could rest in his loving arms as she traveled over mountains and hills, flew over clouds, and as she made her final journey from this life into eternity.

LORD, I look up to the mountains, but my help does not come from there! My help comes from you, who made the heavens and the earth! Because you hold me, I will not stumble and fall. Because you watch over me, I will not fear. Thank you for your constant care and protection. My security is in you. Please bless my going out and coming in, both now and forever.

THE KNOWLEDGE THAT WE ARE NEVER ALONE CALMS THE TROUBLED SEA OF OUR LIVES AND SPEAKS PEACE TO OUR SOULS. A. W. Tozer (1897–1963)

The One Year Bible Readings for today are **Daniel 9:1–11:1; 1 John 2:18–3:6; Psalm 121:1-8;** and **Proverbs 28:27-28.**

peace

Peace in Jerusalem

Pray for the peace of Jerusalem. May all who love this city prosper. O Jerusalem, may there be peace within your walls and prosperity in your palaces. For the sake of my family and friends, I will say, "Peace be with you." For the sake of the house of the Lord our God, I will seek what is best for you, O Jerusalem.
Psalm 122:6-9

Jerusalem had not always been the "holy city." There was a time when Jerusalem was in the hands of the Jebusites, but they had been driven out. The city was now entirely in the possession of the children of God. Justice would be administered according to the heartbeat of God without outside influence or interference. When the people made their annual pilgrimage to Jerusalem to celebrate the three feasts, David penned this psalm as an announcement. He wanted all the people to know that Jerusalem was the city where God would record his name! Though David had a vested interest in Jerusalem, it was not his welfare that he solicited. He was a man of worship and loved the house of God. His desire was that the ark, the temple, and the glory of God would continue to abide in Jerusalem.

Today God's name is still recorded in Jerusalem. Pray for the peace of Jerusalem. Ask the God who never tires and never sleeps to bring rest to his people and to watch over Israel.

JEHOVAH, you created the universe. You are aware of the conflict of the nations, of the pleas of those who call for peace. I pray that you will protect your people. I pray that you will reign in Jerusalem. Help us as a people, a nation, to remember those who are suffering from unrest and conflict. Omnipotent and tireless God, I pray that you will bring peace and restoration to your holy city.

FOR MOST MEN THE WORLD IS CENTERED IN SELF, WHICH IS MISERY: TO HAVE ONE'S WORLD CENTERED IN GOD IS PEACE.
Donald Hankey (1874–1917)

The One Year Bible Readings for today are **Daniel 11:2-35; 1 John 3:7-24; Psalm 122:1-9;** and **Proverbs 29:1.**

DECEMBER

4

Confidence in His Love

God is love, and all who live in love live in God, and God lives in them. And as we live in God, our love grows more perfect. So we will not be afraid on the day of judgment, but we can face him with confidence because we are like Christ here in this world. Such love has no fear because perfect love expels all fear.
1 John 4:16-18

What a remarkable thing that we can rely on the love of God. How amazing that we get to experience that love because all who live in love live in God and God lives in them. That love does not originate in us but in God's love for us. Our love for God is not perfect or complete, but his love is perfect and complete and as we abide in him by his Spirit, our love will grow more complete. In all our trials we can know that God loves us more than we can imagine. This love rescued us from darkness and brought us into his marvelous light. This love covers all of our sins. It will equip us to stand before the Lord on the Day of judgment with confidence, not with fear. This love is so powerful that with it we can live victoriously and fearlessly because "perfect love expels all fear." Take a few moments to meditate on the love of God and to draw near to him in thanksgiving and praise.

LORD OF LOVE, thank you for first loving me! As we live in you, our love grows more complete. Although I don't understand all the trials I may go through, I trust in your love for me. Help me to abide in you. Fill me with your perfect love that casts out all fear so that I can live in confidence and rest in you and share your amazing love with those around me.

EVERYTHING GOD DOES IS LOVE—EVEN WHEN WE DO NOT UNDERSTAND HIM. Mother Basilea Schlink (1904–2001)

The One Year Bible Readings for today are **Daniel 11:36–12:13; 1 John 4:1-21; Psalm 123:1-4;** and **Proverbs 29:2-4.**

thorns

Praying a Hedge of Thorns

I will fence her in with thornbushes. I will block the road to make her lose her way. When she runs after her lovers, she won't be able to catch up with them. She will search for them but not find them.
Hosea 2:6-7

Have you ever felt as if you have run out of prayers for a prodigal in your life (whether a teenager, a niece or nephew, or a spouse) and that person is still running headlong toward destruction? If so, you might identify with Hosea, whose wife, Gomer, was continually on the wrong path and running after other lovers. God said that he would block her path with thornbushes, wall her in so that she couldn't find her way.

When people we love don't have the wisdom to see the destructive paths they are on, we can pray for a "hedge of thorns." We ask God to separate our loved ones from destructive influences, to cause those who lure them into evil to lose interest and to cause the prodigals to lose interest in them. Just as God's actions caused Gomer's lovers to depart, this prayer can form a barricade, or a double hedge, to keep destructive influences out and the prodigal in. This prayer can't change a person's will, but God can remove wrong influences and frustrate the prodigal's attempts to get to them. Then you can pray that in that frustration, the prodigal will turn to God.

LORD, I ask you to build a hedge of thorns around [insert name], to separate my loved one from any influence not ordained by you. I pray that those who are a bad influence will lose interest and flee and that my loved one would lose interest in them as well. May that hedge of thorns defend against any contact with those who are out of your will.

GOD IS EAGER AND ABLE TO DELIVER AND BLESS THE WORLD HE HAS REDEEMED, IF HIS PEOPLE WERE BUT WILLING, IF THEY WERE BUT READY, TO CRY TO HIM DAY AND NIGHT.
Andrew Murray (1828–1917)

The One Year Bible Readings for today are **Hosea 1:1–3:5; 1 John 5:1-21; Psalm 124:1-8;** and **Proverbs 29:5-8.**

DECEMBER

6

significance

Nothing of Significance

Hear the word of the Lord, O people of Israel! The Lord has filed a lawsuit against you, saying: "There is no faithfulness, no kindness, no knowledge of God in your land."
Hosea 4:1

No one looks forward to receiving a summons, but that's exactly what happened with Israel. The King of kings had filed a lawsuit, and the charges were serious. Though the nation had a rich history and God had promised an abundant future, there was nothing of lasting value in the land. A significant nation had become insignificant. How does an entire nation lose their heritage? They lose it in increments, when idols replace God, when one generation fails to teach the precepts of faith to the next, when people call on God only in times of crisis.

Israel did not know the extent of their loss until the summons arrived at their door. We may point to the problems in our own nation, but a country is only as strong as its people. Therefore, it is wise to examine our own lives first. Are we faithful? Are we kind to others? Do we know God and obey his Word? Are we teaching his precepts to the next generation? Take a moment and ask God to shed his light on your heart and home and to sow seeds of significance in your life.

FATHER, I pray that I will be faithful, kind, and knowledgeable of you. Help me to cherish those things that are of lasting value, for I find significance through you. Father, I lift up my nation before you. Help us to recognize what is of value and what is not. Open our eyes so that we will change our ways. Change my nation, Lord, but begin with me.

THE HUMAN VALUE IS NOT THE ULTIMATE, BUT ONLY THE PENULTIMATE VALUE; THE LAST, THE HIGHEST VALUE IS GOD THE FATHER. HE ALONE IS THE CAUSE AND THE MEASURE OF ALL THINGS, CAUSE AND MEASURE OF ALL VALUATIONS, CAUSE AND MEASURE OF ALL LOVE. Karl Adam (1876–1966)

The One Year Bible Readings for today are **Hosea 4:1–5:15; 2 John 1-13; Psalm 125:1-5;** and **Proverbs 29:9-11.**

truth

Living in the Truth

John's joy is unmistakable in this letter. He had received a good report! His dear friend, Gaius, was living in the truth. This was a bright spot in an otherwise dark picture. Diotrephes, the local leader of the church, had mistreated a group of traveling teachers. When people in the church stepped in to defend them, he put them out of the church. He gossiped wickedly about John and undermined the leaders' authority. Somewhere along the way Diotrephes had lost sight of the truth. He loved being a leader but had forgotten how to serve.

What does it mean to live in the truth? It means not only studying God's Word but also putting it into practice. It means avoiding petty quarrels and power trips. It means serving others instead of being self-serving. It is being faithful to the task at hand. Pastors and leaders often carry heavy burdens, and many times they do so at great personal sacrifice. You have the ability to lighten their load. Determine to ease the burdens of those who serve by living in the truth.

Dear friend, I am praying that all is well with you and that your body is as healthy as I know your soul is. Some of the brothers recently returned and made me very happy by telling me about your faithfulness and that you are living in the truth.
3 John 1:2-3

GOD, I lift up all those in authority. Their job is difficult. Help me to be a blessing rather than a burden. Help me to be faithful and to practice what I believe. Lord, I pray not only for my pastor but for all the leaders in my church. Minister to them. Wrap your arms around their families. Help me to be a bright spot in their ministry by living in the truth!

SEEK THE TRUTH
LISTEN TO THE TRUTH
TEACH THE TRUTH
LOVE THE TRUTH
ABIDE BY THE TRUTH
AND DEFEND THE TRUTH UNTO DEATH.
John Huss (1370–1415)

The One Year Bible Readings for today are **Hosea 6:1–9:17; 3 John 1-15; Psalm 126:1-6;** and **Proverbs 29:12-14.**

DECEMBER

8

rest

Glory and Rest

All glory to God, who is able to keep you from stumbling, and who will bring you into his glorious presence innocent of sin and with great joy. All glory to him, who alone is God our Savior, through Jesus Christ our Lord. Yes, glory, majesty, power, and authority belong to him, in the beginning, now, and forevermore.
Jude 24-25

After an extensive defense of the faith and a discussion of the doom awaiting those who reject God's way, Jude's benediction is hopeful and refreshing. It encourages us that although we live in a sinful world, God is able to keep us from falling. For it is his power that saves us, keeps us from stumbling, and will one day present us before his throne completely blameless and innocent of sin. It would be enough for us to be brought safely home to heaven, but Jude says that it will also be "with great joy." This thought can bring us into the rest that comes from believing God is completely adequate to accomplish this feat and we can totally depend on his power and strength. How wonderful to know that it doesn't depend on me to save myself, work hard, and make myself ready to enter God's glorious presence on that great day. My part is to believe and rest in the One who is my salvation, to yield to his refining and purifying work in my heart and life, and to give him honor and glory now and forevermore.

THANK YOU for the great gift of salvation through Jesus Christ our Lord. Glory to you, God, the One who is able to keep me from stumbling and bring me into your glorious presence blameless and with great joy! Help me to depend on your keeping power and strength as you work within me to please you. All glory, majesty, power, and authority belong to you from the beginning, now, and forever!

HOW SHALL WE REST IN GOD? BY GIVING OURSELVES WHOLLY TO HIM. IF YOU GIVE YOURSELF BY HALVES, YOU CANNOT FIND FULL REST; THERE WILL EVER BE A LURKING DISQUIET IN THAT HALF THAT IS WITHHELD.
Jean Nicolas Grou (1731–1803)

The One Year Bible Readings for today are **Hosea 10:1–14:9; Jude 1-25; Psalm 127:1-5;** and **Proverbs 29:15-17.**

return

Repent and Return

The grapevines and the fig trees have all withered. The pomegranate trees, palm trees, and apple trees—yes, all the fruit trees—have dried up. All joy has dried up with them. Dress yourselves in sackcloth, you priests! Wail, you who serve before the altar! Come, spend the night in sackcloth, you ministers of my God! There is no grain or wine to offer at the Temple of your God.
Joel 1:12-13

The first chapter of Joel is a call to "give ear" and is addressed to leaders and elders of Judah. As the plague of locusts descends on the land surrounding Jerusalem, crops and grapevines are destroyed, every palm, pomegranate, and fruit tree is dried up, and the people are devastated. In the face of this plague, the only hope for the people of Judah is to turn to God in true repentance.

Our nation faces different enemies today, but they are no less fierce or destructive, so God calls us to turn to him while there is still time. Give me your hearts, the Lord says. Don't just make an outward show of repentance or grief (tearing your clothes); I want a deep heart repentance, and I want you to return to me as the center of your life and your nation. Throughout the Scriptures God lays out the same pattern: if people will respond to his call, come in humility and repentance and pray, he will forgive their sins, and heal and restore their land, their lives, and their families. His promise to us is the same.

THANK YOU, GOD, for being gracious and merciful, not easily angered but filled with kindness and longing for your people. Grant not only me but our whole nation the gift of repentance, the gift of tears, so that we can return to you with all our hearts. Thank you not only for hearing my cries for help but also for bringing healing and restoration to my life today.

GOD WILL TAKE NINE STEPS TOWARD US, BUT HE WILL NOT TAKE THE TENTH. HE WILL INCLINE US TO REPENT, BUT HE CANNOT DO OUR REPENTING FOR US. A. W. Tozer (1897–1963)

The One Year Bible Readings for today are **Joel 1:1–3:21; Revelation 1:1-20; Psalm 128:1-6;** and **Proverbs 29:18.**

DECEMBER

10

love

First Love

I know all the things you do. I have seen your hard work and your patient endurance. . . . But I have this complaint against you. You don't love me or each other as you did at first! Look how far you have fallen from your first love! Turn back to me again.
Revelation 2:2, 4-5

First love, someone once said, is abandoning all for a love that has abandoned all. It refers to such deep devotion to Christ that we will abandon everything for the One who gave his life for us. Maybe when you first surrendered to Christ, you couldn't wait to spend time with Jesus; you read the Bible hungrily, and you hung on every word. Then you got busy working for the Lord, and along the way you lost the freshness of basking in his presence. People and responsibilities began to take first place. The Lord commended the believers for working hard, persevering, and patiently suffering without giving up, but he was also calling them and all Christians throughout history back to that first loving and vital relationship with him. How encouraging that though we can't force or fabricate this kind of love, Christ our bridegroom is always there wooing us back to him!

LORD, I confess that I have been working for you and "doing" a lot but have lost the simple devotion of loving you. Thank you that you are ever calling me back to intimacy with you. Thank you for your arms that are open wide to receive me. Help me to once again abandon myself to you, to experience your unfailing love for me, and to live in pure devotion close to your heart.

WE MUST SPIRITUALLY RENOUNCE ALL OTHER LOVES FOR LOVE OF GOD OR AT LEAST SO HOLD THEM IN SUBORDINATION TO THIS THAT WE ARE READY TO FOREGO THEM FOR ITS SAKE; YET WHEN WE FIND GOD, OR, RATHER, WHEN WE KNOW OURSELVES AS FOUND OF HIM, WE FIND IN AND WITH HIM ALL THE LOVES WHICH FOR HIS SAKE WE HAD FOREGONE. Sir William Temple (1628–1699)

The One Year Bible Readings for today are **Amos 1:1–3:15; Revelation 2:1-17; Psalm 129:1-8;** and **Proverbs 29:19-20.**

remember

Remember Who He Is

Throughout Amos chapter 5, in the midst of harsh judgment and the announcement of more disasters to come, the Lord mercifully calls his people to leave their idolatry, stop their wickedness, corruption, and injustice, and return to him. "Come back to the Lord and live," he tells them, before I "roar through Israel like a fire, devouring you completely." He calls them to remember what he has done, to look at creation, the constellations and stars at night. He reminds them of who he is: the blessed controller of everything in nature. He turns blackness into morning and day into night. He draws water from the oceans and pours it down as rain. His power destroys the strong and crushes all their defenses, causes the proud to stumble, and strengthens the weak. The Lord Almighty is his name! Just as the Israelites strayed when they forgot God and his deeds, so do we. One of the great values of the Scriptures is that they call us back to the truth of who God is. They give us word pictures of God's power and greatness so that we will return to him in surrender and devotion—that we might live.

Come back to the Lord and live! If you don't, he will roar through Israel like a fire, devouring you completely. . . . It is the Lord who created the stars, the Pleiades and Orion. It is he who turns darkness into morning and day into night. It is he who draws up water from the oceans and pours it down as rain on the land. The Lord is his name! With blinding speed and power he destroys the strong, crushing all their defenses.

Amos 5:6, 8-9

OH, LORD ALMIGHTY, who created the stars and turns darkness into dawn and day into night, I bow before you. I praise you for ruling over heaven and earth and "with blinding speed and power" crushing the wicked. Nothing can withstand your power! Thank you for your Word, which reminds me of who you are and calls me back to devotion and truth. Keep me from evil, and guide me along the path of life.

OH, FOR HEARTS TO BOW TO THE TRUTH SO FREQUENTLY PRESSED IN SCRIPTURE, AND THUS TO BE KEPT FROM THE DEFILEMENT OF EVIL!
H. A. Ironside (1876–1951)

The One Year Bible Readings for today are **Amos 4:1–6:14; Revelation 2:18–3:6; Psalm 130:1-8;** and **Proverbs 29:21-22.**

DECEMBER

12

quiet

Quiet My Heart

Lord, my heart is not proud; my eyes are not haughty. I don't concern myself with matters too great or awesome for me. But I have stilled and quieted myself, just as a small child is quiet with its mother. Yes, like a small child is my soul within me. O Israel, put your hope in the Lord—now and always.
Psalm 131:1-3

When we were in Maryland visiting our son, daughter-in-law, and their baby, I took photographs of my granddaughter. Josephine wasn't eating, demanding anything, or scrambling down to get something; she was just resting on her mother's lap, holding Mom's finger, and enjoying being close to her. This quiet moment may have been short-lived, but it's similar to this psalm's picture of childlike trust in the Lord. David is not arrogant or proud even though he is a great king who has had many victories on the battlefield. He doesn't boast about his own greatness. He doesn't concern himself with "matters too great or awesome," or seek his own agenda. Instead, he rests quietly and depends on the Lord.

You may be thinking, *I could never be that peaceful with everything I'm concerned about.* But the psalmist concludes in verse 3: "Put your hope in the Lord—now and always." Whether we are in darkness or morning light, difficult times or a season of joy, he calls us to humble, childlike trust in the Lord, to be still and wait quietly for God to work, to hope in him for today and for all our tomorrows. Ask God to bring that kind of quietness to your soul as you draw near to him.

LORD, thank you for calling me to childlike trust. You are utterly dependable and faithful! I come to you in humility and ask you to quiet my racing heart, my busy mind. As a small child quietly leaning on her mother, may I rest in you, depend on you, and trust in you fully this day. Help me to leave all my burdens with you and enjoy being in your presence.

IT IS NOT OUR TRUST THAT KEEPS US, BUT THE GOD IN WHOM WE TRUST WHO KEEPS US.
Oswald Chambers (1874–1917)

The ONE YEAR BIBLE

The One Year Bible Readings for today are **Amos 7:1–9:15; Revelation 3:7-22; Psalm 131:1-3;** and **Proverbs 29:23.**

DECEMBER
13

Laying Down Our Crowns

Much of the book of Revelation is puzzling and beyond our understanding; it pictures something that we will experience only in the hereafter. Now we comprehend only snippets of the great panorama of the end of time. One of those is in today's verses. As the heavenly company gathers, the twenty-four elders fall down before God, lay their crowns before him, and unite in praise: "You are worthy! You created everything."

Just as the twenty-four elders lay down their crowns, we are to lay down our best efforts, our victories, giftings and ministries, and bow in worship. We have nothing that we haven't received from God. Corrie ten Boom said that after she spoke, people often showered her with accolades and compliments. But when she got back to her room, she would bow before the Lord and—just like a bouquet—offer to him every word of praise she had received. Someday every knee will bow, and we will join the elders and the company of heaven to worship the King of kings, but in the meantime, we can still worship the creator and sustainer of the universe, who is worthy to receive all glory and honor and power.

LORD, thank you for this picture of your glory being celebrated in heaven. You are worthy! It is for you and because of you that all things exist. Give us glimpses of how infinite, limitless, and majestic you are so that your glory is our focus. Draw us into worship. I lay my crowns before you, Lord—all that I've done or accomplished, all that I am, I give to you.

Whenever the living beings give glory and honor and thanks to the one sitting on the throne, the one who lives forever and ever, the twenty-four elders fall down and worship the one who lives forever and ever. And they lay their crowns before the throne and say, "You are worthy, O Lord our God, to receive glory and honor and power. For you created everything, and it is for your pleasure that they exist and were created."
Revelation 4:9-11

THE GLORY OF GOD, AND, AS OUR ONLY MEANS TO GLORIFYING HIM, THE SALVATION OF HUMAN SOULS, IS THE REAL BUSINESS OF LIFE.
C. S. Lewis (1898–1963)

The One Year Bible Readings for today are **Obadiah 1-21; Revelation 4:1-11; Psalm 132:1-18;** and **Proverbs 29:24-25.**

DECEMBER

14

prayer

A Belly Prayer

The Lord had arranged for a great fish to swallow Jonah. And Jonah was inside the fish for three days and three nights. Then Jonah prayed to the Lord his God from inside the fish. He said, "I cried out to the Lord in my great trouble, and he answered me. I called to you from the world of the dead, and Lord, you heard me! You threw me into the ocean depths, and I sank down to the heart of the sea. I was buried beneath your wild and stormy waves."
Jonah 1:17–2:1-3

Have you ever prayed a prayer from an emergency room? Have you cried out from a broken relationship or a business failure? If so, you might identify with Jonah's prayer from the belly of the fish. Instead of obeying God and warning the people of Nineveh of impending destruction, Jonah had tried to run from the Lord. But God was with Jonah when the crew threw him overboard. He was with Jonah in the belly of the fish he had prepared to swallow him. He was with him in his trouble and that trouble awakened Jonah to repentance and his need of God.

Beneath the waves he lost all hope. But when he cried out in desperation and despair, God heard him and rescued him. There is no place where the Lord cannot hear and respond to us — no pit too deep, no trouble too terrible, no situation too difficult for God. When we cry out to him from whatever "belly" we find ourselves in, he will answer.

LORD, how I thank you that in the deepest trouble when I cry out to you, you hear and answer me just as you did Jonah. I am glad that there is no place so dark or situation so hopeless that you cannot bring deliverance. I will offer sacrifices to you with songs of praise, for my salvation comes from you alone!

PRAYER WAS THE MIGHTY FORCE THAT BROUGHT JONAH FROM "THE BELLY OF HELL." PRAYER, MIGHTY PRAYER, SECURED THE END. PRAYER BROUGHT GOD TO THE RESCUE OF UNFAITHFUL JONAH, DESPITE HIS SIN OF FLEEING FROM DUTY. GOD COULD NOT DENY HIS PRAYER. NOTHING IS BEYOND THE REACH OF PRAYER BECAUSE NO PRAYER IS TOO HARD FOR GOD TO ANSWER.
E. M. Bounds (1835–1913)

The One Year Bible Readings for today are **Jonah 1:1–4:11; Revelation 5:1-14; Psalm 133:1-3;** and **Proverbs 29:26-27.**

limit

There Is No Limit

Agur may have lacked wisdom, but he looked for answers in the right place. He may not have had common sense, but he knew that there was One greater than himself. Can God use us in spite of our limitations? Absolutely! What we lack in human ability we can find in God. He has used the simple things of this world to confound the wise many times. He called Moses, a man who feared public speaking, to lead a nation. He promoted David, a shepherd boy, to the position of king. He sent his own Son to be born in a small town and laid in a manger, just one more illustration of humble beginnings laced with destiny. Though we cannot begin to compare with the Savior, we are instruments in the Father's hands. It is not your abilities that shape the world; it is God, who holds the wind in his fists and wraps the ocean in his cloak. He is majestic and all-powerful! Have you allowed your limitations to keep you from the destiny he has for you? Then place yourself in the hands of the mighty God, for it is he who does great things.

I am too ignorant to be human, and I lack common sense. I have not mastered human wisdom, nor do I know the Holy One. Who but God goes up to heaven and comes back down? Who holds the wind in his fists? Who wraps up the oceans in his cloak? Who has created the whole wide world? What is his name—and his son's name? Tell me if you know!

Proverbs 30:2-4

LORD, who holds the wind in his fist and the oceans in his cloak? It is you, precious Father. You still the wind with your voice. You are the creator of the stars. You command angels and orchestrate the changing of the seasons. It is you who created me and gave me purpose in life. Look into my heart, Father, and make me a willing instrument in your hands.

HOW COMPLETELY SATISFYING TO TURN FROM OUR LIMITATIONS TO A GOD WHO HAS NONE. ETERNAL YEARS LIE IN HIS HEART. FOR HIM TIME DOES NOT PASS, IT REMAINS; AND THOSE WHO ARE IN CHRIST SHARE WITH HIM ALL THE RICHES OF LIMITLESS TIME AND ENDLESS YEAR.
A. W. Tozer (1897–1963)

The One Year Bible Readings for today are **Micah 1:1–4:13; Revelation 6:1-17; Psalm 134:1-3;** and **Proverbs 30:1-4.**

DECEMBER
16

order

A Tall Order

No, O people, the Lord has already told you what is good, and this is what he requires: to do what is right, to love mercy, and to walk humbly with your God.
Micah 6:8

What a tall order God's requirements are for those who have broken his covenant law and now ask what they should do. What a challenge for us today! Does God require his people to be successful? to build a big church? to develop a dynamic radio or TV program? to achieve a significant position in society? None of these makes the list of what the Lord requires of us. Though the requirements may sound simple, they are an important key to pleasing God: First, do what is right; this means not only rendering just decisions but also discovering our particular work and doing it faithfully. Second, love mercy. God expects us to practice steadfast love, pursue and value kindness, and act mercifully toward others, from the greatest to the least. Third, walk in obedience and humility with the Lord. Sound easy? Not in a fallen world. God knew this would be a tall order. But he demonstrated what is good through his merciful acts and steadfast love, and in Jesus he gave the ultimate model of how to live. Through his Spirit living within us he gives us the power to do what is right, to love mercy, and walk humbly with God.

LORD, you are not interested in outward show or performance, elaborate sacrifices, or religious acts. You want to develop in me the heart responses of humility, mercy, love, and justice. Work these attitudes in me. Thank you for showing me what is good through the example of your Son, who perfectly met all of your requirements so that through his Spirit I may abide in you.

MAY MY LIFE BRING YOU GLORY AND HONOR. WE ARE THE FUEL, THE FIRE IS THE LOVE OF GOD; WE ARE THE CHANNEL, THE TIDE IS HIS PERPETUAL FLOW OF GRACE. Richardson Wright (1887–1961)

The One Year Bible Readings for today are **Micah 5:1–7:20; Revelation 7:1-17; Psalm 135:1-21;** and **Proverbs 30:5-6.**

DECEMBER
17

The Prayers of God's People

Another angel with a gold incense burner came and stood at the altar. And a great quantity of incense was given to him to mix with the prayers of God's people, to be offered on the gold altar before the throne. The smoke of the incense, mixed with the prayers of the saints, ascended up to God from the altar where the angel had poured them out.
Revelation 8:3-4

Our prayers matter to God. We don't just "pray into space" and then our prayers are forgotten. These verses tell us that our prayers are like perfume or sweet smelling incense that ascends to the Lord. They rise before him and move his heart. He hears every plea and petition; all the prayers of God's people are set before him. They aren't like letters that get misplaced. God saves them along with our praises in a golden bowl. Some of these prayers he will answer during our lifetimes. We'll get to see the breakthrough in the life of someone we've labored in intercession for. Some of the things we've asked God to do, will perhaps not happen until we are seeing things from heaven's gates. But these prayers are powerful; they have an impact and affect eternity. What a great encouragement when we are tired and discouraged to know that God treasures our prayers!

LORD, how I thank you not only for hearing my prayers but also for treasuring them, storing them up with praise in golden bowls at your throne of grace. Thank you for not forgetting my petitions. Thank you for what this passage conveys: my prayers, with all the prayers of the saints throughout history, are important to you and are part of your eternal plan.

PRAYER IS OF TRANSCENDENT IMPORTANCE, FOR IT IS THE MIGHTIEST AGENT TO ADVANCE GOD'S WORK. . . . ONLY PRAYING HEARTS AND HANDS CAN DO GOD'S WORK. . . . PRAYER SUCCEEDS WHEN ALL ELSE FAILS. PRAYER HAS WON GREAT VICTORIES AND HAS RESCUED, WITH NOTABLE TRIUMPH, GOD'S SAINTS WHEN EVERY OTHER HOPE WAS GONE. E. M. Bounds (1835–1913)

The One Year Bible Readings for today are **Nahum 1:1–3:19; Revelation 8:1-13; Psalm 136:1-26;** and **Proverbs 30:7-9.**

DECEMBER

18

hard

A Prayer for Hard Times

I have heard all about you, Lord, and I am filled with awe by the amazing things you have done. In this time of our deep need, begin again to help us, as you did in years gone by. Show us your power to save us. And in your anger, remember your mercy. . . . Even though the fig trees have no blossoms, and there are no grapes on the vine; even though the olive crop fails, and the fields lie empty and barren; even though the flocks die in the fields, and the cattle barns are empty, yet I will rejoice in the Lord! I will be joyful in the God of my salvation.

Habakkuk 3:2, 17-18

Habakkuk saw injustice and violence, misery, and sin all around him. He had cried to God for help, but no help had come. In fact, the Lord told Habakkuk things were going to get worse—he was raising up the cruel Babylonians to oppress the Israelites even more. *How can you let them get away with this evil? Why aren't you doing anything about this?* Habakkuk cried. God did not change the situation as Habakkuk had asked. He didn't drive out their enemies. But he did reveal his plan to eventually foil those who trust in themselves and succeed because of corruption. When God laid out the big picture and told Habakkuk of the victory to come, the prophet was so humbled and awed by the Lord's greatness that something even more important did change: Habakkuk's heart. He didn't stop asking for the Lord's help, but now he asked with faith and a heart of worship: No matter how bad things get, "I will rejoice in the Lord; I will be joyful in the God of my salvation." Ask God to build that kind of heart in you . . . no matter what.

LORD, I have "heard all about you, and I am filled with awe by the amazing things you have done." In our time of deep need, begin again to help us as you did in years gone by. Show us your power to save us! No matter what happens, whether I see prayers answered or victories, may my heart rejoice in you. I will find my joy in you, for you are my strength!

DO YOU LOOK AROUND AND SEE TURMOIL, EITHER IN THE WORLD OR IN YOUR OWN LIFE? MEET GOD THE WAY HABAKKUK DID. TALK TO HIM—EVEN CRY OUT TO HIM—ABOUT THE EVIL OR INJUSTICE OR HOPELESSNESS. ALLOW GOD TO HELP YOU RECALL THE FINISHED WORK OF CHRIST AND YOUR FUTURE HOPE OF FINAL VICTORY. Lee Brase

The One Year Bible Readings for today are **Habakkuk 1:1–3:19; Revelation 9:1-21; Psalm 137:1-9;** and **Proverbs 30:10.**

fair

Is God Fair?

Zephaniah's message was urgent. God's wrath was impending, and it was time to pray! The prophet was not attempting to drive the people away from God but away from sin. Some might read Zephaniah's warning and say that God is not fair. Perhaps that is true. If God were fair, he would give us what we deserve instead of what we need to find our way back to him. We don't deserve God's mercy, but he extends it. We don't deserve his love, but he pours it out in abundance. We can't earn his goodness, but he pours it out in our lives to lead us to repentance. We don't deserve his grace, but he offers unconditional love to heal our brokenness. Israel deserved God's wrath, but the prophet knew that prayer would move the hand and heart of God. It was unlikely that the rebellious people would hold a prayer meeting, so Zephaniah called for the righteous few to pray instead. Prayer changes not only people and events; it also transforms those who pray. Earthly agendas are altered as God responds.

MERCIFUL FATHER, help us to gather together and pray for your mercy. Forgive us for pushing you out of our lives only to fill them with meaningless pursuits. Forgive us for allowing evil to penetrate our hearts and minds. Open the eyes of our nation to our desperate need for you. Thank you for giving us not what we deserve but what we need to find our way back to you.

TO BELIEVE IN GOD IS TO KNOW THAT ALL THE RULES WILL BE FAIR—AND THAT THERE WILL BE WONDERFUL SURPRISES! Sister Corita (1918–1986)

Gather together and pray, you shameless nation. Gather while there is still time, before judgment begins and your opportunity is blown away like chaff. Act now, before the fierce fury of the Lord falls and the terrible day of the Lord's anger begins. Beg the Lord to save you—all you who are humble, all you who uphold justice. Walk humbly and do what is right. Perhaps even yet the Lord will protect you from his anger on that day of destruction.

Zephaniah 2:1-3

The One Year Bible Readings for today are **Zephaniah 1:1–3:20; Revelation 10:1-11; Psalm 138:1-8;** and **Proverbs 30:11-14.**

DECEMBER

20

All Our Days

You saw me before I was born. Every day of my life was recorded in your book. Every moment was laid out before a single day had passed.
Psalm 139:16

My mother was in Nevada undergoing cancer treatment when her only son's first child was born. Doctors told her she couldn't fly because of brain swelling and couldn't survive the drive to Texas. Mom had always feared flying but wanted more than anything to see her new grandchild, her six children and the other twenty-two grandchildren and to worship at her church once more. When an elderly minister came to her hospital bed that night, he read Psalm 139. When Mom heard, "Every day of my life was recorded in your book, every moment was laid out before a single day had passed," she knew she didn't have to worry about how many days she had left because God knew. Those words set Mom free to check out of the hospital, enjoy a glorious flight, hold her new grandson, and celebrate every day she had left as a gift from God, who had ordained each moment. Through this experience, I came to a renewed sense of God's sovereignty, whether I'm on the ground or in the air, on a jumbo jet after the 9-11 hijackings or on a little prop plane in the snow-covered mountains of Wyoming.

LORD, I praise you for your amazing sovereignty. You wove me together in my mother's womb, saw me before I was born, and have already recorded every day of my life. You charted the path ahead of me and laid out every moment before a single day had passed. I don't have to fear because you are with me, before me, behind me, surrounding me. Such knowledge is too wonderful for me!

TIME IS SO PRECIOUS THAT IT IS DEALT OUT TO US ONLY IN THE SMALLEST POSSIBLE FRACTIONS—A TINY MOMENT AT A TIME. Irish Proverb

The One Year Bible Readings for today are **Haggai 1:1–2:23; Revelation 11:1-19; Psalm 139:1-24;** and **Proverbs 30:15-16.**

love

Unreciprocated Love

In midautumn of the second year of King Darius's reign, the Lord gave this message to the prophet Zechariah son of Berekiah and grandson of Iddo. "I, the Lord, was very angry with your ancestors. Therefore, say to the people, 'This is what the Lord Almighty says: Return to me, and I will return to you, says the Lord Almighty.'"
Zechariah 1:1-3

Unreciprocated love normally fades. But the Lord endured a one-sided love relationship for generations. His love for his people continued to burn long after they had abandoned him. They ran after other gods, yet God remained faithful to his covenant. Finally, he stood at a distance. No longer would he pour out his love and protection on a people who had forgotten his existence. It didn't take long for the people to see that without God, they had nothing. Several years went by, and then one day through the prophet Zechariah, God sent a love letter to his children, which spelled out the terms of their new relationship. He wanted more than unreciprocated love. Affection is a two-way street, and God called for a reunion of the hearts—nothing less would do. You can offer service or loyalty or even sacrifice to God, but more than anything else he desires that you love him. He is faithful to you. He loved you so much that he gave you his Son and forgave all your sins. What he wants is for you to return that love. What he wants is your heart.

PRECIOUS FATHER, you are the almighty Lord of the universe, and yet you are my friend. May I not grieve your Spirit but rather return the love that you have given me without reservation. I give you my heart, Lord. Thank you for walking with me during difficult times. I rejoice in the peace and shelter of your love that comes only from knowing you.

IT IS BUT RIGHT THAT OUR HEARTS SHOULD BE ON GOD, WHEN THE HEART OF GOD IS SO MUCH ON US. Richard Baxter (1615–1691)

The One Year Bible Readings for today are **Zechariah 1:1-21; Revelation 12:1-17; Psalm 140:1-13;** and **Proverbs 30:17.**

DECEMBER

22

safety

Safety Net

Don't let me lust for evil things; don't let me participate in acts of wickedness. Don't let me share in the delicacies of those who do evil. Let the godly strike me! It will be a kindness! If they reprove me, it is soothing medicine. Don't let me refuse it. But I am in constant prayer against the wicked and their deeds.
Psalm 141:4-5

This is a cry to God not only for an uncompromising faith but for accountability. David had tasted the bitter medicine of compromise and wanted nothing more to do with it. He knew that the enemy wanted to destroy him. He also knew that he had almost destroyed himself in the past when he let down his guard. David was willing to allow the godly to strike him if it would keep him from going down that road again.

Accountability between believers can provide a safety net. The act of answering to another holds you responsible for your actions. In the beginning stages of our faith, accountability is the "pause" button that makes us think before we act. But the dangers of temptation and compromise are not reserved only for new believers. Temptation can be as close as the computer in your home or a relationship at work, but God has promised to help you overcome temptation. Pray for strength to walk in integrity, and ask godly friends to help you walk in uncompromising faith. Ask them to believe in you, pray for you, and to speak the soothing medicine of truth. Then listen!

GOD, thank you for good friends who will speak the truth that is like soothing medicine. I don't always want to hear what people have to say, Lord, but help me not to refuse it since it is good for me. I want my life to reflect uncompromising faith. Empower me by your Spirit to take active steps to live a life without compromise.

THE BEST MIRROR IS AN OLD FRIEND.
George Herbert (1593–1633)

The One Year Bible Readings for today are **Zechariah 2:1–3:10; Revelation 12:18–13:18; Psalm 141:1-10;** and **Proverbs 30:18-20.**

all

Lord, You're All I Want

I pray to you, O Lord. I say, "You are my place of refuge. You are all I really want in life."
Psalm 142:5

Perhaps you once thought, as I did, *If I get college and graduate degrees, find a meaningful career, make a lot of money, get the promotion I aim for, get married, have great children, and retire at sixty-five with a hefty savings account, I'll be happy.* Maybe you *were* happy—for a time. But then you began to ask, *Is that all there is?* The truth is that only God can meet our hearts' deepest needs because he designed those hearts for himself.

We live in a world that offers no end of "things" as sources of satisfaction and happiness. But even Solomon, the one who had it all, said that the eye never ceases desiring and the senses are never satisfied, that undertaking great projects, amassing wealth, and enjoying every pleasure will eventually prove meaningless. The things of this world will not satisfy our real longings. Without God we will always come up empty because he designed us for communion with him and he alone can fill our emptiness. Only the soul that has experienced communion and oneness with the Creator will know true fulfillment and be able to say, "You are all I really want in life."

LORD, open my heart to spiritually perceive the truth that you are all I really need and what my heart really longs for. Let me so experience the joy of your presence that I will not look for satisfaction or pleasure in the things of this world. Let me say with the psalmist, "Lord, you are my place of refuge. You are all I really want in life."

YOU CALLED, YOU CRIED, YOU SHATTERED MY DEAFNESS, YOU SPARKLED, YOU BLAZED, YOU DROVE AWAY MY BLINDNESS, YOU SHED YOUR FRAGRANCE, AND I DREW IN MY BREATH, AND I PANT FOR YOU. Augustine of Hippo (354–430)

The One Year Bible Readings for today are **Zechariah 4:1–5:11; Revelation 14:1-20; Psalm 142:1-7;** and **Proverbs 30:21-23.**

DECEMBER
24

marvelous

Great and Marvelous

Great and marvelous are your actions, Lord God Almighty. Just and true are your ways, O King of the nations. Who will not fear, O Lord, and glorify your name? For you alone are holy. All nations will come and worship before you, for your righteous deeds have been revealed.
Revelation 15:3-4

This song, once sung by Moses as the Israelites celebrated their deliverance from Egypt, also appears in today's passage. The redeemed are gathered after triumphing over the forces of evil. The Lord has revealed his marvelous deeds and is about to execute the glorious climax to his purposes on earth. Now true worship pours forth for the King of the nations: "Great and marvelous are your actions, Lord God Almighty!" Imagine being a part of this celebration and thinking, *This is taking too long; I've got people coming for Sunday lunch, and I need to fix food.* We wouldn't even consider it! We'd be so caught up in the glory and majesty of the Lord that everything else would fade in importance.

At Christmastime we have so much to do—family arriving from out of town, last-minute presents to wrap, to-do lists to get done—that we get distracted from the real purpose of the season: to worship the King of kings. God is just as worthy of glory and honor and power today as he will be on that great day depicted in Revelation. Today, put everything else aside if necessary, and take time to honor and worship the Lord.

OH, LORD GOD ALMIGHTY, your deeds are great and marvelous. You are King of the nations and Lord of my life! You alone are holy and worthy to receive glory, honor, and power. May the things that distract me and my excuses for not spending time with you fade in the light of your glory. Fill my heart with a sense of your greatness and majesty. I adore you, Christ the Lord!

WORSHIP IS THE HIGHWAY OF REVERENCE AND WASHES THE DUST OF EARTH FROM OUR EYES.
Unknown

The One Year Bible Readings for today are **Zechariah 6:1–7:14; Revelation 15:1-8; Psalm 143:1-12;** and **Proverbs 30:24-28.**

reached

The Lord Reached Down

O Lord, what are mortals that you should notice us, mere humans that you should care for us? For we are like a breath of air; our days are like a passing shadow. Bend down the heavens, Lord, and come down.
Psalm 144:3-5

This psalm, which contains praise to God for victory in battle and a question—Why should God stoop to help humanity since we are like a vapor and our days like a passing shadow?—also contains a prayer for the Lord to divinely intervene: "Bend down the heavens, Lord, and come down." This cry for deliverance, a desire to be rescued from enemies and drawn out of deep waters, echoes throughout the Psalms. But the fact is, the Lord *did* bend down the heavens and come down when he became a baby born in Bethlehem. God gave his only begotten Son so that everyone who believes in him will not perish but have eternal life. Today on Christmas, join your voice with the praise of believers throughout history and around the world who celebrate the birth of Jesus Christ, and give him thanks and worship for the sacrifice of his Son to heal and save us. Lift up your heart to the Lord who reached down, the One who cares for us though we are mere mortals and who loves us with an everlasting love.

LORD, as we celebrate your birth today, I praise you for coming to earth so that we who believe in you might know your forgiveness and experience your love. You are Emmanuel, God with us! Although as mere humans we are like a breath of air, our days like a passing shadow, you reached down from on high and brought us out of darkness into your marvelous light.

CHRIST HIMSELF IS LIVING AT THE HEART OF THE WORLD; AND HIS TOTAL MYSTERY—THAT OF CREATION, INCARNATION, REDEMPTION, AND RESURRECTION—EMBODIES AND ANIMATES ALL OF LIFE AND ALL OF HISTORY. Michel Quoist (b. 1921)

The One Year Bible Readings for today are **Zechariah 8:1-23; Revelation 16:1-21; Psalm 144:1-15;** and **Proverbs 30:29-31.**

DECEMBER

26

name

In His Name

The Lord is kind and merciful, slow to get angry, full of unfailing love. The Lord is good to everyone. He showers compassion on all his creation. All of your works will thank you, Lord, and your faithful followers will bless you. They will talk together about the glory of your kingdom; they will celebrate examples of your power. . . . For your kingdom is an everlasting kingdom. You rule generation after generation.

Psalm 145:8-11, 13

This marvelous psalm is full to the brim with attributes of God and revelations of his character: he is compassionate ("to all his creation"). He is gracious and generous, loving and all-powerful, righteous, watchful, protective, near to us, great and good, and ever faithful. The passage also reveals some of God's titles: Judge, King, and Lord.

Think of the Savior: Jesus is the Bread of Life, the Light of the World, our Counselor, our Good Shepherd. Prayerfully studying and meditating on the character traits and names of God is one of the most faith-building, encouraging things you can do for your spiritual life. It will dispel your anxiety and boost your faith. It will enable you to trust God more. Knowing the true character of God will renew and transform your mind with the truth, dissolve doubt, and breathe life into your soul. Saying aloud the attributes of the Lord and thinking about how you've experienced different aspects of his character can be a powerful act of worship. Take a few moments to pray this psalm aloud. Ask God to reveal himself to you in greater clarity than you've ever experienced before.

LORD, how blessed I am to know you! You are all mercy and justice, full of loving-kindness and compassion. You are good to all, majestic and rich in grace. And you always do what you promise! Reveal more of yourself to me. I want to tell others about the glory of your kingdom and examples of your power. Help me to tell of your mighty deeds and praise you forever.

THE CHARACTERISTICS OF GOD ALMIGHTY ARE MIRRORED FOR US IN JESUS CHRIST. THEREFORE IF WE WANT TO KNOW WHAT GOD IS LIKE, WE MUST STUDY JESUS CHRIST. Oswald Chambers (1874–1917)

The One Year Bible Readings for today are **Zechariah 9:1-17; Revelation 17:1-18; Psalm 145:1-21;** and **Proverbs 30:32.**

hope

Our Best Hope

What a great contrast this psalm articulates. It contrasts the faithfulness of God and the instability of people, his unchanging nature and our fickle, flighty nature, the insecurity of trusting in people and the security of trusting in God, the injustice of humanity and the justice of the Lord! God delivers the helpless, the oppressed, and the hungry. He frees prisoners and gives sight to the blind. This is the One in whom we are to put our confidence. The Lord who cares for orphans and widows and foreigners is our helper. He is the best hope for all those needing support and help, and he has the ultimate victory over the wicked. Powerful people can't save us. People, no matter how influential, will die, and all their influence will go with them. But God's authority and power remain throughout all generations. In him we have an eternal, unchangeable source of security. People will disappoint us. But if we put our hope in God, we'll know real blessing and joy. Spend some time thanking God for how faithful and true he is. As you pray today, let this psalm fill you with confidence and hope.

Praise the Lord! Praise the Lord, I tell myself. I will praise the Lord as long as I live. I will sing praises to my God even with my dying breath. Don't put your confidence in powerful people; there is no help for you there. When their breathing stops, they return to the earth, and in a moment all their plans come to an end. But happy are those who have the God of Israel as their helper, whose hope is in the Lord their God.
Psalm 146:1-5

DEAR LORD, forgive me for putting my confidence in people instead of in you. You made heaven and earth, the sea, and everything in them. You are unchanging and all-powerful, and you give justice to the oppressed and help to those bent beneath their loads. You keep all your promises. I put my hope in you, and I praise you, Lord!

IN GOD ALONE IS THERE FAITHFULNESS AND FAITH IN THE TRUST THAT WE MAY HOLD TO HIM, TO HIS PROMISE, AND TO HIS GUIDANCE. TO HOLD TO GOD IS TO RELY ON THE FACT THAT GOD IS THERE FOR ME, AND TO LIVE IN THIS CERTAINTY.
Karl Barth (1886–1968)

The One Year Bible Readings for today are **Zechariah 10:1–11:17; Revelation 18:1-24; Psalm 146:1-10;** and **Proverbs 30:33.**

DECEMBER
28

wonder

God of Wonder

Praise the Lord! How good it is to sing praises to our God! How delightful and how right! The Lord is rebuilding Jerusalem and bringing the exiles back to Israel. He heals the brokenhearted, binding up their wounds. He counts the stars and calls them all by name. How great is our Lord! His power is absolute! His understanding is beyond comprehension!
Psalm 147:1-5

I loved seeing my little grandson Noah as he watched snowflakes twirling from the sky, patted our dog's black, furry coat, and later folded his hands and bowed his red head to say thank you to God for his peanut butter sandwich. He is aware and alive, and his wonder was contagious. Kids are full of wonder, amazement, and awe. Many of us adults, however, have lost our sense of wonder and awe. So God gives us psalms such as this one. They draw us from our ho-hum existence that takes such things as rainbows, snowflakes, and sunrises for granted back to a childlike wonder of our great God who fills the sky with clouds, sends the snow like white wool, and hurls hail like stones. He created everything and possesses all power yet cares for the weak and brokenhearted. He calls the stars by name yet supports the humble. He reigns over all creation yet delights in the simple, heartfelt devotion of those who trust him. His understanding is beyond human comprehension. Surely a God like this can inspire our wonder and awe! Meditate today on the amazing greatness of God, and find your own words to sing his praise.

GOD OF WONDER, I am in awe of your creation, your power, and your compassion. I sing out my praise to you. Your understanding is beyond comprehension! Your power is absolute! How good it is to sing praises to my God! How delightful and how right! Praise the Lord!

RECEIVE EVERY DAY AS A RESURRECTION FROM DEATH, AS A NEW ENJOYMENT OF LIFE. . . . LET YOUR JOYFUL HEART PRAISE AND MAGNIFY SO GOOD AND GLORIOUS A CREATOR.
William Law (1686–1761)

The One Year Bible Readings for today are **Zechariah 12:1–13:9; Revelation 19:1-21; Psalm 147:1-20;** and **Proverbs 31:1-7.**

God Wins!

The Devil, who betrayed them, was thrown into the lake of fire that burns with sulfur, joining the beast and the false prophet. There they will be tormented day and night forever and ever. And I saw a great white throne, and I saw the one who was sitting on it. The earth and sky fled from his presence, but they found no place to hide.
Revelation 20:10-11

The Bible tells the story of a jealous angel named Lucifer (Satan) who rebelled and sought equality with God so God cast him out of heaven. Since Satan cannot be God, he opposes those who are precious to God. His game plan is to detour his opponents—God's children—from their destiny. He has only two plays in the handbook. Number one, blind unbelievers to the truth. Number two, distort the focus of believers and throw them off their game. Satan has only a limited amount of time before the buzzer sounds, so he plays hard. But no matter how many times he injures an opponent or fakes a shot, the final score is already flashing on the board. God wins!

One day Satan will be thrown out of the game altogether, but until then how we play is critical. Souls are at stake. If we work together, we can strengthen one another and recruit more players as we depend on our victorious Lord and King. Recognize your true opponent—not people or circumstances but rather an enemy who knows he's already defeated. Shoot for the goal, keep focused on the prize of the high calling in Christ, all the while rejoicing that God has already won!

SOVEREIGN GOD, you are on the throne and have already overcome the enemy! You are the victor. As this year comes to a close and a new year approaches, may I spend less time worrying about a defeated enemy and more time concerned about those who need the truth. Help me remember that time is limited and how I play the game of life is critical.

HAVE PLENTY OF COURAGE. GOD IS STRONGER THAN THE DEVIL. WE ARE ON THE WINNING SIDE.
John Jay Chapman (1862–1933)

The One Year Bible Readings for today are **Zechariah 14:1-21; Revelation 20:1-15; Psalm 148:1-14;** and **Proverbs 31:8-9.**

DECEMBER
30

light

Heaven's Light

The twelve gates were made of pearls—each gate from a single pearl! And the main street was pure gold, as clear as glass. No temple could be seen in the city, for the Lord God Almighty and the Lamb are its temple. And the city has no need of sun or moon, for the glory of God illuminates the city, and the Lamb is its light. The nations of the earth will walk in its light, and the rulers of the world will come and bring their glory to it.
Revelation 21:21-24

Heaven will not need the sun or the moon for the Lamb will be the light. That light will produce new understanding, illuminating our hearts and minds in a way we could never know on earth. It will warm our spirits as we walk freely in the presence of God. The streets of gold will pale in comparison with the beauty of the light. In our earthly state we see only a glimmer, and yet it is enough to change our lives completely! The light of the Lamb draws you to a heavenly Father. It reveals your need for something and Someone greater than yourself, just as it did when the light blinded Paul physically but opened his spiritual eyes to the truth. It is that light that illuminates God's Word and gives you wisdom that comes from above. It is the light that calls you by name and tells you that you are precious to the Savior. No one can withstand the unbridled light of God, but in heaven we will bask in it. Praise God for the light that guides us, but worship him for the Lamb that is the light!

PRECIOUS LAMB, I can't imagine what it will be like to see that light fully for the first time and bask in the light of your glory. Your light has changed my life, given me wisdom, and helped me find my way out of dark places. It has illuminated your Word and comforted me and taught me. What will it be like one day to walk in a city where the Lamb is the light!

I SAW ETERNITY THE OTHER NIGHT
LIKE A GREAT RING OF PURE AND
ENDLESS LIGHT.

Henry Vaughan (1622–1695)

The One Year Bible Readings for today are **Malachi 1:1–2:17; Revelation 21:1-27; Psalm 149:1-9;** and **Proverbs 31:10-24.**

praise

Ending the Year in Praise

Praise the Lord! Praise God in his heavenly dwelling; praise him in his mighty heaven! Praise him for his mighty works; praise his unequaled greatness! Praise him with a blast of the trumpet; praise him with the lyre and harp! . . . Let everything that lives sing praises to the Lord! Praise the Lord!
Psalm 150:1-3, 6

What a way to end the year—praising the Lord for his mighty works, his unequaled greatness. This psalm, also called the last hallelujah, invites us to join the praises to God in the holy place. The praise is not half-hearted; it is full-force praise with musical instruments—tambourine, stringed instruments, the lyre, the cymbals—and dancing, praise from everyone. When we offer God praise, we're doing what we were created for, even if we're not the best musician or dancer. All of us can raise our voices singing hymns, choruses, and new songs to the Lord. How has God blessed you, your family, friends, or church this year? What mighty works has he accomplished? What progress have you made in an area in which you've struggled? What prayers has God answered? What new attributes or aspects of God have you discovered or experienced in the past year? Lift up your voice or whatever instrument you play, and praise the Lord for these specific things as you pray this psalm aloud.

LORD, I join those in your heavenly dwelling to worship you for your mighty works. I praise your unequaled greatness. I praise you with my whole heart for how you've sustained me in the year that is ending, for your faithfulness, love, and provision. Thank you for how you'll be with me each day in the new year. Let everything that lives sing praises to the Lord!

TO THE EAR OF GOD EVERYTHING HE CREATED MAKES EXQUISITE MUSIC, AND MAN JOINED IN THE PAEAN OF PRAISE UNTIL HE FELL, THEN THERE CAME IN THE FRANTIC DISCORD OF SIN. THE REALIZATION OF REDEMPTION BRINGS MAN BY WAY OF THE MINOR NOTE OF REPENTANCE BACK INTO TUNE WITH PRAISE AGAIN.
Oswald Chambers (1874–1917)

The One Year Bible Readings for today are **Malachi 3:1–4:6; Revelation 22:1-21; Psalm 150:1-6;** and **Proverbs 31:25-31.**

The One Year Book of Praying through the Bible is also available as an **e-book.**

INDEX
of Scripture References

ABOUT THE AUTHOR

CHERI FULLER is an inspirational speaker and an award-winning author of twenty-nine books, including the bestselling *When Mothers Pray, When Teens Pray, When Couples Pray, The Mom You're Meant to Be: Loving Your Kids and Leaning on God, Quiet Whispers from God's Heart for Women,* and many others.

Cheri's ministry, Families Pray USA, inspires, motivates, and equips parents, children, teens, and churches to have an impact on their world through prayer. She has taught children to pray and led the "Prayer Class" at her church, led citywide prayer gatherings for children and families, and also led Moms in Touch prayer groups.

Cheri speaks at conferences and events throughout the year, imparting a vision for the power, gift, and invitation of prayer. She has been a frequent guest on national radio and TV programs including *Focus on the Family, At Home—Live! Moody Midday Connection,* and many others. Her articles have appeared in *Focus on the Family, Pray!* magazine, *Family Circle, ParentLife,* and *Guideposts,* among others. She is a contributing editor for *Today's Christian Woman* and *PrayKids!* magazines.

A former teacher, Cheri has a master's degree in English Literature. She and her husband, Holmes, have three grown children and five grandchildren and live in Oklahoma. Her Web site www.cherifuller.com provides resources on prayer, encouragement for moms and families, and information on her ministry and speaking schedule. For information about speaking engagements or conferences contact

Speak Up Speaker's Services at (810) 982-0898 or Speakupinc@aol.com.

Jan ~~20~~ Praise God Psalm 18:3
Good for difficult times

(?) Jan 19 God protects us
Feb 9 - I thank God He wants to
spent time with me (in prayer)
Feb 13 We give God our fears He
gives us faith hope & love

Feb 22 Brevity of life

April 23 "I am your dwelling place"